Illustrated Clipper® 5.0

John Mueller

Wordware Publishing, Inc.

Library of Congress Cataloging-in-Publication Data

Mueller, John (John P.)
   Illustrated Clipper / John Mueller.
      p.   cm.
   ISBN 1-55622-231-9
    1. Compilers (Computer programs)   2. Clipper (computer program)
I. Title.
QA76.76.C65M84   1990
005.75'65—dc20

                          89-29609
                             CIP

ISBN 1-55622-231-9
10 9 8 7 6 5 4 3 2 1
A9105

Clipper is a registered trademark of Nantucket Corporation.
IBM and PC-DOS are trademarks of International Business Machines Corporation.
dBASE is a registered trademark of Ashton-Tate.
MS DOS is a registered trademark of Microsoft Corporation.
Hercules is a registered trademark of Hercules Corporation.

All inquiries for volume purchases of this book should be addressed to Wordware Publishing, Inc., at the
above address. Telephone inquiries may be made by calling:

(214) 423-0090

Contents

Module	Title	Page
1	About This Book	1
2	Clipper Overview	3

Section 1 — Starting a Program Using Clipper

3	Creating a Program Diagram	8
4	Creating the Basic Program Structure	15
5	Creating a Database Using the DBU Utility	17
6	Creating an Index Using the Index Utility	27
7	Creating Reports and Labels Using the RL Utility	30

Section 2 — Clipper Commands

8	ACCEPT	35
9	APPEND	36
10	AT (@) BOX	39
11	AT (@) CLEAR TO (Blanking Display Sections)	41
12	AT (@) PROMPT (Menu Creation)	43
13	AT (@) SAY/GET (Positioning/Retrieving Text and Data)	45
14	AT (@) TO DOUBLE (Line Drawing)	50
15	AVERAGE	52
16	BEGIN SEQUENCE	55
17	CALL	57
18	CANCEL/QUIT	58
19	CLEAR ALL	60
20	CLEAR GETS	61
21	CLEAR MEMORY	62
22	CLEAR SCREEN	64
23	CLEAR TYPEAHEAD	66
24	CLOSE	68
25	COMMIT	70
26	CONTINUE	75
27	COPY FILE	77
28	COPY STRUCTURE	79
29	COPY TO (Data/Structure)	81
30	COUNT	85
31	CREATE, COPY STRUCTURE EXTENDED, CREATE FROM	88
32	DECLARE, FIELD, LOCAL, MEMVAR, STATIC	91
33	DELETE	96
34	DIR	98
35	DISPLAY	100
36	DO CASE	104

Contents (Cont.)

Module	Title	Page
37	DO (Procedure)	107
38	DO WHILE	109
39	EJECT	112
40	ERASE/DELETE FILE	113
41	EXTERNAL	115
42	FIND	117
43	FOR TO (Execute a Loop)	121
44	FUNCTION	124
45	GO/GOTO	126
46	IF, ELSEIF, ELSE, ENDIF	128
47	INDEX ON	131
48	INPUT	134
49	JOIN WITH	136
50	KEYBOARD	139
51	LABEL FORM	141
52	LIST	143
53	LOCATE	146
54	MENU TO	148
55	NOTE (*/&&)	151
56	PACK	153
57	PARAMETERS	155
58	PRINT STATEMENT (?/??)	156
59	PRIVATE	157
60	PROCEDURE	159
61	PUBLIC	162
62	READ	164
63	RECALL	167
64	REINDEX	169
65	RELEASE	172
66	RENAME	174
67	REPLACE	176
68	REPORT FORM	180
69	RESTORE FROM	184
70	RESTORE SCREEN	186
71	RETURN	188
72	RUN/!	190
73	SAVE SCREEN	193
74	SAVE TO	194
75	SEEK	196

Contents (Cont.)

Module	Title	Page
76	SELECT	198
77	SET Commands	201
78	SKIP	210
79	SORT	213
80	STORE	217
81	SUM	219
82	TEXT TO PRINT/FILE	223
83	TOTAL ON	226
84	TYPE TO PRINT/FILE	229
85	UNLOCK	234
86	UPDATE ON	236
87	USE	239
88	WAIT	241
89	ZAP	242

Section 3 — Clipper Functions

Module	Title	Page
90	ABS( ), EXP( ), LOG( ), MAX( ), MIN( ), MOD( ), SQRT( )	245
91	ACHOICE( ), AADD( ), ACLONE( ), ACOPY( ), ADEL( ), ADIR( ), AEVAL( ), AFIELDS( ), AFILL( ), AINS( ), ARRAY( ), ASCAN( ), ASIZE( ), ASORT( ), DBSTRUCT( ), DIRECTORY( )	249
92	ALTD( )	256
93	ASC( ), CHR( )	258
94	AT( )	260
95	BIN2I( ), BIN2L( ), BIN2W( ), I2BIN( ), L2BIN( ), WORD( )	262
96	BOF( ), DBF( ), EOF( ), LASTREC( )/RECCOUNT( ), RECNO( ), RECSIZE( ), ALIAS( )	266
97	CDOW( ), CMONTH( ), CTOD( ), DATE( ), DAY( ), DOW( ), DTOC( ), DTOS( ), MONTH( ), SECONDS( ), TIME( ), YEAR( )	269
98	COL( ), MAXCOL( ), MAXROW( ), PCOL( ), PROW( ), ROW( ), SETPRC( )	272
99	CURDIR( ), DISKSPACE( ), DOSERROR( ), ERRORLEVEL( ), FKLABEL( ), FKMAX( ), GETE( ), GETENV( ), OS( ), VERSION( )	277
100	DBEDIT( ), BROWSE( ), DBCREATE( ), DBEVAL( )	282
101	DBFILTER( )	288
102	DBRELATION( ), DBRSELECT( )	290
103	DELETED( )	292
104	DESCEND( )	293
105	EMPTY( )	296

Contents (Cont.)

Module	Title	Page
106	FCLOSE( ), FCREATE( ), FERROR( ), FILE( ), FOPEN( ), FREAD( ), FREADSTR( ), FSEEK( ), FWRITE( )	298
107	FCOUNT( ), FIELD( )/FIELDNAME( )	305
108	FLOCK( ), RLOCK( )/LOCK( )	307
109	FOUND( )	310
110	HARDCR( )	312
111	HEADER( )	314
112	IF( )/IIF( ), EVAL( )	316
113	INDEXEXT( ), INDEXKEY( ), INDEXORD( )	320
114	INKEY( ), LASTKEY( ), NEXTKEY( ), READKEY( ), SETKEY( )	323
115	INT( ), ROUND( )	326
116	ISALPHA( ), ISDIGIT( ), ISLOWER( ), ISUPPER( )	329
117	ISCOLOR( )/ISCOLOUR( ), SETCOLOR( )	331
118	ISPRINTER( )	333
119	LEFT( ), RIGHT( )	336
120	LEN( )	338
121	LOWER( ), PAD( ), QOUT( ), SPACE( ), STR( ), STRTRAN( ), STUFF( ), TRANSFORM( ), UPPER( ), VAL( )	340
122	LTRIM( ), SUBSTR( ), TRIM( )/RTRIM( ), ALLTRIM( )	344
123	LUPDATE( )	346
124	MEMOEDIT( ), MEMOLINE( ), MEMOREAD( ), MEMOTRAN( ), MEMOWRIT( )	348
125	MEMORY( )	355
126	MLCOUNT( ), MLPOS( )	359
127	NETERR( ), NETNAME( )	361
128	PCOUNT( )	362
129	PROCLINE( ), PROCNAME( )	364
130	RAT( )	366
131	READEXIT( ), READINSERT( ), READVAR( )	369
132	REPLICATE( )	371
133	RESTSCREEN( ), SAVESCREEN( ), SCROLL( )	373
134	SELECT( )	376
135	SETCANCEL( ), SET( )	378
136	SOUNDEX( )	381
137	TONE( )	383
138	TYPE( ), VALTYPE( )	384
139	UPDATED( )	386
140	USED( )	388

Contents (Cont.)

Module	Title	Page

Section 4 — Clipper Debugging

Module	Title	Page
141	BREAK	389
142	BREAK TOGGLE	393
143	DISPLAY EXPRESSION, DISPLAY TRACE, DISPLAY STATUS, DISPLAY DATABASE	395
144	DOS SHELL	401
145	GO, GO (ANIMATION), GO (KEY)	403
146	HELP	406
147	QUIT	408
148	SINGLE STEP	410
149	VARIABLE ASSIGN PRIVATE, VARIABLE VIEW PRIVATE	412
150	VARIABLE ASSIGN PUBLIC, VARIABLE VIEW PUBLIC	416
151	WATCH	419
Appendix A	Terms and Definitions	423
Appendix B	Printing Your Program Using the Line Program	428
Appendix C	Increasing Your Productivity Using Make and Pre-Processor/Compiler Directives	429
Appendix D	dBASE III Plus Commands and Functions Clipper Doesn't Support	434
Appendix E	Clipper Compiler Error Messages	435
Appendix F	Linker Warning and Error Messages	438
Appendix G	Error Messages Displayed During Program Execution	439
Appendix H	Program Source Code Listings	442
Appendix I	Advanced Topics for Clipper 5.0 and 5.01	472
Appendix J	Exercises	500
Index		517

Recommended Learning Sequence

Sequence	Title	Module	Page
1	About This Book	1	1
2	Clipper Overview	2	3
3	Creating a Program Diagram	3	8
4	Creating the Basic Program Structure	4	15
5	Creating a Database Using the DBU Utility	5	17
6	Creating an Index Using the Index Utility	6	27
7	Creating Reports and Labels Using the RL Utility	7	30
8	CLEAR SCREEN	22	64
9	USE	87	239
10	AT (@) SAY/GET, POSITIONING/RETRIEVING TEXT AND DATA	13	45
11	READ	62	164
12	CLOSE	24	68
13	APPEND	9	36
14	IF, ELSEIF, ELSE, ENDIF	46	128
15	RETURN	71	188
16	CANCEL/QUIT	18	58
17	NOTE (*/&&)	55	151
18	AT (@) BOX	10	39
19	ASC( ), CHR( )	93	258
20	AT (@) TO DOUBLE (Line Drawing)	14	50
21	DO WHILE	38	109
22	DELETE	33	96
23	PACK	56	153
24	SKIP	78	210
25	SEEK	75	196
26	BOF( ), DBF( ), EOF( ), LASTREC( )/RECCOUNT( ), RECNO( ), RECSIZE( ), ALIAS	96	266
27	FOUND( )	109	310
28	DELETED( )	103	292
29	EMPTY( )	105	296
30	UPDATED( )	139	386
31	USED( )	140	388
32	RECALL	63	167
33	DO CASE	36	104
34	AT (@) CLEAR TO (Blanking Display Sections)	11	41
35	ACCEPT	8	35
36	AT (@) PROMPT (Menu Creation)	12	43
37	MENU TO	54	148

Recommended Learning Sequence (Cont.)

Sequence	Title	Module	Page
38	SAVE SCREEN	73	193
39	RESTORE SCREEN	70	186
40	SET Commands	77	201
41	ISCOLOR( )/ISCOLOUR( ), SETCOLOR( )	117	331
42	PROCEDURE	60	159
43	DO (Procedure)	37	107
44	PARAMETERS	57	155
45	INKEY( ), LASTKEY( ), NEXTKEY( ), READKEY( ), SETKEY( )	114	323
46	BEGIN SEQUENCE	16	55
47	STORE	80	217
48	FOR TO (Execute a Loop)	43	121
49	FUNCTION	44	124
50	PRIVATE	59	157
51	PUBLIC	61	162
52	ISPRINTER( )	118	333
53	WAIT	88	241
54	PRINT STATEMENT (?/??)	58	156
55	EJECT	39	112
56	TEXT TO PRINT/FILE	82	223
57	REPORT FORM	68	180
58	LABEL FORM	51	141
59	COL( ), MAXCOL( ), MAXROW( ), PCOL( ), PROW( ), ROW( ), SETPRC( )	98	272
60	LOWER( ), PAD( ), QOUT( ), SPACE( ), STR( ), STRTRAN( ), STUFF( ), TRANSFORM( ), UPPER( ), VAL( )	121	340
61	ISALPHA( ), ISDIGIT( ), ISLOWER( ), ISUPPER( )	116	329
62	LEFT( ), RIGHT( )	119	336
63	LEN( )	120	338
64	LTRIM( ), SUBSTR( ), TRIM( )/RTRIM( ), ALLTRIM( )	122	344
65	FCLOSE( ), FCREATE( ), FERROR( ), FILE( ), FOPEN( ), FREAD( ), FREADSTR( ), FSEEK( ), FWRITE( )	106	298
66	SAVE TO	74	194
67	MEMORY( )	125	355
68	RELEASE	65	172
69	RESTORE FROM	69	184
70	CLEAR ALL	19	60
71	CLEAR GETS	20	61
72	CLEAR MEMORY	21	62

Recommended Learning Sequence (Cont.)

Sequence	Title	Module	Page
73	CLEAR TYPEAHEAD	23	66
74	REPLACE	67	176
75	TONE( )	137	383
76	DECLARE, FIELD, LOCAL, MEMVAR, STATIC	32	91
77	ACHOICE( ), AADD( ), ACLONE( ), ACOPY( ), ADEL( ), ADIR( ), AEVAL( ), AFIELDS( ), AFILL( ), AINS( ), ARRAY( ), ASCAN( ), ASIZE( ), ASORT( ), DBSTRUCT( ), DIRECTORY( )	91	249
78	FCOUNT( ), FIELD( )/FIELDNAME( )	107	305
79	DBEDIT( ), BROWSE( ), DBCREATE( ), DBEVAL( )	100	282
80	COMMIT	25	70
81	DBRELATION( ), DBRSELECT( )	102	290
82	DBFILTER( )	101	288
83	CDOW( ), CMONTH( ), CTOD( ), DATE( ), DAY( ), DOW( ), DTOC( ), DTOS( ), MONTH( ), SECONDS( ), TIME( ), YEAR( )	97	269
84	KEYBOARD	50	139
85	FIND	42	117
86	GO/GOTO	45	126
87	COUNT	30	85
88	AVERAGE	15	52
89	SUM	81	219
90	TOTAL ON	83	226
91	INT( ), ROUND( )	115	326
92	ABS( ), EXP( ), LOG( ), MAX( ), MIN( ), MOD( ), SQRT( )	90	245
93	INDEX ON	47	131
94	DESCEND( )	104	293
95	EXTERNAL	41	115
96	SORT	79	213
97	REINDEX	64	169
98	COPY TO (Data/Structure)	29	81
99	LOCATE	53	146
100	CONTINUE	26	75
101	SOUNDEX( )	136	381
102	PCOUNT( )	128	362
103	TYPE( ), VALTYPE( )	138	384
104	PROCLINE( ), PROCNAME( )	129	364
105	READEXIT( ), READINSERT( ), READVAR( )	131	369
106	RESTSCREEN( ), SAVESCREEN( ), SCROLL( )	133	373
107	MEMOEDIT( ), MEMOLINE( ), MEMOREAD( ), MEMOTRAN( ), MEMOWRIT( )	124	348

Recommended Learning Sequence (Cont.)

Sequence	Title	Module	Page
108	MLCOUNT( ), MLPOS( )	126	359
109	RAT( )	130	366
110	AT( )	94	260
111	INPUT	48	134
112	DIR	34	98
113	ERASE/DELETE FILE	40	113
114	RENAME	66	174
115	CURDIR( ), DISKSPACE( ), DOSERROR( ), ERRORLEVEL( ), FKLABEL( ), FKMAX( ), GETE( ), GETENV( ), OS( ), VERSION( )	99	277
116	HEADER( )	111	314
117	COPY STRUCTURE	28	79
118	COPY FILE	27	77
119	CREATE, COPY STRUCTURE EXTENDED, CREATE FROM	31	88
120	RUN/!	72	190
121	DISPLAY	35	100
122	LIST	52	143
123	LUPDATE( )	123	346
124	SELECT	76	198
125	SELECT( )	134	376
126	JOIN WITH	49	136
127	UPDATE ON	86	236
128	TYPE TO PRINT/FILE	84	229
129	HARDCR( )	110	312
130	IF( )/IIF( ), EVAL( )	112	316
131	INDEXEXT( ), INDEXKEY( ), INDEXORD( )	113	320
132	REPLICATE( )	132	371
133	SETCANCEL( ), SET( )	135	378
134	FLOCK( ), RLOCK( )/LOCK( )	108	307
135	NETERR( ), NETNAME( )	127	361
136	UNLOCK	85	234
137	ZAP	89	242
138	CALL	17	57
139	BIN2I( ), BIN2L( ), BIN2W( ), I2BIN( ), L2BIN( ), WORD( )	95	262
140	QUIT	147	408
141	ALTD( )	92	256
142	HELP	146	406
143	DOS SHELL	144	401
144	GO, GO (ANIMATION), GO (KEY)	145	403
145	SINGLE STEP	148	410

Recommended Learning Sequence (Cont.)

Sequence	Title	Module	Page
146	BREAK	141	389
147	BREAK TOGGLE	142	393
148	WATCH	151	419
149	DISPLAY EXPRESSION, DISPLAY TRACE,		
	DISPLAY STATUS, DISPLAY DATABASE	143	395
150	VARIABLE ASSIGN PUBLIC, VIEW PUBLIC	150	416
151	VARIABLE ASSIGN PRIVATE, VIEW PRIVATE	149	412

Module 1
ABOUT THIS BOOK

INTRODUCTION

This book describes how to create database management systems (DBMS) using Nantucket Clipper®. It shows you all you need to know, even if you have never programmed before. This book shows you how to use each command, function, and control structure provided by Clipper. It also provides hints on when and where to use each command. This book also shows you many of the techniques professionals use, including structured/modularized programming. The book does all this by taking you through steps necessary to learn and create useful programs.

I wrote *Illustrated Clipper 5.0* to meet the needs of a broad range of users. For the beginning programmer it provides a very basic background in structured programming techniques. By learning these techniques early, you can save endless hours unlearning the bad habits encouraged by some programming languages. For the intermediate programmer, this book provides a complete and concise index of all the Clipper commands. It also talks about any specialized uses for them. The advanced programmer will learn new methods of creating programs using Clipper. I tested these techniques over a long time in actual use by the business community. Some of these techniques will not only reduce the lines of code a program requires, but make the program more readable as well. Both advanced and intermediate users can use this book to learn about the differences between the Summer 87 and 5.0 versions of Clipper.

Classroom instructors can use *Illustrated Clipper 5.0* as an example of how to program. Since the result of this book is a working program, students will more readily see the benefits of using one command over another in any given situation. Also, this book provides the basics so needed by the novice programmer, yet seldom explained in an easy-to-use format.

ORGANIZATION

This book contains small, easy-to-read modules. Each module describes a specific command, possible applications for use, and examples for learning how each command works.

Module 2 provides an overview on how to start using Clipper. It also introduces you to some of the basic utilities provided as part of Clipper.

Modules 3 and 4 introduce the basics of structured/modularized programming. While this is not a complete and exhaustive work on the subject, these two modules provide enough information to understand why a programmer uses different structures. These modules also explain the need for documentation. This includes both external and source code documentation. Every novice programmer needs to know the information in these two modules before attempting to learn any other material in this book.

Modules 5 through 7 explain how to use some of the utilities provided with Clipper. Besides the in-depth explanation provided by these modules, other modules throughout the book provide good examples of actual utility use. The reader should learn the material in these modules before attempting to learn the material in Modules 8 through 151.

Modules 8 through 151 provide detailed explanations of each command. These modules appear in alphabetical order so you can reference them easily later. By following the recommended learning sequence, you can make sure the example program you create functions correctly by the end of the book. The program listing in Appendix H helps you determine if you obtained the correct result from each Typical Operation and allows you to compare your final program with a standard.

Appendixes A through I provide reference material to enhance your ability to use Clipper. Appendix A provides a listing of terms and definitions required to understand Clipper terminology completely. Appendixes B and C introduce two more utility programs. Both utilities increase the speed at which you create programs, not necessarily how well you create them. Appendix D provides information regarding Clipper compatibility with dBase III Plus. In most cases Clipper adds to dBase III's capabilities. In other cases, it implements a command in a way oriented toward compiled, not interpreted usage. Appendixes E through G describe error messages you may see during different stages of program creation. Appendix H contains the program source code listings for all programs developed throughout the book. Appendix I contains detailed Clipper 5.0/5.01 enhancements and additional coverage of Clipper 5.0 and 5.01 commands and functions. Appendix J contains Clipper exercises for both classroom and self-teaching situations. If you use *Illustrated Clipper 5.0* in a classroom, you may want to include these exercises for student assignments. If you are learning Clipper by yourself, use these exercises to check your understanding of what each module has taught you. When you can answer these questions, you are ready to move on to the next module in the learning sequence.

HARDWARE REQUIREMENTS

Clipper works with versions 2.0 or greater of the PC-DOS and MS-DOS operating systems. The program will also work with the OS/2 operating system in the DOS compatibility window.

You can run the program on an IBM PC, XT, AT, PS/2, or compatible with a minimum of 512K RAM. Your computer should have a minimum of one floppy disk drive and one hard disk.

Clipper will work with a variety of monitors and video adapters. These monitors include: Hercules, Color Graphics Adapter (CGA), Enhanced Graphics Adapter (EGA), Virtual Graphics Array (VGA), IBM 8514/A Graphics Adapter, HP Vectra, AT&T high-resolution graphics, and the Genius Adapter with a full page monitor. In fact, with specialized programming techniques, you can allow Clipper to work with any type of hardware devised for the PC.

For printing your documents, Clipper can work with a variety of name-brand dot-matrix, daisy wheel, ink jet, and laser printers. If you use a printer that Clipper doesn't support, Clipper lets you create custom print drivers. Customized print drivers let you use Clipper with any printer.

WHAT YOU SHOULD KNOW

The descriptions and examples in this book assume you know how to use PC/MS-DOS with your IBM or compatible computer. You should also know how to format a floppy disk and copy, rename, and delete files. If you can do these, you are ready to use this book with Clipper. If you are not familiar with these common PC/MS-DOS commands, you may want to buy the *Illustrated MS/PC-DOS* book from Wordware Publishing, Inc.

Module 2
CLIPPER OVERVIEW

INTRODUCTION

Clipper allows you to create and distribute programs with an ease not usually found in other programming languages. By allowing you to create .EXE files from source code, Clipper provides the means of distributing applications. The extended command set provided by Clipper allows you to create friendlier programs with only a few commands. Clipper even provides many useful utilities in source code form. This allows you to use the utilities, while studying their source code for examples on command usage.

COMPILING WITH CLIPPER

To compile with Clipper you need to create a program, exit to the DOS prompt, and type the compiler command. Clipper produces an object module that you link together with other object modules to create a program. Clipper provides a number of command line parameters as shown below.

SUMMER 87 VERSION

```
CLIPPER <FILENAME> [-l] [-m] [-o <PATH SPECIFIER>] [-p] [-q] [-s] [-t
<DRIVE SPECIFIER>] [> <ERROR FILENAME>]
```

5.0 VERSION

```
CLIPPER <FILENAME> [-a] [-b] [-d <IDENTIFIER>[=<TEXT>]] [-e] [-i
<PATHNAME>] [-l] [-m] [-n] [-o <PATH SPECIFIER>] [-p] [-q] [-r <LIBFILE>]
[-s] [-t <DRIVE SPECIFIER>] [-u [<USER STANDARD HEADER FILE>]] [-v] [-w] [>
<ERROR FILENAME>]
```

The first clause after the Clipper command is the filename. You do not need to specify an extension if your program uses the .PRG extension. Notice the command line shows the filename enclosed by a less-than (<), then a greater-than (>) symbol. Whenever you see text enclosed by these symbols on a command line, you know that Clipper expects an actual parameter, not the text shown. Do not include the greater-than and less-than symbols on the command line.

The command line includes several switches. These switches alter the way Clipper compiles a program. You specify which switch you want to use by typing a dash (-) then a letter. Braces on the command line show that you do not have to include the text enclosed by the braces for Clipper to accept the command. You must use lowercase letters for the switches, or Clipper will ignore them.

The -a switch (Clipper 5.0 only) tells Clipper to declare all variables declared using the private, public, parameters commands as memory variables.

The -b switch (Clipper 5.0 only) tells Clipper to include debugging information in the object file.

The -d switch (Clipper 5.0 only) declares an identifier to the pre-processor. If you do not include TEXT, then the pre-processor assigns the identifier a null value.

The -e switch (Clipper 5.0 only) tells Clipper to produce a pre-processor listing. If you do not specify a list filename, then Clipper sends the output to the screen instead of a file.

The -i switch (Clipper 5.0 only) adds a directory to the list of directories that Clipper searches for include files. These directories are searched before any other directories.

The -l switch tells Clipper not to include line numbers in the object code. If you do not include line number information, you cannot use the built-in debugging features of Clipper (Summer 87 only).

The -m switch tells Clipper to compile only the file included on the command line. Normally, Clipper compiles all the files referenced within your source code automatically.

The -n switch (Clipper 5.0 only) supresses the creation of a main procedure. This is an advanced option used when you create static procedures. A full explanation of this feature is outside the scope of this book.

The -o switch tells Clipper to place object files (an intermediate step to creating a program) in a directory other than the current one.

The -p switch tells Clipper to pause for disk changes. When you specify this option, Clipper loads the source file, then pauses before creating an object file.

The -q switch tells Clipper to stop displaying source code file line numbers on screen during the compilation process. This switch does not affect the placement of line numbers in the object file.

The -r switch (Clipper 5.0 only) adds to the list of directories searched for library files.

The -s switch tells Clipper to check the syntax (the combination of command/function words and variables) without creating an object module.

The -t switch tells Clipper to create its temporary files (a file used during the compilation process) on a separate disk.

The -u switch (Clipper 5.0 only) tells Clipper to use a user-defined header file in place of the standard header file. This is an advanced feature. A full explanation of this feature is outside the scope of this book.

The -v switch (Clipper 5.0 only) tells the pre-processor to assume that all ambiguous variable references are dynamic memory variables. Clipper uses a default of treating all ambiguous references as fields.

The -w switch (Clipper 5.0 only) tells the pre-processor to generate a warning message each time it encounters an ambiguous variable reference.

By adding a greater-than sign and a filename after all the Clipper command line entries, you can redirect the normal screen output to a file. This allows you to review screen output in one window of your word processor, while making source code corrections in another. This is especially useful for large programs with the potential for a large number of errors.

LINKING USING PLINK86 (SUMMER 87 OR 5.0)

Linking is the process of putting several object modules together to create an executable program. In other words, it makes all the final adjustments your program requires to work correctly. The PLINK86 linker provides a higher degree of executable file compression than the standard DOS linker in most cases. This sometimes results in faster code execution times as well.

However, the reduced code size and program execution time comes at the cost of greater link times (about 1 1/2 times longer). The command line interface for the PLINK86 linker appears below.

```
PLINK86 FI <[D:] [\PATH] FILENAME> [, <FILENAME>] ... LIB <[D:] [\PATH]
LIBRARY NAME> [, <LIBRARY NAME>] ... [OUTPUT <\PATH\FILENAME>]
```

The PLINK86 linker requires two types of input. The first input is a list of filenames. The second input is a list of library names. You precede the filenames with the directive FI. Files are any file you create using the Clipper compiler or any Clipper supplied object modules. Clipper lets you add two parameters to the beginning of each filename entry. The first parameter tells Clipper which drive contains the file if the file does not appear in the current directory. The second parameter tells Clipper what directory path to use to look for the file.

Libraries contain the code for all the commands and functions you use with Clipper. Every command/function included in this book requires code contained in a library file. Clipper provides several library files. You tell PLINK86 which library files to add to your executable code using the LIB directive. You must always use at least the CLIPPER.LIB file. In most cases you need the EXTEND.LIB file as well. As with filenames, Clipper lets you designate a drive and path as part of the library name if the library resides someplace other than the current directory.

LINKING USING THE STANDARD LINKER (SUMMER 87 OR 5.0)

NOTE

This chapter describes the standard linker provided with Microsoft Macro Assembler Version 5.1 (linker version 3.64). Refer to the book provided with your specific linker to find other command line parameters. The required command line parameters discussed in the following paragraphs apply to most versions of IBM™ and Microsoft™ linkers.

The standard linker is especially useful while you develop your program. Since its link speed is greater than the PLINK86 linker, and memory size normally becomes an issue after basic program development, the standard linker provides the speed required to quickly develop your application. Although most standard linkers work with Clipper, some require the addition of command line switches, and others will not work at all. The command line interface for the standard linker provided with version 5.1 of Microsoft Macro Assembler appears below.

```
LINK [/HE] [/PAU] [/I] [/E] [/M[:NUMBER]] [/li] [/noi] [/nod] [/st:number]
[/cp:number] [/se:number] [/o:number] [/do] [/ds] [/hi] [/nog] [/co] [/b]
[/f] [/nof] [/pac:number] [/nop] [/q] <[D:] [\PATH] FILENAME [.EXT]> [+
<FILENAME>] ... [, [<[D:] [\PATH] RUN FILENAME [.EXT]>]] [, [<[D:] [\PATH]
MAP FILENAME [.EXT]>]] [, [<[D:] [\PATH] LIBRARY NAME [.EXT]> [+ <LIBRARY
NAME>] ... ]] [;]
```

The /HE switch allows you to obtain help in using the linker. When you specify the /HE switch without any other command line parameters, the linker displays all available switches and their meaning.

The /PAU switch tells the linker to pause before it writes the executable file to disk. This allows you to change floppy disks on a two-disk system.

The /I switch tells the linker to display all linking information on screen. The linker includes the name of the current object file, the link phase, and any other significant link events.

The /E switch tells the linker to create a smaller executable file using a compression technique to remove redundant characters. Standard linkers that include this switch can produce executable files smaller than those produced by the PLINK86 linker.

The /M switch tells the linker to list all public symbols defined in the object files. When you specify this option, the linker includes a listing of all public variables sorted by both name and address in a .MAP file. The optional number lets you specify the maximum number of variables the linker will sort (default 2048). If the object files contain more variables than the linker can sort, the map file will contain an unsorted list only.

The /LI switch controls whether the linker places line numbers in the map file. In most cases this switch has no effect.

The /NOI switch tells the linker to preserve variable and procedure name case sensitivity. You must use this switch with Clipper. Since the Clipper compiler uses C constructs and C is a case sensitive language, you must include this switch to ensure proper program operation.

Never use the /NOD switch with Clipper. By telling the linker to ignore default libraries embedded in the object files, you could create unusable code.

The /ST switch determines the stack size allocated by the program. The stack is a program-related function automatically created by Clipper.

The /CP switch determines the amount of memory used by the program when you load it in memory. This switch requires an advanced knowledge of programming. Do not use this switch for most programming situations since it can cause program execution speed degradation.

The /SE switch determines the number of segments the linker allows. When using a linker with this switch or a switch that performs the same function, set the number to 512. In most cases this will allow you to link the program correctly. If the program fails to execute correctly or the linker displays an out of segments error message, increase the number of segments.

The /O switch determines the interrupt number used by the linker for overlays. By changing this number you can avoid conflicts with device drivers and terminate-and-stay-resident programs. However, use of this switch requires an advanced knowledge of programming and an intimate knowledge of the programs used with the target machine.

The /DO switch lets you change the order in which the linker places the object files in the executable program. Clipper automatically uses this option.

The /DS and /HI switches determine where the operating system places a program in memory. The linker includes these switches for assembly language programs only.

Microsoft included the /NOG switch for compatibility reasons only. Never use this switch with Clipper programs.

The /CO switch provides a method of including debugging information for any modules you write in assembly or C language.

The /B switch places the linker in batch mode. Normally, the linker asks you for a file location if a file you reference does not exist in the correct directory. When you use the /B switch, the linker generates an error message instead of prompting you.

The /F switch tells the linker to optimize FAR calls made between various program procedures. This lets your program operate at a slightly faster speed. In most cases you can use this switch only with Clipper programs.

The /PAC switch reduces code size by reducing the number of segments in a program. This switch does not work with Clipper programs.

The /NOP switch disables segment packing. Use this switch if the environment contains the /PAC switch.

The /Q switch lets you specify libraries used with Microsoft Quick languages.

LINKING USING RTLINK (VERSION 5.0 ONLY)

RTLink provides two modes of operation. You may use the freeform mode, which corresponds to using PLink86, or positional mode, which corresponds to using the standard linker. You invoke one of these two options by adding the /FREEFORM or /POSITIONAL options to the command line. RTLink uses a default of the freeform mode. In all other respects (for the purposes of this book) you use RTLink the same way you use either PLink86 or the standard linker. There are some nuances of difference between linkers that are not covered in this book. All of these differences pertain to the methods used to create overlay files.

USING THE AUTOMATIC BATCH FILES CL AND CLD

The simplest way to compile and link Clipper programs is by using the CL and CLD batch files provided on the Clipper disks. To use these two batch files you merely type CL or CLD and the filename of the main program. The CLD batch file creates programs with the Clipper debugger added. In most cases you will use the CL batch file instead.

THE EDIT, COMPILE, LINK, DEBUG CYCLE

All programming using Clipper consists of four steps. First you edit or create the program file. When you finish editing the file, you compile it using the Clipper compiler. This creates one or more object files. Then you link all the object files with one or more library files to create an executable file. If the program works, then you don't need to perform the debug step. Otherwise, you debug the file by looking for any syntax errors. Generally, you use a combination of the Clipper-supplied debugger and a close inspection of the source code to find any remaining bugs.

SUMMARY

Clipper provides an easy method of creating very complex DBMS programs once you learn the steps required to create a program. This book teaches you these basics and shows you some of the advanced techniques used by professionals.

Module 3
CREATING A PROGRAM DIAGRAM

INTRODUCTION

The most important preparatory step in creating a program is designing it first. You need to determine how different parts of the program will fit together and what tasks each part will perform. By creating a diagram of what you expect of the program, you can find design problems early, before they become major projects to repair. You need to determine what the database will contain, how you need to access that data, and in what order. The program you design needs to address all the user's needs. By outlining what you intend to build, the user can provide input on additional features or areas requiring refinement. For all these reasons and many more, you need to design first, build second.

DESIGNING THE DATABASE

When you design a database, you create the structure used to hold the information you want to maintain. A database structure contains four elements. The first element is the field name. The second element is the field type. The third element is the field width. The fourth element is the number of decimals for numeric fields.

Clipper lets you use up to ten characters for the field name. You may use any combination of letters, numbers, and symbols. The optimum field name is one that describes the contents of the field most adequately. For example, if you create a database with names and addresses and one of the fields contains the person's last name, call the field LAST_NAME. By using descriptive names, you will easily remember why you included a specific field in the database.

The field type describes the information contained in the field. For example, if you place numbers in a field, then the field contains numeric information. Clipper provides for five different types of information. *Character* contains text information. Usually, this is short information like a person's name or address. *Numeric* contains numbers of any type. While you can place numbers in the character field, you cannot readily perform math functions on them. Using the numeric type allows you to create fields you can perform math operations on. *Date* contains date information. Unlike the other fields, this field always contains eight characters in the format ##/##/##. The numbers contain the month, day, and year using one of several formats. *Logical* contains either true or false. Clipper always sets this field to a width of 1. By using special formatting parameters, you can choose to display Y or N in place of T or F. *Memo* contains characters. Unlike any of the other field types, memo does not have a specific length. Instead, it is a variable length character field. You can use this field type for long character entries of variable length. Be careful using this type since its use does not allow you to use many of Clipper's text formatting commands.

The memo field type creates a special problem. How do you store a field with no specific length? Clipper stores a memo reference in the main database, then creates a special database with a

.DBT extension for the actual memo text. By using this technique, Clipper avoids the problems created by using variable length fields.

The field width describes how large the field is; in other words, how many characters the field contains. As mentioned above, date field types are automatically eight characters long, logical field types are one character long. Clipper assigns a default length of 10 characters to memo field types. This is the display length of the field, not its actual length. Of course, you can still change the display length using the formatting clauses of the display commands. The other two field types, character and numeric, require that you consider in advance how long to make them. One rule of thumb for determining field length is to find the longest character or numeric entry used, then add ten characters for character field types and two characters for numeric field types. If you change field length once you start creating the program code, the task of changing all the required code parameters becomes enormous.

The decimals element applies only to numeric field types. In this entry you place how many characters appear after the decimal point. In most cases that number is two (most database applications work with monetary amounts). This entry works with the width field to determine how large a number you can place in a field. For example, if the field width is 10 and you select 2 decimal places, you can place a number 7 digits long before the decimal point (10 characters - 2 decimal places - 1 for the decimal point).

For the sample programs contained in this book we will need to create three databases with the parameters shown below. Remember, this chapter deals with putting all the facts on paper. In the following modules we will actually create the databases. The completed programs are contained in Appendix H.

Table 3-1. Sample Database 1 Structure (MAILLIST.DBF)

Field Name	Type	Width	Decimals
FIRST_NAME	CHARACTER	25	
MIDDLE	CHARACTER	1	
LAST_NAME	CHARACTER	25	
ADDRESS1	CHARACTER	50	
ADDRESS2	CHARACTER	50	
CITY	CHARACTER	40	
STATE	CHARACTER	2	
ZIP	CHARACTER	10	
TELEPHONE	CHARACTER	10	

Table 3-2. Sample Database 2 Structure (CHCKBOOK.DBF)

Field Name	Type	Width	Decimals
DATE	DATE	8	
CHECK_NUM	NUMERIC	5	0
DRAWN_FOR	CHARACTER	50	
AMOUNT	NUMERIC	10	2
DEPOSIT	NUMERIC	10	2
BALANCE	NUMERIC	12	2
TAX_ITEM	LOGICAL	1	

Table 3-3. Sample Database 3 Structure (NOTEPAD.DBF)

Field Name	Type	Width	Decimals
NOTE_NUM	NUMERIC	5	0
SHORT_SUBJ	CHARACTER	50	
CATEGORY	CHARACTER	15	
NOTE	MEMO	10	

Notice the tables all contain easy-to-read, easy-to-decipher field names. The field lengths are more than adequate. Notice the field widths for the numeric entries in database 2. The two fields dealing with withdrawal and deposit information are 10 characters long. Since it is unlikely that anyone would ever withdraw all the money in the account at one time, the balance field contains two extra characters. This provides an overflow area when deposits exceed withdrawals.

ADDING THE INDEXES

The first question this section answers is "What is an index?" An index provides a fast method of accessing information in the database. When you tell the computer to look for information in an unindexed database, the computer compares the search string with every piece of information in the database. This makes searching for something incredibly slow. You could reduce the search time by keeping the database sorted, but that would consume a phenomenal amount of time as well. However, if you keep a small subset of the information in a database sorted, then the response time becomes more reasonable. The work the computer must perform to keep a small file sorted is much less than for a large file. By using efficient search techniques, you can find the information in the small file, then follow a pointer to the main database. The figure below shows the relationship between a database and index file.

Clipper provides many ways of defining an index to your database. In all cases the definition contains the name of one or more database fields. You combine two fields using the plus sign (+). For example, if you wanted to combine the last name and first name fields in the first database, you would type: LAST_NAME + FIRST_NAME. You can combine the field names with any of the appropriate functions described in this book. For example, if you wanted only the first five characters of the last name used in an index, you would type: substr (LAST_NAME, 1, 5).

Now that you know what an index is and how to establish one in Clipper, you need to design indexes to the sample databases. For the first database the sample programs use a single index consisting of the last name, the first name, and the middle initial (LAST_NAME +

FIRST_NAME + MIDDLE). The second database uses two indexes. The first index uses the date, then the check number. The second index uses the check number only. The third database uses three indexes. The first index uses the note number only. The second index uses the short subject and note number. The third index uses the category and note number.

PROGRAMMING SYMBOLOGY

Once you create the database structure and decide what indexes to use, you start to create a program structure. Programmers use a common set of symbols to represent various aspects of program behavior. The figure below shows these symbols.

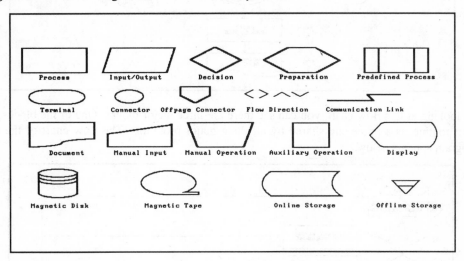

PROGRAM DESIGN

The object of creating a program design using the previously described programming symbols is not to draw every event that might occur within the real program. Instead, you begin by designing the overall structure of the program, then define the subprograms that make up each major block. Finally, you design the procedure blocks and show how they interrelate. Programmers call these charts or block diagrams flow charts. Programmers call them flow charts because they show the flow of code and data that the real program will use.

The reason that you perform this exercise is to find any major flaws in ideology or design before you write the first line of code. By doing this, you reduce the debugging you need to do later. If you go into too much depth, you may find yourself frustrated when you try to follow the overly complex design. If you don't design enough of the program, you may miss flaws that the flow charting process would otherwise find. The superior approach is somewhere between overly complex and not thought out enough. The following figure shows the initial flow chart of the sample programs.

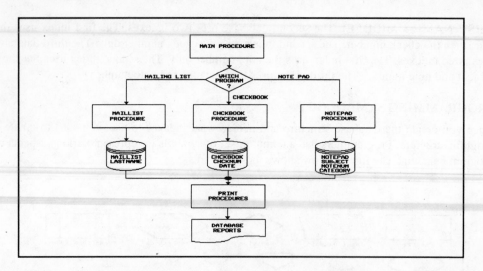

By looking at this flow chart, you can see there are three major blocks. One of the blocks, the print routine, is a procedure shared by all three major programs. The flow chart of the first program appears below.

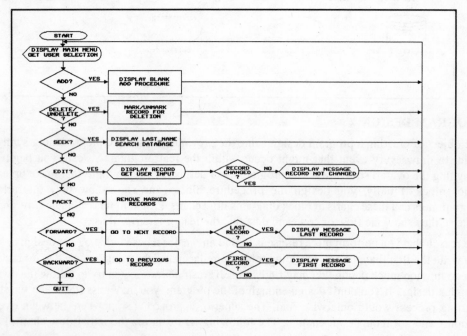

As you can see from this flow chart, the first example is a mailing list database. It allows you to track clients, or friends, or anyone else with an address and telephone number. The flow chart for the second program appears as follows.

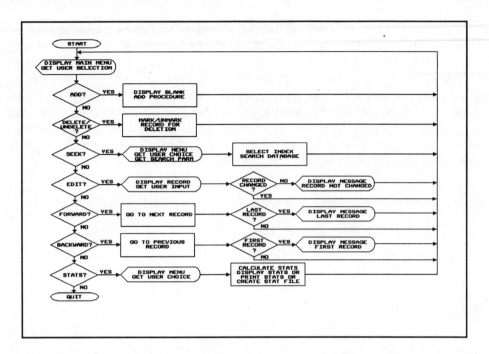

The second program is a checking account manager. Notice the difference between this program and the previous one. The first program had more of the typical database management functions included. This one performs unexpected things like statistical analysis. The flow chart for the third sample program appears below.

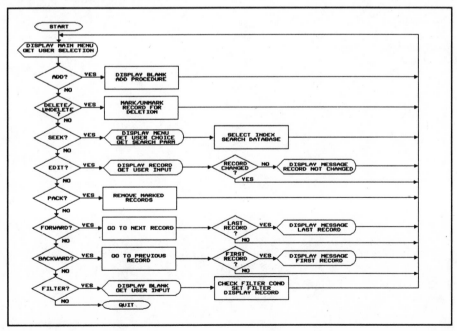

This program performs the very unusual function of tracking your notes. It gives you an idea of how commercial managers that perform the same function might work.

SUMMARY

This chapter has shown you the need for thinking about your database, then designing it, before you start physically creating it. Program design is not an easy task. In fact, some people dislike it so much that they ignore it. Unfortunately, they pay the cost of long hours debugging an undocumented program. Flow charts and database structure charts are not only important, they are essential to creating professional-looking and working programs.

Module 4
CREATING THE BASIC PROGRAM STRUCTURE

INTRODUCTION

This module introduces some important concepts in creating a program quickly and efficiently using the design documents prepared in modules 2 and 3. Creating these design documents is a waste of time if you don't use them to start the actual program. By using the design documents you ensure two things. First, the program you create will work as well as the program you designed. Many programming projects fail not because of poor design, but because of poor design implementation. Using a set of well thought-out design documents reduces the effort necessary to create the program by reducing error.

Second, the documentation update at the end of the programming sequence will involve little or no effort. Since the originators of a program may not perform any program changes later, the originators must create documentation to help those who follow. Reducing the effort required to produce accurate documentation increases the probability of the program originators actually creating it.

USING THE FLOW CHARTS

Reduction of potential programming errors is the most basic reason for creating a flow chart. If you don't use flow charts to create a program, then you lose the effect of designing the program in the first place. In some cases, you take information directly from the flow charts and use it for code and comments within the program. In other cases, you compare the sequence of events within the program against the original design in the flow charts. In either event you end up with a program skeleton. This skeleton may not perform all the work required of the completed program, but it will serve as a structure from which to build. This skeleton ensures the program will meet design specifications. In most cases it also means the program will work better when complete.

To extend this concept further, look at the example below. Compare it to the flow chart for procedure number 1.

```
* Perform this procedure until the user selects quit.
* Display the main menu.
* Get the user menu selection.
do case
   case selection = 'A'
* Do the add procedure.
   case selection = 'D'
* Do the delete procedure.
   case selection = 'U'
* Do the undelete procedure.
   .
   .
endcase
quit
```

Even though the example doesn't show the entire program, you can see the example program follows the flowchart by using either comments or actual code statements. This skeleton will ensure proper program operation later.

ADDING TO THE SKELETON

After you complete a skeleton using the design documents, start filling the skeleton in one procedure at a time. Test each procedure as you complete it to make sure it works. In some cases, you may want to test related procedures as well, since the new procedure may affect their operation. Complete an entire procedure before testing it. The temptation is to test after the addition of a small segment or even a single statement. These tests not only waste time, they really don't test anything.

COMPLETING THE PROGRAM

Completing and testing the procedures in a program is not the final step. The final program step comes in three parts. First, you integrate all subprograms together one at a time. Test each new addition before you add another. Once you create the complete program, test it thoroughly to make absolutely certain that every procedure works correctly. Test the error handling capability by purposely injecting faults. By thoroughly testing the program before you introduce it to a client, you can make sure the client sees the program at its best.

Once you work out all the programming errors, update the design documentation. The design documentation should include database and index design, program flowcharts, source code with plenty of notations, and a narrative of program operation. Anyone, including yourself, who makes changes to the program will require this type of documentation. Program documentation is so important some companies use automated version control software and other programmer's aids to ensure proper program documentation.

SUMMARY

Documentation and programming go hand-in-hand. By using these two mediums of database control together, you can develop a superior application that everyone will enjoy using. Always follow the think, then act rule. Never add anything to a program without first considering the impact to the database it controls. If you follow these simple rules, you can produce elegant applications with the least frustration possible.

Module 5
CREATING A DATABASE
USING THE DBU UTILITY

DESCRIPTION

The DBU utility provides a semi-complete interactive database interface for use with Clipper. The term semi-complete describes accurately the actual functioning of the utility. This utility provides all the functions necessary to create databases, indexes, and views. It also provides some management capabilities (although, you should build those into your program). It doesn't provide any report capabilities.

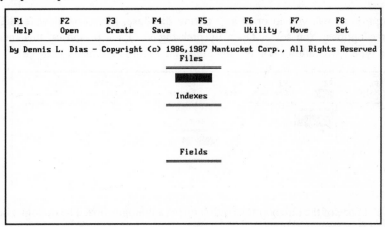

What the DBU utility lacks in essential capability, it makes up for in example. Since Nantucket provides the source code for this utility along with Clipper, you can refer to it to learn how to create a function or use a command. The utility itself will assist you greatly in creating Clipper programs. You will use the DBU utility to perform different functions throughout this book. The command line interface of the DBU utility appears below.

```
DBU [<DATABASE FILENAME>/<VIEW FILENAME>] [/M] [/C]
```

As you can see from the command line interface, the DBU utility allows you to enter three command line parameters. Since you have the source code, you could always add more to suit your needs. The filename clause allows you to specify which database or view to use. Database filenames end in .DBF. View filenames end in .VEW. DBU automatically assumes an extension of .DBF if both a view and a database have the same filename and you do not specify an extension. The /M parameter allows you to select monochrome (two-color) operation. The /C parameter allows you to select multi-color operation even on monochrome displays. Some monochrome displays (for example Hercules™) will allow you to display the additional colors.

The utility always checks the monitor type and defaults to color for color adapters and monochrome for monochrome adapters.

HELP

The Help menu contains a single option, help. When you select this option by pressing F1, DBU provides context sensitive help. To get out of Help, press Esc.

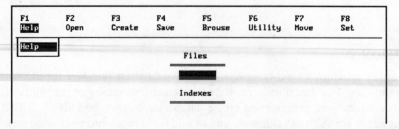

OPEN

The Open option allows you to open an existing database, index, or view. The Open menu contains three options. You select Open by pressing F2. Each option on this menu opens a different file type. DBU allows you to select only the highlighted menu choices.

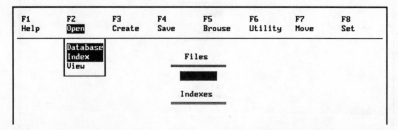

When you select one of the three options, DBU opens a dialogue box. The dialogue box contains two fields and two control buttons.

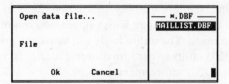

The first field contains the names of all the files in the current directory. By pressing the Up or Down Arrow, you can select one of these files. The second field contains a blank to type the path and name of a file to open. Normally, DBU places the cursor in the first field if any files with the correct extension exist. Otherwise, it places the cursor in the blank field. You can select between the two fields using the Right and Left Arrows when the current directory contains files with the correct extension. Once you press Enter to select the file, DBU highlights the OK control button. If you press Enter again, DBU opens the selected file and displays it. You can select the cancel control button by pressing Right Arrow. Pressing Enter with the cancel control button highlighted returns control to the main menu without opening the selected file. You can always press Esc to get back to the main menu immediately.

CREATE

The Create option allows you to create a new database or index. The Create menu contains two entries, database and index. DBU highlights the index entry only when you have a database open. You can always create a new database.

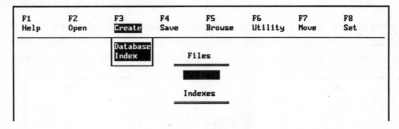

When you select the Create Database option, DBU presents a form containing four entries. Each field in the new database occupies one row in the form. You do not use all four entries for every type of field. To select between options in the field type column, press Spacebar. Module 3 contains a complete description of the four entries and their use.

```
Structure of <new file>    Field 1

Field Name    Type        Width   Dec

██████████    Character    10
```

If you have a database open and want to create an index to it, use the Create Index option. When you select this option, DBU opens a dialog box containing three fields and two control buttons.

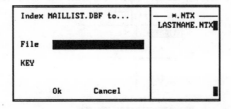

The first field contains a list of index files in the current directory. The second field contains a blank for typing a filename. The third field contains a blank for typing the key fields to use for the index. DBU always places the cursor in the filename field when it opens the dialogue box. If you want to select an existing index, you press Right Arrow to move the cursor to the first field, then press the Up and Down Arrows to highlight the correct file. Press Enter to select the

19

existing index. DBU automatically places the existing key fields in the key field when you select an existing index. In either case, you can type a new set of key field values by selecting the key field using the arrow keys.

Once you select an index file and type a set of key field values, you can highlight the Ok control button by pressing Enter in the key field. If you want to cancel the operation, select cancel using the Right Arrow and press Enter. Otherwise, press Enter with the Ok control button highlighted.

SAVE

The Save option allows you to store the parameters of a view or the structure of a new/changed database on disk. The Save menu contains two options: database and view. DBU never highlights both options at the same time since you will never need to use both at the same time.

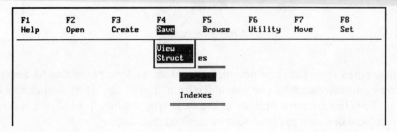

You select the Save Database option while inside the Create Database form. Once you finish creating a database, you can save the structure to disk. You select the Save View option after you set up the database viewing parameters you want to save. DBU does not allow you to select either Save option while in any other menu except Create Database. To save a view, you must set up the parameters, then save it while in the Main menu.

BROWSE

The Browse menu contains two options: database and view. If you select the database option, DBU displays the entire database using any order created by attached indexes. If you select view, DBU checks for the view file, opens it if necessary, and displays the selected portion on screen.

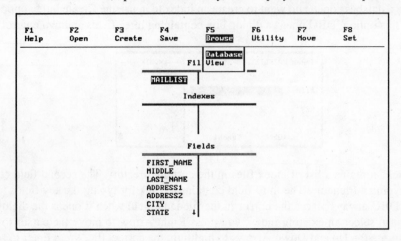

The Browse option presents a spreadsheet style editing environment for your database. Instead of changing one record at a time, this option allows you to see and change several. The database fields appear as columns. The database records appear as rows.

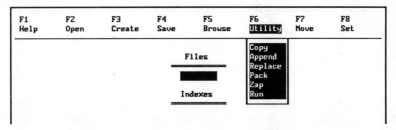

Like any spreadsheet, pressing the arrow keys moves you around the database. Typing a value in a field changes the contents of that field for that record only. Pressing PgUp or PgDn replaces all the records shown with the next or previous set in order. Pressing Esc closes the full screen editor.

UTILITY

The Utility menu contains six options. Each option controls some aspect of utility operation on database files except Run. The Run command invokes a second copy of DOS you can use for running standard DOS commands if you desire. DBU allows you to select the Utility options only at the Main menu. Except for the Run option, DBU also requires a database loaded.

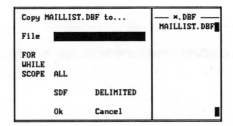

The Utility Copy and Utility Append options open the same dialogue box. The difference between the two is the direction of data flow. The Utility Copy option sends data from the currently selected database to a disk file. The Utility Append option transfers records from a disk file to the currently selected database.

The Utility Copy/Append dialogue box contains five fields and four control buttons. The five fields contain a list of files in the current directory, a blank field for typing the file name, a blank field for selecting a FOR condition, a blank field for selecting a WHILE condition, and a scope field containing the key word ALL. The four control buttons are SDF, Delimited, Ok, and Cancel. Module 9 contains the rules for using Append. Module 29 contains the rules for using Copy.

The Utility Replace option replaces the contents of the field you specify with a new value using the specified conditions. By using this command you avoid having to replace the values contained by one or more fields individually.

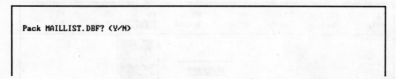

The Utility Replace dialogue box contains six fields and two control buttons. The six fields contain a list of fields in the current database, a blank field for typing the new field value, a blank field for selecting a WITH condition, a blank field for selecting a FOR condition, a blank field for selecting a WHILE condition, and a scope field containing the key word ALL. The two control buttons are Ok, and Cancel. Module 67 contains the rules for using Replace.

The Utility Pack option removes records you mark for deletion from the database. It also reorders any index files attached to the database. Module 56 contains the rules for using Pack.

```
Pack MAILLIST.DBF? (Y/N)
```

The Utility Zap option removes all the records from a database. Unlike the Delete command used in full screen editing, Zap permanently removes the records. Module 89 contains the rules for using Zap.

The Utility Run option allows you to perform any operation you could normally perform at the DOS prompt. The dialogue box created by DBU for Run contains a single field for typing the DOS command. When you use the Run option, the database program remains in memory. This limits the size of the application or task you can perform. Module 72 contains the rules for using Run.

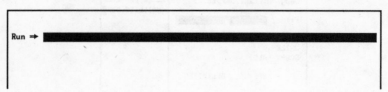

MOVE

The Move menu contains four options. All four options change the current position of the record pointer to a new one. DBU does not allow you to select any of the Move options if you are not in the browse (full screen edit) display. You select Move by pressing F7 at the Main menu.

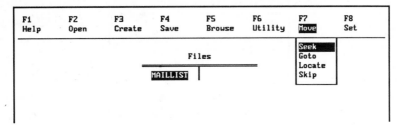

All four Move menu options display the same type of dialogue box when selected. The dialogue box contains a single entry for typing an expression, a record number, or the number of records to move the record pointer.

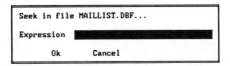

Module 75 contains the rules for using Seek. Module 45 contains the rules for using Goto. Module 53 contains the rules for using Locate. Module 78 contains the rules for using Skip.

SET

The Set menu contains three options. Each option allows you to change how the Browse option displays a database. Two of the options also affect the Utility options as well. These options include Set Relation and Set Filter. Module 77 completely describes all the Set commands. You access the Set menu by pressing F8.

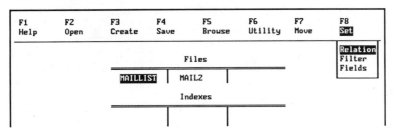

The Set Relation option allows you to link two databases together using some criteria. DBU allows two criteria types. The first type is a numeric expression. When using a numeric expression ensure the child database does not use an index. The second type is a key field. When using a key field, ensure the parent and child databases use indexes with the key field and the first index field.

The Set Relation dialogue box contains one column for each open database. To set a relation, type the first letter of the parent database filename in the left column, then press Enter. The cursor automatically moves to the next column. Type the first letter of the child database filename in the right column, then press Enter. Another row appears below the first one containing the filenames. Type the relation in this row and press Enter.

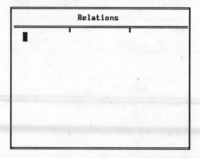

The Set Filter option reduces the number of records displayed to a subset defined by an expression. The expression normally consists of a field name, a field value, and a relational operator. The Set Filter dialogue box contains a single blank in which to place the filter expression.

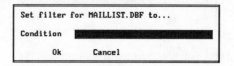

The Set Fields option adjusts how many and in what order DBU displays the fields of a database. Changing the display order does not actually reorder the database. The dialogue box for this option contains one field and two control buttons. The field contains a field name to place in the current cursor position on the field list for the selected database. When you select the field name, the cursor automatically highlights the Ok control button. To cancel the change, select the Cancel control button and press Enter.

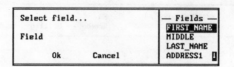

APPLICATIONS

This utility has almost unlimited applications. The main uses for this utility are database/index/view creation during program design, and database maintenance. Since this utility lacks any means for printing the contents of the database, you can't use it as a stand-alone interactive database without modification.

TYPICAL OPERATION

In this example you compile the DBU utility, then perform some simple operations using it. Begin this example at the DOS prompt in the C:\CLIPPER directory.

NOTE

This procedure assumes you created a directory, C:\CLIPPER, and copied all the Clipper files to it. It also assumes that the PATH statement in your AUTOEXEC.BAT file contains the CLIPPER directory. This book uses a subdirectory, C:\CLIPPER\0022, for the sample programs and databases. All typical operations in this book assume you started in the C:\CLIPPER\0022 directory unless otherwise instructed.

1. Type **MAKEDBU** and press **Enter**. A list of compile messages appears as Clipper compiles each section of DBU. Finally, a link message appears, then the DOS prompt.

```
Copyright (c) Nantucket Corp 1985-1987.  All Rights Reserved.
Microsoft C Runtime Library Routines,
Copyright (c) Microsoft Corp 1984-1987.  All Rights Reserved.

Compiling DBUUTIL.PRG
Code size 9754, Symbols 3632, Constants 1126

C:\CLIPPER>clipper dbuhelp -m -q -l
The Clipper Compiler
Copyright (c) Nantucket Corp 1985-1987.  All Rights Reserved.
Microsoft C Runtime Library Routines,
Copyright (c) Microsoft Corp 1984-1987.  All Rights Reserved.

Compiling DBUHELP.PRG
Code size 531, Symbols 496, Constants 93

C:\CLIPPER>plink86 fi dbu,dbuview,dbustru,dbuedit,dbuindx,dbucopy,dbuutil,dbuhel
p lib \clipper\clipper,\clipper\extend
PLINK86plus ( Nantucket ) Version 2.24.
Copyright (C) 1987 by Phoenix Technologies Ltd.,
All Rights Reserved.


DBU.EXE (255 K)
C:\CLIPPER>
```

2. Type **MD 0022**. Press **Enter** to create a new subdirectory. Type **CD 0022**. Press **Enter** to enter the new subdirectory. Type **DBU**. Press **Enter**. The DBU main menu appears.

3. Press **F3**. Select DATABASE by pressing **Enter**. The Create Database structure form appears.

NOTE

From this point on, all DBU displays show the effect of the /M (monochrome) switch.

4. Type the database structure information into the form as shown below.

Structure of <new file>		Field 9	
Field Name	Type	Width	Dec
FIRST_NAME	Character	25	
MIDDLE	Character	1	
LAST_NAME	Character	25	
ADDRESS1	Character	50	
ADDRESS2	Character	50	
CITY	Character	40	
STATE	Character	2	
ZIP	Character	10	
TELEPHONE	Character	13	

5. Press **F4** then **Enter** to select Save Structure. Type **MAILLIST**. Press **Enter** twice. DBU names the new database MAILLIST and saves the structure to disk.

6. Press **F3**. Select Index by pressing **Down Arrow**, then **Enter**. Type **LASTNAME** in the File field. Press **Enter**. Type **LAST_NAME + FIRST_NAME + MIDDLE** in the Key field. Press **Enter** twice. DBU creates the new index and saves it to disk.

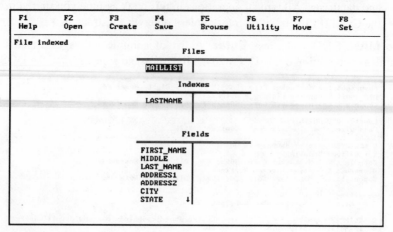

7. Press **Esc**. The DBU utility asks if you want to exit to DOS.

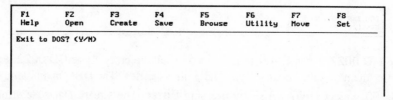

8. Type **Y**. The DOS prompt appears.

9. Turn to Module 6 to continue the learning sequence.

Module 6
CREATING AN INDEX
USING THE INDEX UTILITY

DESCRIPTION

The Index utility lets you quickly create indexes to database files. Since Nantucket provides the source code for this utility, you can modify it to meet your requirements.

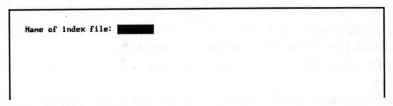

The Index utility requires only the database filename as input. If you don't provide the database name or the database does not exist, it exits with an error message. The command line interface of the Index utility appears below.

```
INDEX <DATABASE FILENAME>
```

APPLICATIONS

Use the Index utility where memory limitations do not allow the use of the DBU utility described in Module 5. Since this utility requires a very small amount of random access memory (RAM), it works in situations where the other utilities may not work. For example, if you need to reindex a database from within another application, you can use the Index utility with a DOS shell.

TYPICAL OPERATION

In this example, you compile the Index utility, create a database using DBU, then index it using Index. Begin this example at the DOS prompt in the C:\CLIPPER directory.

1. Type **CLIPPER INDEX -I**. Press **Enter**. The Clipper compile messages appear.
2. Type **PLINK86 FI INDEX LIB CLIPPER**. Press **Enter**. The PLink86 link messages appear.

```
C:\CLIPPER>CLIPPER INDEX -1
The Clipper Compiler
Copyright (c) Nantucket Corp 1985-1987.  All Rights Reserved.
Microsoft C Runtime Library Routines,
Copyright (c) Microsoft Corp 1984-1987.  All Rights Reserved.

Compiling INDEX.PRG
Code Pass 1
Code Pass 2
Code size 142, Symbols 80, Constants 130

C:\CLIPPER>PLINK86 FI INDEX LIB CLIPPER
PLINK86plus ( Nantucket ) Version 2.24.
Copyright (C) 1987 by Phoenix Technologies Ltd.,
All Rights Reserved.


INDEX.EXE (150 K)
C:\CLIPPER>
```

3. Type **CD 0022** and press **Enter** to change directories to the sample program directory. Type **DBU**. Press **Enter**. The DBU main menu appears.

4. Press **F3**. Select DATABASE by pressing **Enter**. The Create Database structure form appears.

5. Type the database structure information into the form as shown below.

```
Structure of <new file>    Field 7

Field Name     Type         Width    Dec

DATE           Date           8
CHECK_NUM      Numeric        5        0
DRAWN_FOR      Character     50
AMOUNT         Numeric       10        2
DEPOSIT        Numeric       10        2
BALANCE        Numeric       12        2
TAX_ITEM       Logical        1
```

6. Press **F4** then **Enter** to select Save Structure. Type **CHCKBOOK**. Press **Enter** twice. DBU names the new database CHCKBOOK and saves the structure to disk.

7. Press **Esc**. Type **Y** to exit the DBU utility. The DOS prompt appears.

8. Type **INDEX CHCKBOOK**. Press **Enter**. The Index display appears.

9. Type **CHCKNUM**. Press **Enter**. Index asks for the key expression to use.

```
Name of index file: CHCKNUM
Key expression:
```

10. Type **CHECK_NUM**. Press **Enter**. Index displays the number of records indexed. The DOS prompt appears.

```
Name of index file: CHCKNUM
Key expression: CHECK_NUM
     0  Records indexed
C:\CLIPPER\0022>
```

11. Type **INDEX CHCKBOOK**. Press **Enter**. The Index display appears.
12. Type **DATE**. Press **Enter**. Index asks for the key expression to use.
13. Type **DTOC(DATE) + STR(CHECK_NUM, 5, 0)**. Press **Enter**. Index displays the number of records indexed. The DOS prompt appears.
14. Turn to Module 7 to continue the learning sequence.

Module 7
CREATING REPORTS AND LABELS
USING THE RL UTILITY

DESCRIPTION

The RL utility allows you to create reports and labels from the databases created using the DBU utility. The Report command creates .FRM files, while the Label command creates .LBL files. The RL utility does not accept any command line parameters. The command line interface of the RL utility appears below.

    RL

The RL main menu provides three options. The Label option creates mailing label files. You select it by typing L at the Main menu. The Report option creates database report files. You select it by typing R at the Main menu. The Quit option closes all files, then exits to DOS. You select it by typing Q at the Main menu.

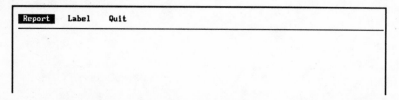

APPLICATIONS

Use the RL utility to quickly create report and label files for the programs you create. If the printouts your program uses are generic in nature, then using these files reduces the amount of time required to create a program. You should always use a report or label form when possible. Reserve customized programs for special circumstances.

Use report forms to create either standard or wide format reports of database information using a tabular format. In most circumstances, a report form has enough flexibility to create the reports you require. Clipper allows you to specify headings, subheadings, and table data. The table data can contain calculated fields, standard database fields, and database fields modified by Clipper functions.

Use label forms to create mailing labels and other continuous form adhesive backed labels. Other uses for labels include shelf markers, binder identification stickers, and bar code labels for inventory control.

TYPICAL OPERATION

In this example you compile the RL utility, create a label form, and create a report form. Each form uses a different database to more adequately show when you would use each form type. Begin this example at the DOS prompt in the C:\CLIPPER directory.

1. Type **MAKERL** and press **Enter**. A list of compile messages appears as Clipper compiles each section of RL. Finally, a link message appears, then the DOS prompt.

```
Copyright (c) Nantucket Corp 1985-1987.  All Rights Reserved.
Microsoft C Runtime Library Routines,
Copyright (c) Microsoft Corp 1984-1987.  All Rights Reserved.

Compiling RLBACK.PRG
Code size 7867, Symbols 2320, Constants 629

C:\CLIPPER>clipper rldialog -q -m
The Clipper Compiler
Copyright (c) Nantucket Corp 1985-1987.  All Rights Reserved.
Microsoft C Runtime Library Routines,
Copyright (c) Microsoft Corp 1984-1987.  All Rights Reserved.

Compiling RLDIALOG.PRG
Code size 4277, Symbols 1072, Constants 395

C:\CLIPPER>plink86 fi rlfront,rldialog,rlback lib \clipper\clipper,\clipper\exte
nd output rl
PLINK86plus ( Nantucket ) Version 2.24.
Copyright (C) 1987 by Phoenix Technologies Ltd.,
All Rights Reserved.


RL.EXE (204 K)
C:\CLIPPER>
```

2. Type **CD 0022** and press **Enter**. Type **RL**. Press **Enter**. The RL main menu appears.

3. Type **L**. A dialogue box asking for a filename appears.

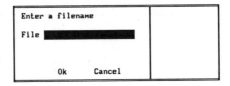

4. Type **MAILLABL**. Press **Enter** twice. The Label form appears.

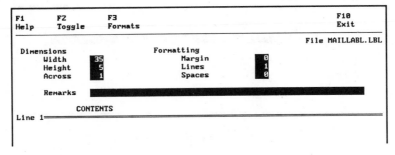

5. Press **F3**. The Label Type Selection dialogue box appears.

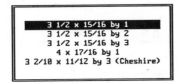

6. Select 3 1/2" by 15/16" by 1 by pressing **Enter**. The Label Type Selection dialogue box disappears.

7. Select the **Margin** field by pressing **Down Arrow** three times. Type **5**. Press **Enter**. Type **F2**. RL highlights the first line of the contents section.

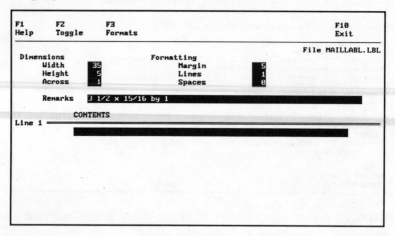

8. Type the information shown below in the first four lines of the contents section.

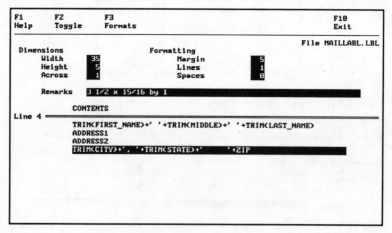

9. Press **F10**. RL asks if you want to save the new label form.

10. Press **Enter** to select OK. The RL main menu reappears.

11. Type **R**. A dialogue box asking for a filename appears.

12. Type **CHCKLIST**. Press **Enter** twice. The Field Definition form appears.

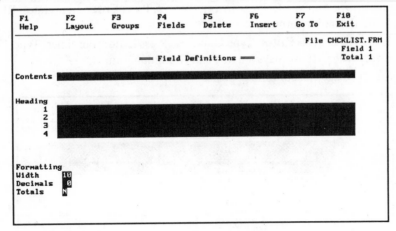

13. Type **DATE**. Press **Enter** to select the first line of the Heading field. Type **DATE**. Press **Enter** four times to select the width field. Type **8**. Press **Enter** three times. RL displays a new Field Definition form. Notice RL automatically updates the current field and total field entries.

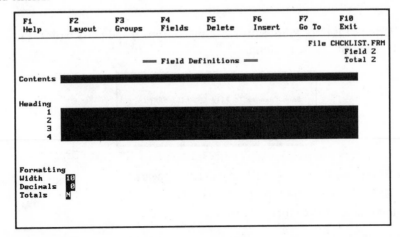

14. Type **CHECK_NUM**. Press **Enter**. Type **Check**. Press **Enter**. Type **Num**. Press **Enter** three times. Type **5**. Press **Enter**. Type **0**. Press **Enter** twice. RL displays a new Field Definition form.

15. Type **DRAWN_FOR**. Press **Enter**. Type **Purpose Drawn For/**. Press **Enter**. Type **Deposit From**. Press **Enter** three times. Type **25**. Press **Enter** twice. RL displays a new Field Definition form.

16. Type **AMOUNT**. Press **Enter**. Type **Check**. Press **Enter**. Type **Amount**. Press **Enter** three times. Type **10**, then **2**. Press **Enter**. Type **Y**. Press **Enter** eight times. RL displays a new Field Definition form.

17. Type **DEPOSIT**. Press **Enter**. Type **Deposit**. Press **Enter**. Type **Amount**. Press **Enter** three times. Type **10**, then **2**. Press **Enter**. Type **Y**. Press **Enter** eight times. RL displays a new Field Definition form.

18. Type **BALANCE**. Press **Enter**. Type **Balance**. Press **Enter** four times. Type **12**, then **2**. Press **Enter** twice. RL displays a new Field Definition form.

19. Press **F2**. The Page Header form appears.

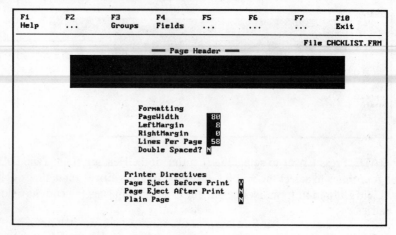

20. Type **Check Listing**. Press **Enter** five times. Type **5** and press **Enter**. Press **F10**. RL asks if you want to save the form.

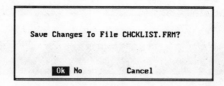

21. Press **Enter** to select OK. The RL Main menu appears.

22. Type **Q**. The DOS prompt appears.

23. Turn to Module 22 to continue the learning sequence.

Module 8
ACCEPT

DESCRIPTION

The Accept command places a user response in a variable. The optional prompt clause lets you place a question or other form of text on the screen. Unlike the At (@) Say/Get command, you cannot directly place the input to an Accept command in a database field. The Accept command does not allow formatting of the input either. The command line interface of the Accept command appears below.

```
ACCEPT [<PROMPT>] TO <MEMVAR>
```

APPLICATIONS

Use the Accept command when you want to obtain user input, and the format of the input and the position of any prompts are not important. An example of this is an opening prompt before any display elements, such as an editing screen, are in place.

TYPICAL OPERATION

In this example you use the Accept command to determine which database the sample program will use. Begin this example in your word processor with MAILLIST.PRG loaded.

1. Add the following text to the variable section at the beginning of the program.
   ```
   ANSWER = 'A'
   DB_NAME = 'Y'
   ```

2. Add the following text before and after the Use command at the beginning of the program as shown below.
   ```
   * chr(013) = carriage return and chr (010) = line feed.
   accept 'Do you want to use the standard database (if no, type the new' +;
      'database name)?' + chr(013) + chr(010) to DB_NAME
   if (DB_NAME = 'Y') .or. (DB_NAME = 'y')
      use MAILLIST index LASTNAME
   endif
   ```

3. Save the document and exit your word processor. Type **CL MAILLIST** at the DOS prompt. Press **Enter**.

4. Type **MAILLIST**. Press **Enter**. The message "Do you want to use the standard database (if no, type the new database name)?" appears.

5. Type **Y** and press **Enter**. The mailing list program display appears.

6. Type **Q** to quit the program. Type **MAILLIST**. Press **Enter**. Type **N**. Press **Enter**. The message "Database not found in current directory." appears. The DOS prompt appears.

7. Turn to Module 12 to continue the learning sequence.

Module 9
APPEND

DESCRIPTION

The Append command adds records to a database. Clipper provides two variations of the Append command. The Append Blank command adds a blank record to the end of a database. The Append From command lets you copy records from an already existing database. The command line interface of the Append command appears below.

```
APPEND BLANK
```

OR

```
APPEND [SCOPE] [FIELDS <FIELD LIST>] FROM <FILE>/<EXPC1> [FOR <CONDITION>]
[WHILE <CONDITION>] [SDF]/[DELIMITED [WITH BLANK/<DELIMITER>/<EXPC2>]]
```

The scope clause determines how many of the source database records Append adds to the target database. Clipper uses three key words to determine the scope. All adds every record in the source database to the target. Next <n> adds the number of records specified by n. Clipper starts adding records from the record pointed to by the record pointer. Record <n> adds a single record; <n> specifies which record to add.

The fields clause specifies which fields to transfer from the source database to the target. If the source database contains fields the target doesn't, Clipper ignores them. Any fields not filled as Clipper adds records to the target database remain blank.

The only required entry when using Append From is the file you wish to append from. Clipper lets you use the actual database filename, or you can place the filename in a variable and use the variable instead.

The for clause lets you describe which records to add from the source database when using a scope of all or next. The condition tells Clipper what criteria a record must meet before the target database accepts it. For example, if you had a listing of people and their ages and wanted to build a new database containing only people 40 years of age and older, you would use the statement append all from <filename> for AGE > 39.

The while clause works somewhat like the for clause. It limits the number of records appended from the source database. However, instead of finding all the records that meet a certain criteria, the while clause appends records while the database meets the criteria and stops when it doesn't. This allows you to find a contiguous section of a database.

The SDF (system data format ASCII file) and delimited clauses let you import records from files that don't use a standard database format. An SDF file contains fixed length records separated by a carriage return and line feed. An end of file marker (Ctrl-Z or ASCII 26) marks the end of the file. A delimited file contains variable length records separated by a carriage return and line feed. A comma (,) separates each field in the record, and double quotes (") mark the boundaries of character fields. An end of file marker marks the end of the file. When you use the delimited clause with the with blank clause, a space marks the boundary between fields. When you use the delimited clause with the with delimiter clause, Clipper uses the specified delimiter as a field boundary. Clipper lets you specify the delimiter or a variable containing the delimiter.

APPLICATIONS

Use the Append Blank command to add blank records to the end of a database. You normally use this command for any type of standard data entry screen program. For example, we will use this version of the Append command in the sample program.

Use the Append From command when you want to convert an ASCII file to a database file. This method of conversion works well when you want to send data from one machine to another. Since the two machines may not use the same database format, printing the contents of the database to an ASCII file and then reconverting it provides the only means of transfer.

TYPICAL OPERATION

In this example you add records to the example database using the Append Blank command. Begin this example at the DOS prompt in the C:\CLIPPER\0022 directory.

1. Add the following text to MAILLIST.PRG between the Use command and the first @ Say command as shown below.

```
use MAILLIST index LASTNAME
append blank
@ 04, 06 say 'Name:'
```

2. Save the document and exit your word processor.

3. Type **CL MAILLIST** at the DOS prompt. Press **Enter**. The Clipper batch file clears the screen, then compiles and links the program.

4. Type **MAILLIST**. Press **Enter**. Type **GEORGE**. Press **Enter**. Type **A**. Type **SMITH**. Press **Enter**. Type **1212 12th Street**. Press **Enter** twice. Type **ANYWHERE**. Press **Enter**. Type **CA**. Type **92111**. Press **Enter**. Type **6192221212**. The DOS prompt appears. Notice the program automatically inserts the parentheses around the telephone area code, and the dash between the third and fourth digits of the number.

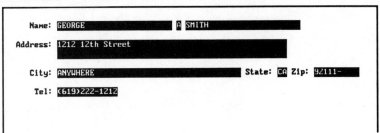

5. Type **DBU** and press **Enter**. The database utility screen appears.

6. Type **MAILLIST** and press **Enter**. The database utility retrieves MAILLIST.DBF.

7. Press **F5**. The Browse menu appears.

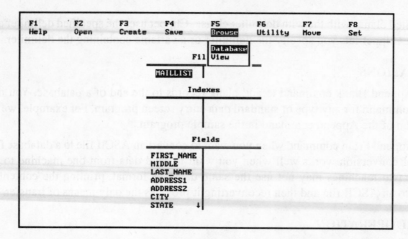

8. Press **Enter**. The database utility displays the contents of MAILLIST.DBF. Notice the first (and only) record contains the previously typed information.

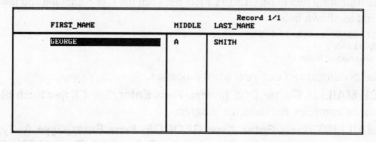

9. Press **Esc** twice to exit the database utility. Type **Y**. The DOS prompt appears.
10. Turn to Module 46 to continue the learning sequence.

Module 10
AT (@) BOX

DESCRIPTION

The At (@) Box command draws a square or rectangle on the display, then fills the box with the requested character. EXPN1 through EXPN4 tell Clipper where to draw the box. EXPN1 contains the highest row. EXPN2 contains the leftmost column. EXPN3 contains the lowest row. EXPN4 contains the rightmost column. The EXPC entry contains nine characters. The first eight characters tell Clipper what extended ASCII characters to use for each corner and side of the box. Clipper begins drawing the box at the upper left corner of the display and proceeds clockwise. The first character in EXPC contains the character to use for the upper left corner. The last character in EXPC contains the fill character Clipper uses to fill in the box. The command line interface of the At (@) Box command appears below.

```
@ <EXPN1>, <EXPN2>, <EXPN3>, <EXPN4> BOX <EXPC>
```

APPLICATIONS

Use the At (@) Box command to draw boxes where needed on your display. For example, you could separate various portions of the data entry display to reduce screen clutter. You could also use a box to surround the data entry area and another to surround the menu area.

TYPICAL OPERATION

In this example you draw a box around the data entry area using the At (@) Box command. Begin this example in your word processor with MAILLIST.PRG loaded.

1. Type the following text.
   ```
   * Display the database information and the editing screen.
   @ 01, 00, 24, 79 box ' ╔═╗║╝═╚║▒ '
   @ 04, 06 say 'Name:'
   ```

   ### NOTE
   You can duplicate the nine characters used for EXPC by pressing Alt and each of the following key sequences on the numeric keypad: 201, 205, 187, 186, 188, 205, 200, 186, and 177. You must use the numeric keypad, not the numbers appearing above the QWERTY section of the keyboard. Release the Alt key after each key sequence.

2. Save the document and exit your word processor.
3. Type **CL MAILLIST** at the DOS prompt. Press **Enter**.
4. Type **MAILLIST**. Press **Enter**. The program asks if you want to add a new record.

5. Type **Y**. The data entry screen appears.

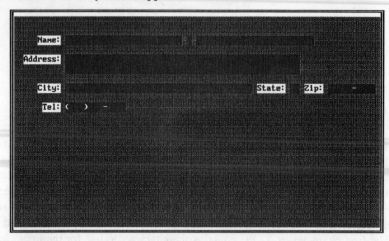

6. Type **SAMUEL**. Press **Enter**. Type **L**. Type **STONE**. Press **Enter**. Type **1234 A Street**. Press **Enter** twice. Type **SOMEPLACE**. Press **Enter**. Type **WI**. Type **532110114**. Type **4141992929**. The DOS prompt appears.

7. Type **DBU** and press **Enter** to execute the database utility program. Type **MAILLIST** and press **Enter** to select the database. Press **Down Arrow** to select the index field. Type **LASTNAME** and press **Enter** to select the index file. The database utility retrieves MAILLIST.DBF and its associated index file.

8. Press **F5**. The Browse menu appears.

9. Press **Enter**. The database utility displays the contents of MAILLIST.DBF. Notice the records appear in order of last name.

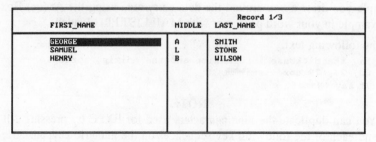

10. Press **Esc** twice to exit the database utility. Type **Y**. The DOS prompt appears.

11. Turn to Module 93 to continue the learning sequence.

Module 11
AT (@) CLEAR TO
(BLANKING DISPLAY SECTIONS)

DESCRIPTION

The At (@) Clear To command clears a rectangular portion of the screen. EXPN1 and EXPN2 contain the upper left screen coordinates with EXPN1 containing the row. The to clause lets you specify the lower right corner of the rectangle. EXPN3 and EXPN4 contain the lower right coordinates with EXPN3 containing the row. If you do not specify the lower right corner, Clipper automatically uses the coordinates 24, 79. The command line interface of the At (@) Clear To command appears below.

```
@ <EXPN1>, <EXPN2> CLEAR [TO <EXPN3>, <EXPN4>]
```

APPLICATIONS

Use the @ Clear To command to clear rectangular portions of the display. This command is especially effective when you create a display containing multiple windows. It allows you to erase the contents of each window as needed. This command also works well with message lines. By using an @ Clear To command, you preserve any borders or other constructs at the right side of the display.

TYPICAL OPERATION

In this example you use the @ Clear To command to enhance previously created routines and to clear the menu area of the display. Begin this example in your word processor with MAILLIST.PRG loaded.

1. Add the following text between the line drawing command and the @ Say record number command at the beginning of the program.

```
@ 20, 01 to 20, 78
@ 21, 01 clear to 23, 78
@ 02, 39 say ' Record Number: '
```

2. Change the following text after the otherwise clause of the Do Case control structure at the beginning of the program.

```
    @ 23,04 say ' Record not updated '
otherwise
    @ 23,04 clear to 23,78
endcase
```

3. Save the document and exit your word processor. Type **CL MAILLIST** at the DOS prompt. Press **Enter**.

4. Type **MAILLIST**. Press **Enter**. The mailing list program display appears.

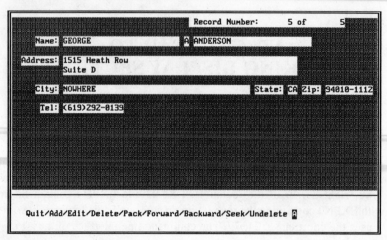

5. Type **B**. The beginning of file message appears.
6. Type **F**. The beginning of file message disappears. Notice the At (@) Clear To command appears to work more efficiently than the At (@) Say command used previously.
7. Type **Q**. The DOS prompt appears.
8. Turn to Module 8 to continue the learning sequence.

Module 12
AT (@) PROMPT
(MENU CREATION)

DESCRIPTION

The At (@) Prompt command works in conjunction with the Menu To command to create menu screens. The At (@) Prompt command defines the menu entries and any messages displayed at the bottom of the screen. EXPN1 defines the row coordinate, and EXPN2 defines the column coordinate of the prompt. The first character expression, EXPC1, contains the menu entry displayed in the window. The message clause and associated character expression contain the message Clipper displays at the bottom of the screen as additional help. Clipper allows you to use character strings delimited by single (') or double quotes ("), or a variable for the character expression. The command line interface of the At (@) Prompt command appears below.

```
@ <EXPN1>, <EXPN2> PROMPT <EXPC1> [MESSAGE <EXPC2>]
```

APPLICATIONS

Use the At (@) Prompt command as the first half of the process of defining a lighted bar menu. A lighted bar menu (like the drop down menus used in many programs) provides the two advantages of nicer appearance and better use of screen space. If the menu appears only when needed, the program can use the space normally used by the menu for other purposes. The addition of messages displayed at the bottom of the screen allows you to create friendly, helpful menus. The user can use the entry as written, or read the prompt at the bottom of the screen for further assistance.

TYPICAL OPERATION

In this example you begin the process of converting the sample program to drop down menus using the At (@) Prompt command. Begin this example in your word processor with MAILLIST.PRG loaded.

1. Change the text between the clear display note and the begin processing loop note to appear as below.
    ```
    * Clear the display and prepare the database for use.
    clear screen
    use MAILLIST index LASTNAME
    * Begin processing loop.
    ```

2. Add the following text between the menu prompt Read command and the beginning of the case statement.
    ```
    read
    @ 03, 04 prompt 'Quit' message 'Leave this application.'
    @ 04, 04 prompt 'Add' message 'Add a new record.'
    @ 05, 04 prompt 'Edit' message 'Change the contents of this record.'
    @ 06, 04 prompt 'Delete' message 'Mark this record for removal.'
    ```

```
@ 07, 04 prompt 'Pack' message 'Remove all marked records.'
@ 08, 04 prompt 'Forward' message 'Go one record forward.'
@ 09, 04 prompt 'Backward' message 'Go one record back.'
@ 10, 04 prompt 'Seek' message 'Find a particular last name.'
@ 11, 04 prompt 'Undelete' message 'Remove this record from the ;
   deletion list.'
* Add a new record.
do case
case ANSWER = 'A'
```

3. Change the record number and deleted messages as follows.

```
@ 21, 45 say ' Record Number: '
@ 21, 60 say recno()
@ 21, 67 say ' of '
@ 21, 71 say reccount()
if deleted()
   @ 21, 04 say ' DELETED '
else
   @ 21, 04 say '         ' && Type space 9 times.
endif
```

4. Save the document and exit your word processor. Type **CL MAILLIST** at the DOS prompt. Press **Enter**.

5. Type **MAILLIST**. Press **Enter**.

6. Type **Q**. The menu prompts appear intertwined with the program display.

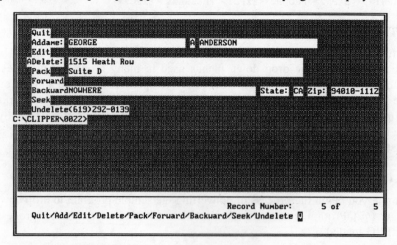

7. Turn to Module 54 to continue the learning sequence.

Module 13
AT (@) SAY/GET
(POSITIONING/RETRIEVING
TEXT AND DATA)

DESCRIPTION

The At (@) Say/Get command places text and data at the requested position on the default output device. In addition, this command obtains user input from the keyboard, displays it on the output device, and checks its validity. The command line interface of the At (@) Say/Get command appears below.

```
@ <EXPN1>, <EXPN2> [SAY <EXP> [PICTURE <EXPC1>]] [GET <VARIABLE> [PICTURE
<EXPC2>] [WHEN <EXPL1>] [RANGE <EXPN3>, <EXPN4>] [VALID <EXPL2>]]
```

The two variables EXPN1 and EXPN2 contain the row and column coordinates that Clipper uses to position the information. EXPN1 contains the row, EXPN2 contains the column. When the default output goes to the screen, the order in which these coordinates appear does not matter. Clipper moves around the screen placing data and text where requested. However, when the default output goes to the printer, all the coordinates must proceed in order from the first to last row, and first to last column within a row. If Clipper sees a row less than the previous row, it ejects the paper and begins at that position on a new sheet. Likewise, if Clipper sees a column less than the previous column for a given row, it ejects the paper and begins at that position on a new sheet.

The say clause sends text or data to the default output device. The EXP variable contains the text, data, or mixture of both to send. You must enclose any text within double (") or single (') quotes. Clipper allows you to mix text and data by using the concatenation symbol (+). For example @ 1, 1 say "Some text: " + VARIABLE is a legal statement in Clipper as long as all elements are characters. You may use a function to convert numeric data within a statement to character data.

The picture clause within the say clause lets you format the output. You place a picture of how you want the text to look within double or single quotes after the picture clause. A picture consists of one or more template symbols. Clipper also provides a picture shorthand called functions. You use a single picture function to format an entire line of output. Clipper differentiates between template symbols and functions by preceding a function with an at (@) sign. Table 13-1 contains a listing of picture template symbols. Table 13-2 contains a listing of picture functions.

Table 13-1. Picture Template Symbols

Template	Result
A	Displays only alphabetic characters. No symbols or numbers allowed.
N	Displays only alphabetic characters or numbers. No symbols allowed.
X	Displays any character.
9	Displays numbers and negative/positive sign symbols only. No alphabetic characters or other symbols allowed.
#	Displays numbers, negative/positive signs, and spaces for any data type. No alphabetic characters or other symbols allowed.
L	Displays only logical operators .T. and .F. No alphabetic characters, numbers, or symbols allowed.
Y	Displays only logical operators Y and N. No alphabetic characters, numbers, or symbols allowed.
!	Displays alphabetic characters in upper case even if input is in lower case. Does not change data in database fields. Does change keyboard input.
$	Displays a dollar sign in place of leading spaces in a numeric variable.
*	Displays an asterisk in place of leading spaces in a numeric variable.
.	Marks the position of a decimal point in numeric variables.
,	Marks the position of a comma in numeric variables.
Symbol	Any symbol other than those described above, displayed and input as characters. Cursor skips these symbols during input.

Table 13-2. Picture Function Symbols

Function	Variable Type	Result
A	C	Allows only alphabetic characters. Does not allow numeric, date, or logical input.
B	N	Displays numbers left justified. Does not regulate input data type.
C	N	Displays CR after all positive numbers. Although normally used with monetary amounts, does not regulate input data type.
D	D, N	Displays date using the format specified using the SET DATE command. The default date format is American (month/day/year). Does not regulate input data type.
E	D, N	Displays dates in British format. Displays numbers in European format (period and comma reversed). Does not regulate input data type.
K	All	If the user presses any key other than a cursor key (indicating they want to change this field), this function clears the get variable.
R	C	Inserts non-template characters into a get. For example, if a user normally inputs a particular value, you could reduce data entry time by placing the value there automatically. This does not prevent the user from changing the value.

Table 13-2. Picture Function Symbols (Cont.)

Function	Variable Type	Result
S	C	Allows scrolling within an input field. If a field allows more input than the space displayed on screen, the user can scroll through the field to see the entire entry.
X	N	Displays DB after negative numbers. Although normally used with monetary amounts, does not regulate input data type.
Z	N	Displays zero as a blank. Does not regulate input data type.
(	N	Encloses negative numbers in parentheses with leading spaces. Although normally used with monetary amounts, does not regulate input data type.
)	N	Encloses negative numbers in parentheses without leading spaces. Although normally used with monetary amounts, does not regulate input data type.
!	C	Displays all alphabetic characters in upper case. Converts input from gets to upper case.

Variable Type Legend
D   Date
C   Character
N   Numeric
L   Logical

The get clause obtains user input for a specific variable. A get does not immediately request the data, instead it waits for activation by a Read command (Module 62). Clipper maintains a list of pending gets until either a Clear Gets or a Read command clears them. Clipper places the user input in the variable appearing after the get clause. You may use a database field in place of a variable by specifying the work area, then the variable. Place an arrow between the variable and the work area (for example, A->Field_Name).

The picture clause within the get clause affects how Clipper formats the keyboard input. Table 13-1 contains a listing of picture template symbols. Table 13-2 contains a listing of picture functions.

The when clause allows you to specify a condition that must exist before the user can enter the get. For example, you could use this clause to specify conditional blanks on a form. In some cases the user may need to fill in the blank, at other times the blank is unnecessary. One instance of this need is an accounting system. When the user fills out a purchase order, some blanks require data. When the company receives the purchase, the user must fill in other blanks. In both cases some blanks remain available. For example, you would fill in the order date only when you initially fill out the purchase order. Likewise, the user fills in the receive date only after the company receives the purchase. However, you always need access to the company name and address information.

The range clause within the get clause limits the range of input for date and numeric variables. EXPN3 contains the lower limit; EXPN4 contains the upper limit. For example, if you placed the statement @ 01, 01, get VARIABLE range 1, 10 within your code, Clipper would limit the input to the range between 1 and 10. If the user input is not within the requested range, Clipper returns control to the affected get until the input is within range.

The valid clause within the get clause validates the input against a logical statement. For example, if you included the statement @ 01, 01, get VARIABLE valid VARIABLE > 10 within your code, Clipper would look for a numeric input greater that 10. If the user input does not set the logical statement true, Clipper returns control to the affected get until the input is valid. Unlike the range clause, the valid clause works with any type of input. Also, the logical statement can have more that one argument: for example, valid VARIABLE = A .or. VARIABLE = B. Clipper also lets you use user-defined functions as an argument for valid. You must never use the range and valid clauses together in the same get.

APPLICATIONS

Use the say clause to send text and/or data to the default output device. Clipper uses the picture clause to format the text or data as desired. By using a mixture of picture symbol templates and functions, you can achieve various formatting effects.

Use the get clause to retrieve user input from the keyboard after a program issues a Read command. Clipper maintains a list of pending gets until a Read or Clear Gets command clears them. The picture clause formats the incoming data. The effects of the various picture symbol templates and functions are the same as those for the say picture clause. The range clause allows you to define the upper and lower limits of numeric and date variables. By using a picture and range together, you can ensure the user inputs only numbers in the desired range. The valid clause allows you to define a logical set of parameters the user input must meet before being accepted. It works on any type of user input. Clipper allows you to use a user-defined function in place of an actual logical statement. This function could compare the input to a list of values and insert the closest correct value in the variable. You could also create a user-defined function to scan text strings for undesirable values.

TYPICAL OPERATION

In this example you add a screen display to MAILLIST.PRG using the At (@) Say/Get command. Begin this example at the DOS prompt in the C:\CLIPPER\0022 directory.

NOTE
This example assumes you built the database using the DBU utility in Module 5. This example will not work without both the database and index files.

1. Edit MAILLIST.PRG using a word processor. Add the highlighted text to the end of MAILLIST.PRG.

```
clear screen
use MAILLIST index LASTNAME
@ 04, 06 say 'Name:'
@ 06, 03 say 'Address:'
@ 09, 06 say 'City:'
@ 09, 53 say 'State:'
@ 09, 63 say 'Zip:'
```

```
@ 11, 07 say 'Tel:'
@ 04, 12 get FIRST_NAME picture '@!'
@ 04, 38 get MIDDLE picture '!'
@ 04, 40 get LAST_NAME picture '@!'
@ 06, 12 get ADDRESS1
@ 07, 12 get ADDRESS2
@ 09, 12 get CITY picture '@!'
@ 09, 60 get STATE picture '!!'
@ 09, 68 get ZIP picture '99999-9999'
@ 11, 12 get TELEPHONE picture '(999)999-9999'
```

2. Press **Enter**. Save the document and exit your word processor.

3. Type **CL MAILLIST** at the DOS prompt. Press **Enter**. The Clipper batch file clears the screen, then compiles and links the program.

4. Type **MAILLIST**. Press **Enter**. The program clears the display. Notice Clipper displays the text and highlighted blocks to receive data but does not stop to retrieve the data.

5. Turn to Module 62 to continue the learning sequence.

Module 14
AT (@) TO DOUBLE
(LINE DRAWING)

DESCRIPTION

The At (@) To Double command draws single or double lines using the extended ASCII character set from one point to another. The two numbers preceding the to clause provide the starting point. The two numbers after the to clause provide the ending point. EXPN1 and EXPN3 provide the row coordinate. If EXPN1 and EXPN3 are equal, Clipper draws a horizontal line. EXPN2 and EXPN4 provide the column coordinates. If EXPN2 and EXPN4 are the same, Clipper draws a vertical line. If neither set of coordinates are the same, Clipper draws a box using the starting point as the upper left corner and the ending point as the lower right corner. The double clause allows you to draw double lines and boxes instead of single lines. The command line interface of the At (@) To Double command appears below.

```
@ <EXPN1>, <EXPN2> TO <EXPN3>, <EXPN4> [DOUBLE]
```

APPLICATIONS

Use the At (@) To Double command to draw lines on the display. You can also use this command to draw boxes if you only want double or single lines. By adding lines between rows of fields, you reduce the visual clutter apparent when the fields appear too close together. You can also use lines to separate the data entry area from the command line.

TYPICAL OPERATION

In this example you use the At (@) To Double command to draw a line separating the command line from the data entry area. Begin this example in your word processor with MAILLIST.PRG loaded.

1. Add the following text at the position shown within the program.

   ```
   * Display the database information and the editing screen.
   @ 01, 00, 24, 79 box DOUBLE_LINE
   @ 20, 01 to 20, 78
   @ 04, 06 say 'Name:'
   ```

2. Save the document and exit your word processor.

3. Type **CL MAILLIST** at the DOS prompt. Press **Enter**.

4. Type **MAILLIST**. Press **Enter**. Type **N**. The program doesn't add a new record to the database. Notice the single line appearing in the lower half of the display.

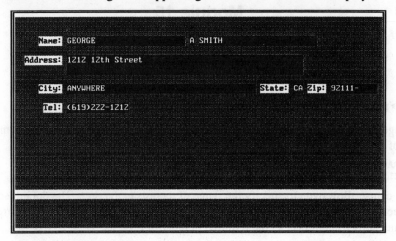

5. Press **Esc**. The DOS prompt appears.
6. Turn to Module 38 to continue the learning sequence.

Module 15
AVERAGE

DESCRIPTION

The Average command computes the average of a range of database records. The command line interface of the Average command appears below.

```
AVERAGE [<SCOPE>] <EXPN LIST> TO <MEMVAR LIST> [FOR <CONDITION>]
[WHILE <CONDITION>]
```

The scope clause allows you to specify the range of records to average. The default scope is all. If you specify next with a number, Clipper starts averaging records from the current record position and stops when it checks the required number of records.

The EXPN TO MEMVAR clause specifies what fields to use, how to average them (math expression), and where Average sends the result. This is the only required parameter for the Average command.

The For condition clause allows you to limit the number of records averaged to those meeting a predefined condition. Normally, the condition contains a field name, then a relational operator (>, <, <>, =), followed by the condition. Clipper averages all records in the database meeting the defined condition and scope.

The While condition clause allows you to limit the number of records averaged to those meeting a predefined condition. Unlike the For condition clause, Clipper stops averaging records as soon as it sees a record not meeting the criteria. In some respects, this clause works like a combination of the for condition and scope clauses.

APPLICATIONS

Use the Average command whenever you need to find the numeric average of a group of records. This command is especially useful in statistical analysis; for example, if you recorded the time required to perform a task each time you performed it, then wanted to find the average time required to perform the task.

TYPICAL OPERATION

In this example you compute the average check size and deposit size using the Average command. Begin this example in your word processor with CHCKBOOK.PRG loaded.

1. Add the following text to the STATS procedure.
    ```
    private TCHECKS, NTCHECKS, DEPOSITS, READY
    private AVE_CHCK, AVE_DEP
    AVE_CHCK = 0
    AVE_DEP = 0
    TCHECKS = 0
    NTCHECKS = 0
    DEPOSITS = 0
    READY = ' '
    ```

```
* Get the statistics
count to TCHECKS for (TAX_ITEM = .T.) .and. (DEPOSIT = 0)
count to NTCHECKS for (TAX_ITEM = .F.) .and. (DEPOSIT = 0)
count to DEPOSITS for DEPOSIT <> 0
average AMOUNT to AVE_CHCK for AMOUNT <> 0
average DEPOSIT to AVE_DEP for DEPOSIT <> 0
* Display the statistics.
@ 12, 04 say 'Number of Tax Deductible Checks:      ' +;
   ltrim(str(TCHECKS, 5, 0))
@ 13, 04 say 'Number of Non-Tax Deductible Checks: ' +;
   ltrim(str(NTCHECKS, 5, 0))
@ 14, 04 say 'Number of Deposits:                  ' +;
   ltrim(str(DEPOSITS, 5, 0))
@ 15, 04 say 'Average Check Amount:                ' +;
   ltrim(str(AVE_CHCK, 10, 2))
@ 16, 04 say 'Average Deposit Amount:              ' +;
   ltrim(str(AVE_DEP, 10, 2))
@ 22, 04 say 'Press any key when ready...' get READY
read
```

2. Save the document and exit your word processor. Type **CL CHCKBOOK** at the DOS prompt. Press **Enter**.

3. Type **MAILLIST**. Press **Enter**. The mailing list program menu appears.

4. Press **F4**. The checkbook program menu appears.

5. Press **Down Arrow** until the Stats option of the menu appears.

6. Press **Enter**. The checkbook statistics appear. Notice the statistics now include average check and deposit size.

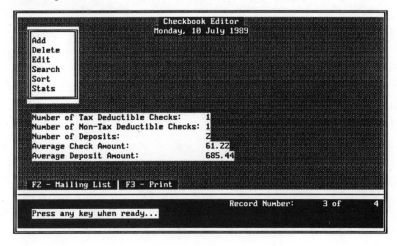

7. Press **Enter** to erase the statistics and return to the menu. Type **A** and press **Enter**. Enter the following information at the fields indicated. Type **N** when asked if you want to add any more checks. The checkbook program menu appears.

Date: 07/10/89
Check: 3
For: JEAN'S SHOES
Amount: 520.00

8. Press **Down Arrow** to select Stats. Press **Enter**. The checkbook statistics appear. Notice the statistics correctly show the addition of a non-tax deductible check and a different average check amount.

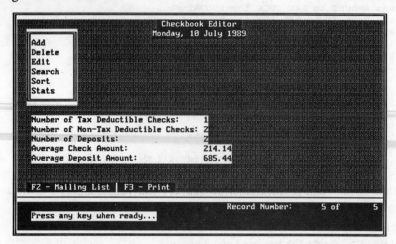

```
                        Checkbook Editor
                     Monday, 10 July 1989
 ┌────────┐
 │Add     │
 │Delete  │
 │Edit    │
 │Search  │
 │Sort    │
 │Stats   │
 └────────┘

 Number of Tax Deductible Checks:      1
 Number of Non-Tax Deductible Checks:  2
 Number of Deposits:                   2
 Average Check Amount:                 214.14
 Average Deposit Amount:               685.44


 F2 - Mailing List │ F3 - Print

                                    Record Number:    5 of      5
 ┌──────────────────────────────┐
 │Press any key when ready...   │
 └──────────────────────────────┘
```

9. Press **Enter** to return to the checkbook program menu. Type **Q** to select quit. Press **Enter**. The DOS prompt appears.

10. Turn to Module 81 to continue the learning sequence.

Module 16
BEGIN SEQUENCE

DESCRIPTION

The Begin Sequence control structure lets you define a section of code as a control structure. Most control structures of this nature provide protection from run-time errors; for example, if the user tries to open a nonexistent file or the computer experiences a hardware error. The command line interface of the Begin Sequence control structure appears below.

```
BEGIN SEQUENCE <STATEMENTS> [BREAK [<ERROR NUMBER>]] <STATEMENTS>
[RECOVER [<VARIABLE>]] <STATEMENTS> [RETRY] END [SEQUENCE]
```

The optional break clause within the control structure allows you to get out of the control structure and execute an error handling procedure. You may optionally try to prompt the user to fix the problem and execute the control structure code again. The error number allows you to specify what error condition occurred. If you specify a recover point within the control structure, Clipper resumes program execution at that point within the control structure. Otherwise, control resumes at the first executable statement after the end clause.

The optional recover clause specifies the point Clipper passes control to in the event of a break. The statements following the recover clause contain code that helps the user get through the error condition. The variable following the recover clause receives the error number from the break. This allows you to perform any special setups or error handling required by certain types of error. If the error is such that the user can retry the sequence of events that led to the error, use the retry clause. Clipper automatically resumes execution at the beginning of the sequence when it sees the retry clause. A printer failure is an example of a sequence you could retry. If the printer is off-line, then the user could retry printing after setting the printer on-line.

APPLICATIONS

Use the Break Sequence control structure whenever you need to define a section of code as a control structure. By defining the code as a control structure, you can compensate for some types of run-time errors that might occur. You can add code that the program doesn't normally execute after the end clause of the control structure to handle the error.

TYPICAL OPERATION

In this example you define a section of the sample program source code as a control structure using the Begin Sequence control structure. Begin this example in your word processor with MAILLIST.PRG loaded.

1. Add the following text to the variable section at the beginning of the sample program.
```
KEYPRESS = 0
CPRESSED = 'Y'
```

2. Add the following text to the database edit menu section. Remove the @ Say command.

```
do DISPLAY_MENU
KEYPRESS = lastkey()
if KEYPRESS = 3    && If the user pressed Ctrl-C
   break           && then exit.
endif
```

3. Add the following text after the Do While command at the beginning of the program.

```
do while ANSWER <> 1
* If the user presses Ctrl-C, then ask if they really want
* to exit.
begin sequence
* Display the editing screen.
```

4. Add the following text between the endcase clause of the Do Case control structure and enddo at the end of the program. Move the enddo clause after the Quit command.

```
endcase
if ANSWER <> 1
   loop                && Back to beginning if no errors occur.
endif
* Close the database and exit to DOS. ; IF ANSWER = I
quit                         ; ENDIF
end               && Begin Sequence    IF ANSWER <> I ; LOOP ; ENDIF
* If the user presses Ctrl-C follow this routine.
@ 23, 04 say 'Are you sure you want to exit? ' get CPRESSED picture '!'
read
if CPRESSED = 'Y'
   quit
endif             && Otherwise go back up and get another menu selection.
enddo
```

5. Save the document and exit your word processor. Type **CL MAILLIST** at the DOS prompt. Press **Enter**.

6. Type **MAILLIST**. Press **Enter**.

7. Type **E**. The Edit display appears.

8. Press **Esc**. The menu reappears. Notice the program operates normally.

9. Press **Ctrl-C**. The program displays the message, "Are you sure you want to exit?"

10. Type **N**. The menu reappears.

11. Press **Ctrl-C**. Type **Y**. The DOS prompt appears.

12. Turn to Module 80 to continue the learning sequence.

Module 17
CALL

DESCRIPTION

The Call command lets you execute separately compiled routines written in assembly language or C. When creating a program in assembly language, you must use C calling conventions. Any separately compiled routine must use FAR calls/returns. PROCESS contains the name of the routine to execute. The optional with clause allows you to pass parameters to the routine. EXP LIST contains the passed parameters. The command line interface of the Call command appears below.

```
CALL <PROCESS> [WITH <EXP LIST>]
```

APPLICATIONS

Use the Call command to add functionality to a Clipper program. By using separately compiled routines, you can add functions not normally found in Clipper. For example, you may want to add a function to check the status of a serial port before using it to print. Or you may want to add a communications module to your program. To use this command you must know either C or assembly language and associated programming techniques.

TYPICAL OPERATION

The Call command requires knowledge of advanced C or assembly language programming techniques. A discussion of how to create separately compiled routines is not within the scope of this book. Turn to Module 95 to continue the learning sequence.

Module 18
CANCEL/QUIT

DESCRIPTION

The Cancel/Quit commands close all files, end the current program, deallocate all memory, and return control to the operating system. These commands operate like a combination of the Close All and Return commands. They perform the same function but require 16 bytes less memory than the close/return combination. By saving memory, you reduce the hardware requirements of a target machine. The command line interface of the Cancel/Quit commands appears below.

    QUIT

    OR

    CANCEL

APPLICATIONS

Use the Cancel/Quit commands whenever you want to stop program execution and return control to the operating system. When placed at the end of a program, it reduces the two-step close and return method of program termination to a single step.

You can enclose a quit statement within control structures to provide a means of conditionally terminating the program. For example, if during startup the program determines the user machine does not contain the correct hardware, you can use a Cancel/Quit command to end the program immediately.

TYPICAL OPERATION

In this example you replace the Close All and Return commands with a Quit command. Begin this example at the DOS prompt in the C:\CLIPPER\0022 directory.

1. Type **CL MAILLIST** at the DOS prompt. Press **Enter**. Notice the size of the program code.

```
C:\CLIPPER\0022>Clipper MAILLIST
The Clipper Compiler
Copyright (c) Nantucket Corp 1985-1987.   All Rights Reserved.
Microsoft C Runtime Library Routines,
Copyright (c) Microsoft Corp 1984-1987.   All Rights Reserved.

Compiling MAILLIST.PRG
Code Pass 1
Code Pass 2
Code size 315, Symbols 192, Constants 245

C:\CLIPPER\0022>IF NOT ERRORLEVEL 1 Plink86 FI MAILLIST LIB \CLIPPER\CLIPPER, \C
LIPPER\EXTEND
PLINK86plus ( Nantucket ) Version 2.24.
Copyright (C) 1987 by Phoenix Technologies Ltd.,
All Rights Reserved.


MAILLIST.EXE (150 K)
C:\CLIPPER\0022>
```

2. Edit MAILLIST.PRG using a word processor. Type **quit** at the end of MAILLIST.PRG.

3. Press **Enter**. Remove the Close All and Return commands which appear directly above the Quit command. Save the document and exit your word processor.

4. Type **CL MAILLIST** at the DOS prompt. Press **Enter**. Notice the size of the program code decreases from the amount in step 1.

```
C:\CLIPPER\0022>Clipper MAILLIST
The Clipper Compiler
Copyright (c) Nantucket Corp 1985-1987.   All Rights Reserved.
Microsoft C Runtime Library Routines,
Copyright (c) Microsoft Corp 1984-1987.   All Rights Reserved.

Compiling MAILLIST.PRG
Code Pass 1
Code Pass 2
Code size 299, Symbols 192, Constants 245

C:\CLIPPER\0022>IF NOT ERRORLEVEL 1 Plink86 FI MAILLIST LIB \CLIPPER\CLIPPER, \C
LIPPER\EXTEND
PLINK86plus ( Nantucket ) Version 2.24.
Copyright (C) 1987 by Phoenix Technologies Ltd.,
All Rights Reserved.


MAILLIST.EXE (150 K)
C:\CLIPPER\0022>
```

5. Type **MAILLIST**. Press **Enter**. Notice the display appears exactly as before.

6. Type **N**. Press **Esc**. The DOS prompt appears. Notice, Clipper does not tell you it closed the files.

7. Turn to Module 55 to continue the learning sequence.

Module 19
CLEAR ALL

DESCRIPTION

The Clear All command closes all databases and associated files, deallocates any memory used by variables, and changes the work area to 1. The command line interface of the Clear All command appears below.

```
CLEAR ALL
```

APPLICATIONS

Use the Clear All command to reset the Clipper environment before executing a procedure. This is especially useful when you link several stand-alone programs together.

TYPICAL OPERATION

In this example you use the Clear All command to reset the environment for both the print and mailing list programs. Begin this example in your word processor with PRINT.PRG loaded.

1. Add the following text to the beginning of the program.
   ```
   * TODAY'S DATE
   * Make sure the environment is clear.
   clear all
   * Perform program setup.
   ```

2. Save the document and exit your word processor. Type **CLIPPER PRINT** at the DOS prompt. Press **Enter**. Clipper compiles the print program.

3. Load MAILLIST.PRG into your word processor. Add the following text to the beginning of the program.
   ```
   * TODAY'S DATE
   * Make sure the environment is clear.
   clear all
   * Program Variables
   ```

4. Save the document and exit your word processor. Type **CL MAILLIST PRINT** at the DOS prompt. Press **Enter**.

5. Type **MAILLIST**. Press **Enter**. Notice the program operates the same as the previous module.

6. Press **F3**. The print program appears. Notice it also operates the same as the previous module. Press **F2** to return to the mailing list program.

7. Select Quit by pressing **Enter**. The DOS prompt appears.

8. Turn to Module 20 to continue the learning sequence.

Module 20
CLEAR GETS

DESCRIPTION

The Clear Gets command clears any pending gets. Clipper considers a get pending only after a Read command in this instance. The command line interface of the Clear Gets command appears below.

```
CLEAR GETS
```

APPLICATIONS

Use the Clear Gets command as another measure to ensure the environment is clear before executing a procedure.

TYPICAL OPERATION

In this example you use the Clear Gets command in both the print and mailing list programs. Begin this example in your word processor with PRINT.PRG loaded.

1. Add the following text to the beginning of the program.
   ```
   * Make sure the environment is clear.
   clear all
   clear gets
   * Perform program setup.
   ```

2. Save the document and exit your word processor. Type **CLIPPER PRINT** at the DOS prompt. Press **Enter**. Clipper compiles the print program.

3. Load MAILLIST.PRG into your word processor. Add the following text to the beginning of the program.
   ```
   * Make sure the environment is clear.
   clear all
   clear gets
   * Program Variables
   ```

4. Save the document and exit your word processor. Type **CL MAILLIST PRINT** at the DOS prompt. Press **Enter**.

5. Type **MAILLIST**. Press **Enter**. Notice the program operates the same as the previous module.

6. Press **F3**. The print program appears. Notice it also operates the same as the previous module. Press **F2** to return to the mailing list program.

7. Select Quit by pressing **Enter**. The DOS prompt appears.

8. Turn to Module 21 to continue the learning sequence.

Module 21
CLEAR MEMORY

DESCRIPTION

The Clear Memory command releases all memory variables, public and private. It performs the same task as the Release All command (which releases private variables only), but its scope is different. The command line interface of the Clear Memory command appears below.

```
CLEAR MEMORY
```

APPLICATIONS

Use the Clear Memory command to release all memory used by variables in a procedure and its associated subprocedures. In most cases, you use this command before leaving one main procedure to enter another; for example, leaving the database maintenance function on a main menu to go to the print function. Since this function releases all variables, you should not use it when you exit to perform some minor procedure and return; for example, when the user presses the F1 key to obtain help. If you used the Clear Memory command in this instance, the program would not operate when you returned from the help routine. However, you could use the Clear Memory command before leaving help to release the memory used by that procedure.

TYPICAL OPERATION

In this example you use the Clear Memory command to release all variables used by the main procedures before executing the next procedure. Begin this example in your word processor with PRINT.PRG loaded.

1. Add and re-order the following text at the beginning of the program.
   ```
   * Make sure the environment is clear.
   clear gets
   clear memory
   clear all
   * Perform program setup.
   ```

2. Save the document and exit your word processor. Type **CLIPPER PRINT** at the DOS prompt. Press **Enter**. Clipper compiles the print program.

3. Load MAILLIST.PRG into your word processor. Add and re-order the following text at the beginning of the program.
   ```
   * Make sure the environment is clear.
   clear gets
   clear memory
   clear all
   * Program Variables
   ```

4. Save the document and exit your word processor. Type **CL MAILLIST PRINT** at the DOS prompt. Press **Enter**.

5. Type **MAILLIST**. Press **Enter**. Notice the program operates the same as the previous module.

6. Press **F3**. The print program appears. Notice it also operates the same as the previous module. Press **F2** to return to the mailing list program.

7. Select Quit by pressing **Enter**. The DOS prompt appears.

8. Turn to Module 23 to continue the learning sequence.

Module 22
CLEAR SCREEN

DESCRIPTION

The Clear Screen command clears any text or graphics appearing on the display. It then places the cursor in the upper left corner of the display. If you use the Clear command without the screen modifier, Clipper clears the screen and any pending gets. The CLS version of the command is the same as using Clear Screen. The command line interface of the Clear Screen command appears below.

```
CLEAR [SCREEN]
```
OR
```
CLS
```

APPLICATIONS

Use the Clear Screen command whenever you need to completely remove any text or graphics from the display. This command usually precedes screen display commands on entry to a new module. By using the Clear command by itself, you also remove any gets created by a previous module.

TYPICAL OPERATION

In this example, you create a Clipper program that clears the display. Begin this example at the DOS prompt in the C:\CLIPPER\0022 directory.

1. Load any word processor capable of producing ASCII (non-formatted) output. Type **clear screen**. Press **Enter**. Save the file using MAILLIST.PRG as the filename. Quit the word processor.

NOTE
The CL.BAT file and Clipper program and library files used in the following step are in the C:\CLIPPER directory. If you encounter problems in the following step, be sure that the DOS path command includes the expression PATH=\CLIPPER. A typical path command might be:

PATH=C:\;\DOS;\CLIPPER

2. Type **CL MAILLIST** at the DOS prompt. Press **Enter**. The Clipper batch file clears the screen, then compiles and links the program.

```
C:\CLIPPER\0022>Clipper MAILLIST
The Clipper Compiler
Copyright (c) Nantucket Corp 1985-1987.   All Rights Reserved.
Microsoft C Runtime Library Routines,
Copyright (c) Microsoft Corp 1984-1987.   All Rights Reserved.

Compiling MAILLIST.PRG
Code Pass 1
Code Pass 2
Code size 48, Symbols 32, Constants 0

C:\CLIPPER\0022>IF NOT ERRORLEVEL 1 Plink86 FI MAILLIST LIB \CLIPPER\CLIPPER, \C
LIPPER\EXTEND
PLINK86plus ( Nantucket ) Version 2.24.
Copyright (C) 1987 by Phoenix Technologies Ltd.,
All Rights Reserved.


MAILLIST.EXE (149 K)
C:\CLIPPER\0022>
```

3. Type **MAILLIST**. Press **Enter**. The program clears the display.

```
C:\CLIPPER\0022>
```

4. Turn to Module 87 to continue the learning sequence.

Module 23
CLEAR TYPEAHEAD

DESCRIPTION

The Clear Typeahead command removes any characters from the typeahead buffer. The typeahead buffer is an area Clipper uses to store user keystrokes until the program has time to process them. You change the size of the typeahead buffer using the Set Typeahead command (Module 77). The command line interface of the Clear Typeahead command appears below.

```
CLEAR TYPEAHEAD
```

APPLICATIONS

Use the Clear Typeahead command to clear the typeahead buffer. One example of this is if the keystrokes in a particular instance required complex processing. If the user entered the wrong keystrokes, you could signal an error and clear the typeahead buffer. Another instance is in menu routines. Some users enter multiple keystrokes hoping to get through the menus more quickly. By clearing the typeahead buffer after each menu, you can prevent errors occurring from too many keystrokes.

The InKey( ), LastKey( ), and NextKey( ) functions (Module 114) help you determine what the typeahead buffer contains. By using these functions in conjunction with the Clear Typeahead command, you can ensure the user always enters keystrokes appropriate to the current situation. In most cases this method is slower than defining ranges for At (@) Get commands. Use this technique when the input parameters are too complex to monitor using standard methods. You can also use this technique in error checking routines.

TYPICAL OPERATION

In this example you enhance the Ctrl-Break checking in MAILLIST.PRG by using the Clear Typeahead command. Begin this example at the mailing list program Main menu.

1. Press **Esc**. Notice the Main menu flickers.
2. Press **Enter** to select Quit. The DOS prompt appears.
3. Load MAILLIST.PRG into your word processor. Add the following text to the menu display section at the beginning of the program (after the Ctrl-Break check).

```
endif
if KEYPRESS = 27          && If the user pressed Esc
   @ 22, 06 say 'Press a menu item letter, function key, Enter, ' +;
      'or Ctrl-Break only!'
   inkey(1)               && Wait 1 second,
   clear typeahead        && clear the buffer, and
   loop                   && go back to the beginning.
endif
* Add a new record.
```

4. Save the document and exit your word processor. Type **CL MAILLIST PRINT** at the DOS prompt. Press **Enter**.

5. Type **MAILLIST**. Press **Enter**.

6. Press **Esc**. The program displays an error message, waits one second, clears the typeahead buffer, and redisplays the menu.

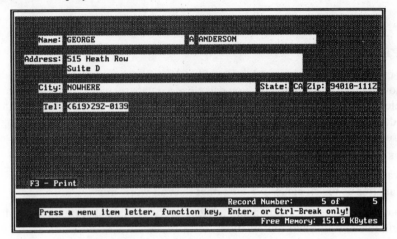

7. Select Quit by pressing **Enter**. The DOS prompt appears.

8. Turn to Module 67 to continue the learning sequence.

Module 24
CLOSE

DESCRIPTION

The Close command provides several different levels of file/variable closure. Depending on the clause following the Close command, you can close a database, index, or format file. Closing a file also releases any filters or relations attached to the file. Close with no clauses automatically closes the database and associated indexes in the current work area. The command line interface of the Close command appears below.

```
CLOSE [<ALIAS>/ALL/ALTERNATE/DATABASES/FORMAT/INDEX]
```

The alias variable allows you to specify a work area where you want all files closed. It performs the same function as the all clause on one rather than all work areas.

The all clause causes the Close command to close every open database, index, and format file. This, in turn, releases all filters and relations.

The alternate clause tells the Close command to close the alternate database and associated indexes. This also releases the filters and relations attached to the alternate database.

The databases clause works much like the all clause, except Clipper does not close the format files.

The format clause tells the Close command to close all open format files. The database and index files remain open. Clipper does not release the filters or relations attached to the databases.

The index clause tells the Close command to close all open index files. The database and format files remain open. Clipper does not release the filters or relations attached to the databases.

APPLICATIONS

Use the Close command whenever you want to release a database, filter, or index file. Closing ensures Clipper updates the database and index files before you leave the program. You can also use this command between program transitions; for example, when you stop editing the database and go back to the Main menu. Using the Close command judiciously also allows better network access times and reduces the chances of database corruption.

TYPICAL OPERATION

In this example you use the Close command to close the mail list database and index before quitting the program. Begin this example at the DOS prompt in the C:\CLIPPER\0022 directory.

1. Edit MAILLIST.PRG using a word processor. Type **close all** at the end of MAILLIST.PRG.
2. Press **Enter**. Save the document and exit your word processor.

3. Type **CL MAILLIST** at the DOS prompt. Press **Enter**. The Clipper batch file clears the screen, then compiles and links the program.

4. Type **MAILLIST**. Press **Enter**. Notice the display appears exactly as before.

5. Press **Esc**. The DOS prompt appears. Notice, Clipper does not tell you it closed the files even though you added a command to perform this task. (The display appears the same as before you added the Close command.)

6. Turn to Module 9 to continue the learning sequence.

Module 25
COMMIT

DESCRIPTION

The Commit command performs the necessary, but almost invisible, function of ensuring that the data input by the user actually gets on disk. DOS uses a system of buffers to temporarily store data before writing it to disk. A buffer consists of 512-byte chunks of RAM. If the machine experiences a failure of any sort before DOS actually writes the data to disk, your database may lose information. Failure to write data correctly also results in corrupted databases as well. The Commit command forces DOS to write all Clipper data to disk at critical times, ensuring you experience no data loss during machine failures. The command line interface of the Commit command appears below.

```
COMMIT
```

APPLICATIONS

Use the Commit command when you edit or add records to a database. This is especially important in loops using DBEdit( ) or other full screen display functions. These functions tend to lose data more easily since you cannot make certain that DOS actually writes the information to disk. As important are loops where you continuously add information to the database. Even if you make sure you use the Replace command as discussed in Module 67, the Commit command adds yet another layer of safety.

TYPICAL OPERATION

In this example you create an add and a delete function for the sample database. Since you normally add checks to a database in groups, this example shows an append loop using the Commit command to ensure data integrity. It also shows how to create a user-defined function for deleting records while in the full screen editing mode. In this case the Commit command appears as part of the delete function. Begin this example in your word processor with CHCKBOOK.PRG loaded.

1. Add/modify the following text in the ADD_REC and DEL_REC procedures.

```
procedure ADD_REC
* This procedure adds records to the database.
* Create procedure variables.
private MORE
MORE = 'Y'
* Create a screen area.
@ 03, 15, 12, 78 box DOUBLE_LINE
@ 04, 16 clear to 11, 77
@ 10, 16 to 10, 77
* Get the new check information.
do while MORE = 'Y'
    @ 04, 16 say 'Date:      ' get M->DATE picture '@D'
    @ 05, 16 say 'Check:     ' get M->CHECK_NUM picture '99999'
```

```
     @ 06, 16 say 'For:        ' get M->DRAWN_FOR picture '@K@!'
     @ 07, 16 say 'Amount:     ' get M->AMOUNT picture '9999999.99'
     @ 08, 16 say 'Deposit:    ' get M->DEPOSIT picture '9999999.99'
     @ 09, 16 say 'Tax Item:   ' get M->TAX_ITEM picture 'Y'
     read
* If the user added a check, put it in the database.
  if (M->AMOUNT <> 0) .or. (M->DEPOSIT <> 0)
     append blank
     replace A->DATE with M->DATE
     replace A->CHECK_NUM with M->CHECK_NUM
     replace A->DRAWN_FOR with M->DRAWN_FOR
     replace A->AMOUNT with M->AMOUNT
     replace A->DEPOSIT with M->DEPOSIT
     replace A->TAX_ITEM with M->TAX_ITEM
     commit
  endif
     @ 11, 16 say 'Add another check? ' get MORE picture '!'
     read
enddo
return
procedure DEL_REC
* This procedure removes records from the database.
* Get user input for record deletions.
set color to N/W,W+/N
dbedit(03, 01, 23, 78, FIELD_ARRAY, 'REMOVE_REC')
set color to 'W/N,N/W,,,W+/N'
* Remove the deleted records from the database.
pack
return
function REMOVE_REC
* This function marks the records for deletion. It does not
* actually remove them.
* Declare variables
private STATUS
STATUS = 1 && Continue with DBEdit() function.
* Check if user wants record deleted.
if lastkey() = 7 .and. .not. deleted()
   delete
   commit
elseif lastkey() = 7 .and. deleted()
   recall
   commit
endif
* Display record status.
if deleted()
   @ 02, 70 say 'DELETED'
else
   @ 02, 70 say '        '
endif
* Check if user wants to exit DBEdit()
if lastkey() = 27
   STATUS = 0       && Exit DBEdit() function.
endif
return STATUS
```

2. Add the following variables to the beginning of the program.

```
FIELD_NUMBER = 1
M->DATE = DATE()
M->CHECK_NUM = 0
M->DRAWN_FOR = space(50)
AMOUNT = 0.00
DEPOSIT = 0.00
```

```
BALANCE = 0.00
TAX_ITEM = .F.
```

3. Save the document and exit your word processor. Type **CL CHCKBOOK** at the DOS prompt. Press **Enter**. The Clipper batch file clears the screen, then compiles and links the program.

4. Type **MAILLIST**. Press **Enter**. The mailing list program menu appears.

5. Press **F4**. The checkbook program menu appears.

6. Type **A**. Press **Enter**. The add checks display appears.

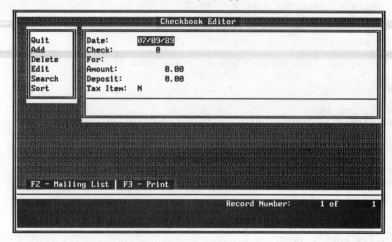

7. Type the text for the first check shown below.

Date: 07/09/89
Check: 1
For: GEORGES RESTAURANT
Amount: 19.99
Deposit: 0.00

8. Type **Y** at the Tax Item field to complete the entry. The program asks if you want to enter another check.

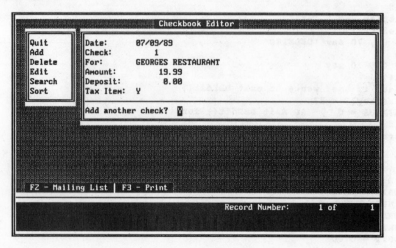

9. Type **Y** to obtain another blank record. Type the following information to enter two more checks. Notice the program retains the previous information for each new entry.

```
Date: 07/09/89
Check: 2
For: ANTHONY'S FOOD STORE
Amount: 102.44
Deposit: 0.00
Tax Item: N
Date: 07/09/89
Check: 0
For: PAYCHECK
Amount: 0.00
Deposit: 550.89
```

10. Type **N** in the Tax Item field to complete the entries. Type **N** when asked if you want to add another check. The checkbook program menu appears.

11. Type **D** and press **Enter** to select the Delete option. The Delete full screen display appears.

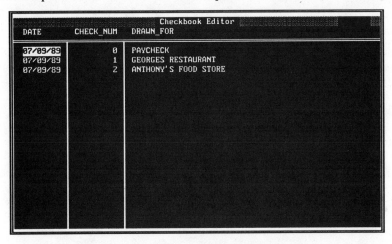

12. Press **Del**. The program displays a DELETED message at the top of the display.

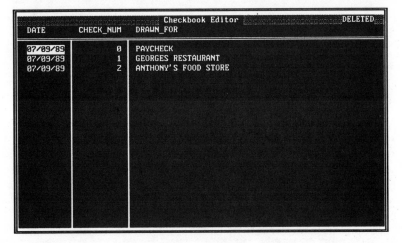

13. Press **Del**. The DELETED message disappears.

14. Highlight the blank record by pressing **Up Arrow**. Press **Del,** then **Esc**. Type **E** and press **Enter**. The program displays the full screen edit display. Notice the program removed the deleted record.

15. Press **Esc**. The checkbook program menu appears.

16. Type **Q** to select quit. Press **Enter**. The DOS prompt appears.

17. Turn to Module 102 to continue the learning sequence.

Module 26
CONTINUE

DESCRIPTION

The Continue command lets you perform another locate using the same for condition specified by the Locate command for the current work area. Clipper only uses the for clause condition; it ignores any while clause condition added to the Locate command. The command line interface of the Continue command appears below.

```
CONTINUE
```

APPLICATIONS

Use the Continue command when you wish to continue locating records using the same criteria specified in the pending locate for the current work area. When you use the Continue command, Clipper begins looking from the current record pointer position through the database.

TYPICAL OPERATION

Begin this example in your word processor with CHCKBOOK.PRG loaded.

1. Change the LOCATE procedure at the end of the program as shown below.
   ```
   FIND_NAME = space(50)
   FIND_AGAIN = 'Y'
   @ 12, 04 say 'Which check entry name do you want to find? '
   @ 13, 04 get FIND_NAME picture '@!'
   read
   locate for DRAWN_FOR = FIND_NAME
   * Display the record.
   do EDIT_REC
   do while FIND_AGAIN = 'Y'
      @ 22, 04 clear to 22, 76
      @ 22, 04 say 'Find the next occurrence of ' + trim(FIND_NAME) +;
         '? ' get FIND_AGAIN picture '!'
      read
      if FIND_AGAIN = 'Y'
         continue
         do EDIT_REC
      endif
   enddo
   return
   ```

2. Save the document and exit your word processor. Type **CL CHCKBOOK** at the DOS prompt. Press **Enter**.

3. Type **MAILLIST**. Press **Enter**. The mailing list program menu appears.

4. Press **F4** to select the checkbook program. Press **Down Arrow** until the Locate option of the menu appears. Press **Enter**. The program asks which entry name you want to locate.

5. Type **PAYCHECK** and press **Enter**. The program displays the edit screen with PAYCHECK highlighted.

6. Press **Esc**. The program asks if you want to find the next occurrence of PAYCHECK.

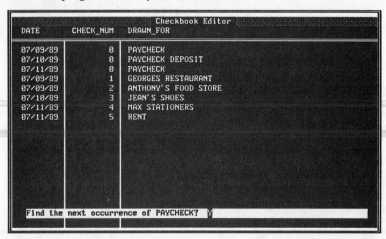

7. Type **Y**. The program displays the edit screen with the third occurrence of PAYCHECK highlighted. It skips the second occurrence because this entry is not an exact match.

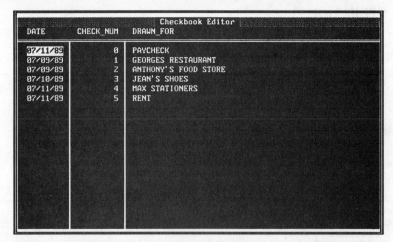

8. Press **Esc**. The program asks if you want to find the next occurrence of PAYCHECK.

9. Type **Y**. The program displays the edit screen with the last entry highlighted. It highlights this entry since no other occurrences of PAYCHECK appeared in the database and you set softseek on.

10. Press **Esc** then type **N** to return to the checkbook menu. Type **Q** to select quit. Press **Enter**. The DOS prompt appears.

11. Turn to Module 136 to continue the learning sequence.

Module 27
COPY FILE

DESCRIPTION

The Copy File command lets you send information contained in one file to a new file. Clipper allows you to express the source and destination filenames as either a literal string or a variable. FILE1.EXT1/EXPC1 contains the name of the source file. FILE2.EXT2/EXPC2 contains the name of the destination file. You cannot use this command to copy only part of the file. It works like its DOS equivalent and copies the entire file. If you copy the source file to a destination file that already exists, Clipper overwrites the old file contents. The command line interface of the Copy File command appears below.

```
COPY FILE <FILE1>.<EXT1>/(<EXPC1>) TO <FILE2>.<EXT2>/(<EXPC2>)
```

APPLICATIONS

Use the Copy File command whenever you need to send information from the database in the current work area to another file. For example, you can use this command in conjunction with the Sort and Reindex commands to create more efficient database files. This reduces the access time required to find information on disk.

You may also use this command to copy any other type of file. For example, you could use it as part of a backup routine. By sending whole files to the backup disk whenever possible, you remove the possibility of creating a non-recoverable disk. However, this method of backup does waste large quantities of disk space. In the case of large database files, you cannot use this command since the disk must contain enough space to hold the entire file.

TYPICAL OPERATION

In this example you complete the backup function of the sample program using the File Copy command. Begin this example in your word processor with MAINT.PRG loaded.

1. Change the following text in the backup section of the maintenance program.
    ```
        ?? ' Header size: ' + ltrim(str(header() + 1, 10, 0)) + ' bytes.'
        copy file &DIR_FILE to a:&DIR_FILE
    next
    ```

2. Save the document and exit your word processor. Type **CLD MAINT** at the DOS prompt. Press **Enter**.

3. Type **MAINT**. Press **Enter**. The program asks for a directory path and skeleton.

4. Type **'*.DBF'** and press **Enter**. The program displays a listing of files ending with .DBF. Then the program asks if you want to delete any files.

5. Type **'N'** and press **Enter**. The program asks if you want to rename any files.

6. Type **'N'** and press **Enter**. The program asks if you want to perform a data file backup.

7. Place a blank, formatted disk in drive A. Type **'Y'** and press **Enter**. The drive light on drive A illuminates. The program displays a file copy message, the amount of memory required, and exits normally. Notice the total bytes copied for each file.

```
Type directory path and skeleton
'*.DBF'
CHCKBOOK DBF    1035   07/15/89
MAILLIST DBF    1625   07/16/89
NOTEPAD  DBF     406   07/16/89
SUMMARY  DBF     550   07/11/89
NEWTEMP  DBF    1035   07/15/89
HELP     DBF     162   07/16/89

Do you want to delete any of the files? 'N'
Do you want to rename any of the files? 'N'
Do you want to backup the data files? 'Y'
Place disk in drive A
Copying files in CLIPPER\0022 to drive A.

Copying database CHCKBOOK.DBF to drive A. 1035 bytes Header size: 259 bytes.
Copying database MAILLIST.DBF to drive A. 1625 bytes Header size: 323 bytes.
Copying database NOTEPAD.DBF to drive A. 406 bytes Header size: 163 bytes.
Copying database SUMMARY.DBF to drive A. 550 bytes Header size: 259 bytes.
Copying database NEWTEMP.DBF to drive A. 1035 bytes Header size: 259 bytes.
Copying database HELP.DBF to drive A. 162 bytes Header size: 131 bytes.
C:\CLIPPER\0022>
```

8. Type **DIR A:*.DBF** and press **Enter**. DOS displays a list of files and their size. Notice the database file sizes exactly match the DOS file sizes and the total bytes copied recorded earlier.

```
C:\CLIPPER\0022>DIR A:*.DBF

 Volume in drive A has no label
 Directory of  A:\

CHCKBOOK DBF    1035    7-18-89   7:46p
MAILLIST DBF    1625    7-18-89   7:46p
NOTEPAD  DBF     406    7-18-89   7:46p
SUMMARY  DBF     550    7-18-89   7:46p
NEWTEMP  DBF    1035    7-18-89   7:46p
HELP     DBF     162    7-18-89   7:46p
        6 File(s)    351232 bytes free

C:\CLIPPER\0022>
```

9. Turn to Module 31 to continue the learning sequence.

Module 28
COPY STRUCTURE

DESCRIPTION

The Copy Structure command lets you create a new database having the same characteristics as an existing one. It does this by copying the database header from the existing database to the new one. You can also create a subset of an existing database using the fields clause. The command line interface of the Copy Structure command appears below.

```
COPY STRUCTURE [FIELDS <FIELD LIST>] TO <FILE>/(<EXPC>)
```

The fields clause specifies which fields to transfer from the existing database to the new one. The Copy Structure always completely erases any file with the same name as the new database before creating it. This means that you lose any existing fields or information by using the same name over again.

The only required entry when using Copy Structure is the file you want to copy a structure to. Clipper allows you to use the actual database filename, or you can place the filename in a variable and use the variable instead.

APPLICATIONS

Use the Copy Structure command when you maintain several versions of the same database and create new copies on a regular basis. For example, an accounting database could use this command to create a new account file.

TYPICAL OPERATION

In this example you copy the structure of the database files in the sample directory to the disk in drive A using the Copy Structure command. You then compare the size of the file to the size of the header reported using the Header( ) function. Begin this example in your word processor with MAINT.PRG loaded.

1. Add the following text to the backup section of the maintenance program.
   ```
   ?? ltrim(str(header() + (lastrec() * recsize()) + 1, 10, 0)) + ' bytes'
   ?? ' Header size: ' + ltrim(str(header() + 1, 10, 0)) + ' bytes.'
   copy structure to a:&DIR_FILE
   next
   ```

2. Save the document and exit your word processor. Type **CLD MAINT** at the DOS prompt. Press **Enter**.

3. Type **MAINT**. Press **Enter**. The program asks for a directory path and skeleton.

4. Type **'*.DBF'** and press **Enter**. The program displays a listing of files ending with .DBF. Then the program asks if you want to delete any files.

5. Type **'N'** and press **Enter**. The program asks if you want to rename any files.

6. Type **'N'** and press **Enter**. The program asks if you want to perform a data file backup.

7. Place a blank, formatted disk in drive A. Type **'Y'** and press **Enter**. The drive light on drive A illuminates. The program displays a file copy message, the amount of memory required, and exits normally. Notice the header sizes for each file.

```
Type directory path and skeleton
'*.DBF'
CHCKBOOK DBF     1035  07/15/89
MAILLIST DBF     1625  07/16/89
NOTEPAD  DBF      406  07/16/89
SUMMARY  DBF      550  07/11/89
NEWTEMP  DBF     1035  07/15/89
HELP     DBF      162  07/16/89

Do you want to delete any of the files? 'N'
Do you want to rename any of the files? 'N'
Do you want to backup the data files? 'Y'
Place disk in drive A
Copying files in CLIPPER\0022 to drive A.

Copying database CHCKBOOK.DBF to drive A. 1035 bytes Header size: 259 bytes.
Copying database MAILLIST.DBF to drive A. 1625 bytes Header size: 323 bytes.
Copying database NOTEPAD.DBF to drive A. 406 bytes Header size: 163 bytes.
Copying database SUMMARY.DBF to drive A. 550 bytes Header size: 259 bytes.
Copying database NEWTEMP.DBF to drive A. 1035 bytes Header size: 259 bytes.
Copying database HELP.DBF to drive A. 162 bytes Header size: 131 bytes.
C:\CLIPPER\0022>
```

8. Type **DIR A:*.DBF** and press **Enter**. DOS displays a list of files and their size. Notice the database file sizes exactly match the header file sizes recorded earlier.

```
C:\CLIPPER\0022>DIR A:*.DBF

 Volume in drive A has no label
 Directory of  A:\

CHCKBOOK DBF     259   7-18-89   2:58p
MAILLIST DBF     323   7-18-89   2:58p
NOTEPAD  DBF     163   7-18-89   2:58p
SUMMARY  DBF     259   7-18-89   2:58p
NEWTEMP  DBF     259   7-18-89   2:58p
HELP     DBF     131   7-18-89   2:58p
        6 File(s)   354304 bytes free

C:\CLIPPER\0022>
```

9. Turn to Module 27 to continue the learning sequence.

Module 29
COPY TO
(DATA/STRUCTURE)

DESCRIPTION

The Copy To command lets you send all or part of the contents of the database in the current work area to another file. Clipper lets you send this information to another database or an ASCII file using one of three methods. The command line interface of the Copy To command appears below.

```
COPY TO <FILE>/(<EXPC1>) [<SCOPE>] [FIELDS <FIELD LIST>] [FOR <CONDITION>]
[WHILE <CONDITION>] [SDF/DELIMITED/DELIMITED WITH <DELIMITER>/(<EXPC2>)]
```

The only required entry when using the Copy To command is the file you wish to copy the database information to. Clipper lets you use the actual database/text filename, or you can place the filename in a variable and use the variable instead. In all cases, Clipper erases the contents of the file if it exists before copying.

The scope clause determines how many of the source database records Copy To adds to the target database/text file. Clipper uses three key words to determine the scope. All adds every record in the source database to the target. Next <n> adds the number of records specified by n. Clipper starts copying records from the record pointed to by the record pointer. Record <n> adds a single record; <n> specifies which record to add.

The fields clause specifies which fields to transfer from the source database to the target. Clipper adds all the fields in the source database to the target database if you do not specify particular fields.

The for clause allows you to describe which records to copy from the source database to the target when using a scope of all or next. The condition tells Clipper what criteria a record must meet before the target database/text file accepts it. For example, if you had a listing of people and their ages and wanted to build a new database containing only people 40 years of age and older, you would use the statement copy to <filename> all for AGE > 39.

The SDF (system data format ASCII file) and delimited clauses allow you to export records to files that don't use a standard database format. In most cases you do this for word processors so you can create specialized reports or import database information as part of a letter. An SDF file contains fixed length records separated by a carriage return and line feed. An end of file marker (Ctrl-Z or ASCII 26) marks the end of the file. A delimited file contains variable length records separated by a carriage return and line feed. A comma (,) separates each field in the record, and double quotes (") mark the boundaries of character fields. An end of file marker marks the end of the file. When you use the delimited clause with the with blank clause, a space marks the boundary between fields. When you use the delimited clause with the with delimiter clause, Clipper uses the specified delimiter as a field boundary. Clipper allows you to specify the delimiter or a variable containing the delimiter.

APPLICATIONS

Use the Copy To command whenever you need to send information from the database in the current work area to another file. For example, you can use this command in conjunction with the Sort and Reindex commands to create more efficient database files. This reduces the access time required to find information on disk.

You could also use this command to export files to word processors or other programs which do not accept standard database files. Another use is sending information to a dissimilar machine. The target machine would get the information and only need to reformat it as necessary.

TYPICAL OPERATION

In this example you complete the Reindex function of the example program. This means the user does not need to exit the program to copy the temporary database to the checkbook database. You also add the capability to export the checkbook database information in SDF format. Begin this example in your word processor with CHCKBOOK.PRG loaded.

1. Add the following text to the menu array declaration at the beginning of the program.

```
declare MENU_ITEM[10]
MENU_ITEM[1] = 'Quit'
MENU_ITEM[2] = 'Add'
MENU_ITEM[3] = 'Delete'
MENU_ITEM[4] = 'Sort'
MENU_ITEM[5] = 'Edit'
MENU_ITEM[6] = 'Search'
MENU_ITEM[7] = 'Stats'
MENU_ITEM[8] = 'Balance'
MENU_ITEM[9] = 'Reindex'
MENU_ITEM[10] = 'Export'
```

2. Add the following text to the menu case statement at the beginning of the program.

```
        do REINDEX
    case MENU_ITEM[ANSWER] = 'Export'
        do EXPORT
endcase
```

3. Change the REINDEX procedure and add the following procedure to the end of the procedure section of the program.

```
set color to N/W,W+/N
@ 22, 04 say 'Sorting Database, Please Wait...'
sort on CHECK_NUM, DATE to TEMPDATA
use TEMPDATA
copy to CHCKBOOK all
@ 22, 04 say 'Reindexing Database, Please Wait...'
use CHCKBOOK index CHCKNUM, DATE
reindex
set color to 'W/N,N/W,,,W+/N'
return
procedure EXPORT
* This procedure exports the database to an SDF formatted file.
* Initialize Variables.
EXP_FILE = space(60)
@ 12, 04 say 'What file do you want to export to? '
@ 13, 04 get EXP_FILE picture '@!'
read
copy to &EXP_FILE all SDF
return
```

4. Save the document and exit your word processor. Type **CL CHCKBOOK** at the DOS prompt. Press **Enter**.

5. Type **MAILLIST**. Press **Enter**. The mailing list program menu appears.

6. Press **F4** to select the checkbook program. Press **Down Arrow** until the Reindex option of the menu appears. Press **Enter**. The program sorts then reindexes the database.

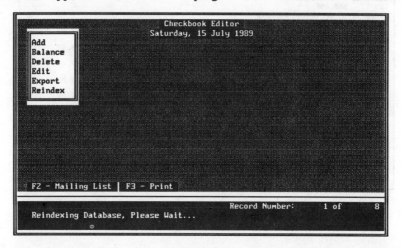

7. Type **E** to select Edit and press **Enter**. Notice the database and index files match.

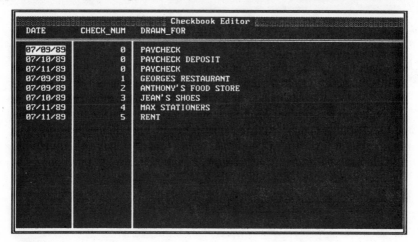

8. Press **Esc** to return to the checkbook program menu. Type **E** twice to select export the database information. Press **Enter**. The prompt asks "What file do you want to export to?"

9. Type **EXAMPLE.SDF** and press **Enter**. The program exports the database information in SDF format.

10. Type **Q** to select quit. Press **Enter**. The DOS prompt appears.

11. Type **TYPE EXAMPLE.SDF**. DOS displays the file. Notice the records appear with evenly spaced fields, each record contains a carriage return to mark the end of the record, and the file ends with a Ctrl-Z.

```
C:\CLIPPER\0022>TYPE EXAMPLE.SDF
19890709    0PAYCHECK                              0.00      550
.89      550.89F
19890710    0PAYCHECK DEPOSIT                      0.00      820
.00     1248.46F
19890711    0PAYCHECK                              0.00     1200
.98          F
19890709    1GEORGES RESTAURANT                   19.99        0
.00      530.90T
19890709    2ANTHONY'S FOOD STORE                102.44        0
.00      428.46F
19890710    3JEAN'S SHOES                        520.00        0
.00      728.46F
19890711    4MAX STATIONERS                       12.22        0
.00      716.24T
19890711    5RENT                               1000.00        0
.00          T

C:\CLIPPER\0022>
```

12. Turn to Module 53 to continue the learning sequence.

Module 30
COUNT

DESCRIPTION

The Count command calculates the number of records matching a given criteria and places the total in a memory variable. The command line interface of the Count command appears below.

```
COUNT [<SCOPE>] [FOR <CONDITION>] [WHILE <CONDITION>] TO <MEMVAR>
```

The scope clause allows you to specify the range of records to count. The default scope is all. If you specify next with a number, Clipper starts counting records from the current record position and stops when it checks the required number of records.

The for condition clause allows you to limit the number of records counted to those meeting a predefined condition. Normally, the condition contains a field name, then a relational operator (>, <, <>, =), followed by the condition. Clipper counts all records in the database meeting the defined condition and scope.

The while condition clause allows you to limit the number of records counted to those meeting a predefined condition. Unlike the for condition clause, Clipper stops counting records as soon as it sees a record not meeting the criteria. In some respects, this clause works like a combination of the for condition and scope clauses.

The to memvar clause specifies where Count sends the tally. This is the only required parameter for the Count command. If you do not intend to specify parameters for the tally, the RecCount( ) function (Module 96) provides a total faster.

APPLICATIONS

Use the Count command when you need a total number of records matching a certain criteria. For example, use Count if you want to know how many items in a database contain a particular value in one of the fields.

TYPICAL OPERATION

In this example you use the Count command to determine how many entries in the sample database are tax deductible, how many are deposits, and then the number matching neither criteria. Begin this example in your word processor with CHCKBOOK.PRG loaded.

1. Add/change the following text to the array at the beginning of the program.

```
declare MENU_ITEM[7]
MENU_ITEM[1] = 'Quit'
MENU_ITEM[2] = 'Add'
MENU_ITEM[3] = 'Delete'
MENU_ITEM[4] = 'Sort'
MENU_ITEM[5] = 'Edit'
MENU_ITEM[6] = 'Search'
MENU_ITEM[7] = 'Stats'
```

2. Add the following text to the case statement at the beginning of the program.

```
    do SEARCH_REC
  case MENU_ITEM[ANSWER] = 'Stats'
    do STATS
endcase
```

3. Add the following procedure to the end of the procedure section of the program.

```
procedure STATS
* This procedure produces a list of statistics about the
* checkbook database.
private TCHECKS, NTCHECKS, DEPOSITS, READY
TCHECKS = 0
NTCHECKS = 0
DEPOSITS = 0
READY = ' '
* Get the statistics
count to TCHECKS for (TAX_ITEM = .T.) .and. (DEPOSIT = 0)
count to NTCHECKS for (TAX_ITEM = .F.) .and. (DEPOSIT = 0)
count to DEPOSITS for DEPOSIT <> 0
* Display the statistics.
@ 12, 04 say 'Number of Tax Deductible Checks:       ' +;
   ltrim(str(TCHECKS, 5, 0))
@ 13, 04 say 'Number of Non-Tax Deductible Checks: ' +;
   ltrim(str(NTCHECKS, 5, 0))
@ 14, 04 say 'Number of Deposits:                   ' +;
   ltrim(str(DEPOSITS, 5, 0))
@ 22, 04 say 'Press any key when ready...' get READY
read
return
```

4. Save the document and exit your word processor. Type **CL CHCKBOOK** at the DOS prompt. Press **Enter**.

5. Type **MAILLIST**. Press **Enter**. The mailing list program menu appears.

6. Press **F4**. The checkbook program menu appears.

7. Press **Down Arrow** until the Stats option of the menu appears. Notice the menu scrolls to show the additional menu entry.

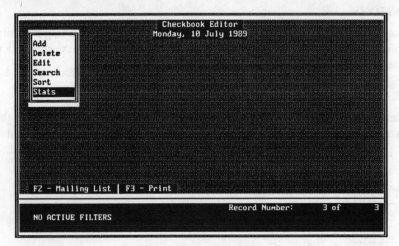

8. Press **Enter**. The checkbook statistics appear.

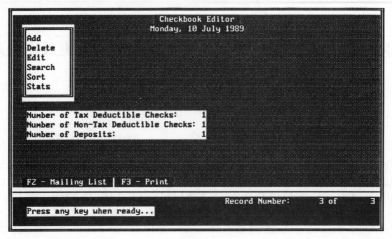

9. Press **Enter** to erase the statistics and return to the menu. Type **A** and press **Enter**. Enter the following information at the fields indicated. Type **N** when asked if you want to add any more checks. The checkbook program menu appears.

   Date: 07/10/89
   For: PAYCHECK DEPOSIT
   Deposit: 820.00
   Tax Item: N

10. Press **Down Arrow** to select Stats. Press **Enter**. The checkbook statistics appear. Notice the statistics correctly show the addition of a deposit.

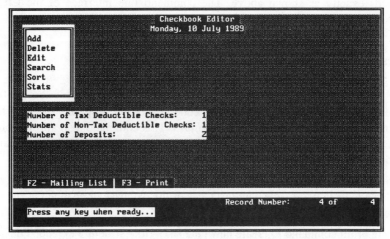

11. Press **Enter** to return to the checkbook program menu. Type **Q** to select quit. Press **Enter**. The DOS prompt appears.

12. Turn to Module 15 to continue the learning sequence.

Module 31
CREATE, COPY STRUCTURE EXTENDED,
CREATE FROM

DESCRIPTION

The Create command produces a file with empty field parameters for a database. The Clipper manual calls these special database files structure extended databases. Each structure extended database contains four fields: FIELD_NAME, FIELD_TYPE, FIELD_LEN, and FIELD_DEC. These fields reflect one of the four attributes of a field in a standard database. Each record is a single instance of a field in a standard database. You may create a structure extended database for an open database using the Copy Structure Extended command. Instead of creating an empty database like the Create command does, this command creates a database containing the field parameters for the database in the current work area. The Create From command creates a new database with the name expressed in FILE1/EXPC1 using the parameters contained in FILE2/EXPC2. FILE2 is a structure extended database. Clipper lets you create databases using structure extended databases with more fields than those described above. For example, you could add a memo field to contain comments about the data contained in each field. This allows you to create data dictionaries of all the databases for a particular project. While Clipper is not sensitive to the order of the fields in the structure extended database, you must name the four essential fields exactly as shown above. The command line interface of the Create, Copy Structure Extended, and Create From commands appears below.

```
CREATE <FILE>/(<EXOC>)
COPY STRUCTURE EXTENDED TO <FILE>/(<EXPC>)
CREATE <FILE1>/(<EXPC1>) FROM <FILE2>/(<EXPC2>)
```

APPLICATIONS

Use the Create command in conjunction with code generation programs to allow the user to create database structures using full screen displays. This command also allows you to create database dictionaries during program development. This is especially important in team projects requiring coordination of effort.

Use the Copy Structure Extended command to create a structure extended database of an existing database. This allows you to create new instances of the database or change the structure of an old database with minimal effort.

Use the Create From command to create new databases from structure extended database files. This command allows you to create new instances of user databases in an accounting system (for example). This command also allows you to coordinate efforts among team members of a database project. By ensuring everyone uses databases of exactly the same structure, you prevent code conflicts at program integration time.

TYPICAL OPERATION

In this example you create an extended database structure from one of the existing databases using the Copy Structure Extended command. Then you display the structure on screen. Finally, you create a new instance of the database using the Create From command. Begin this example in your word processor with MAINT.PRG loaded.

1. Add the following text to the end of the maintenance program.

```
* Create a structure extended database, show the contents on screen,
* then create a new instance of the database, if desired.
input 'Do you want to create a new database? ' to ANSWER
ANSWER = upper(ANSWER)
if len(ANSWER) > 1
   ANSWER = substr(ANSWER, 1, 1)
endif
if ANSWER = 'Y'
   input 'Enter the old database file name. ' to DATA_NAME
   DATA_NAME = upper(DATA_NAME)
   if len(DATA_NAME) > 8
      DATA_NAME = substr(DATA_NAME, 1, 8)
   endif
   use &DATA_NAME
   copy structure extended to TEMP_DAT
   use TEMP_DAT
   ?
   ? 'Database Contains the Following Fields:'
   ?
   ? 'Name        Type Length Decimals'
   do while .not. eof()
      ? FIELD_NAME + ' ' + FIELD_TYPE + '    '
      ?? str (FIELD_LEN,3,0) + '    ' + str(FIELD_DEC,3,0)
      skip
   enddo
   ?
   input 'Enter the new database name. ' to NDAT_NAME
   NDAT_NAME = upper(NDAT_NAME)
   if len(NDAT_NAME) > 8
      NDAT_NAME = substr(NDAT_NAME, 1, 8)
   endif
   create &NDAT_NAME from TEMP_DAT
endif
* Exit this utility
```

2. Save the document and exit your word processor. Type **CLD MAINT** at the DOS prompt. Press **Enter**.

3. Type **MAINT**. Press **Enter**. The program asks for a directory path and skeleton.

4. Type **'*.DBF'** and press **Enter**. The program displays a listing of files ending with .DBF. Then the program asks if you want to delete any files.

5. Type **'N'** and press **Enter**. The program asks if you want to rename any files.

6. Type **'N'** and press **Enter**. The program asks if you want to perform a data file backup.

7. Type **'N'** and press **Enter**. The program asks "Do you want to create a new database?"

8. Type **'Y'** and press **Enter**. The program displays "Enter the old database file name."

9. Type **'MAILLIST'** and press **Enter**. The program displays a listing of the fields in the mailing list database. It then displays "Enter the new database name."

10. Type **'NEW_MAIL'** and press **Enter**. The program creates the new database and exits normally.

```
NOTEPAD   DBF     406  07/16/89
SUMMARY   DBF     550  07/11/89
HELP      DBF     162  07/16/89

Do you want to delete any of the files? 'N'
Do you want to rename any of the files? 'N'
Do you want to backup the data files? 'N'
Do you want to create a new database? 'Y'
Enter old the database file name. 'MAILLIST'

Database Contains the Following Fields:

Name        Type Length Decimals
FIRST_NAME  C     25       0
MIDDLE      C      1       0
LAST_NAME   C     25       0
ADDRESS1    C     50       0
ADDRESS2    C     50       0
CITY        C     40       0
STATE       C      2       0
ZIP         C     10       0
TELEPHONE   C     13       0

Enter the new database name. 'NEW_MAIL'
C:\CLIPPER\0022>
```

11. Type **DBU TEMP_DAT** and press **Enter**. DBU displays the contents of the structure extended database TEMP_DAT (used to create the new database in the maintenance program.)

			Record 1/9
FIELD_NAME	FIELD_TYPE	FIELD_LEN	FIELD_DEC
FIRST_NAME	C	25	0
MIDDLE	C	1	0
LAST_NAME	C	25	0
ADDRESS1	C	50	0
ADDRESS2	C	50	0
CITY	C	40	0
STATE	C	2	0
ZIP	C	10	0
TELEPHONE	C	13	0

12. Press **Esc** to exit the browse display of DBU. Type **NEW_MAIL** in the database field. Press **Enter** to retrieve the database. Press **F5**. Select Database by pressing **Enter**. DBU displays the NEW_MAIL database. Notice it contains exactly the same fields as the original mailing list database.

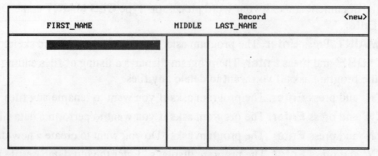

			Record	<new>
FIRST_NAME		MIDDLE	LAST_NAME	

13. Press **Esc** twice then type **Y** to exit DBU. The DOS prompt appears.

14. Turn to Module 72 to continue the learning sequence.

Module 32
DECLARE, FIELD, LOCAL, MEMVAR, STATIC

DESCRIPTION

Clipper provides five different commands for adding variables or arrays to your program. These commands create different sizes and types of variables or arrays. They also create variables or arrays with different scopes. The scope of the variable determines what procedures and functions can use it. Only the function that creates a variable can use it if it has a local scope. Variables with a global scope are available to all functions and procedures in a program. The command line interface of these commands appears below.

NOTE

EXP1 can contain either a variable or array name. If you create an array, then you must follow the array name with a set of brackets ([ ]). You must place the number of array elements within the brackets. To declare a multidimensional array, include more than one number separated by commas. For example, to declare a 2 by 3 array using DECLARE, you would type DECLARE SomeArray [2, 3]. Clipper uses 4,096 as the maximum size for any dimension of an array.

EXP2 contains the value you want to assign to a variable. You cannot initialize the values of an array by placing a value in EXP2. Each value in an array automatically receives a value of NIL.

```
DECLARE <EXP1> [:= <EXP2>] [, <EXP3> [:= <EXP4>]] ...
FIELD <FIELD LIST> [IN <ALIAS/DATABASE NAME>]
LOCAL <EXP1> [:= <EXP2>] [, <EXP3> [:= <EXP4>]] ...
MEMVAR <MEMVAR LIST>
STATIC <EXP1> [:= <EXP2>] [, <EXP3> [:= <EXP4>]] ...
```

The Declare command allows you to create private variables and arrays. Only the function or procedure that creates the variable or array can see it. This command is functionally equivalent to the Private command described in Module 58. It is provided for compatibility with previous versions of Clipper.

The Field command allows you to declare database field names to the compiler. This helps the compiler to resolve unqualified references to a field. For example, if you used the statement REPLACE Employee WITH Employee in your program, the compiler would not know which Employee to replace. A qualified version of the same statement includes a database reference (for example, A->). The optional ALIAS/DATABASE NAME allows you to reference the correct field automatically. For example, to reference the Employee field in the first database you would type FIELD EMPLOYEE IN DATA1. After you make this declaration, every unqualified reference to Employee uses the first database as a reference. If you do not specify a database, then Field supplies the special FIELD reference to the compiler. This command, like all declaration commands, does not affect field references made within macros. In addition, this command does not check for the existence of the referenced database or its fields. The fields declared using this command are valid within the current procedure or function. You can override this default status by using Field prior to any executable statement in the program and including the /N compiler directive. The Field command must precede any executable statements in the procedure or function in which it appears.

The Local command creates arrays or variables with a local scope. Local variables exist for the current procedure or function and any procedures or functions it invokes. Therefore, the variables have an arbitrary scope depending on where you declare them. For example, if you declare a local variable or array at the beginning of the program, it really has a global scope. You must use the Local command before any other executable statement in your program (including Private, Public, and Parameters). Clipper creates local variables each time you execute the procedure or function in which they appear. If you call the procedure or function recursively (a statement within the procedure or function calls itself), Clipper creates a new version of the variables for each recursion. Since the compiler resolves local variables at compile time, your program loses any reference to the variable name. Any variables declared using the Field, Local, or Memvar commands override a local variable of the same name. Local variables take precedence over public, private, or field variables of the same name unless you declare the variable using the Field or Memvar commands. Clipper destroys the contents of a local variable when the procedure ends.

The Memvar command allows you to declare both public and private variables to the compiler. This helps the compiler to resolve unqualified references to a variable. After you make this declaration, every unqualified reference to a variable uses memory as a reference. This command, like all declaration commands, does not affect variable references made within macros. In addition, this command does not check for the existence of the declared variables or create them if they do not exist. You must declare the variable using the Public, Private, or Parameters commands. The variables declared using this command are valid within the current procedure or function. You can override this default status by using Memvar prior to any executable statement in the program and including the /N compiler directive. The Memvar command must precede any executable statements in the procedure or function in which it appears (including Public, Private, and Parameters commands).

The Static command creates arrays and variables with the same scope and properties as local variables. The only difference between the two types is that static variables retain their value when the procedure or function ends. Therefore, you can use static variables when you need to keep track of a value between calls to a procedure or function.

APPLICATIONS

Use the Declare command to create arrays or variables with a private scope. The Local and Static commands allow you to create variables and arrays with an arbitrary scope. The only determining factor when using these two commands is the location of the declaration within the program.

You can use variables to store many different types of single value information. This includes numbers, strings, and dates. Variables take less storage than arrays, but provide less flexibility.

There are two types of arrays: single and multidimensional. Single arrays are useful for a number of programming tasks. For example, you could use an array to store a set of related error message strings. By creating a procedure with a single parameter, the error number, you could display any error message by referencing the correct array element. This centralization reduces code size and improves program readability. Multidimensional arrays are even more useful, but require more memory than single arrays.

Another use for single arrays is menu creation. You place the menu items in an array and use a Clipper supplied function to display the menu. This method of creating menus has advantages over using the Prompt and Menu To commands. For example, you could create arrays containing several standardized menus. By referencing the correct array, you could use the same menus throughout the program without having to redefine the prompts you wish to use.

Multidimensional arrays provide you with even more flexibility. For example, you could place all the values from a directory in one multidimensional array. In essence, a multidimensional array works like a small database stored in memory. Each dimension represents a field. Each array element represents a record. Of course, this is only a rough equivalence. A database is accessed serially. You must read each record and access its fields individually. A multidimensional array is a random access object. You can get the information from any part of the array at any time.

There are many other uses for arrays. Clipper provides many useful functions for manipulating arrays. Module 91 contains a complete listing of these functions and their use.

TYPICAL OPERATION

In this example you begin creating a new program called CHCKBOOK using the Declare command. Begin this example in your word processor with CHCKBOOK.PRG loaded.

1. Add the following text to create the program shell.

```
* CHCKBOOK.PRG
* This program manages a checkbook.
* YOUR NAME
* TODAY'S DATE
* Program Variables
DOUBLE_LINE = chr(201) + chr(205) + chr(187) + chr(186) + chr(188) + ;
   chr(205) + chr(200) + chr(186) + chr(177)
ANSWER = 0
* Create the menu array and place the menu values in it.
declare MENU_ITEM[6]
MENU_ITEM[1] = 'Quit'
MENU_ITEM[2] = 'Add'
MENU_ITEM[3] = 'Delete'
MENU_ITEM[4] = 'Sort'
MENU_ITEM[5] = 'Edit'
MENU_ITEM[6] = 'Search'
* Setup program defaults.
set softseek on
set wrap on
set key -1 to MAILLIST        && Point F2 to the mailing list program.
set key -2 to PRINT           && Point F3 to the print program.
set key -3 to                 && Make sure F4 is clear.
* Clear the display and prepare the database for use.
clear screen
use CHCKBOOK index CHCKNUM, DATE
* Display the screen.
do DISP_SCRN5
* Close the databases and return.
quit
```

```
* Begin procedures here.
procedure DISP_SCRN5
* This procedure displays the screen and status information.
@ 01, 00, 24, 79 box DOUBLE_LINE
@ 20, 01 to 20, 78
set color to N/W,W+/N
@ 02, 31 say ' Checkbook Editor '
@ 19, 03 say ' F2 - Mailing List ' + chr(179) + ' F3 - Print '
@ 21, 01 clear to 23, 78
@ 21, 45 say ' Record Number: '
@ 21, 60 say recno()
@ 21, 67 say ' of '
@ 21, 71 say reccount()
* Show the record status.
if deleted()
    @ 21, 04 say ' DELETED '
else
    @ 21, 04 say '          '
endif
set color to 'W/N,N/W,,,W+/N'
return
```

2. Save the document. Load CL.BAT into your word processor. Change the following text to add the checkbook procedure to the link cycle.

```
Clipper %1
IF NOT ERRORLEVEL 1 Plink86 FI MAILLIST, PRINT, CHCKBOOK LIB ;
\CLIPPER\CLIPPER, \CLIPPER\EXTEND
```

3. Save the document. Load MAILLIST.PRG into your word processor. Add the following text to the beginning of the program.

```
set key -2 to PRINT          && Point F3 to the print program.
set key -3 to CHCKBOOK       && Point F4 to the checkbook program.
* Clear the display and prepare the database for use.
```

4. Add/change the following text in the DISPLAY_STATUS procedure.

```
endif
@ 02, 30 say ' Mailing List Editor '
@ 19, 04 say ' F3 - Print ' + chr(179) + ' F4 - Checkbook '
@ 21, 01 clear to 23, 78
```

5. Save the document and exit your word processor. Type **CLIPPER MAILLIST** at the DOS prompt. Clipper compiles the mailing list program.

6. Load PRINT.PRG into your word processor. Add the following text to the beginning of the program.

```
set key -2 to              && Make sure F3 points to nothing.
set key -3 to CHCKBOOK     && Point F4 to checkbook program.
* Declare standard variables public.
```

7. Add/change the following text in the DISP_SCRN procedure.

```
@ 03, HEADING_CENTER say 'Mailing List Print Program'
@ 20, 04 say ' F2 - Mailing List ' + chr(179) + ' F4 - Checkbook '
@ 21, 04 say 'Free Memory: ' + ltrim(str(memory(0), 12, 1)) + ' KBytes'
```

8. Save the document and exit your word processor. Type **CLIPPER PRINT** at the DOS prompt. Clipper compiles the print program.

9. Type **CL CHCKBOOK** at the DOS prompt. Press **Enter**.

10. Type **MAILLIST**. Press **Enter**. The mailing list program menu appears. Notice a heading appears describing the program function.

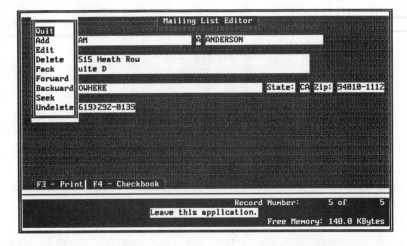

11. Press **F4**. The checkbook program display appears, then the DOS prompt.

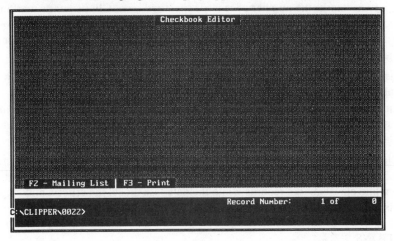

12. Turn to Module 91 to continue the learning sequence.

Module 33
DELETE

DESCRIPTION

The Delete command marks a record or set of records for removal from the database. It does not actually remove the records; you can undelete deleted records. The command line interface of the Delete command appears below.

```
DELETE [<SCOPE>] [FOR <CONDITION>] [WHILE <CONDITION>]
```

The scope clause determines how many records the Delete command marks for removal from the database. Clipper uses three key words to determine the scope. All marks every record in the database. Next <n> marks the number of records specified by n. Clipper starts marking records from the record pointed to by the record pointer. Record <n> marks a single record; <n> specifies which record to mark. If you use the Delete command without a specified scope, Clipper assumes the current record.

The for clause lets you describe which records to mark for removal from the database when using a scope of all or next. The condition tells Clipper what criteria a record must meet before the Delete command marks it. For example, if you had a listing of people and their ages and wanted to remove only people 40 years of age and older, you would use the statement delete all for AGE > 39.

The while clause works somewhat like the for clause. It limits the number of records marked for removal from the database. However, instead of finding all the records that meet a certain criteria, the while clause marks records while the database meets the criteria and stops when it doesn't. This allows you to mark a contiguous section of a database for removal.

APPLICATIONS

Use the Delete command whenever you want to remove records from the database. Even though the database still physically contains the records, and you can retrieve them, most Clipper commands will not display or print them. By marking the records using this command, you can be sure you don't need the records before actually removing them from the database.

TYPICAL OPERATION

In this example you add the capability to mark records for removal using the Delete command in the example program. Begin this example in your word processor with MAILLIST.PRG loaded.

1. Change the menu prompt as shown below.

```
@ 22, 04 say 'Quit/Add Record/Edit Record/Delete Record' get ANSWER picture '!'
```

2. Add the text below between the read and the endif appearing at the end of the program.

```
    read
* Delete the current record.
elseif ANSWER = 'D'
    delete
endif
```

3. Save the document and exit your word processor. Type **CL MAILLIST** at the DOS prompt. Press **Enter**.

4. Type **MAILLIST**. Press **Enter**. Type **A**. The program presents a new record.

5. Type **THIS IS A DELETED RECORD**. Press **PgDn**. Type **D**. The program marks the new record for removal.

6. Type **Q** to quit the program. Type **DBU**. The database utility screen appears.

7. Type **MAILLIST** and press **Enter**. Press **Down Arrow** to select the index field. Type **LASTNAME** and press **Enter**. The database utility retrieves MAILLIST.DBF.

8. Press **F5** to select the Browse menu. Press **Enter**. The database utility displays the contents of MAILLIST.DBF. Notice Clipper displays the deleted record first. The database utility also displays a <Deleted> indicator.

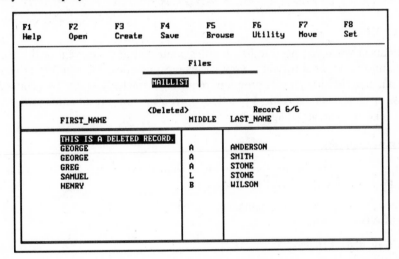

9. Press **Esc** twice to exit the database utility. Type **Y**. The DOS prompt appears.

10. Turn to Module 56 to continue the learning sequence.

Module 34
DIR

DESCRIPTION

The Dir command obtains a directory listing and displays it for the drive, path, and skeleton parameters specified. If the command line does not specify a drive, Clipper uses the default drive (the one selected using the Set Default command). If the command line does not specify a path, Clipper uses the default path (the one set using the Set Path command). If the command line does not contain a skeleton, Clipper displays a standard listing of database files. The skeleton may include both standard DOS wildcard characters (? and *). The command line interface of the Dir command appears below.

```
DIR [<DRIVE>:] [<PATH>\] [<SKELETON>]/(<EXPC>)
```

APPLICATIONS

Use this command when you need to list the files contained in the current or other directory. Since this command does not format the output, its most practical use is utility programs. Use the ADir( ) function (Module 91) for programs requiring formatted output. This command does consume less memory than the ADir( ) function. So you can use it in situations where memory is more of a concern than output appearance.

TYPICAL OPERATION

In this example you add to the maintenance program using the Dir command. Begin this example in your word processor with MAINT.PRG loaded.

1. Add the following text to the maintenance program.
   ```
   * Initialize variables.
   DIR_SKEL = ' '
   * Display a directory.
   clear screen
   input 'Type directory path and skeleton' + chr(13) + chr(10) to DIR_SKEL
   if len(DIR_SKEL) < 2
       dir
   else
       dir &DIR_SKEL
   endif
   ```

2. Save the document and exit your word processor. Type **CLD MAINT** at the DOS prompt. Press **Enter**.

3. Type **MAINT**. Press **Enter**. The program asks for a directory path and skeleton.

4. Press **Enter**. The program displays a listing of the database files, their size, date of last update, and number of records.

98

```
Type directory path and skeleton

Database Files    # Records    Last Update    Size
CHCKBOOK.DBF          8        07/15/89        1035
MAILLIST.DBF          6        07/16/89        1625
NOTEPAD.DBF           3        07/16/89         406
SUMMARY.DBF           3        07/11/89         550
TEMPDATA.DBF          8        07/15/89        1035
HELP.DBF              1        07/16/89         162

C:\CLIPPER\0022>
```

5. Type **MAINT**. Press **Enter**. The program asks for a directory path and skeleton.

6. Type **'*.NTX'** and press **Enter**. The program displays a listing of files ending with .NTX.

```
Type directory path and skeleton
'*.NTX'
CATEGORY NTX    2048    06/28/89
CHCKNUM  NTX    2048    07/15/89
DATE     NTX    2048    07/16/89
LASTNAME NTX    2048    07/09/89
NOTENUM  NTX    2048    06/28/89
SUBJECT  NTX    2048    06/28/89
TEMP_IND NTX    2048    07/15/89
HELP     NTX    2048    07/16/89

C:\CLIPPER\0022>
```

7. Turn to Module 40 to continue the learning sequence.

Module 35
DISPLAY

DESCRIPTION

The Display command lets you quickly list the contents of a database to the display, printer, or file. The command line interface of the Display command appears below.

```
DISPLAY [OFF] [<SCOPE>] <EXP LIST> [FOR <CONDITION>] [WHILE <CONDITION>]
[TO PRINT] [TO FILE <FILE>/(<EXPC>)]
```

The off clause determines if the Display command lists the record number with the information requested. If you specify off, then Clipper does not display the record number.

The scope clause determines how many of the database records the Display command presents. The Display command uses a default scope of next 1 instead of the standard scope of all.

EXP LIST contains the fields or other Clipper functions to display. For example, you could display the date and time using the Date( ) and Time( ) functions. You may also modify the field output using any text, numeric, or date manipulation functions.

The for clause allows you to describe which records to display from the database when using a scope of all or next. The condition tells Clipper what criteria a record must meet before being displayed. For example, if you had a listing of people and their ages and wanted to display only those records containing people 40 years of age and older, you would use the statement display all <exp list> for AGE > 39.

The to print clause allows you to send the output to the standard print output device. If you want to change this device, use the Set Printer command (Module 77). Clipper uses a default of LPT1 for the output port.

The to file clause allows you to send the output to the specified file. FILE is the literal filename, EXPC is a variable containing the filename.

APPLICATIONS

Use the Display command whenever you need to quickly output the contents of a database. This is especially good when you want to locate a specific record number.

The Display command also works well when you want to output a copy of the database for verification purposes. Normally, you do not need the formatted output provided by report forms or custom print routines when verifying the database. Using the Display command in place of a report form or custom print routine saves time.

TYPICAL OPERATION

In this example you add a menu and a database display feature using the Display command to the DOS shell program. Begin this example in your word processor with DOSSHELL.PRG loaded.

1. Add the following text to the beginning of the DOS shell program.

```
* TODAY'S DATE
* Declare the local variables.
declare MENU_ARRAY[3]
MENU_ARRAY[1] = 'Quit'
MENU_ARRAY[2] = 'Dos Shell'
MENU_ARRAY[3] = 'Show Records'
SELECT = 2
* Save the display.
save screen to TEMP2
* Get the user selection.
do while MENU_ARRAY[SELECT] <> 'Quit'
    @ 03, 39 clear to 07, 55
    @ 03, 39 to 07, 55 double
    SELECT = achoice(04, 40, 06, 54, MENU_ARRAY)
    do case
        case MENU_ARRAY[SELECT] = 'Dos Shell'
            do DOS_SHELL
        case MENU_ARRAY[SELECT] = 'Show Records'
            do SHOW_RECS
    endcase
enddo
* Restore the display.
restore screen from TEMP2
return
* Begin the procedures.
procedure SHOW_RECS
* This procedure displays the database records on screen.
* Initialize the variables.
NUM_FIELDS = 0
DISP_STR = ''
COUNTER = 0
FIELD_CONTENTS = ''
* Save the screen and position the record pointer.
save screen to TEMP
goto top
* Obtain the number of fields, get the field names, place
* the contents of the fields in a string, then display the
* string. Cycle the display every 20 names.
NUM_FIELDS = fcount()
declare FIELD_ARRAY[NUM_FIELDS]
afields(FIELD_ARRAY)
clear screen
do while .not. eof()
    for COUNTER = 1 to NUM_FIELDS
        if COUNTER = 1
            FIELD_CONTENTS = FIELD_ARRAY[1]
            do case
                case type(FIELD_CONTENTS) = 'C'
                    DISP_STR = &FIELD_CONTENTS
                case type(FIELD_CONTENTS) = 'D'
                    DISP_STR = dtoc(&FIELD_CONTENTS)
                case type(FIELD_CONTENTS) = 'N'
                    DISP_STR = str(&FIELD_CONTENTS)
                case type(FIELD_CONTENTS) = 'L'
                    if &FIELD_CONTENTS = .T.
                        DISP_STR = '.T.'
                    else
                        DISP_STR = '.F.'
                    endif
            endcase
        else
            FIELD_CONTENTS = FIELD_ARRAY[COUNTER]
```

```
        do case
            case type(FIELD_CONTENTS) = 'C'
                DISP_STR = DISP_STR + '  ' + &FIELD_CONTENTS
            case type(FIELD_CONTENTS) = 'D'
                DISP_STR = DISP_STR + '  ' + dtoc(&FIELD_CONTENTS)
            case type(FIELD_CONTENTS) = 'N'
                DISP_STR = DISP_STR + '  ' + str(&FIELD_CONTENTS)
            case type(FIELD_CONTENTS) = 'L'
                if &FIELD_CONTENTS = .T.
                    DISP_STR = DISP_STR + '  .T.'
                else
                    DISP_STR = DISP_STR + '  .F.'
                endif
        endcase
    endif
next
display DISP_STR
if .not. eof()
    skip
endif
if (row() > 18) .or. (eof())
    wait
    clear screen
endif
enddo
restore screen from TEMP
return
procedure DOS_SHELL
* Execute DOS command processor. This example assumes the
```

2. Save the document and exit your word processor. Type **CL DOSSHELL** at the DOS prompt. Press **Enter**.

3. Type **MAILLIST** and press **Enter**. The mailing list program menu appears.

4. Press **F10**. The DOS shell menu appears.

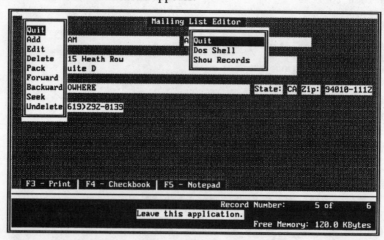

5. Select Show Records by typing **S** and pressing **Enter**. The program displays a complete listing of the mailing list records.

```
      5  SAM                  | A | ANDERSON              | 515 Heath R
ou                           |   | Suite D
       | NOWHERE             |   |                | CA | 94010-1112 | (619
>292-0139
      1  GEORGE               | A | SMITH                 | 1212 12th S
treet
       | ANYWHERE            |   |                | CA | 92111-     | (619
>222-1212
      4  GREG                 | A | STONE                 | 152 Elm Str
eet
       | SOMEPLACE           |   |                | WI | 53211-0125 | (414
>616-3135
      3  SAMUEL               | L | STONE                 | 1234 A Stre
et
       | SOMEPLACE           |   |                | WI | 53211-0114 | (414
>199-2929
      6  AMY                  | B | WILSON                | 8111 North
Hampton
       | ANYWHERE            |   |                | CA | 92111-     | (619
>516-1234
Press any key to continue...
```

6. Press **Enter** twice. The DOS shell menu appears.

7. Type **Q** and press **Enter** to quit the DOS shell menu. Press **F4** to select the checkbook program. Press **F10**, type **S**, and press **Enter** to select Show Records. The program displays a complete listing of the checkbook records. Notice the program automatically compensates for the change in database.

```
   1  07/09/89 |      0 | PAYCHECK                                   |
   0.00 |      550.89 |      550.89 | .F.                             |
   2  07/10/89 |      0 | PAYCHECK DEPOSIT                           |
   0.00 |      820.00 |     1248.46 | .F.                             |
   3  07/11/89 |      0 | PAYCHECK                                   |
   0.00 |     1200.98 |        0.00 | .F.                             |
   4  07/09/89 |      1 | GEORGES RESTAURANT                         |
  19.99 |        0.00 |      530.90 | .T.                             |
   5  07/09/89 |      2 | ANTHONY'S FOOD STORE                       |
 102.44 |        0.00 |      428.46 | .F.                             |
   6  07/10/89 |      3 | JEAN'S SHOES                               |
 520.00 |        0.00 |      728.46 | .F.                             |
   7  07/11/89 |      4 | MAX STATIONERS                             |
  12.22 |        0.00 |      716.24 | .T.                             |
   8  07/11/89 |      5 | RENT                                       |
1000.00 |        0.00 |        0.00 | .T.                             |
Press any key to continue...
```

8. Press any key to continue, then type **Q** and press **Enter** to quit the DOS shell menu. Press **F5** to select the notepad program. Press **F10**, type **S**, and press **Enter** to select Show Records. The program displays a complete listing of the notepad records.

```
   1      1 | This is the first note          | GENERAL

   2      2 | This is the second note         | GENERAL

   3      3 | This is the third note          | 1
Press any key to continue...
```

9. Press **Enter** twice, then select Quit by pressing **Enter**. The DOS prompt appears.

10 Turn to Module 52 to continue the learning sequence.

Module 36
DO CASE

DESCRIPTION

The Do Case control structure works much like a string of If, Elseif, Else, Endif control structures. The difference between these two commands is the way the compiler implements them. The Do Case control structure produces slightly larger, but much faster code than the If, Elseif, Else, Endif control structure. In some cases, using the Do Case control structure also produces more readable source code. Each case clause within the Do Case control structure corresponds to an elseif clause within the If, Elseif, Else, Endif control structure. There is no direct correspondence between the two control structures for the otherwise clause. The otherwise clause lets you cover all other contingencies with a single statement. Clipper executes the commands after the otherwise clause if none of the specified conditions within the Do Case control structure match the current condition. The command line interface of the Do Case control structure appears below.

```
DO CASE ... CASE <CONDITION> ... <COMMANDS> [... CASE <CONDITION>] ...
<COMMANDS> [... OTHERWISE] ... <COMMANDS> ENDCASE
```

APPLICATIONS

Use the Do Case control structure in place of the If, Elseif, Else, Endif control structure when speed is more important than memory requirements. In some cases, one Do Case control structure makes the source code more readable than using several If, Elseif, Else, Endif control structures. The Do Case control structure also lets you cover every contingency with the otherwise clause. While you can implement this feature with the If, Elseif, Else, Endif control structure, the condition part of the statement becomes overly complex.

TYPICAL OPERATION

In this example you replace two of the If, Elseif, Else, Endif control structures with Do Case control structures. You change the structures one at a time to see the effect on code and constant size, then execute the program to see the slight increase in speed. Since this program is small compared to many database management programs, you can normally expect to see much larger increases in speed. Begin this example at the DOS prompt.

1. Type **CL MAILLIST** at the DOS prompt. Press **Enter**. Notice the code and constant sizes.
2. Use a word processor to change the If, Elseif, Else, Endif control structure to a Do Case control structure as shown below.

```
do case
case ANSWER = 'A'
   append blank
   @ 04, 12 get FIRST_NAME picture '@!' valid .not. empty(FIRST_NAME)
   @ 04, 38 get MIDDLE picture '!' valid .not. empty(MIDDLE)
   @ 04, 40 get LAST_NAME picture '@!' valid .not. empty(LAST_NAME)
```

```
   @ 06, 12 get ADDRESS1
   @ 07, 12 get ADDRESS2
   @ 09, 12 get CITY picture '@!'
   @ 09, 60 get STATE picture '!!'
   @ 09, 68 get ZIP picture '99999-9999'
   @ 11, 12 get TELEPHONE picture '(999)999-9999'
   read
* Display the database information and the editing screen.
case ANSWER = 'E'
   @ 04, 12 get FIRST_NAME picture '@!' valid .not. empty(FIRST_NAME)
   @ 04, 38 get MIDDLE picture '!' valid .not. empty(MIDDLE)
   @ 04, 40 get LAST_NAME picture '@!' valid .not. empty(LAST_NAME)
   @ 06, 12 get ADDRESS1
   @ 07, 12 get ADDRESS2
   @ 09, 12 get CITY picture '@!'
   @ 09, 60 get STATE picture '!!'
   @ 09, 68 get ZIP picture '99999-9999'
   @ 11, 12 get TELEPHONE picture '(999)999-9999'
   read
* Delete the current record.
case ANSWER = 'D'
   delete
* Remove the deleted records.
case ANSWER = 'P'
   pack
* Move forward one record.
case ANSWER = 'F'
   skip
* Move backward one record.
case ANSWER = 'B'
   skip -1
* Search for the desired last name.
case ANSWER = 'S'
   SEARCH_NAME = LAST_NAME
   @ 04, 40 get SEARCH_NAME picture '@K@!'
   read
   seek SEARCH_NAME
* Undelete a previously deleted record.
case ANSWER = 'U'
   recall
endcase
enddo
```

3. Save the document and exit your word processor. Type **CL MAILLIST** at the DOS prompt. Press **Enter**. Notice the code size increases.

4. Use a word processor to change the If, Elseif, Else, Endif control structure to a Do Case control structure as shown below. Notice how much more readable these sets of statements become.

```
do case
case bof() .and. ANSWER = 'B'
   @ 23,04 say ' Beginning of File '
case eof() .and. .not. ANSWER='S'
   @ 23,04 say ' End of File '
case .not. found() .and. ANSWER = 'S'
   @ 23,04 say ' Name not found. '
case .not. updated() .and. ANSWER = 'E'
   @ 23,04 say ' Record not updated '
otherwise
   @ 23,04 say ' ███████████████ '    && Press Alt-177 (on keypad) 20 times.
endcase
```

5. Save the document and exit your word processor. Type **CL MAILLIST** at the DOS prompt. Press **Enter**. Notice the code and constant size increase.

6. Type **MAILLIST** and press **Enter**.

7. Type **F, B,** or **S** to use the forward, backward, and seek options. Notice the difference in response time to keystrokes.

8. Type **Q**. The DOS prompt appears.

9. Turn to Module 11 to continue the learning sequence.

Module 37
DO
(PROCEDURE)

DESCRIPTION

The Do command works with the Procedure control structure to create more readable and reliable programs. When you separate a section of code from the main procedure using the Procedure control structure, you need a method to access it. The Do command allows you to access the code separated by the Procedure control structure. The command line interface of the Do command appears below.

```
DO <PROCEDURE> [WITH <PARAMETER LIST>]
```

The procedure name appears after the Do command. You can optionally send the procedure a list of parameters using the with clause. The parameters can contain anything the procedure might need to make it more generic. For example, if you created a menu procedure and wanted to use the same procedure in every program, you could send the menu entries in a parameter list. The procedure, in turn, could place the selection returned by the user in a specific variable.

APPLICATIONS

Use the Do command to execute code contained within Procedure control structures. By naming your procedures descriptively, you can see what a program does without looking at the procedures. In this sense, procedures called by the Do command act much like headings in an outline. To get a basic feel for the content of the document, you look at the headings. To see the detail of a particular section, you look at the subheadings (or procedures in the case of a program). The use of the Do command with Procedure control structures keeps your code well organized and easy to read.

TYPICAL OPERATION

In this example you complete the process of breaking the sample program into generic sections by using the Do command. The object of this sample is to create more readable code without changing program operation. Begin this example in your word processor with MAILLIST.PRG loaded.

1. Add the following text to the beginning of the sample program.

```
* Display the editing screen.
do DISPLAY_STATUS
* Display the edit area.
do DISPLAY_SCRN
do DISPLAY_DATA
* Get user choice.
do DISPLAY_MENU
* Add a new record.
do case
```

```
case ANSWER = 2
    append blank
    do GET_DATA
    read
* Display the database information.
case ANSWER = 3
    do GET_DATA
    read
```

2. Save the document and exit your word processor. Type **CL MAILLIST** at the DOS prompt. Press **Enter**.

3. Type **MAILLIST**. Press **Enter**.

4. Type **E**. The menu disappears and the edit screen appears as before. Notice the program operates exactly as before.

5. Press **Esc**. The menu reappears. Notice the Edit option appears highlighted.

6. Type **S** to select the seek option. Type **D** and press **Enter**. The program does not find a matching record. It does place the record pointer at the first non-matching position greater than D. Notice the program operates exactly as before.

7. Type **Q**. The DOS prompt appears.

8. Turn to Module 57 to continue the learning sequence.

Module 38
DO WHILE

DESCRIPTION

The Do While control structure provides a method of creating program loops. A loop is a control structure where Clipper executes the same set of commands until a certain condition no longer exists. The command line interface of the Do While control structure appears below.

```
DO WHILE <CONDITION> <STATEMENTS> ... [EXIT] <STATEMENTS> ... [LOOP]
<STATEMENTS> ... ENDDO
```

The condition clause contains the argument Clipper monitors for change. When the condition no longer evaluates true, the program exits the Do While control structure.

The statement clauses are lines of code between the various sections of the Do While control structure. They contain the code Clipper executes until the condition is no longer true.

The exit clause provides an alternate method of exiting the control structure. Clipper does not execute the statements following the exit clause, but passes control to the code immediately following the enddo clause. Normally, the exit statement appears nested within a case or if endif control structure.

The loop clause passes control to the first statement of the Do While control structure without executing the lines of code below it. Normally, the loop statement appears nested within a case or if endif control structure.

The enddo clause marks the end of the Do While control structure. Every Do While control structure contains an enddo clause.

APPLICATIONS

Use the Do While control structure whenever you need to execute a set of program instructions more than one time. The Do While control structure is especially effective in instances where you need to evaluate the condition before you execute the statements even one time. The exit clause provides an easy method of leaving the control structure when error handling code detects an error. The loop clause provides the means of restarting the loop. For example, if you needed to execute a set of instructions only occasionally, you could test for the condition required first. Then, you could loop to the top of the Do While control structure if the condition required did not exist.

TYPICAL OPERATION

In this example you add a Do While control structure to MAILLIST.PRG. This will allow you to add more than one record before leaving the program. Begin this example in your word processor with MAILLIST.PRG loaded.

1. Change your program so it looks like the program listing shown below. Make sure you compare your program with the new program listing line-by-line.

```
* MAILLIST.PRG
* This program manages a mailing list.
* YOUR NAME
* TODAY'S DATE
* Program Variables
DOUBLE_LINE = chr(201) + chr(205) + chr(187) + chr(186) + chr(188) + ;
   chr(205) + chr(200) + chr(186) + chr(177)
ANSWER = 'A'
* Clear the display and prepare database for use.
clear screen
use MAILLIST index LASTNAME
* Begin processing loop.
do while ANSWER <> 'Q'
* Display the editing screen.
@ 01, 00, 24, 79 box DOUBLE_LINE
@ 20, 01 to 20, 78
@ 04, 06 say 'Name:'
@ 06, 03 say 'Address:'
@ 09, 06 say 'City:'
@ 09, 53 say 'State:'
@ 09, 63 say 'Zip:'
@ 11, 07 say 'Tel:'
* Get user choice.
@ 22, 04 say 'Quit/Add Record/Edit Record' get ANSWER picture '!'
read
* Add a new record.
if ANSWER = 'A'
   append blank
   @ 04, 12 get FIRST_NAME picture '@!'
   @ 04, 38 get MIDDLE picture '!'
   @ 04, 40 get LAST_NAME picture '@!'
   @ 06, 12 get ADDRESS1
   @ 07, 12 get ADDRESS2
   @ 09, 12 get CITY picture '@!'
   @ 09, 60 get STATE picture '!!'
   @ 09, 68 get ZIP picture '99999-9999'
   @ 11, 12 get TELEPHONE picture '(999)999-9999'
   read
* Display the database information.
elseif ANSWER = 'E'
   @ 04, 12 get FIRST_NAME picture '@!'
   @ 04, 38 get MIDDLE picture '!'
   @ 04, 40 get LAST_NAME picture '@!'
   @ 06, 12 get ADDRESS1
   @ 07, 12 get ADDRESS2
   @ 09, 12 get CITY picture '@!'
   @ 09, 60 get STATE picture '!!'
   @ 09, 68 get ZIP picture '99999-9999'
   @ 11, 12 get TELEPHONE picture '(999)999-9999'
   read
endif
enddo
* Close the database and exit to DOS.
quit
```

2. Save the document and exit your word processor.

3. Type **CL MAILLIST** at the DOS prompt. Press **Enter**.

4. Type **MAILLIST**. Press **Enter**. The data entry screen appears. Notice the cursor appears at the end of the menu.

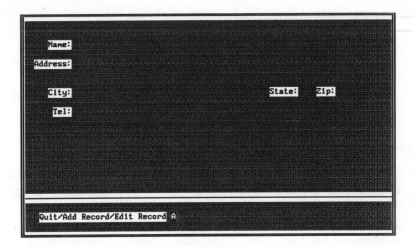

5. Type **E**. The first record in the database appears.

NOTE

If your program freezes or you cannot exit by pressing Q at the menu prompt, press Alt-C. Clipper displays a menu with an option to quit. If you select quit, Clipper exits and the DOS prompt appears. Make sure you check your program for errors after you exit.

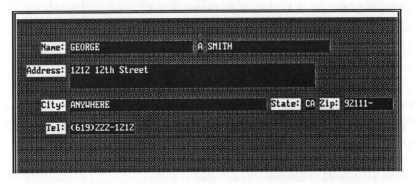

6. Press **PgDn** to go back to the menu. Type **A**. A blank record appears.

7. Type **GEORGE**. Press **Enter**. Type **A**. Type **ANDERSON**. Press **Enter**. Type **1515 Heath Row**. Press **Enter**. Type **Suite D**. Press **Enter**. Type **NOWHERE**. Press **Enter**. Type **CA**. Type **940101112**. Type **6192920139**. The cursor goes back to the menu.

8. Type **Q**. The DOS prompt appears.

9. Turn to Module 33 to continue the learning sequence.

Module 39
EJECT

DESCRIPTION

The Eject command performs the same function as the Form Feed switch on your printer. It advances the paper to the top of next page. The command line interface of the Eject command appears below.

```
EJECT
```

APPLICATIONS

Use this command between pages of customized reports. Also use it at the end of all reports to advance the paper to the top of the next page.

TYPICAL OPERATION

In this example you use the Eject command to advance the paper after sending output to the printer. Begin this example in your word processor with PRINT.PRG loaded.

1. Add the following text at the end of the main procedure.

```
?? ' Records.'
eject
* Reset the display and printer.
```

2. Save the document and exit your word processor. Compile the program.

3. Type **PRINT**. Press **Enter**.

4. Type **LPT1**. Press **Enter**. The printer outputs the last record message and advances the paper to the top of the next page.

5. Press **Enter**. The DOS prompt appears.

6. Turn to Module 82 to continue the learning sequence.

Module 40
ERASE/DELETE FILE

DESCRIPTION

The Erase/Delete File command removes a file from the disk. You must always close any file you want to erase before attempting to erase it. Clipper uses the standard DOS file erasure techniques. This means that you or someone else could recover the file using one of the currently available file recovery programs. The command line interface of the Erase/Delete File command appears below.

```
ERASE FILE <FILENAME>.<EXT>/(<EXPC>)
DELETE FILE <FILENAME>.<EXT>/(<EXPC>)
```

APPLICATIONS

Use the Erase/Delete File command whenever you no longer need a file stored on disk.

TYPICAL OPERATION

In this example you add the capability of removing unneeded disk files using the Erase/Delete File command. Begin this example in your word processor with MAINT.PRG loaded.

1. Add the following text to the maintenance program.
```
* Ask if any files require deletion.
input 'Do you want to delete any of the files? ' to ANSWER
ANSWER = upper(ANSWER)
if len(ANSWER) > 1
   ANSWER = substr(ANSWER, 1, 1)
endif
if ANSWER = 'Y'
   input 'Which file(s) do you want deleted?' + chr(13) + chr(10) to
DEL_FILE
   delete file &DEL_FILE
endif
* Exit this utility
```

2. Save the document and exit your word processor. Type **CLD MAINT** at the DOS prompt. Press **Enter**.

3. Type **MAINT**. Press **Enter**. The program asks for a directory path and skeleton.

4. Type **'*.NTX'** and press **Enter**. The program displays a listing of files ending with .NTX. Then the program asks "Do you want to delete any of the files?"

5. Type **'Y'** and press **Enter**. The program asks "Which file(s) do you want deleted?"

6. Type **'TEMP_IND.NTX'**. Press **Enter**. The program deletes the file and returns to DOS.

7. Type **DIR TEMP_IND.NTX**. Press **Enter**. DOS reports 'File not found' since the program deleted it.

```
Type directory path and skeleton
'*.NTX'
CATEGORY NTX     2048  06/28/89
CHCKNUM  NTX     2048  07/15/89
DATE     NTX     2048  07/15/89
LASTNAME NTX     2048  07/09/89
NOTENUM  NTX     2048  06/28/89
SUBJECT  NTX     2048  06/28/89
TEMP_IND NTX     2048  07/15/89
HELP     NTX     2048  07/16/89

Do you want to delete any of the files? 'Y'
Which file(s) do you want deleted?
'TEMP_IND.NTX'
C:\CLIPPER\0022>DIR TEMP_IND.NTX

 Volume in drive C is JOHN'S DISK
 Directory of  C:\CLIPPER\0022

File not found

C:\CLIPPER\0022>
```

8. Turn to Module 66 to continue the learning sequence.

Module 41
EXTERNAL

DESCRIPTION

The External command tells the compiler and linker that a procedure appears outside the current program. In most cases Clipper finds the external procedures itself. However, if you place the procedure in a macro (&) statement, the compiler does not know that the procedure exists unless you tell it. Any commands or functions appearing in CLIPPER.LIB do not require the use of the External command. Any other functions, even those in EXTEND.LIB, require the use of the External command when the function appears as part of a macro statement. The command line interface of the External command appears below.

```
EXTERNAL <PROCEDURE LIST>
```

APPLICATIONS

Use the External command whenever you use user-defined or extended functions within a macro (&) statement.

TYPICAL OPERATION

In this example you fix the problem noted in Module 104 during the typical operation using the External command. Begin this example in your word processor with CHCKBOOK.PRG loaded.

1. Add the following text to the beginning of the program.
   ```
   set key -3 to                        && Make sure F4 is clear.
   * Declare external procedures.
   external DESCEND
   * Clear the display and prepare the database for use.
   ```

2. Save the document and exit your word processor. Type **CL CHCKBOOK** at the DOS prompt. Press **Enter**.

3. Type **MAILLIST**. Press **Enter**. The mailing list program menu appears.

4. Press **F4**. The checkbook program menu appears.

5. Press **Down Arrow** until the Sort option of the menu appears.

6. Press **Enter**. The Sort menu appears.

7. Select Date by pressing **Down Arrow**. Press **Enter**. The program highlights the Date option and asks in which order you want to sort.

8. Select Descending by pressing **Down Arrow** then **Enter**. The program returns the selector to the quit option on the first menu.

9. Select Drawn For by pressing **Down Arrow** twice. Press **Enter**. Select Descending by pressing **Down Arrow** then **Enter**. Select Quit by pressing **Enter**. The program sorts the database and displays the sorted version on screen. Notice the error message does not appear and the database appears sorted in descending order.

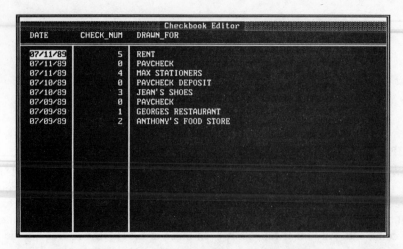

```
                          Checkbook Editor
  DATE        CHECK_NUM   DRAWN_FOR

  07/11/89            5   RENT
  07/11/89            0   PAYCHECK
  07/11/89            4   MAX STATIONERS
  07/10/89            0   PAYCHECK DEPOSIT
  07/10/89            3   JEAN'S SHOES
  07/09/89            0   PAYCHECK
  07/09/89            1   GEORGES RESTAURANT
  07/09/89            2   ANTHONY'S FOOD STORE
```

10. Press **Esc** to return to the checkbook program menu. Type **Q** to select quit. Press **Enter**. The DOS prompt appears.

11. Turn to Module 79 to continue the learning sequence.

Module 42
FIND

DESCRIPTION

The Find command locates a record in a database using a search string. Clipper lets you specify either a literal character string or a variable containing a character string. The command line interface of the Find command appears below.

```
FIND <CHARACTER STRING>/(<EXPC>)
```

APPLICATIONS

Use the Find command to quickly find any record in the database. By using different index files, you can search for any value using any field. The Find command always begins at the top of the database and searches down, making it more thorough than some search methods. In most cases it does not operate as quickly as the Seek command.

TYPICAL OPERATION

Begin this example in your word processor with CHCKBOOK.PRG loaded.

1. Change the SEARCH_REC procedure as shown below. Add the following two functions.

```
procedure SEARCH_REC
* This procedure allows the user to search the database.
private CHECK_VALUE, DATE_VALUE, SEARCH_TYPE, WAIT_VAR
CHECK_VALUE = 0
DATE_VALUE = date()
SEARCH_TYPE = 'C'
WAIT_VAR = ' '
* Get the search type.
@ 14, 04 say 'Search for (C)heck Number or (D)ate? ';
   get SEARCH_TYPE picture '!'
read
* Setup the index.
do case
   case SEARCH_TYPE = 'C'
      set index to CHCKNUM
   case SEARCH_TYPE = 'D'
      set index to DATE
endcase
* Get the search information.
do case
   case SEARCH_TYPE = 'C'
      @ 15, 04 say 'Which check do you want? ' get CHECK_VALUE picture ;
      '99999'
   case SEARCH_TYPE = 'D'
      @ 15, 04 say 'Which date do you want? ' get DATE_VALUE picture ;
      '99/99/99'
endcase
read
* Convert the information to an acceptable format.
```

```
CHECK_VALUE = conv_num(CHECK_VALUE)
DATE_VALUE = conv_date(DATE_VALUE)
* Find the check or date.
do case
   case SEARCH_TYPE = 'C'
      find &CHECK_VALUE
   case SEARCH_TYPE = 'D'
      find &DATE_VALUE
endcase
if .not. found()
   @ 17, 04 say 'Check not found! Press any key.' get WAIT_VAR
   read
else
   do EDIT_REC
endif
set index to CHCKNUM, DATE
return
function CONV_NUM
* Convert CONV_VALUE to a string with leading zeros.
parameters CONV_VALUE
CONV_VALUE = str(CONV_VALUE, 5, 0)
CONV_VALUE = strtran(CONV_VALUE, ' ', '0')
return CONV_VALUE
function CONV_DATE
* Convert CONV_VALUE to a string.
parameters CONV_VALUE
CONV_VALUE = dtoc(CONV_VALUE)
return CONV_VALUE
```

2. Save the document and exit your word processor. Type **CL CHCKBOOK** at the DOS prompt. Press **Enter**.

3. Type **MAILLIST**. Press **Enter**.

4. Press **F4**.

5. Type **S** and press **Enter**. The program asks what type of search to perform.

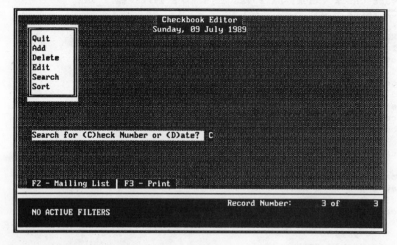

6. Type **C**. The program asks for a check number.

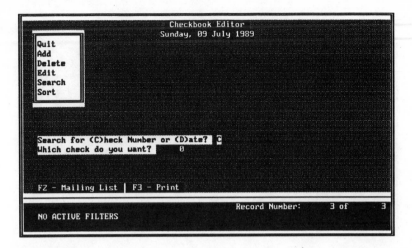

7. Type **1** and press **Enter**. The program displays the edit screen with the correct check number highlighted.

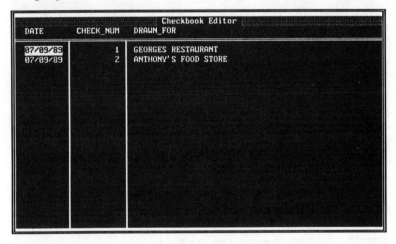

8. Press **Esc**. The checkbook program menu appears.

9. Type **S** and press **Enter**. The program asks what type of search you want to perform.

10. Type **D**. The program asks for a date and suggests today's date.

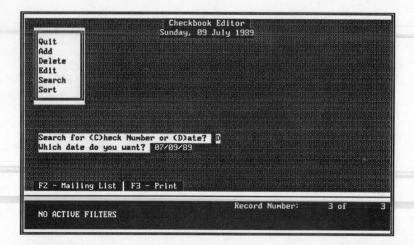

11. Type **07/09/89**. The program displays the edit screen with the correct date highlighted.

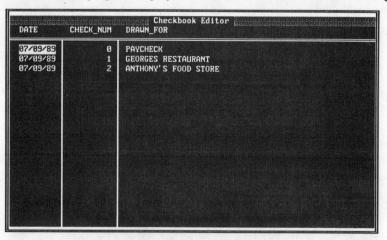

12. Press **Esc**. The checkbook program menu appears.
13. Type **Q** to select quit. Press **Enter**. The DOS prompt appears.
14. Turn to Module 45 to continue the learning sequence.

Module 43
FOR TO
(EXECUTE A LOOP)

DESCRIPTION

The For To control structure provides another means of creating loops in Clipper. This particular control structure has several advantages over the Do While control structure. For example, when you use the Do While control structure, you must think of an appropriate condition for terminating the loop. With a For To control structure, you always know how long the loop will execute and that the loop will end. The command line interface of the For To control structure appears below.

```
FOR <MEMVAR> = <EXPN1> TO <EXPN2> [STEP <EXPN3>] <STATEMENTS> ... [EXIT]
<STATEMENTS> ... [LOOP] NEXT
```

The MEMVAR contains a memory variable used to hold the current count. When Clipper encounters the For To control structure, it places the value of EXPN1 into MEMVAR. When MEMVAR reaches EXPN2, the program exits the For To control structure.

Normally Clipper counts by one. For example, if MEMVAR currently contains 2, then when this loop finishes, Clipper updates it to 3. By placing a different number in EXPN3 and using the step clause, you can cause Clipper to count by some other value.

The exit clause lets you leave the control structure before MEMVAR equals EXPN2. Clipper automatically resumes program execution after the next clause.

The loop clause lets you go back to the first statement in the control structure before Clipper executes all the statements in the control structure.

APPLICATIONS

Use the For To control structure when you know the number of control structure execution cycles in advance. For example, print routines normally execute a fixed number of times. Using the For To control structure avoids some of the problems involved in using a Do While control structure. For example, you must check all conditions in a Do While control structure before you enter it; otherwise, the control structure could end before even one loop occurs. For To control structures always execute at least once.

TYPICAL OPERATION

In this example you start another program using the For To control structure. This example is a print routine for the mailing list program. Begin this example in your word processor.

1. Create PRINT.PRG using the following text.

```
* PRINT.PRG
* This program prints a mailing list.
* YOUR NAME
```

```
* TODAY'S DATE
* Program Variables
DOUBLE_LINE = chr(201) + chr(205) + chr(187) + chr(186) + chr(188) + ;
    chr(205) + chr(200) + chr(186) + chr(177)
PRNT_COUNT = 0
* Display a print screen
do DISP_SCRN
* Setup program defaults.
set print on
set console off
* Open the database and prepare it for use.
use MAILLIST index LASTNAME
for PRNT_COUNT = 1 to reccount()
    do DISP_COUNT
next
* Reset the display and printer.
set print off
set console on
* Close the database and exit.
quit
* Begin Procedures
procedure DISP_SCRN
* This procedure displays a print screen.
clear
@ 01, 00, 24, 79 box DOUBLE_LINE
set color to N/W,W+/N
@ 02, 01 clear to 04, 78
@ 21, 01 clear to 23, 78
@ 03, 27 say 'Mailing List Print Program'
set color to W/N,N/W
return
procedure DISP_COUNT
* This procedure displays the current record being printed
* and the total number to print.
set console on
set print off
set color to N/W,W+/N
@ 22, 04 say 'Printing record'
@ 22, 19 say PRNT_COUNT
@ 22, 30 say 'of'
@ 22, 32 say reccount()
set console off
set print on
set color to W/N,N/W
return
```

2. Save the document and exit your word processor. Type **CL PRINT** at the DOS prompt. Press **Enter**.

NOTE

Some computers operate at a speed too great to actually see the program counting the record numbers at this time. If your computer is in this category, make sure your display matches the following screen shot.

3. Type **PRINT**. Press **Enter**. The record number counts from 1 through 5, then the DOS prompt appears.

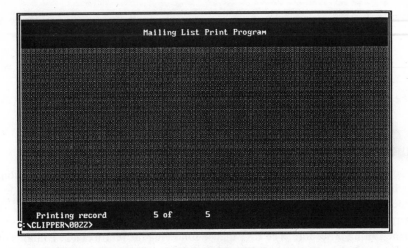

4. Turn to Module 44 to continue the learning sequence.

Module 44
FUNCTION

DESCRIPTION

The Function command allows you to create functions that work much like the functions already supplied with Clipper. The name of the function always appears after the function declaration. The statements following the function name define what task the function performs. The return clause returns program control to the calling procedure. Every user-defined function must return a value to the calling procedure. The EXP clause following the return clause contains this value. EXP contains any legal value including strings, dates, numbers, arrays, NIL, and code blocks. NIL is a special value which refers to no value. It differs from a blank or a 0 in that Clipper looks at it as an empty set. A code block contains executable code. Code blocks are an advanced user function outside the scope of this book. The command line interface of the Function command appears below.

```
FUNCTION <PROCEDURE> [(<PARAMETER LIST>)] [LOCAL <EXP1> [:= <EXP2>] [,
<EXP3> [:= <EXP4>]] ...] [STATIC <EXP5> [:= <EXP6>] [, <EXP7> [:= <EXP8>]]
...] [FIELD <FIELD LIST> [IN <ALIAS/DATABASE NAME>]] [MEMVAR <EXP9>]
<STATEMENTS> ... RETURN <EXP>
```

The parameter list defines the variables that a calling procedure must pass to the function. These variables may consist of any legal value including strings, dates, numbers, and arrays. You may not use a variable name containing leading underscores. Clipper allows you to use any number of characters in the variable name. However, only the first ten characters are significant. Clipper always defines these parameters as local variables. You must enclose the parameter list in parentheses.

The local, static, field, and memvar clauses perform the task of declaring variables. Module 32 contains a complete description of these three clauses. You must use these four declarations in the order specified.

APPLICATIONS

Use the Function command to create any type of function you might need to perform a certain task. For example, if you wanted to create a function that inserted the current date and time as part of a heading, you could use the Function command to create it. Although the uses for functions are as unlimited as procedures, use procedures when you want to perform a task with no return value, and functions when you want a return value. Tasks that usually require return values include equipment status, text/data manipulation, and database/index status.

TYPICAL OPERATION

In this example you begin the process of creating a printer status function using the Function command. Begin this example in your word processor with PRINT.PRG loaded.

1. Add the following text to the variable section at the beginning of the program.

```
PRNT_COUNT = 0
PRNT_PORT = 'PRN  '
```

2. Add this text after the screen display section at the beginning of the program.

```
do DISP_SCRN
* Check the printer status.
@ 06, 04 say 'Enter the printer port you wish to use. ' ;
   get PRNT_PORT picture '@!'
read
do while .not. PRNT_ON (PRNT_PORT)
   @ 06, 04 say 'Enter the printer port you wish to use. ';
      get PRNT_PORT picture '@!'
   read
enddo
```

3. Add the following text at the end of the program.

```
return
function PRNT_ON
* This function checks the status of the printer port and
* returns true if the port exists and the printer is on.
parameters PORT_NAME
* Initialize the return variable.
IS_PORT = .F.
set printer to &PORT_NAME
IS_PORT = .T.
return IS_PORT
```

4. Save the document and exit your word processor. Type **CL PRINT** at the DOS prompt. Press **Enter**.

5. Type **PRINT**. Press **Enter**. The print program asks which printer to use. Notice it automatically suggests the default printer, PRN.

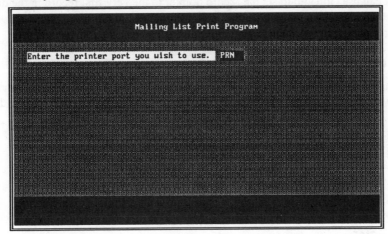

6. Type **LPT1**. Press **Enter**. The record number counts from 1 through 5, then the DOS prompt appears.

7. Turn to Module 59 to continue the learning sequence.

Module 45
GO/GOTO

DESCRIPTION

The Go/Goto command places the record pointer in a precise position in the database. If you specify a number, EXPN, then Go/Goto takes you to that specific record. If you specify the top clause, Go/Goto takes you to the first record. For unindexed databases it takes you to record number 1. When using indexed databases, it takes you to the first record in the index. If you specify the bottom clause, Go/Goto takes you to the last record in the database. Go/Goto follows the same rules for the bottom clause as it does for the top clause. The command line interface of the Go/Goto command appears below.

```
GO/GOTO <EXPN>/BOTTOM/TOP
```

APPLICATIONS

The Go/Goto command has many uses. This is an all-purpose tool used in about every location you can think of. By storing a record number in a variable, then performing a task, you can return the user to the initial record at the end of the task. If you want to perform a customized print routine, you can use Go/Goto to set the record pointer to the very first record in the database. If you want a blank template for an edit or add operation, you can use the Go/Goto command to set the record pointer one past the last record.

TYPICAL OPERATION

In this example you replace a relatively inefficient method of finding the last record in a database with the Go/Goto command. Begin this example in your word processor with MAILLIST.PRG loaded.

1. Change the case statement text for add as shown below.
   ```
   * Add a new record.
   do case
   case ANSWER = 2
      goto bottom
      do GET_DATA
   ```
2. Save the document and exit your word processor. Type **CL MAILLIST** at the DOS prompt. Press **Enter**.
3. Type **MAILLIST**. Press **Enter**. The mailing list program menu appears.
4. Type **A**. Notice the program presents a display showing the last record in the database.

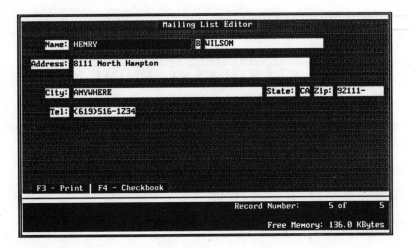

5. Type **AMY** in the First Name field and press **PgDn** to complete the transaction. The mailing list program menu appears.

6. Type **Q** to select Quit. The DOS prompt appears.

7. Turn to Module 30 to continue the learning sequence.

Module 46
IF, ELSEIF, ELSE, ENDIF

DESCRIPTION

The If, Elseif, Else, Endif control structure conditionally executes the statements appearing behind each condition. Every control structure begins with the if clause and ends with an endif clause. The command line interface of the If, Elseif, Else, Endif control structure appears below.

```
IF <CONDITION> <STATEMENTS> ... [ELSEIF <CONDITION> <STATEMENTS> ... ]
[ELSE <STATEMENTS> ... ] ENDIF
```

A condition is a logic statement. For example, VARIABLE = 0 is a logic statement Clipper can test for accuracy. When a condition tests true, Clipper executes the statements following it. Otherwise, the control structure fails, or Clipper executes an alternative set of statements. For example, if the condition of an if clause evaluates false, but the control structure contains an else clause, Clipper executes the statements following the else clause. The elseif clause works in the same manner as the else clause. It waits until the if clause of a control structure fails. However, the elseif clause adds a new set of conditions Clipper must test. If these conditions also fail, Clipper looks for another alternative set of statements to execute. If it finds none, then the control structure fails. Clipper allows you to use as many elseif clauses as needed. You may have only one if, else, and endif clause per control structure.

APPLICATIONS

Use the If, Elseif, Else, Endif control structure to influence program flow. By using this control structure correctly, you can change the program environment to meet changing requirements. You can also check for certain events to occur and take appropriate action. For example, you could use this control structure to perform certain tasks based on user input. You could also check for hardware conditions and issue warnings to the user as needed.

TYPICAL OPERATION

In this example you use the If, Elseif, Else, Endif control structure to influence when the program adds a record to the sample database. Begin this example at the DOS prompt in the C:\CLIPPER\0022 directory.

1. Add the following text to the MAILLIST.PRG as shown below. Notice the indented append blank statement. This identifies it as a statement executing within the If, Elseif, Else, Endif control structure.

```
use MAILLIST index LASTNAME
ANSWER = 'Y'
@ 22, 04 say 'Do you want to add a new record? ' get ANSWER picture '!'
read
if ANSWER = 'Y'
   append blank
else
```

```
    @ 22, 04 say 'No new record was added to the database. '
endif
@ 04, 06 say 'Name:'
```

2. Save the document and exit your word processor.

3. Type **CL MAILLIST** at the DOS prompt. Press **Enter**.

4. Type **MAILLIST**. Press **Enter**. The program asks if you want to add a record.

5. Type **N**. The mailing list display appears. The program displays the message "No new record was added to the database." Notice the record you entered previously appears.

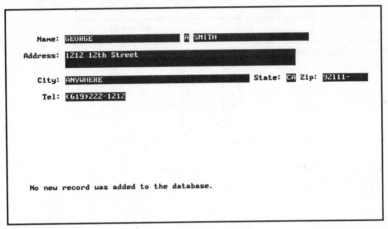

6. Press **Esc**. The DOS prompt appears.

7. Type **MAILLIST** and press **Enter**. The program asks if you want to add a new record.

8. Type **Y**. The mailing list display appears. Notice a new record appears and the add a new record question remains intact.

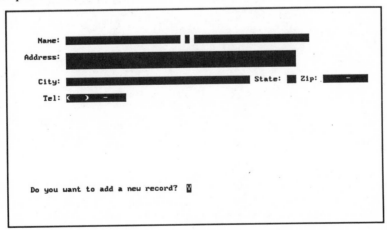

9. Type **HENRY**. Press **Enter**. Type **B**. Type **WILSON**. Press **Enter**. Type **8111 North Hampton**. Press **Enter** twice. Type **ANYWHERE**. Press **Enter**. Type **CA**. Type **92111**. Press Enter. Type **6195161234**. The DOS prompt appears.

10. Type **DBU** and press **Enter** to execute the database utility. Type **MAILLIST** and press **Enter**. The database utility retrieves MAILLIST.DBF.

11. Press **F5** to get into the browse display. Press **Enter**. The database utility displays the contents of MAILLIST.DBF. Notice the database now contains two records containing the previously entered data.

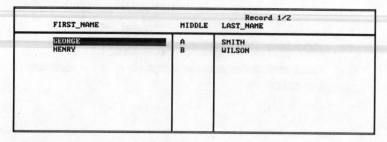

```
                                           Record 1/2
          FIRST_NAME               MIDDLE  LAST_NAME

          GEORGE                    A       SMITH
          HENRY                     B       WILSON
```

12. Press **Esc** twice to exit the database utility. Type **Y**. The DOS prompt appears.

13. Turn to Module 71 to continue the learning sequence.

Module 47
INDEX ON

DESCRIPTION

The Index On command creates a sorted listing of KEY EXP in an index file (FILE/EXPC) separate from the database. This index file also contains a pointer to the record in the database. Clipper uses this index to allow quick access to records within the database. Module 6 contains complete information on indexes and how Clipper implements them. The command line interface of the Index On command appears below.

```
INDEX ON <KEY EXP> TO <FILE>/(<EXPC>)
```

APPLICATIONS

Use the Index On command whenever you need to sort a database in a different order, the index file becomes corrupted, or you change the database without opening the index file as well. Using index files reduces the time required to find information without the need to constantly sort the database. Many Clipper commands require you use an index file.

TYPICAL OPERATION

In this example you begin building the SORT procedure using the Index To command. Begin this example in your word processor with CHCKBOOK.PRG loaded.

1. Add the following text to the SORT_REC procedure.
    ```
    * Initialize Variables.
    private NAME_ARRAY, AVAIL_ARRAY, SORT_STRING, SORT_SELECT
    declare NAME_ARRAY[7]
    NAME_ARRAY[1] = 'Quit'
    NAME_ARRAY[2] = 'Date'
    NAME_ARRAY[3] = 'Check Number'
    NAME_ARRAY[4] = 'Drawn For'
    NAME_ARRAY[5] = 'Check Amount'
    NAME_ARRAY[6] = 'Deposit Amount'
    NAME_ARRAY[7] = 'Tax Ded. Item'
    declare AVAIL_ARRAY[7]
    afill(AVAIL_ARRAY, .T.)
    SORT_STRING = ' '
    SORT_SELECT = 2
    * Keep adding parameters to the sort string until the user
    * quits the sort menu.
    set color to 'N/W,W/N,,,W+/N'
    do while .not. NAME_ARRAY[SORT_SELECT] = 'Quit'
       @ 06, 06 to 14, 21 double
       SORT_SELECT = achoice(07, 07, 13, 20, NAME_ARRAY, AVAIL_ARRAY)
         do case
           case NAME_ARRAY[SORT_SELECT] = 'Date'
               SORT_STRING = ltrim(SORT_STRING) + 'DTOS(DATE) + '
               AVAIL_ARRAY[SORT_SELECT] = .F.
           case NAME_ARRAY[SORT_SELECT] = 'Check Number'
    ```

```
        SORT_STRING = ltrim(SORT_STRING) + 'STR(CHECK_NUM,5,0) + '
        AVAIL_ARRAY[SORT_SELECT] = .F.
   case NAME_ARRAY[SORT_SELECT] = 'Drawn For'
        SORT_STRING = ltrim(SORT_STRING) + 'DRAWN_FOR + '
        AVAIL_ARRAY[SORT_SELECT] = .F.
   case NAME_ARRAY[SORT_SELECT] = 'Check Amount'
        SORT_STRING = ltrim(SORT_STRING) + 'STR(AMOUNT,10,2) + '
        AVAIL_ARRAY[SORT_SELECT] = .F.
   case NAME_ARRAY[SORT_SELECT] = 'Deposit Amount'
        SORT_STRING = ltrim(SORT_STRING) + 'STR(DEPOSIT,10,2) + '
        AVAIL_ARRAY[SORT_SELECT] = .F.
   case NAME_ARRAY[SORT_SELECT] = 'Tax Ded. Item'
        SORT_STRING = ltrim(SORT_STRING) + 'TAX_ITEM + '
        AVAIL_ARRAY[SORT_SELECT] = .F.
   endcase
enddo
* Trim the last plus sign from the end of SORT_STRING.
SORT_STRING = substr(SORT_STRING, 1, len(SORT_STRING) - 3)
* Create then look at index.
index on &SORT_STRING to TEMP_IND
do EDIT_REC
set index to CHCKNUM, DATE
set color to 'W/N,N/W,,,W+/N'
return
```

NOTE

Some 512 KByte RAM equipped machines may run out of RAM during
critical operations from this module to the end of the learning sequence.
For those machines, type CLD CHCKBOOK in place of CL
CHCKBOOK. Type CHCKBOOK to enter the procedure in place of
MAILLIST. All other operations will function normally.

2. Save the document and exit your word processor. Type **CL CHCKBOOK** at the DOS
   prompt. Press **Enter**.

3. Type **MAILLIST**. Press **Enter**. The mailing list program menu appears.

4. Press **F4**. The checkbook program menu appears.

5. Press **Down Arrow** until the Sort option of the menu appears.

6. Press **Enter**. The Sort menu appears.

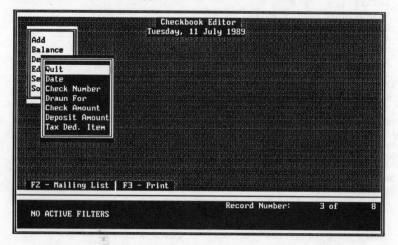

7. Select Date by pressing **Down Arrow**. Press **Enter**. The program highlights the Date option and returns the selector to the Quit option.

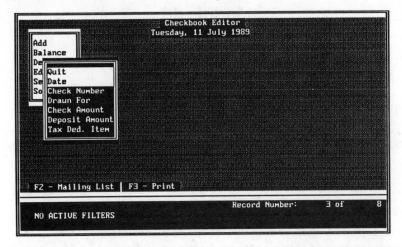

8. Select Drawn For by pressing **Down Arrow** twice. Press **Enter**. Select Quit by pressing **Enter**. The program sorts the database and displays the sorted version on screen.

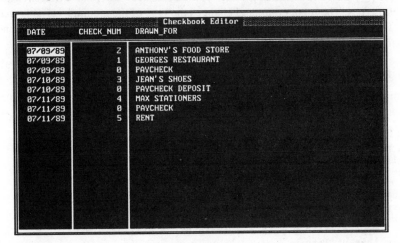

9. Press **Esc** to return to the checkbook program menu. Type **Q** to select quit. Press **Enter**. The DOS prompt appears.

10. Turn to Module 104 to continue the learning sequence.

Module 48
INPUT

DESCRIPTION

The Input command accepts user entry from the keyboard and places it in the specified memory variable. The optional prompt displays a message telling the user what sort of information to type. The command line interface of the Input command appears below.

```
INPUT [<PROMPT>] TO <MEMVAR>
```

APPLICATIONS

Use the Input command when you do not require formatted screen prompts. This command provides an easy method of obtaining input of any type without the problems associated with screen formatting. Since it does less, the Input command requires less memory than an equivalent At (@) Say/Get command. Also, you do not need to create different variables for different entry types. The Input command changes the type of the memory variable to match the user entry. This makes the Input command ideal for programmer utilities where memory is the prime consideration and screen appearance is not as much a concern.

TYPICAL OPERATION

In this example you begin creating a maintenance program that is not part of the sample program created in previous learning sequences. Begin this example in your word processor.

1. Type the following text to create MAINT.PRG.

   ```
   * MAINT.PRG
   * This program is the beginning of a programmer's toolbox
   * for Clipper.
   * YOUR NAME
   * TODAY'S DATE
   * Display a directory.
   clear screen
   input 'Type directory path and skeleton' + chr(13) + chr(10) to DIR_SKEL
   * Exit this utility
   quit
   ```

2. Save the document and exit your word processor. Type **CLD MAINT** at the DOS prompt. Press **Enter**.

3. Type **MAINT**. Press **Enter**. The program displays "Type directory path and skeleton."

4. Type ***.*** and press **Enter**. The program exits with an error.

```
Proc MAINT line 10, expression error (in macro)
C:\CLIPPER\0022>ath and skeleton
*.*
```

134

5. Type **MAINT** and press **Enter**. Type '*.*' for the directory skeleton. Press **Enter**. The program exits normally.

```
Type directory path and skeleton
'*.*'
C:\CLIPPER\0022>
```

6. Type **MAINT** and press **Enter**. Type **300** for the directory skeleton. Press **Enter**. The program exits normally. Notice the program accepts 300 as a number, not a character string.

```
Type directory path and skeleton
300
C:\CLIPPER\0022>
```

7. Turn to Module 34 to continue the learning sequence.

Module 49
JOIN WITH

DESCRIPTION

The Join With command lets you create a composite of two databases, even if the two databases use dissimilar structures. You must open both databases you want merged. Clipper assumes the first database appears in the current work area. ALIAS/EXPC1 contains the name of the second database. FILE/EXPC2 contains the name of a file to send the composite database to. If the specified file exists, Clipper erases the old version first, then creates a new file. The for clause allows you to specify a limited group of records. CONDITION is a Boolean expression containing a field, followed by >, <, <>, or =, and ending with a value. The optional fields clause limits the fields copied from both databases to those in FIELD LIST. The command line interface of the Join With command appears below.

```
JOIN WITH <ALIAS>/(<EXPC1>) TO <FILE>/(<EXPC2>) FOR <CONDITION> [FIELDS
<FIELD LIST>]
```

APPLICATIONS

Use the Join With command when you want to create a composite database of two dissimilar databases. One example of this situation is creating a mail merge database consisting of names, addresses, and amounts due. Normally, the account information appears in one database and the mailing list information in another.

TYPICAL OPERATION

In this example you create a composite database from the mailing list and the checkbook database. The composite database contains only those records appearing in both databases. Notice the fields do not match exactly; the program uses text manipulation functions to match them. Begin this example in your word processor with DOSSHELL.PRG loaded.

1. Remove the following text from the CONSOLIDATE procedure.
   ```
   * Display them one at a time.
   select A
   do SHOW_RECS
   select B
   do SHOW_RECS
   ```

2. Add the following text to the CONSOLIDATE procedure.
   ```
   use CHCKBOOK index CHCKNUM, DATE
   * Create the new database. Note the use of the semicolon at the end
   * of each line. This allows you to create extended commands.

   join with MAILLIST to TEMP_DAT for trim(B->DRAWN_FOR) = ;
   upper(trim(A->FIRST_NAME) + ' ' + A->MIDDLE + ' ' + ;
   trim(A->LAST_NAME)) fields B->DATE, B->CHECK_NUM, ;
   ```

```
B->DRAWN_FOR, B->AMOUNT, B->TAX_ITEM, A->ADDRESS1, ;
A->ADDRESS2, A->CITY, A->STATE, A->ZIP, A->TELEPHONE
```

return

3. Save the document and exit your word processor. Type **CL DOSSHELL** at the DOS prompt. Press **Enter**.

4. Type **MAILLIST** and press **Enter**. The mailing list program menu appears.

5. Press **F4** to select the checkbook program. Add the records shown below using the Add function on the checkbook program menu.

```
Date: 07/22/89
Check: 6
For: GEORGE A SMITH
Amount: 22.50
Tax Item: N

Date: 07/22/89
Check: 7
For: SAMUEL L STONE
Amount: 144.25
Tax Item: N

Date: 07/22/89
Check: 8
For: SAMUEL L STONE
Amount: 199.95
Tax Item: N

Date: 07/22/89
Check: 9
For: AMY B WILSON
Amount: 12.15
Tax Item: N
```

6. Press **F10**. The DOS shell menu appears.

7. Select Consolidate Checks by typing **C** and pressing **Enter**.

8. Type **Q** and press **Enter** to quit the DOS shell menu. Press **Enter** to select Quit. The DOS prompt appears.

9. Type **DBU TEMP_DAT** and press **Enter**. The DBU browse display appears. Notice that the combined database, TEMP_DAT, contains only the four records that match in both databases.

```
                                      Record 1/4
 DATE       CHECK_NUM   DRAWN_FOR

 07/22/89          6    GEORGE A SMITH
 07/22/89          7    SAMUEL L STONE
 07/22/89          8    SAMUEL L STONE
 07/22/89          9    AMY B WILSON
```

10. Press **Ctrl-End**. Notice the combined database contains only the fields requested by the Join With command.

		Record 1/4	
CITY	STATE	ZIP	TELEPHONE
ANYWHERE	CA	92111-	(619)222-1212
SOMEPLACE	WI	53211-0114	(414)199-2929
SOMEPLACE	WI	53211-0114	(414)199-2929
ANYWHERE	CA	92111-	(619)516-1234

11. Press **Esc** twice and answer **Y** when asked if you want to leave DBU. The DOS prompt appears.

12. Turn to Module 86 to continue the learning sequence.

Module 50
KEYBOARD

DESCRIPTION

The Keyboard command lets you place a string of characters into the keyboard buffer. The program reads these characters as if they were input from the keyboard. The command line interface of the Keyboard command appears below.

```
KEYBOARD <EXPC>
```

APPLICATIONS

Use the Keyboard command whenever you want to automate some program feature. For example, by placing a Keyboard command in a procedure called by a Set Key command, you can automate data entry or create macros. You can also use the Keyboard command with the AChoice( ) and DBEdit( ) functions. In these two cases, you place the Keyboard command in the user-defined function.

TYPICAL OPERATION

In this example you assign the current date to a function key using the Set Key and Keyboard commands in conjunction with each other. Begin this example in your word processor with CHCKBOOK.PRG loaded.

1. Add the following text to the beginning of the ADD_REC procedure.
   ```
   * This procedure adds records to the database.
   * Set the Shift-F2 key to output the date.
   set key -11 to DATE_OUT
   * Create procedure variables.
   ```

2. Add the following text and procedure at the end of the ADD_REC procedure.
   ```
   * Release the Shift-F2 key.
   set key -11 to
   return
   procedure DATE_OUT
   * This procedure outputs the date using the Keyboard command.
   keyboard dtoc(date())
   return
   ```

3. Save the document and exit your word processor. Type **CL CHCKBOOK** at the DOS prompt. Press **Enter**.

4. Type **MAILLIST**. Press **Enter**.

5. Press **F4**.

6. Type **A** and press **Enter** to select the Add option. Select the For field by pressing **Down Arrow** twice. Press **Shift-F2**. The program places the current date in the For field.

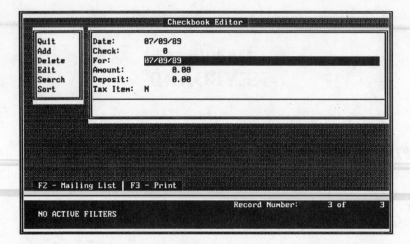

7. Press **PgDn**. Type **N** when asked if you want to add another record. The checkbook program menu appears.

8. Type **Q** to select quit. Press **Enter**. The DOS prompt appears.

9. Turn to Module 42 to continue the learning sequence.

Module 51
LABEL FORM

DESCRIPTION

The Label Form command lets you combine the information in your database with the parameters in a preformatted label file. A label file differs from a report file in the size and type document the label file works with. The label form creates labels while the report form creates full size reports. You can create a label form file using the RL utility discussed in Module 7. The command line interface of the Label Form command appears below.

```
LABEL FORM <FILE1>/(<EXPC1>) [<SCOPE>] [FOR <CONDITION>] [WHILE
<CONDITION>] [SAMPLE] [TO PRINT] [TO FILE <FILE2>/(<EXPC2>)]
```

The file clause contains the name of the label form file. Clipper lets you specify the actual file name or use a variable. This is the only required input to the label form command.

The scope clause lets you specify the range of records to print using the formatting commands contained in the label form file. The default scope is all. If you specify next with a number, Clipper starts printing records from the current record position and stops when it prints the required number of records.

The for condition clause lets you limit the number of records printed to those meeting a predefined condition. Normally, the condition contains a field name, then a relational operator (>, <, <>, =), followed by the condition. Clipper prints all the records in the database meeting the defined condition and scope. The while condition clause lets you limit the number of records printed to those meeting a predefined condition. Unlike the for condition clause, Clipper stops printing the report as soon as it sees a record not meeting the criteria. In some respects, this clause works like a combination of the for condition and scope clauses.

The sample clause lets you check the alignment of your labels before printing. Clipper sends asterisks (*) approximating the area used by the data for each label. After Clipper sends the data for one label, it asks if you want another sample. If you want another sample, type Y. Otherwise, Clipper starts printing the actual database information.

The to print clause specifies where Clipper sends the labels. The default destination is the display. If you specify the printer and set the console to off, Clipper outputs to the printer only. By keeping the console on, you can send the output to both the printer and display.

The to file clause lets you send the label output to the specified file. Clipper does not provide a default filename, so the filename must appear after the clause. If you do not specify an extension, Clipper automatically adds the TXT extension. Clipper lets you send the label output to the display, printer, and a file simultaneously.

APPLICATIONS

Use the Label Form command to output labels of any type to the display, a file, or the printer. One excellent use of the Label command is for mailing labels or stock labels. Another excellent use is creating merge files for many different word processors. By outputting the data in the merge format required by the word processor, you save the time required inputting the names and addresses for letters or other form correspondence.

TYPICAL OPERATION

In this example you add a print routine for printing the contents of the mailing list database using the Label Form command. Begin this example in your word processor with PRINT.PRG loaded.

1. Add the following text to the menu selection check section of the main program.

```
        set console off
        use CHCKBOOK
        set console on
        do DISP_MENU3
        report form CHCKLIST to print
    case MENU_SEL = 3
        use MAILLIST index LASTNAME
        set console off
        @ 22, 04
        label form MAILLABL sample to print
        set console on
endcase
```

2. Add the following text to the DISP_MENU2 procedure.

```
@ 07, 03 prompt 'Check Book' message 'Print the Check Book Database.'
@ 08, 03 prompt 'Mailing List' message 'Print the Mailing List Database.'
menu to MENU_SEL
```

3. Save the document and exit your word processor. Compile the program.

4. Type **PRINT**. Press **Enter**.

5. Type **LPT1**. Press **Enter** to select a printer. Type **N** to forego running the printer test. The program displays a menu for selecting the database you want to print.

6. Select Mailing List by pressing **Down Arrow**. Press **Enter**. The program prints a sample label, then displays a message asking if you want another sample.

NOTE
If the next step does not work properly and Clipper returns an error in .LBL file message, use RL to determine that the form does not contain any extra entries. Check the file contents with those appearing in Module 7.

7. Type **N**. The program prints five labels corresponding to the contents of MAILLIST.DBF.

8. Select Quit by pressing **Up Arrow** twice. Press **Enter**. The DOS prompt appears.

9. Turn to Module 98 to continue the learning sequence.

Module 52
LIST

DESCRIPTION

The List command lets you quickly list the contents of a database to the display, printer, or file. While it provides the functionality of the Display command, the List command executes slightly faster and produces slightly larger executable files. The command line interface of the List command appears below.

```
LIST [OFF] [<SCOPE>] <EXP LIST> [FOR <CONDITION>] [WHILE <CONDITION>] [TO
PRINT] [TO FILE <FILE>/(<EXPC>)]
```

The off clause determines if the List command lists the record number with the information requested. If you specify off, then Clipper does not list the record number.

The scope clause determines how many of the database records the List command presents. The List command uses a default scope of all. This is the essential difference between the List command and the Display command (Module 35).

EXP LIST contains the fields or other Clipper functions to list. For example, you could list the date and time using the Date( ) and Time( ) functions. You may also modify the field output using any text, numeric, or date manipulation functions.

APPLICATIONS

Use the List command whenever you need to quickly output the contents of a database. This is especially good when you want to locate a specific record number.

The List command also works well when you want to output a copy of the database for verification purposes. Normally, you do not need the formatted output provided by report forms or custom print routines when verifying the database. Using the List command in place of a report form or custom print routine saves time.

TYPICAL OPERATION

In this example you compare the size of the object and executable files using the Display and List commands. You also change the previously added menu and database list feature using the List command. Begin this example at the DOS prompt.

1. Type **DIR DOSSHELL.OBJ** at the DOS prompt and press **Enter** to display the DOS shell program object file size. Type **DIR MAILLIST.EXE** at the DOS prompt and press **Enter** to display the mailing list program executable file size.

```
C:\CLIPPER\0022>DIR DOSSHELL.OBJ

 Volume in drive C is JOHN'S DISK
 Directory of  C:\CLIPPER\0022

DOSSHELL OBJ    2031   7-22-89  11:58a
        1 File(s)  12824576 bytes free

C:\CLIPPER\0022>DIR MAILLIST.EXE

 Volume in drive C is JOHN'S DISK
 Directory of  C:\CLIPPER\0022

MAILLIST EXE   240000   7-22-89  11:59a
        1 File(s)  12824576 bytes free

C:\CLIPPER\0022>
```

2. Load DOSSHELL.PRG into your word processor. Change the following text at the middle of the SHOW_RECS procedure of the DOS shell program.

   ```
   next
   list next 1 DISP_STR
   if .not. eof()
   ```

3. Save the document and exit your word processor. Type **CL DOSSHELL** at the DOS prompt. Press **Enter**.

4. Type **DIR DOSSHELL.OBJ** at the DOS prompt and press **Enter** to display the DOS shell program object file size. Type **DIR MAILLIST.EXE** at the DOS prompt and press **Enter** to display the mailing list program executable file size. Notice both files are slightly larger.

```
C:\CLIPPER\0022>IF NOT ERRORLEVEL 1 Plink86 FI MAILLIST, PRINT, CHCKBOOK, NOTEPA
D, HELP, DOSSHELL LIB \CLIPPER\CLIPPER, \CLIPPER\EXTEND
PLINK86plus ( Nantucket ) Version 2.24.
Copyright (C) 1987 by Phoenix Technologies Ltd.,
All Rights Reserved.


MAILLIST.EXE (224 K)
C:\CLIPPER\0022>DIR DOSSHELL.OBJ

 Volume in drive C is JOHN'S DISK
 Directory of  C:\CLIPPER\0022

DOSSHELL OBJ    2050   7-22-89  12:01p
        1 File(s)  12812288 bytes free

C:\CLIPPER\0022>DIR MAILLIST.EXE

 Volume in drive C is JOHN'S DISK
 Directory of  C:\CLIPPER\0022

MAILLIST EXE   240016   7-22-89  12:03p
        1 File(s)  12812288 bytes free

C:\CLIPPER\0022>
```

5. Type **MAILLIST** and press **Enter**. The mailing list program menu appears.

6. Press **F10**. The DOS shell menu appears.

7. Select Show Records by typing **S** and pressing **Enter**. The program lists a complete listing of the mailing list records. Notice the program operates exactly as before.

```
    5  SAM            | A | ANDERSON         | 515 Heath R
ow                    |   | Suite D
         | NOWHERE                  | CA | 94010-1112 | <619
>292-0139
    1  GEORGE         | A | SMITH            | 1212 12th S
treet                 |   |
         | ANYWHERE                 | CA | 92111-     | <619
>222-1212
    4  GREG           | A | STONE            | 152 Elm Str
eet                   |   |
         | SOMEPLACE                | WI | 53211-0125 | <414
>616-3135
    3  SAMUEL         | L | STONE            | 1234 A Stre
et                    |   |
         | SOMEPLACE                | WI | 53211-0114 | <414
>199-2929
    6  AMY            | B | WILSON           | 8111 North
Hampton               |   |
         | ANYWHERE                 | CA | 92111-     | <619
>516-1234
Press any key to continue...
```

8. Press **Enter** twice. The DOS shell menu appears.

9. Type **Q** and press **Enter** to quit the DOS shell menu.

10. Select Quit by pressing **Enter**. The DOS prompt appears.

11. Turn to Module 123 to continue the learning sequence.

Module 53
LOCATE

DESCRIPTION

The Locate command searches for the first occurrence of the condition specified by the for clause. When you use the Locate command, the database does not require an index. Locate searches record by record through the database. If it finds the required condition, Locate sets Found( ) to true. Each work area containing an open database may have its own active locate. Each Locate command condition remains active until you close the database associated with it or assign a new condition using another Locate command. The command line interface of the Locate command appears below.

```
LOCATE [<SCOPE>] FOR <CONDITION> [WHILE <CONDITION>]
```

The scope clause determines how many of the database records the Locate command searches for.

The for clause lets you describe which records to locate using a scope of all or next. The condition tells Clipper what criteria a record must meet before the Locate command accepts it. For example, if you had a listing of people and their ages, and wanted to locate all records containing only people 40 years of age and older, you would use the statement locate all for AGE > 39. The Locate command, unlike other commands using a for or while clause, requires you include the for clause even if you use the while clause. In other words, the while clause amplifies the for clause.

APPLICATIONS

Use the Locate command when you want to perform multiple locations on the same key and when you did not index the database key field. This allows you to maintain the current index for most operations and still perform searches for peculiar information. One example of this situation is an accounting database where you indexed the database using the vendor name. If you wanted to search for overdue bills, you could use the Locate command to search for them. The database would automatically appear in the correct order for checking the individual account history since you never changed the index.

TYPICAL OPERATION

In this example you add the capability to search the sample database by the DRAWN_FOR field without changing the index. Begin this example in your word processor with CHCKBOOK.PRG loaded.

1. Add the following text to the menu array declaration at the beginning of the program.
    ```
    declare MENU_ITEM[11]
    MENU_ITEM[1] = 'Quit'
    MENU_ITEM[2] = 'Add'
    MENU_ITEM[3] = 'Delete'
    ```

```
MENU_ITEM[4] = 'Sort'
MENU_ITEM[5] = 'Edit'
MENU_ITEM[6] = 'Search'
MENU_ITEM[7] = 'Stats'
MENU_ITEM[8] = 'Balance'
MENU_ITEM[9] = 'Reindex'
MENU_ITEM[10] = 'Export'
MENU_ITEM[11] = 'Locate'
```

2. Add the following text to the menu case statement at the beginning of the program.

```
        do EXPORT
     case MENU_ITEM[ANSWER] = 'Locate'
        do LOCATE
   endcase
```

3. Add the following procedure to the end of the procedure section of the program.

```
procedure LOCATE
* This procedure locates the desired checkbook entry name
* without changing the index.
* Set softseek on so we can find names that are close to the
* correct name.
set softseek on
* Initialize Variables
private FIND_NAME
FIND_NAME = space(50)
@ 12, 04 say 'Which check entry name do you want to find? '
@ 13, 04 get FIND_NAME picture '@!'
read
locate for DRAWN_FOR = FIND_NAME
* Display the record.
do EDIT_REC
return
```

4. Save the document and exit your word processor. Type **CL CHCKBOOK** at the DOS prompt. Press **Enter**.

5. Type **MAILLIST**. Press **Enter**. The mailing list program menu appears.

6. Press **F4** to select the checkbook program. Press **Down Arrow** until the Locate option of the menu appears. Press **Enter**. The program asks "Which check entry name do you want to find?"

7. Type **PAYCHECK** and press **Enter**. The program displays the edit screen with PAYCHECK highlighted.

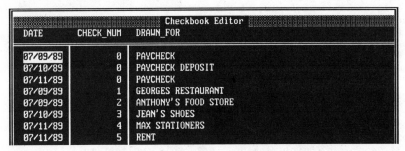

8. Press **Esc** to exit the edit screen. Type **Q** to select quit. Press **Enter**. The DOS prompt appears.

9. Turn to Module 26 to continue the learning sequence.

Module 54
MENU TO

DESCRIPTION

The Menu To command follows an @ Prompt command. This command displays the prompts created by the @ Prompt command, waits for a user selection, then passes that selection as a number to the memory variable (MEMVAR). The command line interface of the Menu To command appears below.

```
MENU TO <MEMVAR>
```

APPLICATIONS

Use the Menu To command in conjunction with the @ Prompt command to create a light-bar menu. This command returns the user selection as a number. The number corresponds to the order of the menu selection. For example, menu selection 1 (usually the top) corresponds to a 1 in the memory variable.

TYPICAL OPERATION

In this example you finish the light-bar menu started in Module 12. This example finishes showing you what you need to do to convert most dBase III programs to a Clipper program using light-bar menus. Begin this example in your word processor with MAILLIST.PRG loaded.

1. Change the ANSWER program variable as follows.
   ```
   ANSWER = 0
   ```

2. Change the Do While command condition as shown below.
   ```
   do while ANSWER <> 1
   ```

3. Change the status line Do Case control structure as shown below.
   ```
   case bof() .and. ANSWER = 7
      @ 23,04 say ' Beginning of File '
   case eof() .and. .not. ANSWER = 8
      @ 23,04 say ' End of File '
   case .not. found() .and. ANSWER = 8
      @ 23,04 say ' Name not found. '
   case .not. updated() .and. ANSWER = 3
      @ 23,04 say ' Record not updated '
   ```

4. Delete the @ Say command used as a menu and add the following text.
   ```
   * Get user choice.
   @ 03, 04 clear to 11, 11
   @ 02, 03 to 12, 12 double
   @ 03, 04 prompt 'Quit' message 'Leave this application.'
   .
   .
   .
   @ 11, 04 prompt 'Undelete' message 'Remove this record from the deletion
   list.'
   menu to ANSWER
   ```

5. Change the Do Case control structure as follows.

```
do case
case ANSWER = 2
.

.
* Display the database information.
case ANSWER = 3
.

.
case ANSWER = 4
   delete
* Remove the deleted records.
case ANSWER = 5
   pack
* Move forward one record.
case ANSWER = 6
   skip
* Move backward one record.
case ANSWER = 7
   skip -1
* Search for the desired last name.
case ANSWER = 8
   SEARCH_NAME = LAST_NAME
   @ 04, 40 get SEARCH_NAME picture '@K@!'
   read
   seek SEARCH_NAME
* Undelete a previously deleted record.
case ANSWER = 9
```

6. Save the document and exit your word processor. Type **CL MAILLIST** at the DOS prompt. Press **Enter**.

7. Type **MAILLIST**. Press **Enter**. Notice the menu now appears as a light-bar menu.

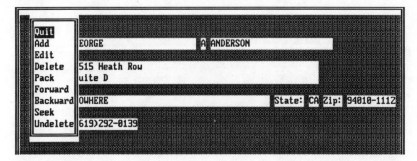

8. Type **E**. The program goes into edit mode. Notice the menu does not disappear as it should.

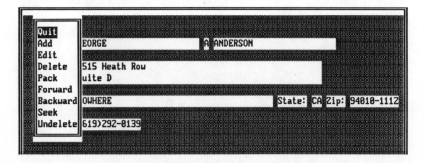

9. Press **Esc**. The standard display reappears. Notice the get statements no longer overwrite the menu and the Edit selection remains highlighted.

10. Highlight Quit by pressing **Up Arrow** twice and press **Enter**. The DOS prompt appears.

11. Turn to Module 73 to continue the learning sequence.

Module 55
NOTE (*/&&)

DESCRIPTION

The Note (*/&&) command lets you add comments to your program. The Note command and the asterisk (*) abbreviation can appear on any line without a command. The && (double ampersand) abbreviation of the Note command can appear on a line by itself, or after a command. The command line interface of the Note command appears below.

```
NOTE <TEXT>
```
OR
```
* <TEXT>
```
OR
```
[<COMMAND>] && <TEXT>
```

APPLICATIONS

Use the Note command to document various aspects of your program. Even if you know exactly how a program or procedure works when you create it, you may forget. When you need to update the procedure, relearning what it does wastes time. By adequately annotating what a procedure or program does, you reduce the time required to update it later. Also, if two or more people work on a project together, documentation reduces the time required to create it. If a program does not contain proper documentation, the people working on the project spend more time talking than programming.

One of the best ways to document a program is to add a heading at the beginning of each program, subprogram, and procedure telling what that section of program code does and who created it. Then add more documentation whenever needed to reveal why you programmed a particular section in a certain way and how that section works. When programming, there is no such thing as too much documentation.

TYPICAL OPERATION

In this example you add comments to MAILLIST.PRG. Begin this example in your word processor with MAILLIST.PRG loaded.

1. Add the following notes to your program. Notice the use of spaces to help document the program.

```
* MAILLIST.PRG
* This program manages a mailing list.
* YOUR NAME
* TODAY'S DATE

* Clear the display and prepare database for use.
```

```
clear screen
use MAILLIST index LASTNAME
ANSWER = 'Y'
@ 22, 04 say 'Do you want to add a new record? ' get ANSWER picture '!'
read
if ANSWER = 'Y'
   append blank
else
   @ 22, 04 say 'No new record was added to the database. '
endif

* Display the database information and the editing screen.

@ 04, 06 say 'Name:'
@ 06, 03 say 'Address:'
@ 09, 06 say 'City:'
@ 09, 53 say 'State:'
@ 09, 63 say 'Zip:'
@ 11, 07 say 'Tel:'
@ 04, 12 get FIRST_NAME picture '@!'
@ 04, 38 get MIDDLE picture '@!'
@ 04, 40 get LAST_NAME picture '@!'
@ 06, 12 get ADDRESS1
@ 07, 12 get ADDRESS2
@ 09, 12 get CITY picture '@!'
@ 09, 60 get STATE picture '!!'
@ 09, 68 get ZIP picture '99999-9999'
@ 11, 12 get TELEPHONE picture '(999)999-9999'
read

* Close the database and exit to DOS.

quit
```

2. Turn to Module 10 to continue the learning sequence.

Module 56
PACK

DESCRIPTION

The Pack command physically removes the records previously marked for deletion by the Delete command. After it removes the records from the database, it reindexes any open indexes attached to the database. It does not automatically reindex any closed index files. The command line interface of the Pack command appears below.

    PACK

APPLICATIONS

Use the Pack command to physically remove database files marked for deletion by the Delete command. In most cases, the Pack command appears as a separate command, not as part of the Delete command. There are two reasons for this arrangement. The Pack command requires full use of the database, blocking other users from database access when used in a network scenario. The second reason is that the Pack command can take a long period of time to execute on large databases. In most cases, therefore, the database administrator uses the Pack command at the end of the day or on the weekend.

TYPICAL OPERATION

In this example you add the Pack command to the sample database and see its effect on records previously marked for deletion. Begin this example in your word processor with MAILLIST.PRG loaded.

1. Change the menu prompt as shown below.

    ```
    @ 22, 04 say 'Quit/Add Record/Edit Record/Delete Record' +;
       '/Pack' get ANSWER picture '!'
    ```

2. Add the text below between the Delete command and the endif appearing at the end of the program.

    ```
    delete

    * Remove the deleted records.
    elseif ANSWER = 'P'
       pack
    endif
    ```

3. Save the document and exit your word processor. Type **CL MAILLIST** at the DOS prompt. Press **Enter**.

4. Type **MAILLIST**. Press **Enter**. Type **P** to select the Pack option.

5. Type **Q** to quit the program. Type **DBU MAILLIST** and press **Enter**. The database utility displays the MAILLIST database. Notice that the MAILLIST program removed the deleted file from the database.

NOTE

Use extreme caution when you open the database file without opening the associated index files. Any inadvertent changes to the database will destroy the index files.

6. Press **Esc** twice to exit the database utility. Type **Y**. The DOS prompt appears.

7. Turn to Module 78 to continue the learning sequence.

Module 57
PARAMETERS

DESCRIPTION

The Parameters statement lets you define variables used to hold information passed to a procedure using the with clause of the Do command. The memvar clause of the Parameters statement holds a list of variable names separated by commas. Clipper keeps the variables active only while the program executes within the Procedure control structure. When the program exits the procedure, Clipper deallocates the memory and allows another procedure to use it. The command line interface of the Parameters statement appears below.

```
PARAMETERS <MEMVAR LIST>
```

APPLICATIONS

Use the Parameters statement to define variables used to hold passed information. By using the Parameters statement in conjunction with a Do command, the calling procedure need not know the variable names of the called procedure.

TYPICAL OPERATION

In this example you use the Parameters statement to define a variable used to hold information. Begin this example in your word processor with MAILLIST.PRG loaded.

1. Add the following text to the Do command used to call DISPLAY_STATUS.
   ```
   do DISPLAY_STATUS with ANSWER
   ```
2. Add the following text to the beginning of the DISPLAY_STATUS procedure.
   ```
   procedure DISPLAY_STATUS

   parameters MENU_VAR              && Contains the current menu selection.

   * This procedure displays status information including the
   ```
3. Save the document and exit your word processor. Type **CL MAILLIST** at the DOS prompt. Press **Enter**.
4. Type **MAILLIST**. Press **Enter**.
5. Type **E**. The menu disappears and the edit screen appears. Notice the program operates exactly as before.
6. Press **Esc**. The menu reappears. Notice the DISPLAY_STATUS procedure displays the correct message.
7. Type **S** to select the seek option. Type **STONE** and press **Enter**. The program finds a matching record.
8. Type **Q**. The DOS prompt appears.
9. Turn to Module 114 to continue the learning sequence.

Module 58
PRINT STATEMENT (?/??)

DESCRIPTION

The Print Statement (?/??) command lets you place text on the printer or display. If you use a single question mark (?), then Clipper places the output on a separate line. If you use a double question mark (??), Clipper places the output on the same line as the previous output. The command line interface of the Print Statement (?/??) command appears below.

```
?/?? <EXP LIST>
```

APPLICATIONS

Use the Print Statement (?/??) command when you need to output text to the display or printer and the text does not require formatting.

TYPICAL OPERATION

In this example you use the Print Statement (?/??) command to output text at the end of the sample program. Begin this example in your word processor with PRINT.PRG loaded.

1. Type the following text after the print loop in the main procedure.

```
for PRNT_COUNT = 1 to reccount()
    do DISP_COUNT
    do REC_PRINT
next

* Place a last page message on the printed output before leaving
* this routine.

? 'Last Page of Output.'
? 'Printed'
?? PRNT_COUNT
?? ' of '
?? reccount()
?? ' Records.'

* Reset the display and printer.
```

2. Save the document and exit your word processor. Compile your program.

3. Type **PRINT**. Press **Enter**.

4. Type **LPT1**. Press **Enter**. The record number counts from 1 through 5. The printer outputs the last record message. The program clears the display and prints "Leaving the Print Program."

5. Press **Enter**. The DOS prompt appears.

6. Turn to Module 39 to continue the learning sequence.

Module 59
PRIVATE

DESCRIPTION

The Private command creates, then defines the scope of a memory variable or array. By using the Private command before you initialize a variable the first time, you tell Clipper that you want only the current procedure and its subprocedures to know about the variable. When you declare a variable using private, Clipper creates it, but does not assign a value to it. The optional initializer allows you to declare, create, and initialize the variable in one step. You must use the Private command within the body of a procedure or function. It must appear after any Field, Local, Memvar, and Static commands. Clipper allows a maximum of 2,048 private variables and arrays within a single program. The command line interface of the Private command appears below.

NOTE

EXP1 can contain either a variable or array name. If you create an array, then you must follow the array name with a set of brackets ([ ]). You must place the number of array elements within the brackets. To declare a multidimensional array, include more than one number separated by commas. For example, to declare a 2 by 3 array using PRIVATE, you would type PRIVATE SomeArray [2, 3]. Clipper uses 4,096 as the maximum size for any dimension of an array.

EXP2 contains the value you want to assign to a variable. You cannot initialize the values of an array by placing a value in EXP2. Each value in an array automatically receives a value of NIL.

```
PRIVATE <EXP1> [:= <EXP2>] [, <EXP3> [:= <EXP4>]] ...
```

APPLICATIONS

The Private command can save memory within a program. If a variable is not needed by any other procedure, then you can save memory by using the Private command. Each time you enter a procedure using private variables, Clipper allocates space for that variable. When you exit, Clipper deallocates the memory for use by another procedure.

TYPICAL OPERATION

In this example you add private variables to some of the procedures and functions in the example program. Begin this example in your word processor with PRINT.PRG loaded.

1. Add the following text between the initial comment and the Parameters command in the PRNT_ON function.

```
* This function checks the status of the printer port and
* returns true if the port exists and the printer is on.
```

157

```
private PORT_NAME, IS_PORT

parameters PORT_NAME
```

2. Save the document and exit your word processor. Type **CL PRINT** at the DOS prompt. Press **Enter**.

3. Type **PRINT**. Press **Enter**.

4. Type **LPT1**. Press **Enter**. The record number counts from 1 through 5, then the DOS prompt appears. Notice the program operates exactly as before, even with the declaration of private variables.

5. Turn to Module 61 to continue the learning sequence.

Module 60
PROCEDURE

DESCRIPTION

The Procedure control structure lets you break up large chunks of code into smaller pieces. There are two reasons for doing this. First, by reducing the size of each code section, you reduce the amount of time needed to learn what task each section performs and how it performs it. Second, you can reuse the code in other programs. By making procedures generic in nature, you can use the same code more than once, reducing the expense and time required to create each program. The command line interface of the Procedure control structure appears below.

```
PROCEDURE <PROCEDURE NAME> [(<PARAMETER LIST>)] [LOCAL <EXP1> [:= <EXP2>]
[, <EXP3> [:= <EXP4>]] ...] [STATIC <EXP5> [:= <EXP6>] [, <EXP7> [:=
<EXP8>]] ...] [FIELD  <FIELD LIST> [IN <ALIAS/DATABASE NAME>]] [MEMVAR
<EXP9>] ... <STATEMENTS> ... [RETURN]
```

Each procedure control structure contains two essential parts and one optional clause. The first clause is the procedure name. To use the procedure, you must include a procedure name, so Clipper will know which code section to use. The statements clause contains the executable code the procedure needs to perform a task. The optional return clause allows you to return to the calling program when the procedure finishes. See Module 71 for more information on the Return command.

The parameter list defines the variables that a calling procedure or function must pass to the procedure. These variables may consist of any legal value including strings, dates, numbers, and arrays. You may not use a variable name containing leading underscores. Clipper allows you to use any number of characters in the variable name. However, only the first ten characters are significant. Clipper always defines these parameters as local variables. You must enclose the parameter list in parentheses.

The local, static, field, and memvar clauses perform the task of declaring variables. Module 32 contains a complete description of these four clauses. You must use these four declarations in the order specified.

APPLICATIONS

Use the Procedure control structure to create more readable and reliable code. By using the Procedure control structure, you can also reduce programming time by reusing sections of code for more than one program.

TYPICAL OPERATION

In this example you begin the process of breaking the sample program into generic sections by using the Procedure control structure. Begin this example in your word processor with MAILLIST.PRG loaded.

1. Add the following text at the end of the program.

```
quit
* Begin Procedures
procedure DISPLAY_DATA
* This procedure displays the data in the current record.
return
procedure DISPLAY_MENU
* This procedure displays the program menu.
return
procedure DISPLAY_SCRN
* This procedure displays the edit area of the database
* display. It does not display the data.
return
procedure DISPLAY_STATUS
* This procedure displays status information including the current record
* number, file status messages, and menu entry prompts.
return
procedure GET_DATA
* This procedure gets the data from the current record.
return
```

2. Move the following text from the beginning of the program to between the procedure and return clauses of DISPLAY_DATA.

```
@ 04, 12 say FIRST_NAME picture '@!'
@ 04, 38 say MIDDLE picture '!'
@ 04, 40 say LAST_NAME picture '@!'
@ 06, 12 say ADDRESS1
@ 07, 12 say ADDRESS2
@ 09, 12 say CITY picture '@!'
@ 09, 60 say STATE picture '!!'
@ 09, 68 say ZIP picture '99999-9999'
@ 11, 12 say TELEPHONE picture '(999)999-9999'
```

3. Move the following text from the beginning of the program to between the procedure and return clauses of DISPLAY_MENU.

```
save screen
set message to 22 center
@ 03, 04 clear to 11, 11
@ 02, 03 to 12, 12 double
@ 03, 04 prompt 'Quit' message 'Leave this application.'
@ 04, 04 prompt 'Add' message 'Add a new record.'
@ 05, 04 prompt 'Edit' message 'Change the contents of this record.'
@ 06, 04 prompt 'Delete' message 'Mark this record for removal.'
@ 07, 04 prompt 'Pack' message 'Remove all marked records.'
@ 08, 04 prompt 'Forward' message 'Go one record forward.'
@ 09, 04 prompt 'Backward' message 'Go one record back.'
@ 10, 04 prompt 'Seek' message 'Find a particular last name.'
@ 11, 04 prompt 'Undelete' message 'Remove this record from the ;
    deletion list.'
menu to ANSWER
restore screen
```

4. Move the following text from the beginning of the program to between the procedure and return clauses of DISPLAY_SCRN.

```
@ 04, 06 say 'Name:'
@ 06, 03 say 'Address:'
@ 09, 06 say 'City:'
@ 09, 53 say 'State:'
@ 09, 63 say 'Zip:'
@ 11, 07 say 'Tel:'
```

5. Move the following text from the beginning of the program to between the procedure and return clauses of DISPLAY_STATUS.

```
@ 01, 00, 24, 79 box DOUBLE_LINE
@ 20, 01 to 20, 78
if iscolor()
   set color to GR+/B,W+/G
else
   set color to N/W,W+/N
endif
@ 21, 01 clear to 23, 78
@ 21, 45 say ' Record Number: '
@ 21, 60 say recno()
@ 21, 67 say ' of '
@ 21, 71 say reccount()
if deleted()
   @ 21, 04 say ' DELETED '
else
   @ 21, 04 say '         '          && Type space 9 times.
endif
do case
case bof() .and. ANSWER = 7
   @ 23, 04 say ' Beginning of File '
case eof() .and. .not. ANSWER = 8
   @ 23, 04 say ' End of File '
case .not. found() .and. ANSWER = 8
   @ 23, 04 say ' Name not Found '
case .not. updated() .and. ANSWER = 3
   @ 23, 04 say ' Record not Updated '
otherwise
   @ 23, 04 clear to 23, 78
endcase
if iscolor()
   OLD_COLOR = setcolor(COLOR1)
else
   OLD_COLOR = setcolor(NO_COLOR1)
endif
```

6. Move the following text from the append section of the program to between the procedure and return clauses of GET_DATA. Remove the second occurrence of the text from the edit section. Notice how much easier the program is to understand.

```
@ 04, 12 get FIRST_NAME picture '@!' valid .not. empty(FIRST_NAME)
@ 04, 38 get MIDDLE picture '@!' valid .not. empty(MIDDLE)
@ 04, 40 get LAST_NAME picture '@!' valid .not. empty(LAST_NAME)
@ 06, 12 get ADDRESS1
@ 07, 12 get ADDRESS2
@ 09, 12 get CITY picture '@!'
@ 09, 60 get STATE picture '!!'
@ 09, 68 get ZIP picture '99999-9999'
@ 11, 12 get TELEPHONE picture '(999)999-9999'
```

7. Turn to Module 37 to continue the learning sequence.

Module 61
PUBLIC

DESCRIPTION

The Public command creates, then defines arrays and variables as available to all modules and procedures within a program. By declaring the variable public, you can refer to it in procedures at the same or higher levels. Unlike the Private command, the Public command initializes the variables you create using it to false (.F.). If you intend to use the variable as anything other than a Boolean operator, you must still initialize it. You may perform this task using the optional initialization clause. You must use the Public command within the body of a procedure or function. It must appear after any Field, Local, Memvar, and Static commands. Clipper allows a maximum of 2,048 public variables and arrays within a single program. Clipper does not allow you to declare private variables public. It does allow you to hide a public variable temporarily by declaring it private. The command line interface of the Public command appears below.

NOTE

EXP1 can contain either a variable or array name. If you create an array, then you must follow the array name with a set of brackets ([ ]). You must place the number of array elements within the brackets. To declare a multidimensional array, include more than one number separated by commas. For example, to declare a 2 by 3 array using PRIVATE you would type PRIVATE SomeArray [2, 3]. Clipper uses 4,096 as the maximum size for any dimension of an array.

EXP2 contains the value you want to assign to a variable. You cannot initialize the values of an array by placing a value in EXP2. Each value in an array automatically receives a value of NIL.

```
PUBLIC <EXP1> [:= <EXP2>] [, <EXP3> [:= <EXP4>]] ...
```

APPLICATIONS

Use the Public command to declare public variables. One example of this is when you link two modules together and want them to share some conditional or static data. The variable which holds the line characters used to draw a display using the @ Box command is a good example of a shareable variable. By declaring the variable only one time, you save memory. Another good use of public variables is menus. If you use a menu structure more than one time throughout a program, but user selection results vary from module to module, you can still save memory by using a public variable.

TYPICAL OPERATION

In this example you declare several variables in the example program public. Begin this example in your word processor with PRINT.PRG loaded.

1. Add the following text below the heading at the beginning of the sample program.

```
* TODAY'S DATE
* Declare standard variables public.
public DOUBLE_LINE, PRNT_PORT
* Program Variables
```

2. Save the document and exit your word processor. Compile PRINT.PRG.

3. Type **PRINT**. Press **Enter**.

4. Type **LPT1**. Press **Enter**. The record number counts from 1 through 5, then the DOS prompt appears. Notice the program operates exactly as before, even with the declaration of public variables.

5. Turn to Module 118 to continue the learning sequence.

Module 62
READ

DESCRIPTION

The Read command lets you enter the full screen editing mode using the currently pending gets. Clipper lets you move between gets by pressing the arrow keys or control key sequences. Clipper also provides a number of editing keys to help in the editing process. Table 62-1 lists the editing keys that Clipper provides while in full screen edit mode. The table lists the keys by functional area. The command line interface of the Read command appears below.

```
READ [SAVE]
```

Table 62-1. Read Editing Keys

Key	Function
Navigation	
Left Arrow, Ctrl-S	Move the cursor one character to the left within the current get only. Will not move the cursor to the previous get.
Right Arrow, Ctrl-D	Move the cursor one character to the right within the current get only. Will not move the cursor to the previous get.
Ctrl-Left Arrow, Ctrl-A	Move the cursor one word to the left within the current get only. Will not move the cursor to the previous get.
Ctrl-Right Arrow, Ctrl-F	Move the cursor one word to the right within the current get only. Will not move the cursor to the previous get.
Up Arrow, Ctrl-E	Move to the previous get.
Down Arrow, Ctrl-X, Return, Ctrl-M	Move to the next get. This control key sequence is not active at the last get in the list.
Home	Move the cursor to the first character of the current get.
End	Move the cursor to the last character of the current get.
Ctrl-Home	Move the cursor to the first character of the first get.
Ctrl-End	Move the cursor to the last character of the last get.
Text Manipulation	
Del, Ctrl-G	Deletes character at the cursor position.
Backspace, Ctrl-H	Remove character to the left of the cursor position. Move the cursor one character left.
Ctrl-T	Remove the word to the right of the current cursor position.
Ctrl-Y	Delete from the current cursor position to the end of the get.
Ctrl-U	Restore the current get to its original condition.
Mode	
Ins, Ctrl-V	Toggle between insert and overwrite modes.
Escape	
Ctrl-W, Ctrl-C, PgUp, PgDn	Terminate the Read command and save the current get.
Return, Ctrl-M	Terminate the Read command. This control key sequence is only active at the last get in the list.

Table 62-1. Read Editing Keys (Cont.)

Key	Function
Esc	Terminate the Read command without saving the current get.
Up Arrow	Terminate the Read command. This control key sequence is only active at the first get in the list and when readexit( ) = .T..
Down Arrow	Terminate the Read command. This control key sequence is only active at the last get in the list and when readexit( ) = .T..

The save clause of the Read command lets you save the pending gets status. Normally Clipper clears its list of pending gets after a read occurs. By using the save clause you tell Clipper to keep the list intact.

APPLICATIONS

Use the Read command to enter the full screen editing mode after you position data entry fields using the Get command. The save clause of the read command lets you keep the pending gets active after the read ends. Using the save clause could save programming steps. For example, you could place a data entry screen on the display, then read the pending gets with the Read command. By using the save statement, you need not redraw the data entry screen for the next record. There are few, if any, instances where the Read command does not follow a list of Get commands.

TYPICAL OPERATION

In this example you add a Read command to the end of MAILLIST.PRG. This lets you enter the full screen editing mode of the data entry screen. Begin this example at the DOS prompt in the C:\CLIPPER\0022 directory.

1. Edit MAILLIST.PRG using a word processor. Type **read** at the end of MAILLIST.PRG.

2. Press **Enter**. Save the document and exit your word processor.

3. Type **CL MAILLIST** at the DOS prompt. Press **Enter**. The Clipper batch file clears the screen, then compiles and links the program.

4. Type **MAILLIST**. Press **Enter**. The program clears the display and you see the data entry screen. Notice the cursor appears in the upper left data entry field.

5. Type **JOHN**. Press **Enter**. The word JOHN appears in the first data entry screen until you press Enter. The cursor advances to the next field. This is because the Get command does not have a database record field or Clipper variable to use for data storage. In other words, even though you entered the information, Clipper has no place to store it.

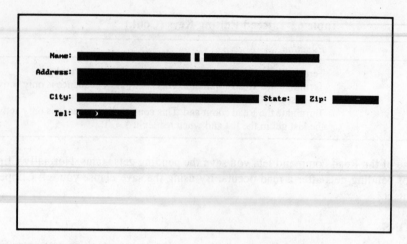

6. Press **Esc**. The DOS prompt appears.
7. Turn to Module 24 to continue the learning sequence.

Module 63
RECALL

DESCRIPTION

The Recall command unmarks any records marked for deletion by the Delete command. The command line interface of the Recall command appears below.

```
RECALL [<SCOPE>] [FOR <CONDITION>] [WHILE <CONDITION>]
```

The scope clause determines how many records the Recall command unmarks (undeletes). The for clause allows you to describe which records to unmark when using a scope of all or next.

APPLICATIONS

Use the Recall command to unmark (undelete) any record marked for deletion by the Delete command. This command does not work on records removed from the database using the Pack command.

TYPICAL OPERATION

In this example you add the capability to unmark (undelete) records to the sample program using the Recall command. Begin this example in your word processor with MAILLIST.PRG loaded.

1. Change the menu prompt as shown below.
   ```
   @ 22, 04 say 'Quit/Add/Edit/Delete/Pack/Forward/Backward/Seek/Undelete';
      get ANSWER picture '!'
   ```

2. Add the following text between the seek command and the endif appearing at the end of the program.
   ```
       seek SEARCH_NAME
   * Undelete a previously deleted record.
   elseif ANSWER = 'U'
       recall
   endif
   ```

3. Save the document and exit your word processor. Type **CL MAILLIST** at the DOS prompt. Press **Enter**.

4. Type **MAILLIST**. Press **Enter**.

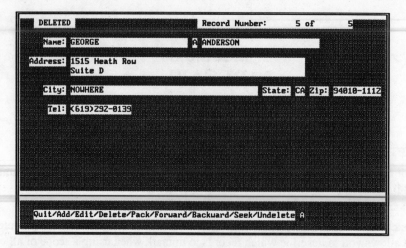

5. Type **U**. The deleted message disappears from the top of the display.
6. Type **Q**. The DOS prompt appears.
7. Turn to Module 36 to continue the learning sequence.

Module 64
REINDEX

DESCRIPTION

The Reindex command rebuilds any indexes attached to any currently opened database in all work areas. The command line interface of the Reindex command appears below.

```
REINDEX
```

APPLICATIONS

Use the Reindex command to rebuild any indexes for a particular database when conditions in the database change without affecting the index file. For example, you may need an index only when printing. Therefore, you need to reindex each time you print to reflect added and deleted records. Or, as the database gets larger, you sort the database to improve access time. Use the Reindex command to rebuild the index files after sorting.

Another occasion to use the Reindex command is to update unique indexes. When you use the Set Unique On command to create unique indexes, Clipper places only one instance of each index key in the index file, even if more than one record uses the same key. This allows quicker access to the records and reduces the disk space required for index files. Clipper points the index to the first record in the database containing that key. You access the rest of the records using the Skip or Goto commands. However, as you add records to the database, the unique key may no longer point to the first record. Using the Reindex command readjusts the pointers.

TYPICAL OPERATION

In this example you add the capability to reindex after sorting the sample database. Begin this example in your word processor with CHCKBOOK.PRG loaded.

1. Add the following text to the menu array declaration at the beginning of the program.
```
declare MENU_ITEM[9]
MENU_ITEM[1] = 'Quit'
MENU_ITEM[2] = 'Add'
MENU_ITEM[3] = 'Delete'
MENU_ITEM[4] = 'Sort'
MENU_ITEM[5] = 'Edit'
MENU_ITEM[6] = 'Search'
MENU_ITEM[7] = 'Stats'
MENU_ITEM[8] = 'Balance'
MENU_ITEM[9] = 'Reindex'
```

2. Add the following text to the menu case statement at the beginning of the program.
```
        do BALANCE
    case MENU_ITEM[ANSWER] = 'Reindex'
        do REINDEX
endcase
```

3. Add the following procedure to the end of the procedure section of the program.

```
procedure REINDEX

* This procedure reindexes the database after sorting.
use CHCKBOOK index CHCKNUM, DATE
reindex
return
```

4. Save the document and exit your word processor. Type **CL CHCKBOOK** at the DOS prompt. Press **Enter**.

5. Type **COPY TEMPDATA.DBF CHCKBOOK.DBF**. Press **Enter**. DOS copies the temporary database to the checkbook database.

6. Type **DBU** and press **Enter**. The DBU main menu appears.

7. Type **CHCKBOOK** in the database field and press **Enter**. Press **Down Arrow**. Type **CHCKNUM** in the index field, and press **Enter**. Press **Down Arrow**. Type **DATE** and press **Enter**. Press **F5**. The DBU browse menu appears.

8. Press **Enter** to select the database option. The browse display appears. Notice the index files no longer match the database.

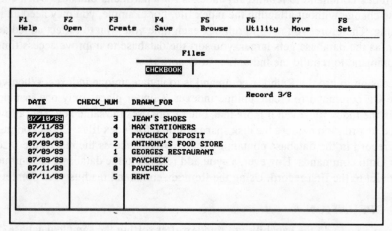

9. Press **Esc** twice. Type **Y** when asked if you want to leave DBU. The DOS prompt appears.

10. Type **MAILLIST**. Press **Enter**. The mailing list program menu appears.

11. Press **F4** to select the checkbook program. Press **Down Arrow** until the Reindex option of the menu appears. Press **Enter**. The program reindexes the database.

12. Type **E** to select Edit and press **Enter**. Notice the database and index files match again.

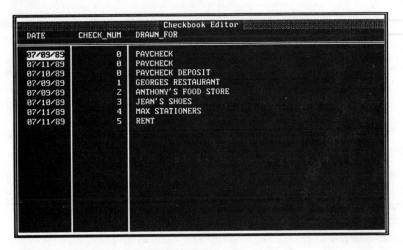

13. Press **Esc** to return to the checkbook program menu. Type **Q** to select quit. Press **Enter**. The DOS prompt appears.

14. Turn to Module 29 to continue the learning sequence.

Module 65
RELEASE

DESCRIPTION

The Release command deallocates the memory used by variables no longer required by the program. By releasing memory you can reduce the RAM requirements of a program. In addition, you can increase the memory available for other purposes. The command line interface of the Release command appears below.

```
RELEASE <MEMVAR LIST>/[ALL [LIKE/EXCEPT <SKELETON>]]
```

The memvar list contains a listing of all the variables you explicitly want to release. The all clause allows you to release all private memory variables in the current procedure when used in place of the memvar list. Adding the like clause with a skeleton (mask) allows you to perform wildcard matches of variables. Clipper releases the variables that match the wildcard mask. Adding the except clause also allows you to perform wildcard matches. In this case you release all memory variables except the ones that match the skeleton. When you create a mask, use the asterisk (*) to identify a group of characters. For example, the mask ch*ch identifies a word starting and ending with ch. The word contains any number of characters in between. The question mark (?) identifies a single character. For example, the mask ch?ch identifies a word starting with ch, followed by a single letter, and ending with ch.

APPLICATIONS

Use the Release command to deallocate the memory used by variables no longer needed by a program. For example, if you use a particular variable only once during program execution, you can release it and use the memory for another purpose.

TYPICAL OPERATION

Begin this example in your word processor with PRINT.PRG loaded.

1. Add the following text to the DISP_SCRN procedure.
    ```
    set color to W/N,N/W
    * Deallocate all variables used in this procedure.
    release all
    return
    ```

2. Add the following text to the PRNT_ON function.
    ```
    endif
    * Deallocate only non-essential variables used in this
    * procedure.
    release all like PORT_NAME
    return IS_PORT
    ```

3. Add the following text to the DISP_MENU3 procedure.
    ```
    endif
    * Deallocate all variables used in this procedure.
    ```

```
release all
return
```

4. Add the following text to the DISP_MENU4 procedure.

```
endcase
* Deallocate all variables used in this procedure.
release all
return
```

5. Add the following text to the NOTE_PRNT procedure.

```
set device to screen
* Deallocate all variables used in this procedure.
release all
return
```

6. Add the following text to the CENTER_LINE function.

```
START_SPOT = (80 - CLENGTH) / 2
* Deallocate the non-essential variables used in this
* procedure.
release all except START_SPOT
return START_SPOT
```

7. Save the document and exit your word processor. Type **CL PRINT MAILLIST** at the DOS prompt. Press **Enter**. The Clipper batch file clears the screen, then compiles and links the print program.

NOTE

The memory amounts displayed in these screen shots may not match those shown on your display. This is due to differences between individual machine configurations.

8. Type **PRINT**. Press **Enter**. The mailing list print program display appears. Notice the program displays the free memory left in KBytes. The program now consumes less memory (leaving more free) than in Module 125.

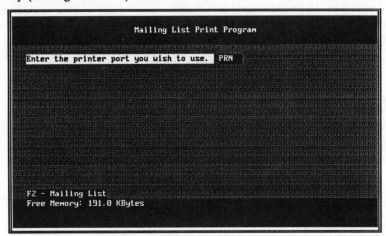

9. Type **LPT1** and press **Enter** to select printer output. Type **N** to forego the printer test. The program displays a menu.

10. Select Quit by pressing **Up Arrow** and then **Enter**. The DOS prompt appears.

11. Turn to Module 69 to continue the learning sequence.

Module 66
RENAME

DESCRIPTION

The Rename command lets you change the name of a file and its associated extension. FILE1.EXT1 contains the original filename. FILE2.EXT2 contains the new name you want to assign. Clipper lets you use a variable containing the filenames EXPC1 and EXPC2 in place of an actual filename. You must close a file before renaming it. Failure to do so will cause program failure. It could also cause file directory damage, making other files inaccessible as well. The command line interface of the Rename command appears below.

```
RENAME <FILE1>.<EXT1>/(<EXPC1> TO <FILE2>.<EXT2>/(<EXPC2>)
```

APPLICATIONS

Use this command when you need to rename a file. For example, if you have several databases that contain similar information for different occasions and you want to simplify user interaction with the program, you could use a master file system. In this system, the program always uses the same filename for operations. You rename the file the user wants to use to match the master filename. When the user completes the operation, you change the name of the file back to its original state.

TYPICAL OPERATION

In this example you add the capability to rename a file to the maintenance program. Begin this example in your word processor with MAINT.PRG loaded.

1. Add the following text to the maintenance program.
   ```
   * Ask if any files require renaming.
   input 'Do you want to rename any of the files? ' to ANSWER
   ANSWER = upper(ANSWER)
   if len(ANSWER) > 1
      ANSWER = substr(ANSWER, 1, 1)
   endif
   if ANSWER = 'Y'
      input 'Which file do you want renamed?' + chr(13) + chr(10) to REN_FILE
      if file(REN_FILE)
         input 'Enter a new filename.' + chr(13) + chr(10) to RENTO_FILE
         rename &REN_FILE to &RENTO_FILE
      endif
   endif
   * Exit this utility
   ```

2. Save the document and exit your word processor. Type **CLD MAINT** at the DOS prompt. Press **Enter**.

3. Type **MAINT**. Press **Enter**. The program asks for a directory path and skeleton.

4. Type '*.DBF' and press **Enter**. The program displays a listing of files ending with .DBF. Then the program asks if you want to delete any files.

5. Type 'N' and press **Enter**. The program asks "Do you want to rename any of the files?"

6. Type 'Y' and press **Enter**. The program asks "Which file do you want to rename?"

7. Type 'TEMPDATA.DBF'. Press **Enter**. The program displays "Enter a new filename."

8. Type 'NEWTEMP.DBF'. Press **Enter**. The program changes the filename and exits normally.

9. Type **DIR NEWTEMP.DBF**. Press **Enter**. DOS displays the file with a new name.

```
Type directory path and skeleton
'*.DBF'
CHCKBOOK DBF     1035   07/15/89
MAILLIST DBF     1625   07/16/89
NOTEPAD  DBF      406   07/16/89
SUMMARY  DBF      550   07/11/89
TEMPDATA DBF     1035   07/15/89
HELP     DBF      162   07/16/89

Do you want to delete any of the files? 'N'
Do you want to rename any of the files? 'Y'
Which file do you want renamed?
'TEMPDATA.DBF'
Enter a new filename.
'NEWTEMP.DBF'
C:\CLIPPER\0022>DIR NEWTEMP.DBF

 Volume in drive C is JOHN'S DISK
 Directory of  C:\CLIPPER\0022

NEWTEMP  DBF     1035   7-15-89   2:56p
        1 File(s)   9893888 bytes free

C:\CLIPPER\0022>
```

10. Turn to Module 99 to continue the learning sequence.

Module 67
REPLACE

DESCRIPTION

The Replace command places the contents of a variable or an expression in the specified field of a database. You can place this value in one, some, or all of the records. Clipper also allows you to replace more than one variable using a single Replace command. However, replacing more than one field with a single command reduces the readability of your code. You gain the advantage of speed by performing multiple replacements with a single command. The code executes faster and Clipper produces smaller EXE files. The command line interface of the Replace command appears below.

```
REPLACE [<SCOPE>] [<ALIAS>] <FIELD1> WITH <EXP1> [, <FIELD2> WITH <EXP2>,
...] [FOR <CONDITION>] [WHILE <CONDITION>]
```

The scope clause allows you to specify the range of record fields to replace. The default scope is all. If you specify next with a number, Clipper starts replacing record fields from the current record position and stops when it replaces the required number of record fields.

The alias clause lets you tell Clipper what you called the database within your program. If you do not specify an alias, Clipper automatically uses the database in the current work area for field replacements.

The field with the exp clause determines what you place in the field. You can use a variable, actual value, or another field. For example, you could place the contents of edit screens in a variable, then replace that value in the appropriate field of the database after you complete an edit. You can also set a relation between two databases and perform multiple replacements from one database to the other.

The for condition clause allows you to limit the number of record fields replaced to those meeting a predefined condition. Normally, the condition contains a field name, then a relational operator (>, <, <>, =), followed by the condition. Clipper replaces all the record fields in the database meeting the defined condition and scope.

The while condition clause allows you to limit the number of record fields replaced to those meeting a predefined condition. Unlike the for condition clause, Clipper stops replacing data in the record fields as soon as it sees a record not meeting the criteria. In some respects, this clause works like a combination of the for condition and scope clauses.

APPLICATIONS

Use the Replace command in three instances. In the first instance, you can make certain that power failures and other mechanical disturbances do not corrupt the database by placing edits in variables first. Then, when the user completes an edit, you can quickly open the database just long enough to replace the values. This also works well when you create new records.

The second instance is when you want the fields of two databases to match in contents. By setting a relation between the two databases and specifying a while or for condition, you can control which records receive new information.

In the third instance, you create a boilerplate record, then request the user modify it as required. By using this method, you normally reduce the time required to enter information into the database.

TYPICAL OPERATION

In this example you change the mailing list program so that it uses variables instead of directly manipulating the database. Then you replace the old field values with new ones using the Replace command. Begin this example in your word processor with MAILLIST.PRG loaded.

1. Add the following variable statements to the beginning of the program.

```
CPRESSED = 'Y'
* Database Variables
public FIRST_NAME, MIDDLE, LAST_NAME, ADDRESS1, ADDRESS2, CITY, STATE
public ZIP, TELEPHONE
do INIT_FIELDS
* Setup program defaults.
```

2. Add/modify the following procedures at the end of the procedure section.

NOTE

The A-> identifies fields within the database. The M-> identifies variables with the same name.

```
procedure GET_DATA
* This procedure gets the data from the current record.
    do SET_VARIABLES
    @ 04, 12 get M->FIRST_NAME picture '@!' valid .not. ;
      empty(M->FIRST_NAME)
    @ 04, 38 get M->MIDDLE picture '!' valid .not. empty(M- >MIDDLE)
    @ 04, 40 get M->LAST_NAME picture '@!' valid .not. empty (M->LAST_NAME)
    @ 06, 12 get M->ADDRESS1
    @ 07, 12 get M->ADDRESS2
    @ 09, 12 get M->CITY picture '@!'
    @ 09, 60 get M->STATE picture '!!'
    @ 09, 68 get M->ZIP picture '99999-9999'
    @ 11, 12 get M->TELEPHONE picture '(999)999-9999'
return
procedure INIT_FIELDS
* This procedure initializes the memory variables used in
* place of actual database fields.
M->FIRST_NAME = space(25)
M->MIDDLE = ' '
M->LAST_NAME = space(25)
M->ADDRESS1 = space(50)
M->ADDRESS2 = space(50)
M->CITY = space(40)
M->STATE = space(2)
M->ZIP = space(10)
M->TELEPHONE = space(13)
return
procedure SET_VARIABLES
* This procedure gets the contents of the current database
* record and places it in the database variables.
M->FIRST_NAME = A->FIRST_NAME
M->MIDDLE = A->MIDDLE
M->LAST_NAME = A->LAST_NAME
```

```
M->ADDRESS1 = A->ADDRESS1
M->ADDRESS2 = A->ADDRESS2
M->CITY = A->CITY
M->STATE = A->STATE
M->ZIP = A->ZIP
M->TELEPHONE = A->TELEPHONE
return
```

3. Save the document and exit your word processor. Type **CL MAILLIST PRINT** at the DOS prompt. Press **Enter**.

4. Type **MAILLIST**. Press **Enter**.

5. Type **E**. Notice the first name of the record contains GEORGE.

6. Type **SAM**. Press **Enter**. Notice the first name field retains the name SAM as normal.

7. Press **PgDn**. The menu reappears. Notice the first name returns to GEORGE, since the program did not replace the database field with the value of the database variable. This is how the Replace command works in conjunction with variables to reduce the risk of corrupting your database.

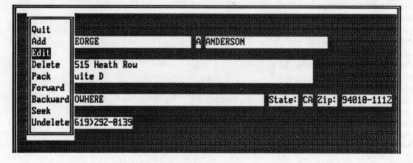

8. Select Quit by pressing **Up Arrow** twice. Press **Enter**. The DOS prompt appears. Load MAILLIST.PRG into your word processor. Add the following procedure to the end of the procedure section.

```
procedure SET_FIELDS
* This procedure gets the contents of the database variables
* and places it in the current database record.
replace A->FIRST_NAME with M->FIRST_NAME
replace A->MIDDLE with M->MIDDLE
replace A->LAST_NAME with M->LAST_NAME
replace A->ADDRESS1 with M->ADDRESS1
replace A->ADDRESS2 with M->ADDRESS2
replace A->CITY with M->CITY
replace A->STATE with M->STATE
replace A->ZIP with M->ZIP
replace A->TELEPHONE with M->TELEPHONE
return
```

9. Add/change the following text in the case statement section at the beginning of the program.

```
case ANSWER = 2
    seek 'ZZZZZ'
    do GET_DATA
    read
    append blank
    do SET_FIELDS
* Display the database information.
case ANSWER = 3
    do GET_DATA
    read
    do SET_FIELDS
```

10. Save the document and exit your word processor. Type **CL MAILLIST PRINT** at the DOS prompt. Press **Enter**.

11. Type **MAILLIST**. Press **Enter**.

12. Type **E**. Notice the first name of the record contains GEORGE.

13. Type **SAM**. Press **Enter**. Notice the first name field retains the name SAM as normal.

14. Press **PgDn**. The menu reappears. Notice the first name does not return to GEORGE as it did the last time.

15. Select Quit. The DOS prompt appears.

16. Turn to Module 137 to continue the learning sequence.

Module 68
REPORT FORM

DESCRIPTION

The Report Form command lets you combine the information in your database with the parameters in a preformatted report file. You can create a report form file using the RL utility discussed in Module 7. The command line interface of the Report Form command appears below.

```
REPORT FORM <FILE1>/(<EXPC1>) [<SCOPE>] [FOR <CONDITION>] [WHILE
<CONDITION>] [TO PRINT] [TO FILE <FILE2>/(<EXPC2>)] [SUMMARY] [PLAIN]
[HEADING <EXPC3>] [NOEJECT]
```

The file clause contains the name of the report form file. Clipper lets you specify the actual file name or use a variable. This is the only required input to the report form command.

The scope clause lets you specify the range of records to print using the formatting commands contained in the report form file. The default scope is all. If you specify next with a number, Clipper starts printing records from the current record position and stops when it prints the required number of records.

The for condition clause lets you limit the number of records printed to those meeting a predefined condition. Normally, the condition contains a field name, then a relational operator (>, <, <>, =), followed by the condition. Clipper prints all the records in the database meeting the defined condition and scope.

The while condition clause lets you limit the number of records printed to those meeting a predefined condition. Unlike the for condition clause, Clipper stops printing the report as soon as it sees a record not meeting the criteria. In some respects, this clause works like a combination of the for condition and scope clauses.

The to print clause specifies where Clipper sends the report. The default destination is the display. If you specify the printer and set the console to off, Clipper outputs to the printer only. By keeping the console on, you can send the output to both the printer and display.

The to file clause lets you send the report output to the specified file. Clipper does not provide a default filename, so the filename must appear after the clause. If you do not specify an extension, Clipper automatically adds the TXT extension. Clipper lets you send the report output to the display, printer, and a file simultaneously.

The summary clause suppresses report detail lines during printing. Clipper prints only the heading, subheading, group, subgroup, and total lines. If the report does not contain any of the above information, Clipper prints a blank report (a form feed).

The plain clause lets you suppress the date, page number, and pagination. Clipper prints the report title (heading and subheadings) and column headings only at the top of the report.

The heading clause lets you create a report heading. Clipper places text or variables on the first line of every page. You specify the report heading using EXPC3 following the heading clause.

The noeject clause suppresses the initial form feed Clipper normally adds at the beginning of a report. This clause applies only when using the to print clause.

APPLICATIONS

Use this command whenever you want to output a standard columnar report. The report form allows headings, subheadings, groups, and subgroups. However, this will not print forms or other specially formatted data.

TYPICAL OPERATION

In this example you add the code required to use the report form created in Module 7. Begin this example in your word processor with PRINT.PRG loaded.

1. Remove the following text.

```
* Setup program defaults.
set print on
set console off
* Open the database and prepare it for use.
use MAILLIST index LASTNAME
for PRNT_COUNT = 1 to reccount()
   do DISP_COUNT
   do REC_PRINT
next
* Reset the display and printer.
set print off
set console on
```

2. Add the following text at the indicated cursor position.

```
    !@#$%^&*()
   endtext
   eject
   wait
   do DISP_SCRN
endif
* Perform this procedure until the user wants to stop.
do while MENU_SEL <> 1
* Display the print menu.
do DISP_SCRN
do DISP_MENU2
* Check the user selection.
do case
   case MENU_SEL = 2
      use CHCKBOOK
      do DISP_MENU3
      report form CHCKLIST to print
endcase
enddo
* Close the database and exit.
```

3. Add the following variable to the beginning of the program.

```
PRNT_TEST = 'Y'
MENU_SEL = 2
```

4. Add the following procedures to the end of the procedure section.

```
procedure DISP_MENU2
* This procedure displays the program menu.
save screen
set message to 22 center
@ 06, 02 clear to 09, 15
```

```
@ 05, 01 to 10, 16 double
@ 06, 03 prompt 'Quit' message 'Leave this application.'
@ 07, 03 prompt 'Check Book' message 'Print the Check Book Database.'
menu to MENU_SEL
restore screen
return
procedure DISP_MENU3
* This procedure displays a menu for selecting an index for
* printing the check book.
private ANSWER2
save screen
set message to 22 center
@ 06, 02 clear to 07, 15
@ 05, 01 to 08, 16 double
@ 06, 03 prompt 'Check Number' message 'Print in Check Number Order.'
@ 07, 03 prompt 'Check Date' message 'Print in Check Date Order.'
menu to ANSWER2
restore screen
* Set the index to match user response.
if ANSWER2 = 1
   set index to CHCKNUM
else
   set index to DATE
endif
return
```

5. Save the document and exit your word processor. Compile the program.

6. Type **PRINT**. Press **Enter**.

7. Type **LPT1**. Press **Enter** to select a printer. Type **N** to forego running the printer test. The program displays a menu for selecting the database you want to print.

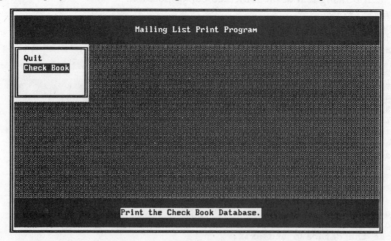

8. Press **Enter** to select Check Book. The program displays another menu.

NOTE

If the next step does not work properly and Clipper returns an error in .FRM file message, use RL to determine that the form does not contain any extra fields. The form should contain only six fields. Use F5 to delete extra blank fields. Check the file contents with those appearing in Module 7. If the form prints but extends over the right margin, use RL to reduce the report left margin.

9. Select Check Date by pressing **Down Arrow**. Press **Enter**. The program prints the report header and totals. It does not print any data since the database does not contain any. Notice Clipper displays the report on screen as well. The Main menu appears.

10. Select Quit by pressing **Up Arrow**. Press **Enter**. The DOS prompt appears.

11. Turn to Module 51 to continue the learning sequence.

Module 69
RESTORE FROM

DESCRIPTION

The Restore From command restores variables stored on disk with the Save To command. You need to supply a file name from which to restore variables. If you use the additive clause, Clipper keeps all the current variables as well. Otherwise, Clipper removes all variables from memory before restoring the disk file. The command line interface of the Restore From command appears below.

```
RESTORE FROM <FILE>/(<EXPC>) [ADDITIVE]
```

APPLICATIONS

Use the Restore From command to obtain variables stored to disk using the Save To command. This command works with the Save To command to create programs that remember previous configuration information.

TYPICAL OPERATION

In this example you restore the printer configuration information previously stored to disk using the Save To command. Begin this example in your word processor with PRINT.PRG loaded.

1. Remove the following text at the beginning of the program.
   ```
   PRNT_PORT = 'PRN  '
   ```

2. Add the following text at the beginning of the program.
   ```
   public DOUBLE_LINE, PRNT_PORT
   * Restore the previous printer configuration information.
   restore from PRNTPORT additive
   * Check variable length, if too long use default setting.
   if len(PRNT_PORT) > 6
      PRNT_PORT = 'PRN  '
   endif
   * Program Variables
   ```

3. Save the document and exit your word processor. Type **CL PRINT MAILLIST** at the DOS prompt. Press **Enter**.

4. Type **PRINT**. Press **Enter**. Notice the program displays LPT1 instead of PRN as usual.

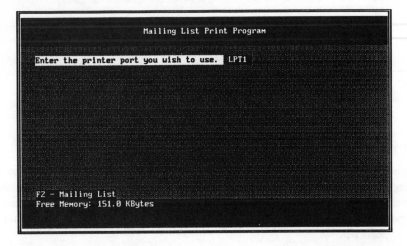

```
                    Mailing List Print Program

 Enter the printer port you wish to use.   LPT1




 F2 - Mailing List
 Free Memory: 151.0 KBytes
```

5. Type **FILE** and press **Enter** to select printer output. Type **EXAMPLE.TXT** for the filename. Type **Y** when the program asks if you want to overwrite the file. Type **N** to forego the printer test. The program displays a menu.

6. Select Quit. The DOS prompt appears.

7. Type **PRINT**. Press **Enter**. The mailing list print program display appears. Notice the program displays PRN as usual (a file is not a printer port).

8. Type **LPT1** and press **Enter** to select printer output. Type **N** to forego the printer test. The program displays a menu.

9. Select Quit. The DOS prompt appears.

10. Turn to Module 19 to continue the learning sequence.

Module 70
RESTORE SCREEN

DESCRIPTION

The Restore Screen command places the contents of a previously saved screen buffer on the display. You save a screen using the Save Screen command. If the screen buffer exists in a memory variable rather than the screen buffer, use the from clause. Place the name of the memory variable after the from clause. The command line interface of the Restore Screen command appears below.

```
RESTORE SCREEN [FROM <MEMVAR>]
```

APPLICATIONS

Use the Restore Screen command in conjunction with the Save Screen command to save and restore a copy of the current display. These two commands work well with pop-up windows and pop-down (lighted-bar) menus. By saving the screen contents before you do the pop-up, you can quickly restore the display with the Restore Screen command. By using a memory variable with the Save Screen command, you could display several levels of menus and remove them as the user presses Esc. Simply use a Restore Screen command with a from clause for the memory variable holding each level. There are other uses for this command as well. For example, you could use it to quickly change between screens for menus, print routines, editors, and database analysis routines.

TYPICAL OPERATION

Begin this example in your word processor with MAILLIST.PRG loaded.

1. Add the following text after the Menu To command and before the Do Case control structure.
   ```
   menu to ANSWER
   restore screen
   * Add a new record.
   ```
2. Save the document and exit your word processor. Type **CL MAILLIST** at the DOS prompt. Press **Enter**.
3. Type **MAILLIST**. Press **Enter**.
4. Type **E**. The menu disappears and the edit screen appears as before. Notice no menu appears along the bottom.

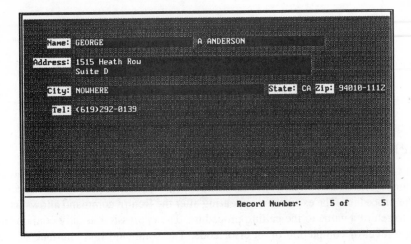

5. Press **Esc**. The menu reappears. Notice the Edit option appears highlighted.

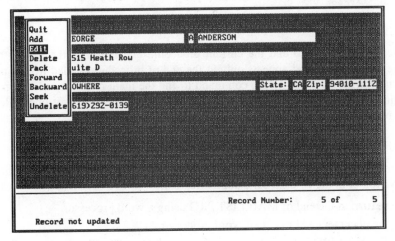

6. Type **Q**. The DOS prompt appears.
7. Turn to Module 77 to continue the learning sequence.

Module 71
RETURN

DESCRIPTION

The Return command ends the current procedure and returns control to the parent procedure or the operating system. After Return ends the current procedure, it deallocates any local variables used by the procedure. The expression appearing after the Return command allows user defined functions to return a value to the calling procedure. The expression usually contains a number indicating a level of completion or an error code. The command line interface of the Return command appears below.

```
RETURN <EXPRESSION>
```

APPLICATIONS

Use the Return command to end the current procedure and return to the calling procedure. Usually the Return command appears only at the end of procedures called from a program or subprogram. You may use the Return command to end the main program and return control to the operating system. Executing a Return command does not close any open files; it does deallocate memory used by the procedure and associated variables.

TYPICAL OPERATION

In this example you add a Return command to the end of MAILLIST.PRG. Begin this example at the DOS prompt in the C:\CLIPPER\0022 directory.

1. Type **return** at the end of MAILLIST.PRG using a word processor.
2. Save the document and exit your word processor.
3. Type **CL MAILLIST** at the DOS prompt. Press **Enter**. The Clipper batch file clears the screen, then compiles and links the program.
4. Type **MAILLIST**. Press **Enter**. The program asks if you want to add a new record.
5. Type **N**. The mailing list edit screen appears.
6. Press **PgDn**. The DOS prompt appears. Notice the effect of the return command is not noticeable. It merely acts as a termination at the end of the program.

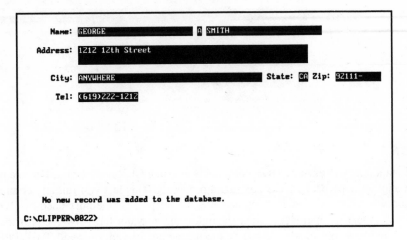

7. Turn to Module 18 to continue the learning sequence.

Module 72
RUN/!

DESCRIPTION

The Run/! command lets you execute DOS commands within a Clipper program. For example, you can create another copy of the DOS command processor. This lets you run any command within the memory limitations of your machine (total memory - (2 * memory used by DOS) - memory used by Clipper). Clipper lets you use the buffer memory normally reserved for sorting and indexing to run DOS commands. To use this extra memory, simply type SET CLIPPER= R<MEMORY>. To determine the amount of memory your application normally reserves for buffers, use the Memory( ) function. This function shows the total memory you can set aside using the R parameter. The command line interface of the Run/! command appears below.

```
RUN <DOS COMMAND>/(<EXPC>)
```

or

```
! <DOS COMMAND>/(<EXPC>)
```

APPLICATIONS

Use the Run/! command whenever you need to execute a DOS command from within your program. This means that you can allow the user access to a DOS shell or use any separately compiled programs you want (within memory limitations). You can also change the program environment dynamically using this command. The DOS Set commands allow you to do this. Use the GetEnv( )/GetE( ) function to store the original environment variable value.

TYPICAL OPERATION

In this example you add the capability of using DOS within the sample program. Begin this example in your word processor with MAILLIST.PRG loaded.

1. Add the following text to the mailing list program.
   ```
   set key -4 to NOTEPAD      && Point F5 to the notepad.
   set key -9 to DOSSHELL     && Point F10 to the DOS Shell.
   * Clear the display and prepare database for use.
   ```

2. Save the document and exit your word processor. Type **CLIPPER MAILLIST** at the DOS prompt. Press **Enter**. Clipper compiles the program.

3. Load CL.BAT into your word processor. Change the text as shown below.
   ```
   IF NOT ERRORLEVEL 1 Plink86 FI MAILLIST, PRINT, CHCKBOOK, NOTEPAD, HELP, ;
   DOSSHELL LIB \CLIPPER\CLIPPER, \CLIPPER\EXTEND
   ```

4. Save the changes and create a new program named DOSSHELL.PRG using your word processor. Add the following text.
   ```
   * DOSSHELL.PRG
   * This program allows the user to exit to DOS from within
   * Clipper.
   ```

```
* YOUR NAME
* TODAY'S DATE
* Execute DOS command processor.  This example assumes the
* command processor is in the root directory of drive C.
save screen to TEMP
clear screen
set cursor on
run C:\COMMAND
restore screen from TEMP
return
```

5. Save the document and exit your word processor. Type **CL DOSSHELL** at the DOS prompt. Press **Enter**.

NOTE

Your machine will show a different amount of RAM depending on your configuration, memory resident programs loaded, and other factors. Therefore, your displays may differ from those shown below. You may also need to use a smaller number after the R parameter of the DOS Set command. This depends on the size memory pool your machine provides after loading the sample program.

6. Type **SET CLIPPER=R100** at the DOS prompt to change Clipper's runtime environment. Type **CHKDSK** and press **Enter**. Notice the amount of RAM displayed.

```
C:\CLIPPER\0022>IF NOT ERRORLEVEL 1 Plink86 FI MAILLIST, PRINT, CHCKBOOK, NOTEPA
D, HELP, DOSSHELL LIB \CLIPPER\CLIPPER, \CLIPPER\EXTEND
PLINK86plus ( Nantucket ) Version 2.24.
Copyright (C) 1987 by Phoenix Technologies Ltd.,
All Rights Reserved.


MAILLIST.EXE (222 K)
C:\CLIPPER\0022>SET CLIPPER=R100

C:\CLIPPER\0022>CHKDSK
Volume JOHN'S DISK created Feb 17, 1989 11:04a

 32598016 bytes total disk space
    90112 bytes in 4 hidden files
   129024 bytes in 46 directories
 23496704 bytes in 1855 user files
  8882176 bytes available on disk

   655360 bytes total memory
   530848 bytes free

C:\CLIPPER\0022>
```

7. Type **MAILLIST** and press **Enter**. The mailing list program menu appears.

8. Press **F10**. The DOS prompt appears.

9. Type **CHKDSK** and press **Enter**. Notice CHKDSK displays a much smaller amount of available RAM. If you used the R100 parameter in the Set command, CHKDSK displays 100 Kbytes — the memory used by DOS.

```
The IBM Personal Computer DOS
Version 3.10 (C)Copyright International Business Machines Corp 1981, 1985
               (C)Copyright Microsoft Corp 1981, 1985

C:\CLIPPER\0022>CHKDSK
Volume JOHN'S DISK created Feb 17, 1989 11:04a

 32598016 bytes total disk space
    90112 bytes in 4 hidden files
   129024 bytes in 46 directories
 23513088 bytes in 1857 user files
  8865792 bytes available on disk

   655360 bytes total memory
    95696 bytes free

C:\CLIPPER\0022>
```

10. Type **EXIT** and press **Enter**. The mailing list program menu appears.

11. Select Quit by pressing **Enter**. The DOS prompt appears.

12. Turn to Module 35 to continue the learning sequence.

Module 73
SAVE SCREEN

DESCRIPTION

The Save Screen command places a copy of the current screen contents in memory. By using the to clause and specifying a memory variable, you can keep copies of several screens by assigning each screen a unique name. If you only need to store one screen at a time, use the Save Screen by itself to conserve memory. The command line interface of the Save Screen command appears below.

```
SAVE SCREEN [TO <MEMVAR>]
```

APPLICATIONS

Use the Save Screen command to save a copy of the current display contents. This command works well with pop-up windows and pop-down (lighted-bar) menus. By saving the screen contents before you do the pop-up, you can quickly restore the display with the Restore Screen command. By using a memory variable with the Save Screen command, you could display several levels of menus and remove them as the user presses Esc. There are other uses for this command as well. For example, you could use it to quickly change between screens for menus, print routines, editors, and database analysis routines.

TYPICAL OPERATION

In this example you save the contents of the screen before placing the menu on the display. Begin this example in your word processor with MAILLIST.PRG loaded.

1. Add the following text after the screen display and before the menu prompts.
    ```
    * Get user choice.
    save screen
    @ 03, 04 clear to 11, 11
    ```

2. Save the document and exit your word processor. Type **CL MAILLIST** at the DOS prompt. Press **Enter**.

3. Type **MAILLIST**. Press **Enter**. The mailing list program display appears. Notice the Save Screen command does not change program operation or increase execution speed.

4. Type **Q**. The DOS prompt appears.

5. Turn to Module 70 to continue the learning sequence.

Module 74
SAVE TO

DESCRIPTION

The Save To command provides a method of saving variables from one program session to another. Clipper saves the variables in the specified file. All memory files use a .MEM extension. The optional all clause allows you to specify a scope. Using all by itself specifies the default scope of all non-hidden (private) variables. You can add the key word like or except to specify a limited scope. The skeleton clause contains the mask that Clipper uses to include or exclude variables. When you use the like clause, Clipper includes the variables in the mask. When you use the except clause, Clipper excludes the variables defined by the mask. The command line interface of the Save To command appears below.

```
SAVE TO <FILE>/(<EXPC>) [ALL [LIKE/EXCEPT <SKELETON>]]
```

APPLICATIONS

Use the Save To command to store variables from one database session to the next. This is especially convenient for configuration and database status variables. By storing the values contained in the variables, you reduce the amount of preliminary work the user must perform for each program execution.

You can also use this command to pass data between two different programs. This is especially convenient in large database situations where one department in a corporation may use one program, another department may use a different program. Using separate programs reduces the RAM requirement for each one. Passing variables between the programs allows asynchronous program communications. For example, you could use this feature as a rudimentary electronic mail system.

TYPICAL OPERATION

In this example you use the Save To command to save the current status of the printer port to a file. Begin this example in your word processor with PRINT.PRG loaded.

1. Add the following text to the end of the main procedure.
   ```
   enddo
   * Save the user printer port selection.
   save to PRNTPORT all like PRNT_PORT
   * Close the database and exit.
   ```

2. Save the document and exit your word processor. Type **CL PRINT** at the DOS prompt. Press **Enter**.

3. Type **PRINT**. Press **Enter**.

4. Type **FILE**. Press **Enter** to select file output instead of printer output. The program displays an entry asking for a filename.

5. Type **EXAMPLE.TXT** and press **Enter**. The program displays a message saying the file already exists.

6. Type **Y** to overwrite the file. Type **N** to forego running the printer test. The program displays a menu for selecting the database you want to print.

7. Press **Enter** to select Check Book. The program displays another menu.

8. Select Check Date by pressing **Down Arrow**. Press **Enter**. The Main menu appears.

9. Select Quit by pressing **Up Arrow**. Press **Enter**. The DOS prompt appears.

NOTE

Although you can type a memory (.MEM) file, you cannot always read the contents. In all cases, the file contains control characters which make reading difficult.

10. Type **CLS** and press **Enter** to clear the display. Type **TYPE PRNTPORT.MEM**. Press **Enter**. The contents of the printer port memory file appear. Notice the file contains the name of the variable, the variable contents, and some control characters.

```
C:\CLIPPER\0022>TYPE PRNTPORT.MEM
PRNT_PORT }|p o+K   .?.?$
~TEXAMPLE.TXT
C:\CLIPPER\0022>
```

11. Turn to Module 125 to continue the learning sequence.

Module 75
SEEK

DESCRIPTION

The Seek command lets you find records by the key field used in an index file. The key field is the database field used by Clipper to order or sort the database. The expression following the Seek command contains the information you want to find. For example, if you are looking for a name, then the expression contains the name. If more than one record matches the search value, then Clipper places the record pointer to the first one in the set. You can page through all the records that match the search value using the Skip command. Clipper lets you use either the actual value or a variable containing the value as the seek expression. The command line interface of the Seek command appears below.

```
SEEK <EXP>
```

APPLICATIONS

Use the Seek command to quickly find any record in the database. By using different index files, you can search for any value using any field. Unlike other methods of finding records, the Seek command only uses a single execution to find the desired record.

TYPICAL OPERATION

In this example you add the capability to find records using the Seek command in the sample database. Begin this example in your word processor with MAILLIST.PRG loaded.

1. Change the menu prompt as shown below.
   ```
   @ 22, 04 say 'Quit/Add/Edit/Delete/Pack/Forward/Backward/Seek';
      get ANSWER picture '!'
   ```

2. Add the text below between the last skip command and the endif appearing at the end of the program.
   ```
      skip -1
   * Search for the desired last name.
   elseif ANSWER = 'S'
      SEARCH_NAME = LAST_NAME
      @ 04, 40 get SEARCH_NAME picture '@K@!'
      read
      seek SEARCH_NAME
   endif
   ```

3. Save the document and exit your word processor. Type **CL MAILLIST** at the DOS prompt. Press **Enter**.

4. Type **MAILLIST**. Press **Enter**.

5. Type **S**. Clipper highlights the last name field of the current record.

6. Type **STONE**. Press **Enter**. Clipper finds the first record with a last name of STONE and displays it.

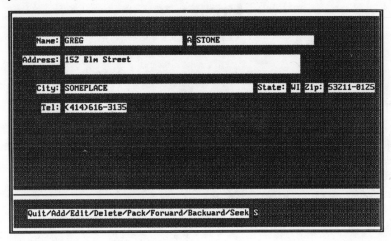

7. Type **Q**. The DOS prompt appears.
8. Turn to Module 96 to continue the learning sequence.

Module 76
SELECT

DESCRIPTION

The Select command selects a work area. Clipper lets you select the work area using a letter (WORK AREA), the database alias, or a number (work area A = 1, B = 2, etc.) Never confuse the Select command with the Select( ) function (Module 134). The command line interface of the Select command appears below.

```
SELECT <WORK AREA>/<ALIAS>/(<EXPN>)
```

APPLICATIONS

Use the Select command to change work areas when using more than one database.

TYPICAL OPERATION

In this example you open two databases and select between them using the Select command. Begin this example in your word processor with DOSSHELL.PRG loaded.

1. Add the following text to the menu selection routine at the beginning of the program.

```
declare MENU_ARRAY[4]
MENU_ARRAY[1] = 'Quit'
MENU_ARRAY[2] = 'Dos Shell'
MENU_ARRAY[3] = 'Show Records'
MENU_ARRAY[4] = 'Consolidate Checks'
SELECT = 2
* Save the display.
save screen to TEMP2
* Get the user selection.
do while MENU_ARRAY[SELECT] <> 'Quit'
   @ 03, 39 clear to 08, 58
   @ 03, 39 to 08, 58 double
   SELECT = achoice(04, 40, 07, 57, MENU_ARRAY)
   do case
      case MENU_ARRAY[SELECT] = 'Dos Shell'
         do DOS_SHELL
      case MENU_ARRAY[SELECT] = 'Show Records'
         do SHOW_RECS
      case MENU_ARRAY[SELECT] = 'Consolidate Checks'
         do CONSOLIDATE
   endcase
```

2. Add the following text to the end of the procedure section of the program.

```
procedure CONSOLIDATE
* This procedure creates a new database by using the
* contents of two previously created databases.
* Open the databases.
select A
use MAILLIST index LASTNAME
select B
use CHCKBOOK index CHCKNUM, DATE
```

```
* Display them one at a time.
select A
do SHOW_RECS
select B
do SHOW_RECS
return
```

3. Save the document and exit your word processor. Type **CL DOSSHELL** at the DOS prompt. Press **Enter**.

4. Type **MAILLIST** and press **Enter**. The mailing list program menu appears.

5. Press **F10**. The DOS shell menu appears. Notice the new menu option.

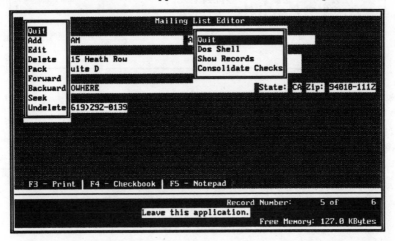

6. Select Consolidate Checks by typing **C** and pressing **Enter**. The program displays the contents of the mailing list database.

```
              Database Last Updated: 07/20/89

     5   SAM              | A | ANDERSON           | 515 Heath R
ou                        |   | Suite D
           | NOWHERE                      | CA | 94010-1112 | <619
>292-0139
     1   GEORGE           | A | SMITH              | 1212 12th S
treet
           | ANYWHERE                     | CA | 92111-     | <619
>222-1212
     4   GREG             | A | STONE              | 152 Elm Str
eet
           | SOMEPLACE                    | WI | 53211-0125 | <414
>616-3135
     3   SAMUEL           | L | STONE              | 1234 A Stre
et
           | SOMEPLACE                    | WI | 53211-0114 | <414
>199-2929
Press any key to continue...
```

7. Press **Enter** twice. The program displays the contents of the checkbook database.

```
                   Database Last Updated: 07/15/89

     1  07/09/89  |        0  |  PAYCHECK                              |
     0.00  |        550.89  |        550.89  |  .F.                    |
     2  07/10/89  |        0  |  PAYCHECK DEPOSIT                      |
     0.00  |        820.00  |       1248.46  |  .F.                    |
     3  07/11/89  |        0  |  PAYCHECK                              |
     0.00  |       1200.98  |          0.00  |  .F.                    |
     4  07/09/89  |        1  |  GEORGES RESTAURANT                    |
    19.99  |          0.00  |        530.90  |  .T.                    |
     5  07/09/89  |        2  |  ANTHONY'S FOOD STORE                  |
   102.44  |          0.00  |        428.46  |  .F.                    |
     6  07/10/89  |        3  |  JEAN'S SHOES                          |
   520.00  |          0.00  |        728.46  |  .F.                    |
     7  07/11/89  |        4  |  MAX STATIONERS                        |
    12.22  |          0.00  |        716.24  |  .T.                    |
     8  07/11/89  |        5  |  RENT                                  |
  1000.00  |          0.00  |          0.00  |  .T.                    |
Press any key to continue...
```

8. Press **Enter**. The DOS shell menu appears.

9. Type **Q** and press **Enter** to quit the DOS shell menu.

10. Select Quit by pressing **Enter**. The DOS prompt appears.

11. Turn to Module 134 to continue the learning sequence.

Module 77
SET COMMANDS

DESCRIPTION

The Set command group consists of 38 different commands. In general, each of these commands toggles a Clipper switch controlling how the compiler creates code. The result is a difference in the overall performance of the program produced by Clipper. The following paragraphs describe each command in detail. The command line interface for each of the Set Command group appears below.

```
SET ALTERNATE TO [<FILE>/(<EXPC>)]
SET ALTERNATE ON/OFF/(<EXPL>)
SET BELL ON/OFF/(<EXPL>)
SET CENTURY ON/OFF/(<EXPL>)
SET COLOR/COLOUR TO [<STANDARD> [, <ENHANCED>] [, <BORDER>]
[, <BACKGROUND>] [, <UNSELECTED>]]/(<EXPC>)
SET CONFIRM ON/OFF/(<EXPL>)
SET CONSOLE ON/OFF/(<EXPL>)
SET CURSOR ON/OFF/(<EXPL>)
SET DATE AMERICAN/ANSI/BRITISH/FRENCH/GERMAN/ITALIAN
SET DECIMALS TO <EXPN>
SET DEFAULT TO <DRIVE> [:<PATH>]/(<EXPC>)
SET DELETED ON/OFF/(<EXPL>)
SET DELIMITERS ON/OFF/(<EXPL>)
SET DELIMITERS TO [<EXPC>/DEFAULT]
SET DEVICE TO SCREEN/PRINT
SET EPOCH TO <EXPN>
SET ESCAPE ON/OFF/(<EXPL>)
SET EXACT ON/OFF/(<EXPL>)
SET EXCLUSIVE ON/OFF/(<EXPL>)
SET FILTER TO [<CONDITION>]
SET FIXED ON/OFF/(<EXPL>)
SET FORMAT TO <PROCEDURE>
SET FUNCTION <EXPN> TO <EXPC>
SET INDEX TO [<FILE LIST>/(<EXPC1>), ...]
SET INTENSITY ON/OFF/(<EXPL>)
SET KEY <EXPN> TO [<PROCEDURE>]
SET MARGIN TO <EXPN>
SET MESSAGE TO [<EXPN> [CENTER/CENTRE]]
SET ORDER TO [<EXPN>]
SET PATH TO (<PATH LIST>)/(<EXPC>)
SET PRINT ON/OFF/(<EXPL>)
SET PRINTER TO [<DEVICE>/<FILE>/(<EXPC>)]
SET PROCEDURE TO [<FILE>]
SET RELATION [ADDITIVE] TO [<KEY EXP1>/<EXPN1> INTO <ALIAS1>/(<EXPC1>)]
[, TO <KEY EXP2>/<EXPN2> INTO <ALIAS2>/(<EXPC2>)] ...
SET SCOREBOARD ON/OFF/(<EXPL>)
SET SOFTSEEK ON/OFF/(<EXPL>)
SET TYPEAHEAD TO <EXPN>
SET UNIQUE ON/OFF/(<EXPL>)
SET WRAP ON/OFF/(<EXPL>)
```

SET ALTERNATE TO The Set Alternate To command lets you select a file as the output area for all commands except At (@) Say/Get. Clipper lets you specify the actual file name or use a variable containing the file name. This file does not constitute a work area since it is not a database. The output appears in the form of standard ASCII text. The Set Alternate On command tells Clipper to send the output to the alternate file; likewise, the off clause sends the output to the normal output device. Setting the alternate file off does not close the file. You must use a Close Alternate command to do this.

SET BELL The Set Bell command lets you turn the error alarm on or off. The error alarm sounds each time the user tries to perform a function contrary to normal operating procedure. For example, placing a character in a numeric field sounds the alarm. In some situations the alarm becomes more of an annoyance than an aid to learning. In these situations you should turn the bell off.

SET CENTURY The Century command turns the hundreds and thousands position of the year portion of a date on or off. For example, if you set century on and output 01/01/89, Clipper would actually output 01/01/1989.

SET COLOR TO The Set Color To command lets you enhance the appearance of your display by changing the display colors. The standard color is the color of all non-enhanced text (display prompts, menus, etc.). The enhanced color determines the appearance of selected text. For example, Clipper enhances all gets during a Read command. Clipper also enhances the selected menu item on a light-bar menu. The border clause changes the color of the text surrounding the normal edit area. No monitors currently support the background entry. The unselected entry changes the color of non-selected light-bar menu entries or get fields. Besides using characters to show which colors to use, Clipper lets you place the values in a memory variable. Every color entry appears as a color pair. The first color specifies the foreground; the second color specifies the background. For example, Set Color To W/N would make the foreground standard color white, the background black. Table 77-1 contains a listing of acceptable color choices for Clipper.

Table 77-1. Clipper Color Selection Table

Color	Number	Letter
Black	0	N
Blue	1	B
Green	2	G
Cyan	3	BG
Red	4	R
Magenta	5	RB
Brown	6	GR
White	7	W
Gray		N+
Yellow		GR+
Blank		X
Underline		U
Inverse Video		I

NOTE:

1. Clipper supports underlining and inverse video only, on monochrome monitors. It does not support colors.
2. When linking with ANSI.OBJ you cannot use numbers for colors.

SET CONFIRM The Set Confirm command determines if Clipper asks before automatically terminating a Get command when the user fills it. If you set confirm to off, Clipper automatically terminates full gets. Otherwise, the user must terminate full gets manually.

SET CONSOLE The Set Console command determines if the output of most display commands appears on the display. If you set console off, then Clipper does not send the output to the display. This command does not affect the full screen display commands: At (@) Say/Get, At (@) Prompt, At (@) Box, At (@) Clear To, At (@) To, and Clear.

SET CURSOR The Set Cursor command determines if Clipper does or does not display a cursor. This command does not affect data entry, it merely hides the cursor from view. The primary use of this command is to hide the cursor while Clipper paints the display on screen.

SET DATE The Set Date command determines how Clipper displays dates. Table 77-2 shows the various display types supported by Clipper.

Table 77-2. Clipper Supported Date Formats

Date Type	Format
American	MM/DD/YY
ANSI	YY.MM.DD
British	DD/MM/YY
French	DD/MM/YY
German	DD.MM.YY
Italian	DD.MM.YY

SET DECIMALS The Set Decimals command changes the number of digits displayed by Clipper after the decimal point. For example, if you set decimals to 3, then performed a division of 1 by 3, Clipper would output 0.333.

SET DEFAULT The Set Default command tells Clipper where to find your database, index, and other operational files. Clipper lets you specify a drive, or a drive and a path. You may use either the actual path as an argument, or a variable containing the path.

SET DELETED The Set Deleted command toggles the display of deleted records on and off. Most commands ignore deleted records when you set deleted on. You may still refer to deleted records by actual record number even after you set deleted on. Clipper still places deleted records in an index file with set deleted on as well.

SET DELIMITERS The Set Delimiters command provides two services. When you set delimiters on, Clipper displays a set of delimiters (characters) before and after each get. The Set Delimiters To command tells Clipper which characters to use. The two most common character pairs are colons (:) and braces ([ ]). If you use a space for either of the two characters, Clipper uses a space in place of the character for that position. The character expression always consists of two characters: the left character determines the left delimiter; the right character determines the right delimiter. The default clause sets Clipper to its default state of using spaces for delimiters. This has the same effect as turning delimiters off.

SET DEVICE TO The Set Device To command provides a means of sending all Clipper output to either the screen or the printer. This command affects all display statements including the @ Say/Get command. By using this command to set the device to the printer, you can better control printer output using @ Say/Get commands.

SET EPOCH The Set Epoch command lets you define the century in which a two-digit year falls. For example, if you set the epoch to 0800 and enter the year 14, then Clipper assumes you mean the year 0814. Clipper assumes a default of 1900 for the epoch setting. You may enter epoch values from 0100 to 2900.

SET ESCAPE The Set Escape command toggles the Esc key on and off. In this instance, the key still works; Clipper ignores it if the Set Escape command turns it off.

SET EXACT The Set Exact command determines how Clipper compares two character strings. When you set exact on, Clipper returns true for exact character matches of strings only. For example, the statement "1234" = "123" returns false. When you set exact off, Clipper returns true if the second string matches all or most of the first string. For example, the statement "1234" = "123" returns true, while the statement "123" = "1234" returns false.

SET EXCLUSIVE The Set Exclusive command determines how Clipper opens files for use. If you set exclusive on, Clipper opens all database and associated files for non-shared use. If you set exclusive off, Clipper allows file sharing. When you open a file for shared use on a network, you must lock each record as you need it.

SET FILTER TO The Set Filter To command provides a means of displaying a subset of all the records contained in a database. For example, the statement Set Filter To AGE > 40 lets Clipper display only those records where the field AGE is greater than 40. Using the Set Filter To command with no condition releases any previous filter conditions. This lets Clipper display all database records.

SET FIXED The Set Fixed command toggles display of numbers using the value set by the Set Decimals command. For example, if you set decimals to 2, then set fixed on, Clipper would display only two digits after the decimal point for any number. If you set fixed off, Clipper would display the actual number of digits allowed by the requesting At (@) Say/Get or other display statement.

SET FORMAT TO The Set Format To command determines which format file Clipper uses for Read commands. A format file contains a listing of At (@) Say/Get, Clear, and other display commands. Using a format file lets you reduce the amount of code needed by a program when the same display appears more than once. Clipper lets you use files with either a .PRG or a .FMT extension. In some cases, you must use a file with a .PRG extension. One of these instances is when you use the Make utility to create a program. See Appendix C for further details.

SET FUNCTION The Set Function command lets you assign a character string to a function key. Clipper recognizes 40 different function key combinations. They include the function key by itself, the function and Shift key together, the function and Alt key together, and the function and Ctrl key together. Clipper assigns each function key a number. The function keys by themselves range from 1 through 10. The Shift-function key combination ranges from 11 through 20. The Ctrl-function key combination ranges from 21 through 30. Finally, the Alt-function key combination ranges from 31 through 40.

SET INDEX TO The Set Index To command determines which index file Clipper uses with the database in the current work area. Clipper allows up to 15 indexes open at any time. You may precede the index filename with a drive and path specifier. The first index in a list of indexes is the master. Clipper uses the master to order the database. It only updates the other indexes in a list. To change the index order, use the Set Order command described below.

SET INTENSITY The Set Intensity command toggles the display of gets and prompts between the standard and enhanced color settings. By placing set intensity to on, you select the enhanced color setting.

SET KEY The Set Key command lets you assign a procedure name to a function key. Clipper assigns the same key numbers as in the Set Function command above. When the user presses the function key during any wait state (read for instance), Clipper passes the procedure name (PROCNAME( )), procedure line number (PROCLINE( )), and the current read variable/get (READVAR( )). This lets you write procedures taking these three factors into account. Clipper allows only 32 active keys at a time using this command. It automatically sets F1 to a procedure called help.

SET MARGIN TO The Set Margin To command defines the beginning column number (left margin) for all print routines. For example, if you set margin to 10 and use 10-pitch type, Clipper places the first text 1 inch from the left margin.

SET MESSAGE TO The Set Message To command determines where Clipper places messages defined as part of an At (@) Prompt command. The number determines the row number on screen (normally 0 - 24). The center clause lets you automatically center the message on the line. Using the Set Message To command without a row number suppresses the display of messages.

SET ORDER TO The Set Order To command lets you change the master index without issuing another Set Index To command. Since the Set Index To command reads the disk and this command doesn't, this command performs the function of master index selection faster. Clipper numbers the indexes from 1 through the number of open indexes in order of their appearance in the file list. If you issue the Set Order To command with a 0, Clipper sets the database back to its natural order without closing the indexes.

SET PATH TO The Set Path To command lets you change the path used to locate all files not located in the default directory. Clipper lets you provide the actual delimited path name or a variable containing the path name.

SET PRINT The Set Print command lets you turn the printer on or off. When you set print on, Clipper sends any output to both the display and the printer. Otherwise, Clipper normally sends the output to the console only.

SET PRINTER TO The Set Printer To command changes the destination for all print output. In some cases, your computer may have more than one printer or other output device attached. Each output device connects to a different computer port. By using the Set Printer To command to redirect the output to the correct port, you can use any output device attached to your computer. Clipper uses a standard output port of LPT1. Besides using actual devices, you can print to a file by replacing the output port name with a file name.

SET PROCEDURE TO The Set Procedure To command tells Clipper to include a separate procedure (.PRG) file when it compiles a program. This command is especially useful for procedures called using the Set Key command. Clipper does not automatically compile these procedure files; you must specify you want them compiled or add them during link time by using a plus sign (+) between object modules.

SET RELATION The Set Relation command lets you link two or more database files together using a specific indexed field. For example, if you had two database files — one had the family name and information, the other had individual family members — you could link the two databases together using the last name. This way each time you changed to a different individual family member, the family name information would change accordingly without any additional commands. The additive clause lets you specify more than one relation. When you leave out the additive clause, Clipper clears all old relations before starting a new one. Clipper allows up to eight relations per work area (eight relations per database).

The way you specify a relation is by selecting the master database (in the example above family member), then telling Clipper what field to relate to the slave database. For example, to implement the example above you would select the work area used by the family member database, then write: "set relation to LAST_NAME into Family_Name."

SET SCOREBOARD The Set Scoreboard command toggles the display of messages, while in a read or memo field edit mode, on or off. If you set scoreboard off, Clipper does not display range error or insert mode messages.

SET SOFTSEEK The Set Softseek command toggles the relative seeking mode on or off. Relative seeking is where the condition in a Seek command does not match an entry in the database. Clipper places the record pointer next to the record with the next higher seek value instead of the end of file. If there is no higher seek value, Clipper places the record pointer at the end of file (last record + 1) position. For example, if you seek the value abc in a database containing abb and abd, then Clipper places the record pointer at the abd position.

SET TYPEAHEAD The Set Typeahead command defines the size keyboard buffer Clipper allocates. You can specify a number from 0 to 32,767 bytes. Each byte holds one character. Using a large typeahead buffer compensates for the typing speed of trained personnel. Unfortunately, it reduces the amount of memory left for code and data.

SET UNIQUE The Set Unique command tells Clipper to allow duplicate key field entries when off, or not to allow duplicate entries when on. By ensuring each key field entry contains unique information, you reduce the chance of duplicate database entries.

SET WRAP The Set Wrap command toggles end of menu wrapping for menus. In other words, when the cursor appears at the end of a light-bar menu, Clipper normally keeps it there when you press the Down Arrow. If you set wrap on, pressing the Down Arrow selects the first menu entry.

APPLICATIONS

Use the Set commands as described above to change the way Clipper operates. By optimizing the program environment, you can reduce the amount of code required to produce an application and reduce frustration using the program. For example, allowing a softseek in some applications, such as a mailing list database, will reduce frustration produced by misspelling a word. In other applications it will increase frustration because the user is never sure if the item exists or not. Frustration increases if the user does not want the record changed if no match exists; for example, an accounting program using account numbers as the key field.

The Set commands are unique because they directly affect Clipper rather than program execution. Successful program implementation often depends on correct settings for these commands. In some cases, it is better to let the user manipulate the Set command settings. Some Set commands reflect personal taste. For example, the Set Color command does not really affect program operation. Instead, it changes the appearance of the program.

TYPICAL OPERATION

In this example you begin to enhance program operation using a series of Set commands. Begin this example in your word processor with MAILLIST.PRG loaded.

1. Add the following text after the program variables at the beginning of the program.

```
DB_NAME = 'Y'
* Setup program defaults.
set softseek on
set wrap on
* Clear the display and prepare the database for use.
```

2. Add the following text after the begin processing loop note.

```
* Display the editing screen.

@ 01, 00, 24, 79 box DOUBLE_LINE
@ 20, 01 to 20, 78
set color to N/W,W+/N
@ 21, 01 clear to 23, 78
```

3. Add the following text before the first edit area At (@) Say command.

```
endcase
set color to W/N,N/W,,,W+/N
* Display the edit area.
@ 04, 06 say` 'Name:'
```

4. Add the following text between the Save Screen command and the At (@) Clear To command in the edit menu section.

```
save screen
set message to 22 center
@ 03, 04 clear to 11, 11
```

5. Save the document and exit your word processor. Type **CL MAILLIST** at the DOS prompt. Press **Enter**.

6. Type **MAILLIST**. Press **Enter**. Notice the program now displays help messages centered in the second line of the message area. Also see how the difference in color makes different parts of the application stand out.

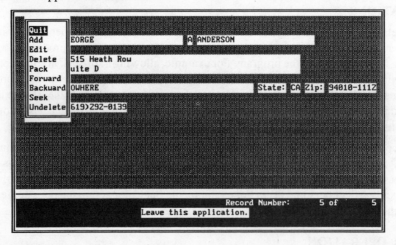

7. Press **Down Arrow** eleven times. Notice the cursor wraps around to the beginning of the menu.

8. Press **Enter**. The edit display appears. Notice how the selected get appears in a different color than the rest of the gets.

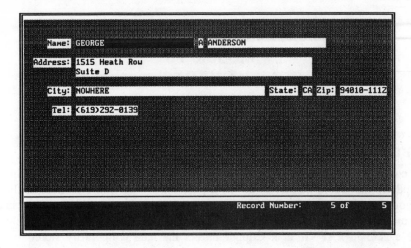

9. Press **Esc**. The menu reappears.

10. Type **S** to execute the seek option. Type **D** and press **Enter**. Notice the program now finds the first record after the requested name instead of going to the end of the file.

11. Type **Q**. The DOS prompt appears.

12. Turn to Module 117 to continue the learning sequence.

Module 78
SKIP

DESCRIPTION

The Skip command lets you move from one record to the next. Each time you skip a record, Clipper updates the record pointer to the next position. By placing a number in the EXPN1 variable, you can skip more than one record at a time. If you place a positive number in EXPN1, Clipper moves the record pointer forward. A negative number moves the record pointer back. If you place a zero in EXPN1, then Clipper moves the data temporarily stored in RAM to permanent storage on disk. The command line interface of the Skip command appears below.

```
SKIP [EXPN1] [ALIAS <ALIAS>/<EXPN2>]
```

The alias clause lets you skip records in a database other than the one in the current work area. Clipper allows you to use the database alias or the work area number as identifiers.

APPLICATIONS

Use the Skip command to move between records in a database. When used in conjunction with a database editor, you normally move only one record forward or backward. If you use the skip command with a database browse program, you can skip the number of record browsed to simulate a page up/page down function. You also use the Skip command in print routines to move from beginning to end of the database, since the print command normally works on the current record only.

TYPICAL OPERATION

In this example you add the capability to move from one record to the next using the Skip command. Begin this example in your word processor with MAILLIST.PRG loaded.

1. Change the menu prompt as shown below.
   ```
   @ 22, 04 say 'Quit/Add Record/Edit Record/Delete Record' +;
      '/Pack/Forward/Backward' get ANSWER picture '!'
   ```

2. Add the text below between the Pack command and the endif appearing at the end of the program.
   ```
       pack
   * Move forward one record.
   elseif ANSWER = 'F'
       skip
   * Move backward one record.
   elseif ANSWER = 'B'
       skip -1
   endif
   ```

3. Add the text below between the last display area @ Say command and the menu prompt as shown.

```
@ 11, 07 say 'Tel:'
@ 04, 12 say FIRST_NAME picture '@!'
@ 04, 38 say MIDDLE picture '!'
@ 04, 40 say LAST_NAME picture '@!'
@ 06, 12 say ADDRESS1
@ 07, 12 say ADDRESS2
@ 09, 12 say CITY picture '@!'
@ 09, 60 say STATE picture '!!'
@ 09, 68 say ZIP picture '99999-9999'
@ 11, 12 say TELEPHONE picture '(999)999-9999'
* Get user choice.
@ 22, 04 say 'Quit/Add Record/Edit Record/Delete Record' +;
    '/Pack/Forward/Backward' get ANSWER picture '!'
```

4. Save the document and exit your word processor. Type **CL MAILLIST** at the DOS prompt. Press **Enter**.

5. Type **MAILLIST**. Press **Enter**. Notice the program now places the field data on screen.

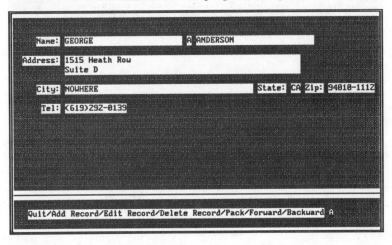

6. Type **F**. The next record appears.

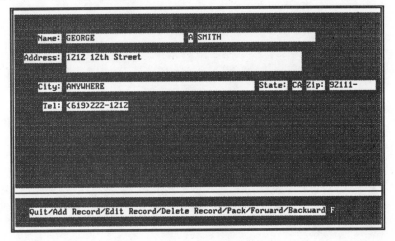

7. Type **F** four times. The end of file record appears (no data displayed in the fields).

8. Type **B**. The last record in the database appears.

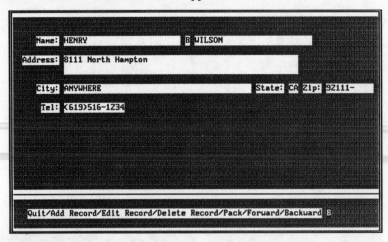

9. Type **B** four times to select the first record in the database. Type **B**. The record does not change.

10. Type **Q** to exit to DOS.

11. Turn to Module 75 to continue the learning sequence.

Module 79
SORT

DESCRIPTION

The Sort command physically reorders a database using the specified parameters. Unlike the Index On command, the Sort command does not create an index file. Instead, it sorts the contents of the database with no index files open. The Sort command places the sorted database in a different file from the original. The command line interface of the Sort command appears below.

```
SORT [<SCOPE>] ON <FIELD1> [/A] [/C] [/D] [, <FIELD2> [/A] [/C] [/D]] ...
TO <FILE>/(<EXPC>) [FOR <CONDITION>] [WHILE <CONDITION>]
```

The fields clause determines which fields the Sort command uses as a key for reordering. In this case, Sort uses the fields in place of the expression used by Index On. You may not use functions within the argument of a Sort command. Clipper allows field names only. This means that if you want to use macro (&) expansions, you must create a program structure to support them. Clipper does provide three modifiers for the fields used as a sort key. The /A modifier tells Clipper to place the field values in ascending order. This is the standard method used by Clipper. The /C modifier tells Clipper to ignore case when sorting. Normally, Clipper views "a" differently from "A." The /D modifier tells Clipper to place the field values in descending order.

The TO FILE/EXPC clause specifies where the Sort command sends the result. If you do not specify an extension for the new database, Clipper automatically adds the .DBF extension.

APPLICATIONS

Use the Sort command to reorder a database using specific criteria. This is a convenient method of performing a clean-up on the database and associated indexes. Even using indexes, the access time for database searches increases as the database becomes larger and more disorganized. This is a result of the number of hard disk accesses required to obtain information. The program must ask the hard disk for information more often when using a disorganized database. Using the Sort command to reorder the database and then creating a new index decreases the time spent searching. Never use Sort in a networking situation without first locking all other database users out (see Set Exclusive On, Module 77 and FLock( ), Module 108).

TYPICAL OPERATION

In this example you create a sorted version of the checkbook database using the Sort command. Notice that since the Sort command does not accept expressions, the method of using variable fields is different from the Index command. Begin this example in your word processor with CHCKBOOK.PRG loaded.

1. Add the following text to the SORT_REC procedure.
```
private VARA, VARB, VARC, VARD, VARE, VARF, NUM
declare NAME_ARRAY[7]
NAME_ARRAY[1] = 'Quit'
```

```
        NAME_ARRAY[2] = 'Date'
        NAME_ARRAY[3] = 'Check Number'
        NAME_ARRAY[4] = 'Drawn For'
        NAME_ARRAY[5] = 'Check Amount'
        NAME_ARRAY[6] = 'Deposit Amount'
        NAME_ARRAY[7] = 'Tax Ded. Item'
        declare AVAIL_ARRAY[7]
        afill(AVAIL_ARRAY, .T.)
        declare ORDER_ARRAY[2]
        ORDER_ARRAY[1] = 'Ascending Order'
        ORDER_ARRAY[2] = 'Descending Order'
        SORT_STRING = ' '
        TEMP_STRING = ' '
        SORT_SELECT = 2
        ORDER_SELECT = 1
        PREV_LEN = 1
        VARA = ' '
        VARB = ' '
        VARC = ' '
        VARD = ' '
        VARE = ' '
        VARF = ' '
        NUM = 'A'
        * Keep adding parameters to the sort string until the user
        * quits the sort menu.
        set color to 'N/W,W/N,,,W+/N'
        do while .not. NAME_ARRAY[SORT_SELECT] = 'Quit'
           @ 06, 06 to 14, 21 double
           SORT_SELECT = achoice(07, 07, 13, 20, NAME_ARRAY, AVAIL_ARRAY)
           do case
              case NAME_ARRAY[SORT_SELECT] = 'Date'
                 SORT_STRING = ltrim(SORT_STRING) + 'DTOS(DATE) + '
                 VAR&NUM = 'DATE'
                 NUM = chr(asc(NUM) + 1)
                 AVAIL_ARRAY[SORT_SELECT] = .F.
              case NAME_ARRAY[SORT_SELECT] = 'Check Number'
                 SORT_STRING = ltrim(SORT_STRING) + 'STR(CHECK_NUM,5,0) + '
                 VAR&NUM = 'CHECK_NUM'
                 NUM = chr(asc(NUM) + 1)
                 AVAIL_ARRAY[SORT_SELECT] = .F.
              case NAME_ARRAY[SORT_SELECT] = 'Drawn For'
                 SORT_STRING = ltrim(SORT_STRING) + 'DRAWN_FOR + '
                 VAR&NUM = 'DRAWN_FOR'
                 NUM = chr(asc(NUM) + 1)
                 AVAIL_ARRAY[SORT_SELECT] = .F.
              case NAME_ARRAY[SORT_SELECT] = 'Check Amount'
                 SORT_STRING = ltrim(SORT_STRING) + 'STR(AMOUNT,10,2) + '
                 VAR&NUM = 'AMOUNT'
                 NUM = chr(asc(NUM) + 1)
                 AVAIL_ARRAY[SORT_SELECT] = .F.
              case NAME_ARRAY[SORT_SELECT] = 'Deposit Amount'
                 SORT_STRING = ltrim(SORT_STRING) + 'STR(DEPOSIT,10,2) + '
                 VAR&NUM = 'DEPOSIT'
                 NUM = chr(asc(NUM) + 1)
                 AVAIL_ARRAY[SORT_SELECT] = .F.
              case NAME_ARRAY[SORT_SELECT] = 'Tax Ded. Item'
                 SORT_STRING = ltrim(SORT_STRING) + 'TAX_ITEM + '
                 VAR&NUM = 'TAX_ITEM'
                 NUM = chr(asc(NUM) + 1)
                 AVAIL_ARRAY[SORT_SELECT] = .F.
           endcase
        * If the user selects quit, exit the loop.
           if NAME_ARRAY[SORT_SELECT] = 'Quit'
```

```
            exit
        endif
* Ask the user to select between ascending and descending order.
        save screen to TEMP_SCRN
        set color to 'W/N,N/W,,,W+/N'
        @ 12, 12 to 15, 29 double
        ORDER_SELECT = achoice(13, 13, 14, 28, ORDER_ARRAY)
* Change the SORT_STRING variable to match the descending
* order requirement.
        if ORDER_ARRAY[ORDER_SELECT] = 'Descending Order'
            TEMP_STRING = substr(SORT_STRING, PREV_LEN, len(SORT_STRING) - ;
                PREV_LEN - 2)
            if PREV_LEN = 1
                SORT_STRING = ''
            else
                SORT_STRING = substr(SORT_STRING, 1, PREV_LEN)
            endif
            SORT_STRING = SORT_STRING + 'DESCEND(' + TEMP_STRING + ') + '
        endif
        restore screen from TEMP_SCRN
        set color to 'N/W,W/N,,,W+/N'
* Set PREV_LEN to the new length of SORT_STRING for use with the
* descending order function.
        PREV_LEN = len(SORT_STRING)
enddo
* Trim the last plus sign from the end of SORT_STRING.
SORT_STRING = substr(SORT_STRING, 1, len(SORT_STRING) - 3)
* Sort the database.
do case
    case NUM = 'B'
        sort on &VARA to TEMPDATA
    case NUM = 'C'
        sort on &VARA, &VARB to TEMPDATA
    case NUM = 'D'
        sort on &VARA, &VARB, &VARC to TEMPDATA
    case NUM = 'E'
        sort on &VARA, &VARB, &VARC, &VARD to TEMPDATA
    case NUM = 'F'
        sort on &VARA, &VARB, &VARC, &VARD, &VARE to TEMPDATA
    case NUM = 'G'
        sort on &VARA, &VARB, &VARC, &VARD, &VARE, &VARF to TEMPDATA
endcase
```

2. Save the document and exit your word processor. Type **CL CHCKBOOK** at the DOS prompt. Press **Enter**.

3. Type **MAILLIST**. Press **Enter**. The mailing list program menu appears.

4. Press **F4** to select the checkbook program. Press **Down Arrow** until the Sort option of the menu appears. Press **Enter**. The Sort menu appears.

5. Select Drawn For by pressing **Down Arrow** three times. Press **Enter**. Select Ascending by pressing **Enter**. The program returns the selector to the quit option on the first menu.

6. Select Date by pressing **Down Arrow**. Press **Enter**. Select Ascending by pressing **Enter**. Select Quit by pressing **Enter**. The program sorts the database and displays the sorted version on screen.

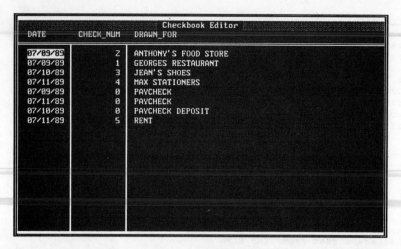

7. Press **Esc** to return to the checkbook program menu. Type **Q** to select quit. Press **Enter**. The DOS prompt appears.

8. Type **DBU TEMPDATA**. Press **Enter**. The DBU edit display appears with TEMPDATA shown in the browse mode. Notice the database appears sorted the same as the edit display in the program without using an index.

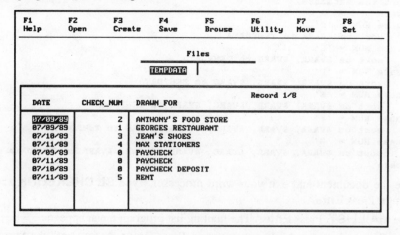

9. Press **Esc** twice. Type **Y** when asked if you want to exit DBU. The DOS prompt appears.

10. Turn to Module 64 to continue the learning sequence.

Module 80
STORE

DESCRIPTION

The Store command lets you place a value in one or more memory variables. In essence, it works the same as the equals (=) sign on variables. The advantage in using the Store command is that you can initialize more than one variable using a single line of code. The EXP clause contains the value you want to place in the memory variables. The MEMVAR LIST clause contains a list of memory variables to initialize. The command line interface of the Store command appears below.

```
STORE <EXP> TO <MEMVAR LIST>
```

OR

```
<MEMVAR> = <EXP>
```

OR

```
<MEMVAR1> := [<MEMVAR2> := ...] <EXP>
```

When you use the Store command, be sure you reference the correct variable. If you give a memory variable the same name as a field in a database, Clipper assumes you want to use the database field unless you specify otherwise. There are two methods of telling Clipper you want to use the memory variable. The first method is using the -v option when you compile the program. When you use this option, Clipper automatically assumes all references are memory variables, not database fields. The second method is using the memory variable alias (M->).

The := (in-line assignment) operator supersedes the Store command. This operator allows you to assign the same value to any number of variables. Memvar contains the names of the variables. You set each variable equal to its predecessor until there are no more variables. Exp is the final entry. It contains the value you wish to assign to all the variables. For example, if you had two variables that you wanted to assign a zero to, you would use the command VAR1 := VAR2 := 0. There are other assignment variables described in the glossary of this book. They include the increment (++), decrement (– –), and compound assignment operators (+=, –=, *=, /=).

APPLICATIONS

Use the Store command whenever you want to change the value of one or more memory variables. The Store command is especially convenient for memory variable initialization at the beginning of a program. By using the Store command, you can reduce the number of lines of code in your program. The Store command does have the side effect of reducing the readability of your code.

TYPICAL OPERATION

In this example you use the Store command to reset the value of ANSWER when the user presses Ctrl-Break during program operation. Begin this example at the DOS prompt in the C:\CLIPPER\0022 directory.

1. Type **MAILLIST**. Press **Enter**.
2. Press **Ctrl-C**. The program displays a prompt asking if you really want to quit.
3. Type **N**. The program should take you to the Main menu. Instead, the DOS prompt appears because ANSWER still contains 1, causing the Do While control structure to end.

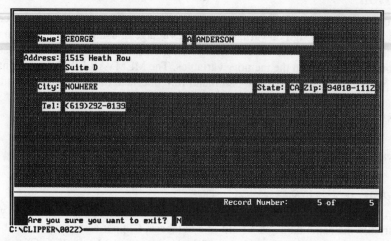

4. Loads MAILLIST.PRG in your word processor. Add the following text at the end of the program before the enddo clause.

```
endif        && Otherwise go back up and get another menu selection.
store 0 to ANSWER
enddo
```

5. Save the document and exit your word processor. Compile your program.
6. Type **MAILLIST**. Press **Enter**. The mailing list program display appears.
7. Press **Ctrl-C**. The program displays a prompt asking if you really want to quit.
8. Type **N**. The Main menu reappears.
9. Press **Ctrl-C**. Type **Y**. The DOS prompt appears.
10. Turn to Module 43 to continue the learning sequence.

Module 81
SUM

DESCRIPTION

The Sum command computes the total value of a range of database records. The command line interface of the Sum command appears below.

```
SUM [<SCOPE>] <EXP LIST> TO <MEMVAR LIST> [FOR <CONDITION>]
[WHILE <CONDITION>]
```

The scope clause allows you to specify the range of records to tally. The default scope is all. If you specify next with a number, Clipper starts adding records from the current record position, and stops when it checks the required number of records.

The EXPN TO MEMVAR clause specifies what fields to use, how to total them (math expression), and where Sum sends the result. This is the only required parameter for the Sum command.

APPLICATIONS

Use the Sum command whenever you need to find the numeric total of a group of records. This command is especially useful in statistical analysis; for example, if you recorded the time required to perform a task each time you performed it, then wanted to find the total time spent performing the task.

This command also works well with financial programs. For example, you could use this command to balance each account in a financial system, then create grand totals.

You can also use this command in custom reports. Many reports require totals at the end of a page, section, group, or end of report. The Sum command makes calculating these totals easier than using variables to track totals as the report prints.

TYPICAL OPERATION

In this example you find the sum of all the tax deductible checks, non-tax deductible checks, and deposits. You also create a new menu entry for balancing the checkbook database. Begin this example in your word processor with CHCKBOOK.PRG loaded.

1. Add/change the following text to the STATS procedure. Then, add the BALANCE procedure.

```
DEPOSITS = 0
CHCKAMT1 = 0
CHCKAMT2 = 0
DEPOSITT = 0
READY = ' '
* Get the statistics
count to TCHECKS for (TAX_ITEM = .T.) .and. (DEPOSIT = 0)
count to NTCHECKS for (TAX_ITEM = .F.) .and. (DEPOSIT = 0)
count to DEPOSITS for DEPOSIT <> 0
```

```
average AMOUNT to AVE_CHCK for AMOUNT <> 0
average DEPOSIT to AVE_DEP for DEPOSIT <> 0
sum DEPOSIT, AMOUNT to DEPOSITT, CHCKAMT1 for TAX_ITEM = .F.
sum AMOUNT to CHCKAMT2 for TAX_ITEM = .T.
* Display the statistics.
@ 12, 04 say 'Number/Amount of Tax Deductible Checks:    ' +;
   str(TCHECKS, 5, 0) + ' / ' + str(CHCKAMT2, 12, 2)
@ 13, 04 say 'Number/Amount of Non-Tax Deductible Checks: ' +;
   str(NTCHECKS, 5, 0) + ' / ' + str(CHCKAMT1, 12, 2)
@ 14, 04 say 'Number/Amount of Deposits:                  ' +;
   str(DEPOSITS, 5, 0) + ' / ' + str(DEPOSITT, 12, 2)
@ 15, 04 say 'Average Check Amount:                       ' +;
   ltrim(str(AVE_CHCK, 10, 2))
@ 16, 04 say 'Average Deposit Amount:                     ' +;
   ltrim(str(AVE_DEP, 10, 2))
@ 22, 04 say 'Press any key when ready...' get READY
read
return
procedure BALANCE
* This procedure balances the checkbook database using the
* Sum command.
* Initialize variables.
private PREV_TOTAL, NEW_TOTAL
PREV_TOTAL = 0
NEW_TOTAL = 0
* Initialize the database. Place the database in date order
* first, then check number within that date.
set index to DATE, CHCKNUM
goto top
* Perform this procedure on all records.
do while .not. eof()
   sum next 1 PREV_TOTAL + A->DEPOSIT - A->AMOUNT to NEW_TOTAL
   replace A->BALANCE with NEW_TOTAL
   PREV_TOTAL = NEW_TOTAL
   skip
enddo
* Set database back to its original status.
set index to CHCKNUM, DATE
return
```

2. Add/change the following text to the array at the beginning of the program.

```
declare MENU_ITEM[8]
MENU_ITEM[1] = 'Quit'
MENU_ITEM[2] = 'Add'
MENU_ITEM[3] = 'Delete'
MENU_ITEM[4] = 'Sort'
MENU_ITEM[5] = 'Edit'
MENU_ITEM[6] = 'Search'
MENU_ITEM[7] = 'Stats'
MENU_ITEM[8] = 'Balance'
```

3. Add the following text to the case statement at the beginning of the program.

```
         do STATS
      case MENU_ITEM[ANSWER] = 'Balance'
         do BALANCE
   endcase
```

4. Save the document and exit your word processor. Type **CL CHCKBOOK** at the DOS prompt. Press **Enter**.

5. Type **MAILLIST**. Press **Enter**. The mailing list program menu appears.

6. Press **F4**. The checkbook program menu appears. Notice the new menu entry, Balance.

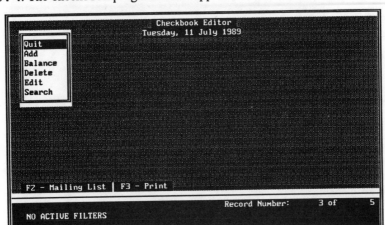

7. Press **Down Arrow** until the Stats option of the menu appears.
8. Press **Enter**. The checkbook statistics appear. Notice the statistics now include check amounts for tax deductible checks, non-tax deductible checks, and deposits.

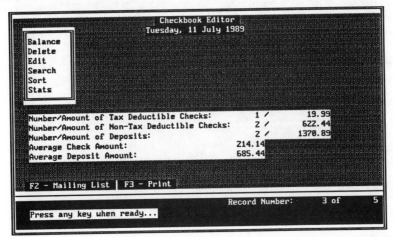

9. Press **Enter** to erase the statistics and return to the menu. Type **A** and press **Enter**. Enter the following information at the fields indicated. Type **N** when asked if you want to add any more checks. The checkbook program menu appears.

```
Date: 07/11/89
Check: 4
For: MAX STATIONERS
Amount: 12.22
Tax Item: Y
```

10. Press **Down Arrow** to select Stats. Press **Enter**. The checkbook statistics appear. Notice the statistics correctly show the addition of a tax deductible check and a different total tax deductible check amount.

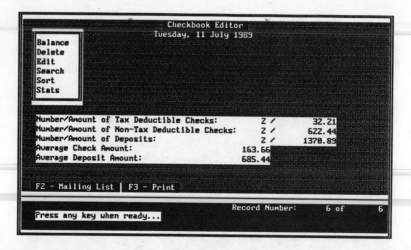

11. Press **Enter** to return to the checkbook program menu. Type **B** to select Balance and press **Enter**. Wait until the program highlights the Quit entry (balance complete). Type **E** to select Edit and press **Enter**. Press **Right Arrow** five times to display the Balance column. Notice every balance column entry contains a total.

AMOUNT	DEPOSIT	BALANCE	TAX_ITEM
0.00	550.89	550.89	F
0.00	820.00	1248.46	F
19.99	0.00	530.90	T
102.44	0.00	428.46	F
520.00	0.00	728.46	F
12.22	0.00	716.24	T

12. Press **Esc** to return to the checkbook program menu. Type **Q** to select quit. Press **Enter**. The DOS prompt appears.

13. Turn to Module 83 to continue the learning sequence.

Module 82
TEXT TO PRINT/FILE

DESCRIPTION

The Text To Print/File command lets you send text to the display, printer, and a file simultaneously. In this instance text does not refer to variables or database fields. This command allows only pure text output. The optional printer and file destinations allow you to send data more than one place using a single command. When you specify the To File clause, you must also specify a file to send the output to. Clipper does not provide a default destination. The command line interface of the Text To Print/File command appears below.

```
TEXT [TO PRINT] [TO FILE <FILE>/(<EXPC>)] <TEXT> ... ENDTEXT
```

APPLICATIONS

Use the Text To Print/File command to send data to display, printer, and a file simultaneously. One use for this command is keeping a log of critical database events. By using this command, you could send display or printer output to a file as well, allowing you to recover from a major fault with ease.

Another use for this command is help files. By using this command you can place the text on screen and allow the user to send it to a file or printer as well. Since the program overwrites the help screen before the user actually uses the help, sending the text to a printer is an excellent method of providing extended help.

TYPICAL OPERATION

In this example you output a printer test pattern to the display, printer, and a file. Begin this example in your word processor with PRINT.PRG loaded.

1. Add the following variable at the beginning of the program.

```
PRNT_PORT = 'PRN
PRNT_TEST = 'Y'
ANSWER = 'C'
```

2. Add the following text after the printer status check.

```
enddo
* Perform the printer test, if desired.
set color to N/W,W+/N
@ 22, 04 say 'Do you want to perform the printer test? ';
   get PRNT_TEST picture '!'
read
set color to W/N,N/W
if PRNT_TEST = 'Y'
   clear
   text to print
   abcdefghijklmnopqrstuvwxyz
   ABCDEFGHIJKLMNOPQRSTUVWXYZ
   1234567890
```

```
         !@#$%^&*()
         endtext
         eject
         wait
         do DISP_SCRN
      endif
      * Setup program defaults.
```

3. Remove the following text near the end of the main program.

```
* Place a last page message on the printed output before leaving this
routine.
? 'Last Page of Output.'
? 'Printed'
?? PRNT_COUNT
?? ' of '
?? reccount()
?? ' Records.'
eject
```

4. Remove the following text near the end of the main program.

```
clear
wait 'Leaving the Print Program'
```

5. Save the document and exit your word processor. Compile the program.

6. Type **PRINT**. Press **Enter**.

7. Type **LPT1**. Press **Enter**. The program asks if you want to perform the printer test.

8. Type **Y** and press **Enter**. The program clears the display and outputs the test pattern to both the printer and the display. The program automatically advances the paper to the top of the next page.

```
abcdefghijklmnopqrstuvwxyz
ABCDEFGHIJKLMNOPQRSTUVWXYZ
1234567890
!@#$%^&*()
Press any key to continue...
```

9. Press **Enter**. The program displays a record count. The DOS prompt appears.

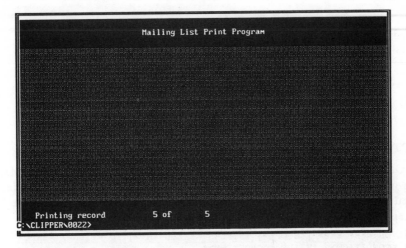

10. Type **TYPE PRINTER.TST**. Press **Enter**. DOS displays the contents of the printer test file. The printer test file contents match the test pattern.

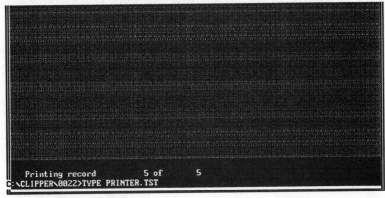

11. Turn to Module 68 to continue the learning sequence.

Module 83
TOTAL ON

DESCRIPTION

The Total On command totals the contents of numeric database fields by group. It places these totals in a new database containing all the fields of the old one. In this way it produces a summarized version of the original database. The command line interface of the Total On command appears below.

```
TOTAL ON <KEY EXP> [<SCOPE>] [FIELDS <FIELD INT>] TO <FILE>/(<EXPC>)
[FOR <CONDITION>] [WHILE <CONDITION>]
```

The KEY EXP clause determines what field or expression Total On uses to group the records as it finds them. For example, if you index or sort a financial database in date order and specify the account number as the key expression, Total On will group checks first by date, second by account number.

The fields clause determines which numeric fields Total On adds. The Total On command will not add expressions, only fields. For example, if you had two fields — one called disbursements, the other credits — and specified both fields using the field clause, the Total On command would produce two totals. If you do not specify a fields clause, each numeric field contains the values of the first record matching the key expression instead of a total.

The TO FILE/EXPC clause specifies where the Total On command sends the result. If you do not specify an extension for the new database, Clipper automatically adds the .DBF extension.

APPLICATIONS

Use the Total On command to produce summarized databases for reports, security reasons, and ease in transmitting. If you want to produce a summary report, using the Total On command often produces results more quickly than any other method. By placing these results in a database, you can reorder the information without a time penalty at print time. For example, if you needed the same summary in two different orders, you would save time on the second report since the computer would not compute the totals a second time.

If you wanted to send another department in your organization the bottom line figures for a sales campaign but not reveal the sources of those numbers, you could use the Total On command to quickly produce a summary database. By providing the information in this format, you eliminate the risk of disclosing proprietary information without reducing the flexibility.

If an office in another area required the totals for a given months sales, you could use the Total On command to produce a summary database. The time required to transmit the summary database is less since it consumes less memory.

TYPICAL OPERATION

In the example you use the Total On command to produce a summary database. Begin this example in your word processor with CHCKBOOK.PRG loaded.

1. Add/change the following text to the BALANCE procedure.

```
enddo
* Create a summary report.
total on DATE fields DEPOSIT, AMOUNT to SUMMARY
use SUMMARY
replace all DRAWN_FOR with 'DATE TOTALS'
goto top
PREV_TOTAL = 0
do while .not. eof()
   replace BALANCE with PREV_TOTAL + DEPOSIT - AMOUNT
   PREV_TOTAL = BALANCE
   skip
enddo
* Set database back to its original status.
use CHCKBOOK index CHCKNUM, DATE
```

2. Save the document and exit your word processor. Type **CL CHCKBOOK** at the DOS prompt. Press **Enter**.

3. Type **MAILLIST**. Press **Enter**. The mailing list program menu appears.

4. Press **F4**. The checkbook program menu appears.

5. Type **B** to select Balance and press **Enter**. Wait until the program highlights the Quit entry (balance complete). Type **Q** to select quit. Press **Enter**. The DOS prompt appears.

6. Type **DBU SUMMARY** and press **Enter**. The DBU utility displays the summary database. Notice the database contains one entry for each date.

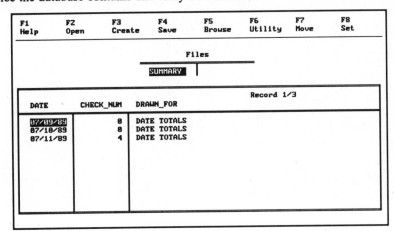

7. Press **Right Arrow** five times. DBU displays the Amount, Deposit, and Balance fields. Notice the Balance field contains the correct total for each entry (yesterday's total, plus today's deposits, minus today's withdrawals).

```
F1        F2        F3        F4        F5        F6        F7        F8
Help      Open      Create    Save      Browse    Utility   Move      Set
─────────────────────────────────────────────────────────────────────────
                              Files
                        ┌─────────┐
                        │ SUMMARY │
                        └─────────┘
        ┌──────────────────────────────────────────────────────────────┐
        │                                       Record 1/3              │
        │     AMOUNT      DEPOSIT      BALANCE       TAX_ITEM            │
        │─────────────────────────────────────────────────────────────│
        │     122.43      550.89     ▐ 428.46▌        F                │
        │     520.00      820.00       728.46         F                │
        │      12.22        0.00       716.24         T                │
        │                                                               │
        │                                                               │
        │                                                               │
        │                                                               │
        │                                                               │
        │                                                               │
        └──────────────────────────────────────────────────────────────┘
```

8. Press **Esc** twice then type **Y** to exit DBU. The DOS prompt appears.

9. Turn to Module 115 to continue the learning sequence.

Module 84
TYPE TO PRINT/FILE

DESCRIPTION

The Type To Print/File command lets you send the contents of any file to the display, printer, and/or a file. Clipper allows you to send the contents to any combination of outputs. It always sends the output to the display unless you use the Set Console Off command to turn the display off. Unlike other file display commands provided by Clipper, this command sends the entire contents of a file to the desired output. This includes any control characters embedded within the file. You cannot stop the display by pressing Esc as usual. To stop the display momentarily, type Ctrl-S instead. FILE1.EXT1/EXPC1 contains the name of the file to type. The to print clause tells Clipper to send the output to the printer. The to file clause sends the output to a file. FILE1.EXT1/EXPC1 contains the name of the output file. The command line interface of the Type To Print/File command appears below.

```
TYPE <FILE1>.<EXT1>/(<EXPC1>) [TO PRINT] [TO FILE <FILE2>.<EXT2>/(<EXPC2>)]
```

APPLICATIONS

Use the Type To Print/File command whenever you need to display the exact unformatted contents of a file. This is useful for two types of display. First, you can use this command to display ASCII text files. Since Clipper also displays the control characters, you can partially format the file before displaying it. This is useful for displaying screens using the extended line-draw characters at the beginning of a program.

Second, you can also use this command to display files with control codes. This is especially useful within debug routines or programmer tool boxes. By knowing the control characters within a file, you can see why and how a program performs certain tasks.

TYPICAL OPERATION

In this example you add the capability to display ASCII or other files to screen, print, or a file using the Type To Print/File command. Begin this example in your word processor with DOSSHELL.PRG loaded.

1. Add the following text to the beginning of the program.

```
declare MENU_ARRAY[5]
MENU_ARRAY[1] = 'Quit'
MENU_ARRAY[2] = 'Dos Shell'
MENU_ARRAY[3] = 'Show Records'
MENU_ARRAY[4] = 'Consolidate Checks'
MENU_ARRAY[5] = 'Type Text File'
SELECT = 2
* Save the display.
save screen to TEMP2
* Get the user selection.
do while MENU_ARRAY[SELECT] <> 'Quit'
```

```
@ 03, 39 clear to 08, 58
@ 03, 39 to 08, 58 double
SELECT = achoice(04, 40, 07, 57, MENU_ARRAY)
do case
   case MENU_ARRAY[SELECT] = 'Dos Shell'
      do DOS_SHELL
   case MENU_ARRAY[SELECT] = 'Show Records'
      do SHOW_RECS
   case MENU_ARRAY[SELECT] = 'Consolidate Checks'
      do CONSOLIDATE
   case MENU_ARRAY[SELECT] = 'Type Text File'
      do TYPE_FILE
```

2. Add the following procedure to the end of the procedure section of the program.

```
procedure TYPE_FILE
* This procedure accepts any filename as input and sends its contents
* to the display, printer, a file, or any combination of the three as
* output.
* Declare the variables.
DIR_ENTRIES = 0
DIR_CHOICE = 2
FILE_NAME = space(12)
OUT_SELECT = 2
OUT_FILE = space(12)
DO_SCREEN = .F.
DO_PRINT = .F.
DO_FILE = .F.
save screen to TYPE1
* Get the user's text file selection.
DIR_ENTRIES = adir('*.*')
declare DIR_ARRAY[DIR_ENTRIES]
adir('*.*', DIR_ARRAY)
asort(DIR_ARRAY)
@ 05, 47 clear to 13, 61
@ 05, 47 to 13, 61 double
DIR_CHOICE = achoice(06, 48, 12, 60, DIR_ARRAY)
FILE_NAME = DIR_ARRAY[DIR_CHOICE]
* Get the user's output selection
declare OUT_ARRAY[4]
OUT_ARRAY[1] = 'Quit'
OUT_ARRAY[2] = 'Display'
OUT_ARRAY[3] = 'Printer'
OUT_ARRAY[4] = 'File'
do while OUT_ARRAY[OUT_SELECT] <> 'Quit'
   @ 09, 54 clear to 14, 62
   @ 09, 54 to 14, 62 double
   OUT_SELECT = achoice(10, 55, 13, 61, OUT_ARRAY)
   do case
      case OUT_ARRAY[OUT_SELECT] = 'Display'
         DO_SCREEN = .T.
      case OUT_ARRAY[OUT_SELECT] = 'Printer'
         DO_PRINT = .T.
      case OUT_ARRAY[OUT_SELECT] = 'File'
         DO_FILE = .T.
         @ 17, 40 say 'Output Filename: ' get OUT_FILE
         read
      endcase
enddo
* Output the file.
if .not. DO_SCREEN
   set console off
endif
clear screen
```

```
do case
   case DO_PRINT .and. .not. DO_FILE
      type &FILE_NAME to print
   case .not. DO_PRINT .and. DO_FILE
      type &FILE_NAME to file &OUT_FILE
   case DO_PRINT .and. DO_FILE
      type &FILE_NAME to print
   otherwise
      type &FILE_NAME
endcase
set console on
if DO_SCREEN
   wait
endif
restore screen from TYPE1
return
```

3. Save the document and exit your word processor. Type **CL DOSSHELL** at the DOS prompt. Press **Enter**.

4. Type **MAILLIST** and press **Enter**. The mailing list program menu appears.

5. Press **F10** to activate the DOS shell menu. Press **T**. A new menu entry appears.

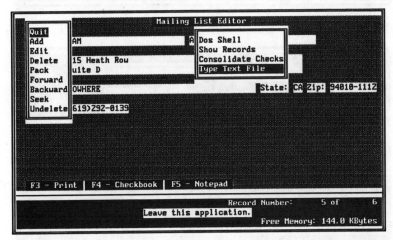

6. Press **Enter**. The program displays a directory of files in the current directory.

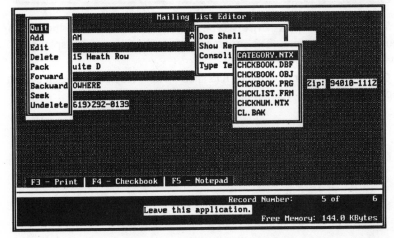

7. Select CL.BAT by pressing **Down Arrow**. Press **Enter** to select the file. The program displays another menu asking where to send the output.

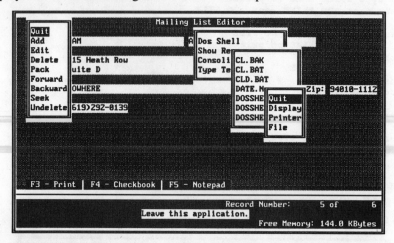

8. Type **F** and press **Enter** to select file. The program asks which file to send the output to.

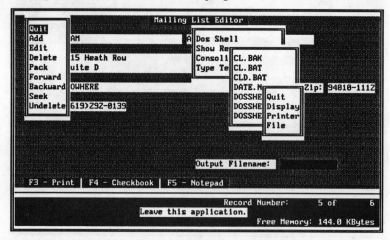

9. Type **TEMP.TXT** and press **Enter**. Type **Q** and press **Enter** when the program displays the output selection menu. The program outputs the file and redisplays the DOS shell menu.

10. Type **Q** and press **Enter** to quit the DOS shell menu. Press **Enter** to select Quit. The DOS prompt appears.

11. Type **TYPE TEMP.TXT** and press **Enter**. DOS displays TEMP.TXT.

```
C:\CLIPPER\0022>TYPE TEMP.TXT

CLS
Clipper %1
IF NOT ERRORLEVEL 1 Plink86 FI MAILLIST, PRINT, CHCKBOOK, NOTEPAD, HELP, DOSSHEL
L LIB \CLIPPER\CLIPPER, \CLIPPER\EXTEND
C:\CLIPPER\0022>
```

12. Turn to Module 110 to continue the learning sequence.

Module 85
UNLOCK

DESCRIPTION

The Unlock command releases any file or record locks for the current work station. The all clause determines if Clipper releases the locks in the current work area or all work areas. When you specify the all clause, Clipper removes the locks in all work areas. The command line interface of the Unlock command appears below.

```
UNLOCK [ALL]
```

APPLICATIONS

Use the Unlock command when you want to release the database locks initiated by the current work station. A work station may not release locks created by another work station. Normally you use this command when you complete all modifications to a database.

TYPICAL OPERATION

In this example you see the effect of using the Unlock command on a file lock and a record lock. This example works with both networked and stand-alone machines. However, you can see the effect of the Unlock command better when using a networked machine. Begin this example at the DOS prompt.

1. Type **NETWORK MAILLIST** and press **Enter**. Type **N** when asked if you want to open the database for exclusive use. The network menu appears. Notice the program automatically opens the MAILLIST database for shared use.

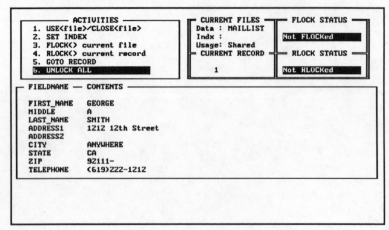

2. Type **3**. The program displays MAILLIST FLOCKed.
3. Type **6**. The program displays Not FLOCKed.
4. Type **4**. The program displays Rec 1 RLOCKed.
5. Type **6**. The program displays Not RLOCKed.
6. Press **Esc**. The DOS prompt appears.
7. Turn to Module 89 to continue the learning sequence.

Module 86
UPDATE ON

DESCRIPTION

The Update On command lets you update the contents of the current database with the contents of another database. The command line interface of the Update On command appears below.

```
UPDATE ON <KEY EXP> FROM <ALIAS>/(<EXPC>) REPLACE <FIELD1> WITH <EXP1>
[, <FIELD2> WITH <EXP2>] ... [RANDOM]
```

The KEY EXP clause contains an expression composed of fields, functions, and operators. In most cases this field contains the same key as the index used to order the database. If you use a sorted database in place of an indexed database, the key normally contains the same key used to sort the database. Both the source and destination databases must use the same key. The source database must contain only a single instance of each key. The destination database may contain more than one instance of each key.

The ALIAS/EXPC clause contains the name of the source database. The destination database in this case is the one in the current work area. The source database is an unopened database on disk. In network situations, open both the source and destination databases using the Set Exclusive On command.

The FIELD clause contains the name of the destination database to replace with EXP. EXP may contain any field, function, or equation desired. Normally EXP contains fields from the source database. Otherwise, you could update the destination database using the Replace command.

The random clause allows you to use an unindexed source database. Clipper looks throughout the entire source database for the key used to order the destination database. When using this clause, the destination database must use an index. This clause greatly reduces the speed of updating, especially when the destination database contains many records. Therefore, use this clause with caution.

APPLICATIONS

Use the Update On command when you need to update a secondary, composite, or backup database using the database normally altered by the user. This provides a method of ensuring all databases contain the same information without requiring the user to make multiple entries.

You can also use this command when one database contains a mathematic equivalent of another database. For example, if one database contains the total amount owed by a customer and another database contains the purchases made by the customer, you could use the Update On command to automatically update the total owed.

TYPICAL OPERATION

In this example you simplify the previously created composite database by eliminating the redundant records. Then you update the amount field to show the total of all checks written to that person using the Update On command. Begin this example in your word processor with DOSSHELL.PRG loaded.

1. Add the following text to the end of the CONSOLIDATE procedure.

```
A->ADDRESS2, A->CITY, A->STATE, A->ZIP, A->TELEPHONE
* Eliminate any redundant records.
select A
use TEMP_DAT
index on DRAWN_FOR to TEMP
goto top
do while .not. eof()
   OLD_NAME = DRAWN_FOR
   skip
   if OLD_NAME = DRAWN_FOR
      delete
   endif
enddo
pack
* Update the composite database using CHCKBOOK.
goto top
replace all AMOUNT with 0
update on DRAWN_FOR from CHCKBOOK replace A->AMOUNT with A->AMOUNT + ;
   B-> AMOUNT random
return
```

2. Save the document and exit your word processor. Type **CL DOSSHELL** at the DOS prompt. Press **Enter**.

3. Type **MAILLIST** and press **Enter**. The mailing list program menu appears.

4. Press **F10**. The DOS shell menu appears.

5. Select Consolidate Checks by typing **C** and pressing **Enter**.

6. Type **Q** and press **Enter** to quit the DOS shell menu. Press **Enter** to select Quit. The DOS prompt appears.

7. Type **DBU TEMP_DAT** and press **Enter**. The DBU browse display appears. Notice the combined database contains no redundant records.

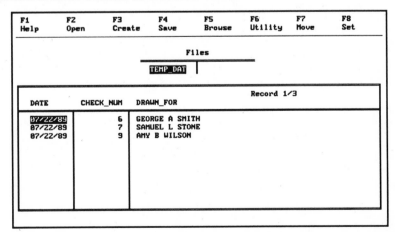

8. Press **Left Arrow** three times. The Amount field appears. Notice the column represents the total of all previously written checks for that particular person.

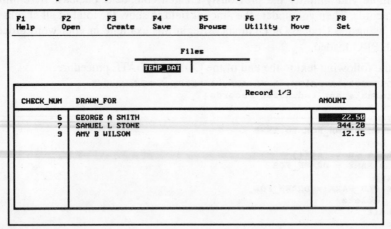

F1	F2	F3	F4	F5	F6	F7	F8
Help	Open	Create	Save	Browse	Utility	Move	Set

Files

TEMP_DAT

Record 1/3

CHECK_NUM	DRAWN_FOR	AMOUNT
6	GEORGE A SMITH	22.50
7	SAMUEL L STONE	344.20
9	AMY B WILSON	12.15

9. Press **Esc** twice and answer **Y** when asked if you want to leave DBU. The DOS prompt appears.

10. Turn to Module 84 to continue the learning sequence.

Module 87
USE

DESCRIPTION

The Use command opens a database and its associated index files. When using the command in a network environment, you can open the file for use by one person only. You can also assign the database an alias, a name to call it within your program. The Use command is one of the few commands, used in every program, which produces a visual effect only when absent. When you don't see anything happen, the Use command executed correctly; otherwise, Clipper displays an error message. The command line interface of the Use command appears below.

```
USE [<FILE>/(<EXPC1>)] [INDEX <FILE LIST>/(<EXPC2>) [,(<EXPC3>)]...]
[EXCLUSIVE] [ALIAS <ALIAS>]
```

The database filename appears after the use clause in the command line interface. You may use the actual database filename, or place the database filename in a variable. If you don't specify a filename, Clipper closes the database in the current work area.

The index clause lets you open one or more indexes associated with the database. As with the database filename, you may specify the filename itself, or use a variable to hold the database filename. You must specify a filename when using the index clause.

The exclusive clause lets you open the database for the private use of the requesting terminal on a network. If you don't specify the exclusive clause, Clipper will allow other terminals to access the database. Clipper denies requests for exclusive use of a database when another terminal is using it. The shared clause specifically opens the database for use with other terminals. When you open a database in shared mode on a network, the application must use locks to make sure the database does not lose integrity. If you open a database without specifying either the exclusive or shared clauses, Clipper uses the value set using the Set Exclusive command.

The alias clause lets you tell Clipper what to call the database within your program. If you do not specify an alias, Clipper automatically uses the database filename as a reference.

The new clause opens the database in the next available work area. If you do not specify this clause, Clipper opens the database in the current work area. It automatically closes any previously opened database in the current work area.

The readonly clause lets you open a database for reading purposes only. Clipper will not allow you to modify the contents of the database. This also lets you open databases with the readonly attribute set. If you try to open a readonly database without using this clause, Clipper generates an error message.

APPLICATIONS

Employ the Use command when you want to open a database. You can reduce program execution time by simultaneously opening any associated indexes using the index clause. Both the use and index clauses let you specify either an actual filename, or a variable containing a filename. Using a variable provides a method of opening a database when you don't know the database name during program conception. For example, you could create a generic program to create database indexes. By using a variable, you could ask the user for a database filename, then open the database without actually knowing what the user would input.

The exclusive clause lets you open a database for an individual terminal's use. For example, if you needed to sort or reindex the database, the exclusive clause would prevent other terminals from interfering.

The alias clause lets you use a generic name for a database. One instance where the alias clause is especially useful is in generic procedures. By using a variable to open the database and an alias to refer to it throughout your code, you need not know the database filename in advance.

The new clause lets you open a database in a new work area without changing the current work area. This lets you save time and code. In addition, you do not need to know the location of an empty work area before opening the database.

The readonly clause can help you maintain the integrity of a database. Some examples of readonly databases include help files. There are many situations where you want the user to view the contents of a database without modifying it. This clause helps you make sure the database remains intact.

TYPICAL OPERATION

In this example you open a database by adding the Use command to the mailing list program. Begin this example at the DOS prompt in the C:\CLIPPER\0022 directory.

1. Edit MAILLIST.PRG using a word processor. Add the following text to the end of MAILLIST.PRG.
   ```
   use MAILLIST index LASTNAME
   ```
2. Press **Enter**. Save the document and exit your word processor.
3. Type **CL MAILLIST** at the DOS prompt. Press **Enter**. The Clipper batch file clears the screen, then compiles and links the program.
4. Type **MAILLIST**. Press **Enter**. The program clears the display. Notice that you cannot see Clipper opening and closing the database.
5. Turn to Module 13 to continue the learning sequence.

Module 88
WAIT

DESCRIPTION

The Wait command lets you insert a pause in the sequence of program events. The optional prompt clause lets you place a message on screen. If you don't use the prompt clause, Clipper places the message "Press any key to continue..." on screen. The optional to memvarc clause lets you place the result of the user keystroke in a variable. In this instance, the Wait command works much like the InKey( ) function. Unlike the InKey( ) function, the Wait command will not return non-printable characters. If the user presses a non-printable character (like a function key), Wait returns 0 in memvarc. The command line interface of the Wait command appears below.

```
WAIT [<PROMPT>] [TO <MEMVARC>]
```

APPLICATIONS

Use the Wait command whenever you need to place a pause in the sequence of program events. There are many instances where you can use the Wait command. For example, if you do not need user input or you need one character, then Wait consumes less memory than the @ Get command or InKey( ) function. Wait works well when you need to display a message, then need to pause while the user reads it. You cannot, however, use Wait when you need to obtain non-printable key input.

TYPICAL OPERATION

In this example you add a message to the sample program, print it, then use the Wait command to add a pause while the user reads it. Begin this example in your word processor with PRINT.PRG loaded.

1. Add the following text at the end of the main section of the sample program.
   ```
   * Close the database and exit.
   clear
   wait 'Leaving the Print Program'
   ```
2. Save the document and exit your word processor. Compile your program.
3. Type **PRINT**. Press **Enter**.
4. Type **LPT1**. Press **Enter**. The record number counts from 1 through 5. The program clears the display and prints "Leaving the Print Program."
5. Press **Enter**. The DOS prompt appears.
6. Turn to Module 58 to continue the learning sequence.

Module 89
ZAP

DESCRIPTION

The Zap command removes all records from the database in the current work area and updates any associated open index and memo files. This command works like a combination of the Delete followed by the Pack command. However, this command works much faster than using the Delete and Pack commands separately. The command line interface of the Zap command appears below.

```
ZAP
```

APPLICATIONS

Use this command when you want to empty the current database, open index files, and any associated memo files. For example, if you want to create an empty copy of a database, you could use the Copy command, open the new database, then empty it using the Zap command.

TYPICAL OPERATION

In this example you create a new copy of the current database, open it, then remove the records using the Zap command. Begin this example in your word processor with DOSSHELL.PRG loaded.

1. Add the following text to the beginning of the program.

```
declare MENU_ARRAY[7]
MENU_ARRAY[1] = 'Quit'
MENU_ARRAY[2] = 'Dos Shell'
MENU_ARRAY[3] = 'Show Records'
MENU_ARRAY[4] = 'Consolidate Checks'
MENU_ARRAY[5] = 'Type Text File'
MENU_ARRAY[6] = 'Index File Status'
MENU_ARRAY[7] = 'Copy Database'
SELECT = 2
* Save the display.
save screen to TEMP2
* Get the user selection.
do while MENU_ARRAY[SELECT] <> 'Quit'
    @ 03, 39 clear to 08, 58
    @ 03, 39 to 08, 58 double
    SELECT = achoice(04, 40, 07, 57, MENU_ARRAY)
    do case
        case MENU_ARRAY[SELECT] = 'Dos Shell'
            do DOS_SHELL
        case MENU_ARRAY[SELECT] = 'Show Records'
            do SHOW_RECS
        case MENU_ARRAY[SELECT] = 'Consolidate Checks'
            do CONSOLIDATE
        case MENU_ARRAY[SELECT] = 'Type Text File'
            do TYPE_FILE
```

```
        case MENU_ARRAY[SELECT] = 'Index File Status'
            do IFILE_STATS
        case MENU_ARRAY[SELECT] = 'Copy Database'
            do COPY_DB
```

2. Add the following procedure to the end of the procedure section of the program.

```
procedure COPY_DB
* This procedure copies the current database to a new  database,
* then removes the records from the new database.
private OLD_NAME
* Store the current database name.
OLD_NAME = alias()
* Copy the database to a new one, then zap the new one.
copy to TEMP_DAT
use TEMP_DAT
zap
* Restore the database.
use &OLD_NAME
do case
    case OLD_NAME = 'MAILLIST'
        set index to LASTNAME
    case OLD_NAME = 'CHCKBOOK'
        set index to CHCKNUM, DATE
    case OLD_NAME = 'NOTEPAD'
        set index to NOTENUM, CATEGORY, SUBJECT
endcase
return
```

3. Save the document and exit your word processor. Type **CL DOSSHELL** at the DOS prompt. Press **Enter**.

4. Type **MAILLIST** and press **Enter**. The mailing list program menu appears.

5. Press **F10** to activate the DOS shell menu. Press **C** twice. A new menu entry appears.

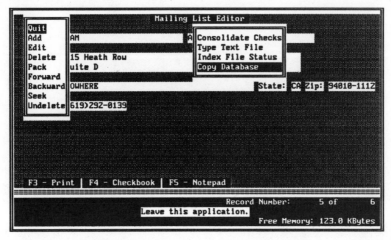

6. Press **Enter**. The program copies the current database, opens the new database, and removes the records.

7. Type **Q** and press **Enter** to quit the DOS shell menu. Press **Enter** to select Quit. The DOS prompt appears.

8. Type **DBU TEMP_DAT** and press **Enter**. The DBU browse display appears. Notice the database uses the mailing list database structure but contains no records.

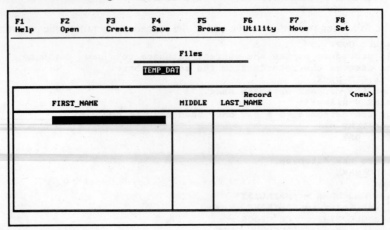

9. Press **Esc** twice. Type **Y** when asked if you want to exit DBU. The DOS prompt appears.
10. Turn to Module 17 to continue the learning sequence.

Module 90
ABS( ), EXP( ), LOG( ), MAX( ),
MIN( ), MOD( ), SQRT( )

DESCRIPTION

The ABS( ), EXP( ), LOG( ), MOD( ), and SQRT( ) functions perform calculations on numeric information. These functions output a numeric derivation of EXPN. In the case of the MOD( ) function, EXPN1 contains the dividend, while EXPN2 contains the divisor. The Clipper MOD( ) function provides compatibility with the dBase III Plus function of the same name. The MAX( ) and MIN( ) functions perform comparisons of numeric information. Both functions compare EXPN1 to EXPN2. The MIN( ) function outputs the lesser of the two numbers. The MAX( ) function outputs the greater of the two numbers. The command line interface of the ABS( ), EXP( ), LOG( ), MAX( ), MIN( ), MOD( ), and SQRT( ) functions appears below.

```
ABS(<EXPN)
EXP(<EXPN>)
LOG(<EXPN>)
MAX(<EXPN1>/<EXPD1>, <EXPN2>,<EXPD2>)
MIN(<EXPN1>/<EXPD1>, <EXPN2>,<EXPD2>)
MOD(<EXPN1>, <EXPN2>)
SQRT(<EXPN>)
```

APPLICATIONS

Use the ABS( ) function when you want to obtain the absolute of any number. What this means is any negative numbers become positive in form. This is especially useful in situations where a negative number would result in an incorrect statistical result.

Use the EXP( ) function to obtain the natural exponentiation (e^x) of a number. The natural exponentiation appears in many financial and statistical calculations to represent growth or decline.

Use the LOG( ) function to obtain the natural logarithm ($\log_e x$) of a number. The natural logarithm appears in many financial and statistical calculations to represent growth or decline.

Use the MAX( ) function to determine the greater of two numbers or dates. This is an effective method of searching a database for the largest number or latest date.

Use the MIN( ) function to determine the least of two numbers or dates. This is an effective method of searching a database for the smallest number or earliest date.

Use the MOD( ) function when you need to find the modulus (the remainder of a division) of two numbers. For example, the output of MOD(4, 3) is 1. This function provides compatibility with the dBase III Plus function of the same name. The Clipper % (modulus) operator supersedes this function.

Use the SQRT( ) function to determine the square root of a number. Many scientific, statistical, and financial equations require the square root of a number.

TYPICAL OPERATION

In this example you use the MIN( ) and MAX( ) functions to determine the smallest and largest check/deposit in the checkbook database. Begin this example in your word processor with CHCKBOOK.PRG loaded.

1. Add the following text to the STATS procedure.

```
private MIN_CHCK, AVE_CHCK, MAX_CHCK, MIN_DEP, AVE_DEP, MAX_DEP
MIN_CHCK = 9999999.99
AVE_CHCK = 0
MAX_CHCK = 0
MIN_DEP = 9999999.99
AVE_DEP = 0
MAX_DEP = 0
TCHECKS = 0
NTCHECKS = 0
DEPOSITS = 0
CHCKAMT1 = 0
CHCKAMT2 = 0
DEPOSITT = 0
READY = ' '
* Get the statistics
count to TCHECKS for (TAX_ITEM = .T.) .and. (DEPOSIT = 0)
count to NTCHECKS for (TAX_ITEM = .F.) .and. (DEPOSIT = 0)
count to DEPOSITS for DEPOSIT <> 0
average AMOUNT to AVE_CHCK for AMOUNT <> 0
average DEPOSIT to AVE_DEP for DEPOSIT <> 0
sum DEPOSIT, AMOUNT to DEPOSITT, CHCKAMT1 for TAX_ITEM = .F.
sum AMOUNT to CHCKAMT2 for TAX_ITEM = .T.
goto top
do while .not. eof()
   if AMOUNT <> 0
      MIN_CHCK = MIN(MIN_CHCK, AMOUNT)
      MAX_CHCK = MAX(MAX_CHCK, AMOUNT)
   else
      MIN_DEP = MIN(MIN_DEP, DEPOSIT)
      MAX_DEP = MAX(MAX_DEP, DEPOSIT)
   endif
   skip
enddo
* Display the statistics.
@ 12, 04 say 'Number/Amount of Tax Deductible Checks:     ' +;
   str(TCHECKS, 5, 0) + ' / ' + str(CHCKAMT2, 12, 2)
@ 13, 04 say 'Number/Amount of Non-Tax Deductible Checks: ' +;
   str(NTCHECKS, 5, 0) + ' / ' + str(CHCKAMT1, 12, 2)
@ 14, 04 say 'Number/Amount of Deposits:                  ' +;
   str(DEPOSITS, 5, 0) + ' / ' + str(DEPOSITT, 12, 2)
@ 15, 04 say 'Average Check Amount:                    $' +;
   ltrim(str(int(AVE_CHCK), 10, 0))
@ 16, 04 say 'Average Deposit Amount:                  $' +;
   ltrim(str(int(AVE_DEP), 10, 0))
@ 17, 04 say 'Minimum/Maximum Check Amount:            ' +;
   ltrim(str(MIN_CHCK, 10, 2)) + '/' + ltrim(str(MAX_CHCK, 10, 2))
@ 18, 04 SAY 'Minimum/Maximum Deposit Amount:          ' +;
   ltrim(str(MIN_DEP, 10, 2)) + '/' + ltrim(str(MAX_DEP, 10, 2))
```

2. Save the document and exit your word processor. Type **CL CHCKBOOK** at the DOS prompt. Press **Enter**.

3. Type **MAILLIST**. Press **Enter**. The mailing list program menu appears.

4. Press **F4**. The checkbook program menu appears.

5. Press **Down Arrow** until the Stats option of the menu appears.

6. Press **Enter**. The checkbook statistics appear. Notice the display now shows the minimum and maximum checks and deposits.

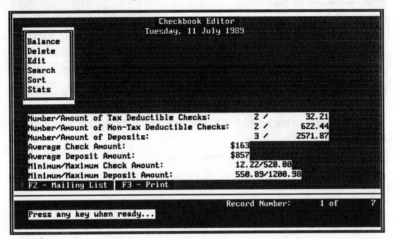

7. Press **Enter** to erase the statistics and return to the menu. Type **A** and press **Enter**. Enter the following information at the fields indicated. Type **N** when asked if you want to add any more checks. The checkbook program menu appears.

   Date: 07/11/89
   Check: 5
   For: RENT
   Amount: 1000.00
   Tax Item: Y

8. Press **Down Arrow** to select Stats. Press **Enter**. The checkbook statistics appear. Notice the statistics correctly show the addition of a tax deductible check and a different maximum check amount.

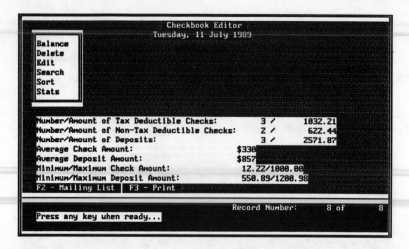

9. Press **Enter** to return to the checkbook program menu. Type **Q** to select quit. Press **Enter**. The DOS prompt appears.

10. Turn to Module 47 to continue the learning sequence.

Module 91
ACHOICE( ), AADD( ), ACLONE( ), ACOPY( ), ADEL( ), ADIR( ), AEVAL( ), AFIELDS( ), AFILL( ), AINS( ), ARRAY( ), ASCAN( ), ASIZE( ), ASORT( ), DBSTRUCT( ), DIRECTORY( )

DESCRIPTION

The AChoice( ), AAdd( ), AClone( ), ACopy( ), ADel( ), ADir( ), AEval( ), AFields( ), AFill( ), AIns( ), AScan( ), ASize( ), and ASort( ) functions allow you to manipulate arrays created using the Declare command. You may also create arrays using the AClone( ) or Array( ) functions. The DBStruct( ), and Directory( ) functions create arrays containing specialized information. The command line interface for these functions appears below.

```
ACHOICE (<EXPN1>, <EXPN2>, <EXPN3>, <EXPN4>, <ARRAY1> [, <ARRAY2> ;
[, <EXPC> [, <EXPN5> [, <EXPN6>]]]])
AADD (<ARRAY>, <EXP>)
ACLONE (<ARRAY1>)
ACOPY (<ARRAY1>, <ARRAY2> [, <EXPN1> [, <EXPN2> [, <EXPN3>]]])
ADEL (<ARRAY>, <EXPN>)
ADIR (<DIRECTORY SKELETON> [, <ARRAY1> [, <ARRAY2> [, <ARRAY3> ;
[, <ARRAY4> [, <ARRAY5>]]]]])
AEVAL (<ARRAY>, <CODE BLOCK> [, <EXPN1> [, <EXPN2>]])
AFIELDS ([<ARRAY1> [, <ARRAY2> [, <ARRAY3> [, <ARRAY4>]]]])
AFILL (<ARRAY>, <EXP> [, <EXPN1> [, <EXPN2>]])
AINS (<ARRAY>, <EXPN>)
ARRAY (<EXPN1> [, <EXPN2> ...])
ASCAN (<ARRAY>, <EXP> [, <EXPN1> [, <EXPN2>]])
ASIZE (<ARRAY>, <EXPN>)
ASORT (<ARRAY> [, <EXPN1> [, <EXPN2> [, <CODE BLOCK>]]])
DBSTRUCT()
DIRECTORY (<EXPC1> [, <EXPC2>])
```

The AChoice( ) function executes a pop-up menu using the character strings in ARRAY1. EXPN1 through EXPN4 define where the menu appears on the display. EXPN1 defines the top, EXPN2 defines the left side, EXPN3 defines the bottom, and EXPN4 defines the right side coordinates. ARRAY2 contains the same number of elements as ARRAY1. Clipper uses ARRAY2 to determine which items in ARRAY1 the user may select. If an element in ARRAY2 contains .F., then the corresponding element in ARRAY1 is not available. Likewise, if the element contains .T., then Clipper allows the user to choose the corresponding selection. You may also use character strings in place of true or false values. When you use character strings, Clipper treats them as macros and evaluates the character string for a value of true or false. EXPC contains the name of a function Clipper executes if the user presses a key not defined for use with the AChoice( ) function. Table 91-1 contains a listing of standard AChoice( ) keystrokes. A discussion of how to create advanced user-defined functions is not within the scope of this book. Refer to Module 44 for a discussion of how to create functions using the Function command.

EXPN5 contains a number which Clipper uses to select the initially highlighted item. For example, if EXPN5 contains 2, then Clipper highlights element 2 of ARRAY1. EXPN6 contains an offset for the first item appearing in the menu window. For example, if ARRAY1 contains 10 items, the window contains room to display 6, and EXPN6 contains 3, then the first menu item displayed at the top of the menu window is element 3 of ARRAY1. To get to menu items 1 and 2 you have to scroll up.

Table 91-1. Standard ACHOICE( ) Keystrokes

Keystroke	Action
Up Arrow	The highlight goes up one menu item.
Down Arrow	The highlight goes down one menu item.
Home	The first menu item appears highlighted.
End	The last menu item appears highlighted.
PgUp	Clipper advances up the menu by the number of elements appearing in the window. The highlight appears in the same place. For example, if the current window contains five items (elements 6 through 10) with element 8 highlighted, then pressing PgUp would display elements 1 through 5 with element 3 highlighted.
PgDn	Clipper advances down the menu by the number of elements appearing in the window. The highlight appears in the same place. For example, if the current window contains five items (elements 1 through 5) with element 3 highlighted, then pressing PgDown would display elements 6 through 10 with element 8 highlighted.
Ctrl-PgUp	The first menu item appears highlighted.
Ctrl-PgDn	The last menu item appears highlighted.
Enter	Return the value of the selected array element to the program.
Esc	Select nothing. Return 0 to the program.
Left Arrow	Select nothing. Return 0 to the program.
Right Arrow	Select nothing. Return 0 to the program.
First Letter of a Menu Item	Select the next item in the menu containing that letter as its first character.

The AAdd( ) function allows you to add an element to an array, effectively increasing its size. This allows you to create dynamic arrays. A dynamic array grows and shrinks to the size needed for a particular task. AAdd( ) function always places the new array element at the end of the array. ARRAY contains the name of the array you want to modify. EXP contains any legal Clipper value including strings, dates, logical values, and numbers.

The AClone( ) function creates an exact duplicate of an array. You set a variable equal to the value returned by AClone( ). ARRAY contains the name of the array you want to duplicate. For example, if you wanted to create a duplicate of an array you would type DUPARRAY := AClone(ARRAY).

The ACopy( ) function allows you to place a copy of array elements in ARRAY1 into ARRAY2. Clipper refers to ARRAY1 as the source array and ARRAY2 as the target array. When you use this function without any of the accompanying optional clauses, Clipper directly copies the source array to the target array in its entirety. EXPN1 defines the starting array element in the source array. If you use this clause, Clipper starts copying at an element other than the first element in the array. EXPN2 defines how many array elements Clipper copies from the source array to the target. EXPN3 defines the starting position in the target array. This allows you to copy the elements from the source array to a different position in the target array.

The ADel( ) function removes the specified element, EXPN, from the array defined by the ARRAY clause. After Clipper removes the array element, it advances the elements below it one position. Using this function does not alter the actual size of the array.

The ADir( ) function retrieves the filenames and associated information selected by DIRECTORY SKELETON contained in the specified directory. If DIRECTORY SKELETON does not contain a directory path, then Clipper uses the current directory. If you do not specify any arrays to fill with the directory contents, then Clipper returns the number of files matching DIRECTORY SKELETON. ARRAY1 contains the filenames. ARRAY2 contains the file size. ARRAY3 contains the file dates. ARRAY4 contains the file times. ARRAY5 contains the file attributes. Table 91-2 contains a listing of file attributes returned by the ADir( ) function. If the directory contains more files matching DIRECTORY SKELETON than the declared arrays have elements, Clipper fills all the array elements and stops. If you do not want a particular component of file information, but that component appears between two components you want, then use a dummy variable (dummy = " ") in place of an array for that array position.

Table 91-2. File Attributes Returned By ADIR( )

Attribute	Description
R	Read-Only
H	Hidden
S	System
D	Directory
A	Archive

The AEval( ) function provides the means of studying the contents of an array. ARRAY contains the name of an array to study. CODE BLOCK is a special construct containing code that you want to use to analyze each array element. EXPN1 contains the number of the first array element you want to study. EXPN2 contains the number of array elements to study. This function provides advanced features outside the scope of this book. Refer to your Clipper manual for a thorough understanding of this topic.

The AFields( ) function returns the field names, field type, field width, and number of decimals for each field in a database. As with the ADir( ) function, each array contains a different component of field information. ARRAY1 contains the field name. ARRAY2 contains the field type. ARRAY3 contains the field width. ARRAY4 contains the number of decimals for numeric field types. As with the ADir( ) function, use dummy variables in place of arrays for field components you do not want to retrieve.

The AFill( ) function provides a means of filling all or part of the elements of an array with the same value. The array clause contains the name of an array to fill. EXPC contains a character string to place in the array. If you do not specify EXPN1 and EXPN2, Clipper fills all array elements with the specified value. EXPN1 contains the array element to start filling at. Clipper always starts at the least numbered element and proceeds to the highest numbered element. EXPN2 contains the number of elements to fill starting at position EXPN1.

The AIns( ) function performs the opposite task of the ADel( ) function. It allows you to insert a new undefined element at position EXPN in ARRAY. As with the ADel( ) function the array does not increase in size. Instead, Clipper discards the last array element and moves the other array elements down one position starting at position EXPN.

The Array( ) function allows you to create an array of a specific length. EXPN contains the number of array elements in each dimension of the array. Clipper allows you to specify a length of up to 4,096 elements for each array dimension. An array can have an unlimited number of dimensions. To create a multidimensional array, specify the length of each dimension and separate each length by a comma. For example, to create a 3 by 4 by 10 array you would type NEWARRAY := Array(3, 4, 10). You may use the Array( ) function within other functions to dynamically create arrays of a specific size as needed.

The AScan( ) function allows you to search for a value within an array. This function returns the numeric position of the element containing the search expression (EXP). If the array does not contain the search expression, AScan( ) returns 0. If you do not specify EXPN1 and EXPN2, AScan( ) searches the entire array. EXPN1 contains the element number for AScan( ) to start searching at. EXPN2 contains the number of elements to scan.

The ASize( ) function changes the size of an array. ARRAY contains the name of the array you want to change. EXPN contains the new array size. If you shorten an array, then ASize( ) removes elements from the end of the array. Any values contained in those elements are lost. When you lengthen an array ASize( ) adds elements to the end of the array and assigns them a value of NIL.

ASort( ) orders the contents of an array in ascending order. If you do not specify EXPN1 and EXPN2, ASort( ) sorts the entire array. EXPN1 contains the element number for ASort( ) to start sorting at. EXPN2 contains the number of elements to sort. In addition to performing a standard sort, you can perform specialized sorts by adding a CODE BLOCK. For example, you could give some array elements a higher precedence based on criteria other than a standard ASCII value. You could use a code block to create a weighted sort. Any discussion of code block execution is outside the scope of this book. Refer to your Clipper manual for a thorough discussion of this topic.

The DBStruct( ) function creates an array containing the structure of a database. Each element of the array refers to one field of the database. To use this function you simply set a variable equal to its output. For example, to obtain the structure of the database in work area A, you would type SARRAY := A->DBStruct( ). There are four subarrays within each array element. These subarrays contain the field name, type, width, and decimals. You access each subarray using a special name. The name subarray uses DBS_NAME. The type subarray uses DBS_TYPE. The length subarray uses DBS_LEN, and decimals uses DBS_DEC. To use these special names you would place the name in brackets after the element number. For example, to display the name of the second field you would type ? SARRAY [1 [DBS_NAME]].

The Directory( ) function places the contents of the current directory in an array. EXPC1 contains the directory string. This string can contain a drive letter, any valid path, and a file specification. EXPC2 contains one or more letters that tell Clipper what file attributes you wish to search for. H includes hidden files, S includes system files, D includes subdirectories, and V includes the DOS volume label and excludes all other files. To use this function you set a variable equal to its output. For example, to get the contents of the current directory including hidden and system files you would type SARRAY := Directory ("*.*", "HS"). Clipper creates one array element for each file it finds in the specified location. Each array element contains five subarrays. These subarrays are labeled F_NAME, F_SIZE, F_DATE, F_TIME, and F_ATT. Each subarray addresses a specific aspect of the file. For example, F_ATT contains the attributes of the file. To display the contents of a specific part of an array element you place the special subarray name in brackets after the array element number. For example, to display the name of the fourth array element you would type ? SARRAY [1 [F_NAME]].

APPLICATIONS

Use these functions as described above to manipulate arrays created using the Declare command or Array( ) or AClone( ) functions. The AChoice( ) function allows you to create very flexible menus. By adding user-defined functions, you can create menus that perform many functions not possible with standard menu handling routines. The ACopy( ) function allows you to quickly reproduce all or part of an array. The ADel( ) function allows you to remove unneeded array elements; for example, if you create a directory listing and then want to remove the hidden files. The AFields( ) function allows you to create flexible database manipulation routines like those found in the DBU utility program provided with Clipper. The AFill( ) function provides a quick method of initializing an array before or even during use. The AIns( ) function allows you to add elements to an array. The AScan( ) function allows you to quickly search an array for a specific value. Searching this way reduces the time required to find values in unformatted text. The ASort( ) function allows you to quickly sort array elements. For example, if you wanted to use the directory obtained with ADel( ) as a menu but wanted the menu choices sorted, the ASort( ) could order the array elements for you. The DBStruct( ) and Directory( ) functions provide you with advanced methods of obtaining the structure of databases or the contents of the DOS file directory.

TYPICAL OPERATION

In this example you use the functions described above to create a menu for the checkbook program. Begin this example in your word processor with CHCKBOOK.PRG loaded.

1. Add the following text to the beginning of the main program.

```
MENU_ITEM[6] = 'Search'
* Sort the menu items then place Quit at the top.
asort(MENU_ITEM)
ANSWER = ascan(MENU_ITEM, 'Quit')
adel(MENU_ITEM, ANSWER)
ains(MENU_ITEM, 1)
MENU_ITEM[1] = 'Quit'
* Setup program defaults.
```

2. Add the following text near the middle of the main program.

```
use CHCKBOOK index CHCKNUM, DATE
* Perform this procedure until the user selects quit.
ANSWER = 2
do while MENU_ITEM[ANSWER] <> 'Quit'
* Display the screen.
   do DISP_SCRN5
* Perform the user requested function.
   do case
      case MENU_ITEM[ANSWER] = 'Add'
         do ADD_REC
      case MENU_ITEM[ANSWER] = 'Delete'
         do DEL_REC
      case MENU_ITEM[ANSWER] = 'Sort'
         do SORT_REC
      case MENU_ITEM[ANSWER] = 'Edit'
         do EDIT_REC
      case MENU_ITEM[ANSWER] = 'Search'
         do SEARCH_REC
```

```
        endcase
* Turn cursor back on.
set cursor on
enddo
* Close the databases and return.
```

3. Add the following procedures to the end of the procedure section.

```
return
procedure ADD_REC
* This procedure adds records to the database.
return
procedure DEL_REC
* This procedure removes records from the database.
return
procedure SORT_REC
* This procedure changes the index used by the database.
return
procedure EDIT_REC
* This procedure allows the user to edit the database.
return
procedure SEARCH_REC
* This procedure allows the user to search the database.
return
```

4. Add the following text to the end of the DISP_SCRN5 procedure.

```
set color to 'W/N,N/W,,,W+/N'
* Obtain the user selection.
@ 03, 03, 10, 13 box DOUBLE_LINE
ANSWER = achoice(04, 04, 09, 12, MENU_ITEM)
return
```

5. Save the document and exit your word processor. Type **CL CHCKBOOK** at the DOS prompt. Press **Enter**.

6. Type **MAILLIST**. Press **Enter**.

7. Press **F4**. The checkbook program menu appears.

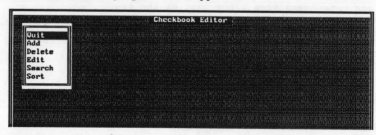

8. Type **S**. The program highlights Search but does not select it. Only the Enter key selects when using arrays.

9. Type **S**. The program selects Sort.

10. Type **Q** to select quit. Notice, the program does not automatically perform the quit function, it only highlights the menu entry. Only the Enter key causes the actual selection of a menu item when using arrays.

11. Press **Enter**. The DOS prompt appears.

12. Turn to Module 107 to continue the learning sequence.

Module 92
ALTD( )

DESCRIPTION

The ALTD( ) function lets you automatically invoke the debug program. If you use ALTD( ) with no parameters, Clipper displays the last debug screen you looked at. The default last screen is the control menu. EXPN contains a modifier to this behavior. When you specify option 2, Clipper displays the View Privates dialogue box. The ALTD( ) function also disables/enables Alt-D. If you want to invoke the debugger without using the ALTD( ) function, normally you press Alt-D. When you disable Alt-D, the program executes faster. To disable Alt-D, specify option 0. To enable Alt-D, specify option 1. The command line interface of the ALTD( ) function appears below.

```
ALTD([<EXPN>])
```

APPLICATIONS

Use the ALTD( ) function to invoke the debugger in places where the program does not use a wait state. For example, if you ask the user for information using an At (@) Get command, the Read command constitutes a wait state. If you wanted to interrupt program execution after that wait state, then you could use the ALTD( ) function.

You can also use the ALTD( ) function to enable or disable the debugger in various program sections. When you disable the debugger, Clipper no longer spends time looking at the keyboard for the Alt-D control code. Instead, the program runs at normal speed. By using this option of the ALTD( ) function, you can run most of the program at full speed and look for Alt-D only in problem areas.

TYPICAL OPERATION

In this example you add the ALTD( ) function to the beginning of the mailing list program. This allows you to debug even the very first line of code in the program. Begin this example in your word processor with MAILLIST.PRG loaded.

1. Add the following text to the beginning of the mailing list program.
   ```
   * TODAY'S DATE
   * Invoke the debugger.
   altd()
   * Make sure the environment is clear.
   ```

2. Save the document and exit your word processor. Type **CLD MAILLIST** at the DOS prompt. Press **Enter**. The Clipper batch file clears the screen, then compiles and links the program.

3. Type **MAILLIST** and press **Enter**. The Debug Control menu appears.

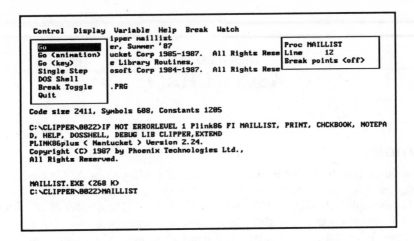

4. Type **Q** and press **Enter**. The DOS prompt appears.

5. Turn to Module 146 to continue the learning sequence.

Module 93
ASC( ), CHR( )

DESCRIPTION

The ASC( ) function converts the leftmost character of a string to its ASCII equivalent. For example, the letter A converts to 65. The CHR( ) function converts a three-digit number to a character. For example, the number 065 converts to the letter A. The number or character string each function converts appears in parentheses after the function name. You must enclose character strings in quotes. The command line interface of the ASC( ) and CHR( ) functions appears below.

```
ASC(<EXPC>)
CHR(<EXPN>)
```

APPLICATIONS

Use the ASC( ) function whenever you need to convert characters to their ASCII numeric equivalent. Use the CHR( ) function whenever you need to convert numbers to their ASCII character. For example, if you wanted to convert an uppercase A to a lowercase, you would use the ASC( ) function to convert it to a number. Next, you add 32 to it, then convert it back to a character using the CHR( ) function.

The CHR( ) function also produces more readable source code when you use control characters. This is especially true when your printer does not support the full ASCII character set. By using the CHR( ) function with the number of the extended ASCII line drawing character, you can always be sure you know which character will appear on the display.

TYPICAL OPERATION

In this example you make the source code of MAILLIST.PRG more readable using the CHR( ) function. Begin this example in your word processor with MAILLIST.PRG loaded.

1. Type the following text after the heading in MAILLIST.PRG.
   ```
   * TODAY'S DATE
   * Program Variables
   DOUBLE_LINE = chr(201) + chr(205) + chr(187) + chr(186) + chr(188) + ;
       chr(205) + chr(200) + chr(186) + chr(177)
   * Clear the display and prepare database for use.
   ```

2. Press **Enter**. Delete the line drawing characters after the At (@) Box command. Type **DOUBLE_LINE** as shown below.
   ```
   @ 01, 00, 24, 79 box DOUBLE_LINE
   ```

3. Save the document and exit your word processor.

4. Type **CL MAILLIST** at the DOS prompt. Press **Enter**.

5. Type **MAILLIST**. Press **Enter**. Type **Y** at the add a new record prompt. The data entry screen appears. Notice it appears exactly the same as before.

6. Type **GREG**. Press **Enter**. Type **A**. Type **STONE**. Press **Enter**. Type **152 Elm Street**. Press **Enter** twice. Type **SOMEPLACE**. Press **Enter**. Type **WI**. Type **532110125**. Type **4146163135**. The DOS prompt appears.

7. Type **DBU** to execute the database utility program. Type **MAILLIST** and press **Enter** to select the database. Press **Down Arrow** to select the index field. Type **LASTNAME** and press **Enter** to select the index file. The database utility retrieves MAILLIST.DBF and its associated index file.

8. Press **F5**.

9. Press **Enter**. The database utility displays the contents of MAILLIST.DBF. Notice the records appear in order of last then first name.

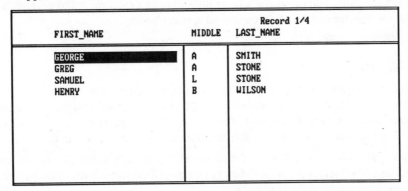

10. Press **Esc** twice to exit the database utility. Type **Y**. The DOS prompt appears.

11. Turn to Module 14 to continue the learning sequence.

Module 94
AT( )

DESCRIPTION

The AT( ) function searches for the last occurrence of EXPC1 in EXPC2. It lets you perform searches within character strings and memo fields. It differs from the RAT( ) function by the direction of search. AT( ) searches from beginning to end, while RAT( ) searches from end to beginning. This distinction can make a large difference in time required to perform a task. The command line interface of the AT( ) command appears below.

```
AT(<EXPC1>, <EXPC2>)
```

APPLICATIONS

Use the AT( ) command when you want to find the first occurrence of a search string in a target string. This is especially useful in conducting searches of text based databases. You can also use it in conjunction with other functions to separate component parts of a string used for control purposes. For example, you could use it to separate the path of a file from the filename.

Always use AT( ) when the majority of searches end at the beginning of a string. Use RAT( ) when the majority of searches end at the end of a string. Use either if the chances of finding the search string are equally likely at either end.

TYPICAL OPERATION

In this example you substitute the AT( ) function for the RAT( ) function used in the previous module in the learning sequence. Then you perform the same sequence of events to test if AT( ) usually produces the same results as RAT( ). Begin this example in your word processor with NOTEPAD.PRG loaded.

1. Change the SRCH_REC2 procedure at the end of the procedure section as follows.
   ```
   BUFFER = memoline(NOTE, 80, CURR_CHCK)
   FOUND_IT = at(NOTE_TEXT, BUFFER) <> 0
   if FOUND_IT = .T.
   ```

2. Save the document and exit your word processor. Type **CL NOTEPAD** at the DOS prompt. Press **Enter**.

3. Type **MAILLIST**. Press **Enter**. The mailing list program menu appears.

4. Press **F5**. The notepad menu appears.

5. Select Search by pressing **Down Arrow**. Press **Enter**. The program asks what type of search you want to conduct.

6. Type **T** to select note text. The program asks you to type the note text to find.

7. Type **special**. Press **Enter**. The program displays note number 3.

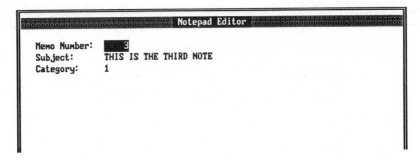

8. Press **PgDn**. The program reveals the note text containing the word special.

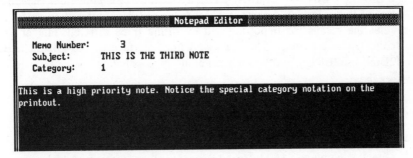

9. Press **Esc**. The notepad menu appears.
10. Press **Q** to quit. Press **Enter**. The DOS prompt appears.
11. Turn to Module 48 to continue the learning sequence.

Module 95
BIN2I( ), BIN2L( ), BIN2W( ),
I2BIN( ), L2BIN( ), WORD( )

DESCRIPTION

The BIN2I( ), BIN2L( ), BIN2W( ), I2BIN( ), L2BIN( ), and Word( ) functions change a foreign number format to Clipper format. A computer uses many different representations for numbers. Clipper provides the means for importing and exporting three different integer (a number without a decimal point) formats. The command line interface of the BIN2I( ), BIN2L( ), BIN2W( ), I2BIN( ), L2BIN( ), and Word( ) functions appears below.

```
BIN2I(<EXPC>)
BIN2L(<EXPC>)
BIN2W(<EXPC>)
I2BIN(<EXPN>)
L2BIN(<EXPN>)
WORD(<EXPN>)
```

The BIN2I( ) function converts a 16-bit signed integer to Clipper format. A 16-bit signed integer uses 15 bits to represent the number and one bit to represent the sign. If the sign bit is 1, then the number is negative. A 16-bit signed integer can have a value ranging from -32,767 to +32,767. The I2BIN( ) function performs the opposite conversion. It changes a Clipper number to a 16-bit integer. In both cases Clipper uses a character string to represent the 16-bit signed integer.

The BIN2L( ) function converts a 32-bit signed integer to Clipper format. Like the 16-bit signed integer described above, a 32-bit signed integer uses 31 bits to represent the number and one bit to represent the sign. A signed 32-bit signed integer can have a value between -2,147,483,647 and +2,147,483,647. The L2BIN( ) function performs the opposite conversion. Clipper uses a character string to represent the 32-bit signed integer.

The BIN2W( ) function converts a 16-bit unsigned integer to Clipper format. Unlike the other two integer representations, this integer does not allow negative numbers. Instead it uses all 16 bits to represent a number. A 16-bit unsigned integer can range in value from 0 to 65535. The I2BIN( ) function performs the opposite conversion. It changes a Clipper number to a 16-bit integer.

The Word( ) function converts a Clipper formatted number ranging in value from -32,767 to +32,767 to an integer. The Word( ) function converts numbers passed to a routine using the Call command from DOUBLE to INT format. This reduces program overhead, allowing the program to execute more quickly.

APPLICATIONS

Use the BIN2I( ), BIN2L( ), BIN2W( ), I2BIN( ), and L2BIN( ) functions when you need to import numeric information from another application or perform low-level tasks on Clipper files. This is especially convenient when you need to repair the headings of Clipper database files.

You can also use this when you want to import integer based information from other programs. However, most spreadsheets store their information in real (numbers with decimal points) format. You cannot use these functions to import real numbers.

Use the Word( ) function when you need to pass numeric information to a separately compiled program using the Call command. By using this function to convert the number, you reduce the amount of work the called program must perform. This in turn increases program execution speed.

TYPICAL OPERATION

In this example you create a simple program for manipulating the header of a Clipper database using the BIN2I( ), BIN2L( ), BIN2W( ), I2BIN( ), and L2BIN( ) functions. Use this program with great care since it can damage your database files. Begin this example in your word processor with nothing loaded.

1. Type the text shown below to create the HEADER.PRG file.

```
* HEADER.PRG
* This program allows you to display and edit the header of a database.
* YOUR NAME
* TODAY'S DATE
* Initialize the variables.
DB_NAME = space(12)
HANDLE = 0
YEAR = 0
MONTH = 0
DAY = 0
NUM_RECS = space(4)
REC_SIZE = space(2)
DATE_STR = space(8)
* Get the filename and open the file.
clear screen
@ 01, 00 to 24, 79 double
@ 02, 02 say 'Enter a database filename: ' get DB_NAME picture '@!'
read
if at('DBF', DB_NAME) = 0
    DB_NAME = trim(DB_NAME) + '.DBF'
endif
if .not. file(DB_NAME)
    @ 03, 02 say 'File not found!'
    quit
endif
HANDLE = fopen(DB_NAME, 2)
* Get the date.
fseek(HANDLE, 1, 0)
YEAR = bin2i(freadstr(HANDLE, 1))
MONTH = bin2i(freadstr(HANDLE, 1))
DAY = bin2i(freadstr(HANDLE, 1))
* Get the number of records.
fseek(HANDLE, 4, 0)
fread(HANDLE, @NUM_RECS, 4)
NUM_RECS = bin2l(NUM_RECS)
* Get the record size.
fseek(HANDLE, 10, 0)
fread(HANDLE, @REC_SIZE, 2)
REC_SIZE = bin2w(REC_SIZE)
* Display the information.
DATE_STR = str(MONTH, 2) + '/' + str(DAY, 2) + '/' + str(YEAR, 2)
@ 04, 02 say 'File Date: ' get DATE_STR picture '99/99/99'
@ 05, 02 say 'Number of Records: ' get NUM_RECS picture '@9'
```

```
@ 06, 02 say 'Record Size: ' get REC_SIZE picture '@9'
read
* Place the new information in the database header.
* Replace the date.
MONTH = i2bin(val(substr(DATE_STR, 1, 2)))
DAY = i2bin(val(substr(DATE_STR, 4, 2)))
YEAR = i2bin(val(substr(DATE_STR, 7, 2)))
fseek(HANDLE, 1, 0)
fwrite(HANDLE, YEAR, 1)
fwrite(HANDLE, MONTH, 1)
fwrite(HANDLE, DAY, 1)
* Replace the number of records.
NUM_RECS = l2bin(NUM_RECS)
fseek(HANDLE, 4, 0)
fwrite(HANDLE, NUM_RECS, 4)
* Replace the record size.
REC_SIZE = l2bin(REC_SIZE)
fseek(HANDLE, 10, 0)
fwrite(HANDLE, REC_SIZE, 2)
fclose(HANDLE)
clear screen
return
```

2. Save the document and exit your word processor. Type **CLD HEADER** at the DOS prompt. Press **Enter**.

3. Type **COPY MAILLIST.DBF TEMP_DAT.DBF** and press **Enter**. DOS copies the contents of the mailing list database to the temporary database.

4. Type **HEADER** and press **Enter**. The program asks which file you want to use.

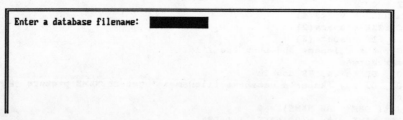

5. Type **TEMP_DAT** and press **Enter**. The program displays the header information for the temporary database.

6. Write the old header information on a sheet of paper. Type **08/23/89** in the date file. Type **10** in the number of records field. Type **300** in the record size field and press **Enter**. The program saves the new header information.

7. Type **DBU TEMP_DAT** and press **Enter**. Notice DBU displays the wrong number of records and copies the last record twice. Also notice DBU distorts the bottom two record entries.

```
                                      Record 1/18
        FIRST_NAME              MIDDLE  LAST_NAME

        GEORGE                    A     SMITH
        HENRY                     B     WILSON
        SAMUEL                    L     STONE
        GREG                      A     STONE
        SAM                       A     ANDERSON
        AMY                       B     WILSON
        AMY                       B     WILSON
        AMY                       B     WILSON
                   ANYWHERE
             (619)516-1234 SAMUEL                    LSTONE
```

8. Press **Esc** twice and type **Y** when asked if you want to leave DBU.

9. Type **HEADER** and press **Enter**. The program asks which file you want to use.

10. Type **TEMP_DAT** and press **Enter**. The program displays the header information for the temporary database. Notice the information reflects the previously entered values.

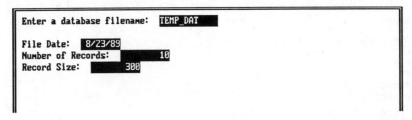

```
   Enter a database filename:   TEMP_DAT

   File Date:    8/23/89
   Number of Records:          10
   Record Size:          300
```

11. Type the previously recorded values in the appropriate fields. Press **Enter** while in the record size field to exit the program. The DOS prompt appears.

12. Turn to Module 147 to continue the learning sequence.

Module 96
BOF( ), DBF( ), EOF( ), LASTREC( )/RECCOUNT( ), RECNO( ), RECSIZE( ), ALIAS( )

DESCRIPTION

These functions provide information about the current state of your database. In most cases you make a variable equal to the function value and display the variable on the screen or printer. For example, to store the current record number in a variable you would type SOMEVAR := RecNo( ). In some cases, especially in print routines, you will output the function value directly. You may also place these functions within other functions. The command line interface of the Alias( ), BOF( ), DBF( ), EOF( ), LastRec( )/RecCount( ), RecNo( ), and RecSize( ) functions appears below.

```
ALIAS([<EXPN>])
BOF()
DBF()
EOF()
LASTREC()
RECCOUNT()
RECNO()
RECSIZE()
```

The Alias( ) function returns the alias of the specified work area. EXPN contains the number of the work area. If the specified work area does not contain an open database, Alias( ) returns a null string (""). Using Alias without specifying a work area number returns the alias of the database in the current work area. This performs the inverse function of the Select( ) function described in Module 134.

The BOF( ) function becomes true when the database is at the beginning of the file. If the database uses an index, Clipper uses the beginning of the index instead.

The DBF( ) function returns the alias of the current database. If there is no database in use, DBF( ) returns a null string (""). This is a dBase III Plus compatibility function. Use the Clipper Alias( ) function whenever possible.

The EOF( ) function becomes true at the end of the file. If the database uses an index, Clipper uses the end of the index instead.

The LastRec( ) and RecCount( ) functions provide the means of obtaining the total number of database records. If you use the database without an index, the last record number is the same as the number of records. However, these two functions provide different outputs if you use them with an index. LastRec( ) reports the number of the last record in the index, while RecCount( ) always returns the number of records.

The RecNo( ) function provides the current record number. However, if you use this function on a database that does not contain any records, then RecNo( ) returns one. In this case both BOF( ) and EOF( ) return true. If you move the record pointer past the EOF( ), then RecNo( ) returns LastRec( ) + 1.

The RecSize( ) function provides the size of the records in the selected database. RecSize( ) returns zero if there is no open database in the current work area. RecSize( ) returns the size of the fields plus any status flags in the database. This means it returns the true record size.

APPLICATIONS

Use this set of functions when you need to determine the state of the currently selected database. For example, many programs use the BOF( ) and EOF( ) functions for control structures and error messages. Many While Do control structures use the EOF( ) function to determine the stopping point for the loop. By displaying a message when BOF( ) or EOF( ) indicate the beginning or end of the database, you prevent user frustration in using move forward or backward menu selections.

You could use the RecNo( ) and LastRec( )/RecCount( ) functions in tandem to show the current database position. Some programs use these functions in print routines to show the remaining number of records.

Finally, you can use the RecSize( ) and LastRec( )/RecCount( ) functions in tandem to determine database backup or storage requirements. By determining the disk size, you could estimate the number of floppies required for a backup.

TYPICAL OPERATION

In this example you add database status messages to the sample program using the BOF( ), EOF( ), LastRec( )/RecCount( ), RecNo( ), and RecSize( ) functions. Begin this example in your word processor with MAILLIST.PRG loaded.

1. Add the following text between the At (@) To command and the At (@) Say command at the top of the document as follows.

```
@ 20, 01 to 20, 78
@ 02, 39 say ' Record Number: '
@ 02, 54 say recno()
@ 02, 61 say ' of '
@ 02, 65 say reccount()
if bof()
   @ 23,04 say ' Beginning of File '
endif
if eof()
   @ 23,04 say ' End of File '
endif
if .not. (bof() .or. eof())
   @ 23,04 say '  ███████████      ' && Press Alt-177 (on the numeric;
*     keypad) 20 times.
endif
@ 04, 06 say 'Name:'
```

2. Save the document and exit your word processor. Type **CL MAILLIST** at the DOS prompt. Press **Enter**.

3. Type **MAILLIST**. Press **Enter**. Notice the program now displays the total number of records and current record number.

4. Type **B**. The program displays a beginning of database message.

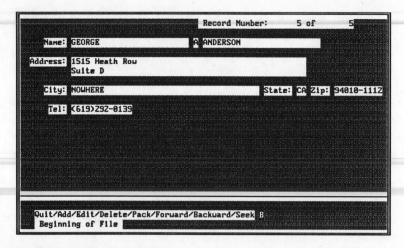

5. Type **F**. The message disappears.
6. Type **F** four times. The program displays an end of database message. Notice the record number is 6, showing the record pointer is actually at the end of the database.

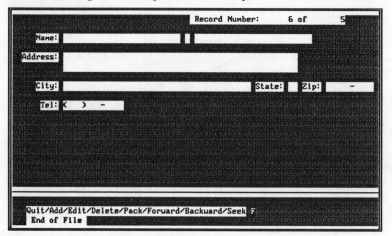

7. Type **Q**. The DOS prompt appears.
8. Turn to Module 109 to continue the learning sequence.

Module 97
CDOW( ), CMONTH( ), CTOD( ), DATE( ), DAY( ), DOW( ), DTOC( ), DTOS( ), MONTH( ), SECONDS( ), TIME( ), YEAR( )

DESCRIPTION

The CDOW( ), CMonth( ), CTOD( ), Date( ), Day( ), DOW( ), DTOC( ), DTOS( ), Month( ), Seconds( ), Time( ), and Year( ) functions all manipulate time or date information. The command line interface of the these functions appears below.

```
CDOW(<EXPD>)
CMONTH(<EXPD>)
CTOD(<EXPC>)
DATE()
DAY(<EXPD>)
DOW(<EXPD>)
DTOC(<EXPD>)
DTOS(<EXPD>)
MONTH(<EXPD>)
SECONDS()
TIME()
YEAR(<EXPD>)
```

The CDOW( ) function accepts a date as input. It returns the day of the week (for example Wednesday) as a character string. If you provide a null date (a date with blanks in place of numbers), CDOW( ) returns a null string ("").

The CMonth( ) function performs almost the same task as the CDOW( ) function. Instead of returning the day of the week, CMonth( ) returns the month as a character string. If you provide a null date, CMonth( ) returns a null string ("").

The CTOD( ) function accepts a formatted character string as input. The string must contain eight or ten characters in the form '99/99/99' or '99/99/9999', where each group of numbers represents the day, month, or year in the current date format. CTOD( ) returns a date with the day, month, and year set as they appear in the character string. If you do not provide the century in the year portion of the character string, Clipper assumes you want the 20th century. If you provide a null string ' / / ', then CTOD( ) returns a null date.

The Date( ) function returns the current date as a date variable. It uses the default format (mm/dd/yy) or the format set using the Set Date command for output.

The DOW( ) function accepts a date as input. It returns the day of week as a numeric. The first day of the week is Sunday, DOW( ) returns 1. The last day of the week is Saturday, DOW( ) returns 7. If you provide a null date, DOW( ) returns 0.

The DTOC( ) function accepts a date as input. It returns the date as a character string in the same format as input. You must supply a date using the default or set date format. The default format is 'mm/dd/yy.' You may change the default using the Set Date command. If you provide DTOC( ) with a null date, it returns a character string containing blanks instead of numbers (' / / ').

The DTOS( ) function performs exactly the same task as the DTOC( ) function. It accepts the same input. It does not however, provide the same output. DTOS( ) outputs a character string suitable for index files in the format year, month, day. There are no spaces or other delimiters between the numbers. For example, DTOS( ) converts the date 3 February 1989 to 19890203.

The Month( ) function accepts a date as input. It outputs a number corresponding to the month in the date as a numeric. January is month 1, December is month 12.

The Seconds( ) function returns the number of seconds elapsed since 12 a.m. (midnight) according to the system clock of the computer as a numeric. Seconds( ) uses a 24-hour format and therefore returns a different amount of seconds for times after 12 p.m. (noon).

The Time( ) function returns the computer system time in the format hh:mm:ss as a character string. Time( ) returns the time in a 24-hour format.

The Year( ) function accepts a date as input. It returns the year as a numeric. The year includes the two century digits. If you provide a date without century digits, Clipper assumes a date in the 20th century. If you provide a null date, Year( ) returns 0.

APPLICATIONS

Use these functions as described above to manipulate time and date information. By using the correct function, you can obtain the date or time in any format required to perform any task.

Use the CDOW( ) and CMonth( ) functions to obtain text day of week and month for report headings and displays.

Use the DOW( ), Day( ), Month( ), and Year( ) functions to obtain the day of week, day, month, and year as numbers. You can use these numbers to perform date arithmetic. Likewise, the Seconds( ) function allows you to obtain the time as a numeric suitable for math operations.

Use the CTOD( ), DTOC( ), and DTOS( ) functions to convert the date to and from string format. This allows you to perform any required manipulation with the date as a string. You can also use strings for report headings and displays easier than the original date format.

Use the Date( ) and Time( ) functions when you need the current system time. By knowing system time you can time/date stamp files to show when you last modified them, time stamp reports, and perform any conversions you require for other uses as well.

TYPICAL OPERATION

In this example you enhance some of the displays by adding the date, time, or both using the functions described above. Begin this example in your word processor with CHCKBOOK.PRG loaded.

1. Add the following variable to the beginning of the program.
   ```
   FIELD_NUMBER = 1
   DATE_STR = cdow(date()) + ', ' + substr(dtoc(date()), 4, 2) +;
       ' ' + cmonth(date()) + ' ' + ltrim(str(year(date()))))
   ```

2. Add the following text to the DISP_SCRN5 procedure.

```
@ 02, 31 say ' Checkbook Editor '
@ 03, 40 - (len(DATE_STR)/2) say DATE_STR
@ 19, 03 say ' F2 - Mailing List ' + chr(179) + ' F3 - Print '
```

3. Add the following text to the REMOVE_REC procedure.

```
endif
* Display time and date.
@ 02, 04 say dtoc(date()) + '   ' + time()
* Check if user wants to exit DBEdit()
```

4. Save the document and exit your word processor. Type **CL CHCKBOOK** at the DOS prompt. Press **Enter**.

5. Type **MAILLIST**. Press **Enter**.

6. Press **F4**. The checkbook program menu appears. Notice the program displays the date and day of week.

7. Type **D** then press **Enter**. Notice the delete procedure now displays the time and date.

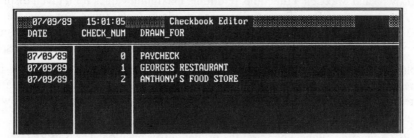

8. Press **Esc** to exit the delete procedure. Type **Q** to select Quit. Press **Enter**. The DOS prompt appears.

9. Turn to Module 50 to continue the learning sequence.

Module 98
COL( ), MAXCOL( ), MAXROW( ), PCOL( ), PROW( ), ROW( ), SETPRC( )

DESCRIPTION

The following functions help you position information on the printer and display. As your programs become more complex, you need to emphasize the aesthetic value of proper text placement. Using these functions can help you perform this task. The command line interface of the Col( ), MaxRow( ), MaxCol( ), PCol( ), PRow( ), Row( ), and SetPRC( ) functions appears below.

```
COL( )
MAXCOL( )
MAXROW( )
PCOL( )
PROW( )
ROW( )
SETPRC(<EXPN1>, <EXPN2>)
```

The Col( ) and Row( ) functions help you determine the current display cursor position. Col( ) returns the vertical, or column, position. Row( ) returns the horizontal, or row, position.

The MaxRow( ) and MaxCol( ) functions return the maximum values for a given display. They allow you to compensate for differences between display adapter types. For example, you can use the 43-line mode of the EGA. MaxRow( ) always returns the value of the bottom-most line of the display. MaxCol( ) always returns the value of the right-most column of the display.

The PCol( ) and PRow( ) functions help you determine the current printer cursor position. PCol( ) returns the vertical, or column, position. Clipper resets the PCol( ) value after each carriage return. PRow( ) returns the horizontal, or row, position. Clipper resets the PRow( ) value at the beginning of each new page.

The SetPRC( ) function allows you to set the printer cursor position. The SetPRC( ) function is the only one of these functions that requires input. EXPN1 contains the row coordinate. EXPN2 contains the column coordinate. This function also automatically resets the values of PCol( ) and PRow( ).

APPLICATIONS

Use the Row( ) and Col( ) functions to obtain the current display cursor coordinates. This is especially effective in help routines where knowing the exact cursor position can alter the help required. These functions also assist you in determining screen position when you send printouts to both the screen and printer.

Use the MaxRow( ) and MaxCol( ) functions to help you determine the current screen size. This allows you to make better use of advanced displays. For example, you could use the 132-column or 50-line mode provided by some VGA display adapters. This allows you to provide the user with an overall view of the data before zeroing in on some specific piece of information.

Use the PRow( ) and PCol( ) functions when you need to know the current print head position. These functions help you place headers and footers correctly when creating custom reports.

Use the SetPRC( ) function to set the internal printer row and column counters. One good use for this function is to reset the head indicators after downloading font or printer control information.

TYPICAL OPERATION

In this example you use the PRow( ) and PCol( ) functions to create a custom print program. You also use the Row( ) and Col( ) functions to send the same customized report to the display. Begin this example at the C:\CLIPPER\0022 prompt.

1. Type **DBU** and press **Enter**. The DBU main menu appears.
2. Press **F3**. Select DATABASE by pressing **Enter**. The Create Database structure form appears.
3. Type the database structure information into the form as shown below.

```
┌─────────────────────────────────────────────┐
│ Structure of <new file>   Field 4           │
│                                             │
│ Field Name    Type       Width   Dec        │
│                                             │
│ NOTE_NUM      Numeric        5     0         │
│ SHORT_SUBJ    Character     50               │
│ CATEGORY      Character     15               │
│ NOTE          Memo          10               │
│                                             │
└─────────────────────────────────────────────┘
```

4. Press **F4** then **Enter** to select Save Structure. Type **NOTEPAD**. Press **Enter** twice. DBU names the new database NOTEPAD and saves the structure to disk.
5. Press **F5** then **Enter** to access the Browse mode. Enter the database records as shown below.

NOTE
To enter the memo field, highlight the field and press Enter. To exit the memo field and save the changes, press Ctrl-W. To obtain any other help on using memo fields within the DBU utility, press F1 while in the memo field.

Table 98-1. Notepad Database Entries

NOTE	SHORT_SUBJ	CATEGORY	MEMO
1	This is the first note.	GENERAL	This is a note.
2	This is the second note.	GENERAL	This is a note too!

6. Press **Esc** to exit the Browse mode. Press **F3**. Select Index by pressing **Down Arrow**, then **Enter**. Type **SUBJECT** in the File field. Press **Enter**. Type **SHORT_SUBJ +** **STR(NOTE_NUM,5,0)** in the Key field. Press **Enter** twice. DBU creates the new index and saves it to disk.

7. Press **F3**. Select Index by pressing **Down Arrow**, then **Enter**. Press **Up Arrow** twice. Type **NOTENUM** in the File field. Press **Down Arrow**. Type **NOTE_NUM** in the Key field. Press **Enter** twice. DBU creates the new index and saves it to disk.

8. Press **F3**. Select Index by pressing **Down Arrow**, then **Enter**. Press **Up Arrow** twice. Type **CATEGORY** in the File field. Press **Down Arrow**. Type **CATEGORY +** **STR(NOTE_NUM,5,0)** in the Key field. Press **Enter** twice. DBU creates the new index and saves it to disk.

9. Press **Esc**. The DBU utility asks if you want to exit to DOS.

10. Type **Y**. The DOS prompt appears.

11. Enter your word processor and load PRINT.PRG. Add the following text to the menu selection check section of the main program.

```
    set console on
case MENU_SEL = 4
    use NOTEPAD
    do DISP_MENU4
    do NOTE_PRNT
endcase
```

12. Add the following text to the DISP_MENU2 procedure.

```
@ 08, 03 prompt 'Mailing List' message 'Print the Mailing List Database.'
@ 09, 03 prompt 'Note Pad' message 'Print the contents of the Note ' + ;
   'Pad Database.'
```

13. Add the following text to the DISP_COUNT procedure.

```
set print off
set device to screen
set color to N/W,W+/N
@ 22, 04 say 'Printing record'
@ 22, 20 say PRNT_COUNT
@ 22, 31 say 'of'
@ 22, 34 say reccount()
set device to print
set console off
```

14. Add the following text to the end of the procedure section.

```
procedure DISP_MENU4
* This procedure displays a menu for selecting an index for
* printing the note pad.
private ANSWER2
save screen
set message to 22 center
@ 06, 02 clear to 08, 14
@ 05, 01 to 09, 15 double
@ 06, 03 prompt 'Note Number' message 'Print in Note Number Order.'
@ 07, 03 prompt 'Subject' message 'Print in Subject then Note Number ;
   Order.'
@ 08, 03 prompt 'Category' message 'Print in Category then Note Number ;
   Order.'
menu to ANSWER2
restore screen
* Set the index to match user response.
do case
```

```
      case ANSWER2 = 1
          set index to NOTENUM
      case ANSWER2 = 2
          set index to SUBJECT
      case ANSWER2 = 3
          set index to CATEGORY
   endcase
   return
   procedure NOTE_PRNT
   * This is a customized print routine for the notepad.
   private ROW, COL
   * Setup initial conditions.
   set console off
   set print on
   set device to print
   setprc (5, 10) && Set the margins.
   PRNT_COUNT = 1
   ROW = prow()
   COL = pcol()
   * Perform this procedure until we print all the records.
   do while .not. eof()
   * Print the information
      @ ROW, COL say chr(13)        && Place print head at beginning.
      @ ROW, COL say 'Note Number:'
      @ ROW, pcol() + 2 say NOTE_NUM
      ROW = ROW + 1
      @ ROW, COL say 'Subject: ' + SHORT_SUBJ
      ROW = ROW + 1
      @ ROW, COL say 'Category: ' + CATEGORY
      ROW = ROW + 2
      @ ROW, COL say NOTE
      ROW = ROW + 1
   * Show the number of records printed.
      do DISP_COUNT
   * See if we need a new page.
      if ROW > 55
          eject
          setprc (5, 10)
          ROW = prow()
          COL = pcol()
      endif
   * Go to the next record.
      skip
      PRNT_COUNT = PRNT_COUNT + 1
   enddo
   * Return the setup to normal.
   set print off
   set console on
   set device to screen
   return
```

15. Save the document and exit your word processor. Type **CL PRINT** at the DOS prompt.
    Press **Enter**.

16. Type **PRINT**. Press **Enter**.

17. Type **LPT1**. Press **Enter** to select a printer. Type **N** to forego running the printer test. The
    program displays a menu for selecting the database you want to print.

18. Select Note Pad by pressing **Down Arrow** twice. Press **Enter**. The program displays another menu.

19. Select Category by pressing **Down Arrow** twice. Press **Enter**. The program prints the two note entries in note number order. It also displays the record number as it prints. The Main menu appears.

20. Select Quit by pressing **Up Arrow** three times. Press **Enter**. The DOS prompt appears.

21. Turn to Module 121 to continue the learning sequence.

Module 99
CURDIR( ), DISKSPACE( ), DOSERROR( ), ERRORLEVEL( ), FKLABEL( ), FKMAX( ), GETE( ), GETENV( ), OS( ), VERSION( )

DESCRIPTION

The CurDir( ), DiskSpace( ), DOSError( ), ErrorLevel( ), FKLabel( ), FKMax( ), GetE( ), GetEnv( ), and OS( ) functions all perform a DOS-related function. The Version( ) function performs a Clipper specific DOS-like function. The command line interface of these functions appears below.

```
CURDIR(<EXPC>)
DISKSPACE([<EXPN>])
DOSERROR()
ERRORLEVEL([<EXPN>])
FKLABEL(<EXPN>)
FKMAX()
GETE(<EXPC>)
GETENV(<EXPC>)
OS()
VERSION()
```

The CurDir( ) and DiskSpace( ) functions retrieve disk drive status information. EXPC, used with CurDir( ), holds the drive letter. If you do not supply a drive letter, CurDir( ) returns the current directory for the default drive. EXPN, used with DiskSpace( ), contains a drive number to check (A = 1, B = 2, etc.) If you do not supply a drive number, DiskSpace( ) returns the amount of space left on the default drive. Supplying a value of zero also returns the amount of space left on the default drive.

The DOSError( ) and ErrorLevel( ) functions retrieve/set system error information. DOSError( ) returns an error number indicating why DOS could not perform a particular operation. Table 99-1 contains a complete listing of these error codes. ErrorLevel( ) retrieves the current DOS error level. This differs from the error number retrieved by DOSError( ). The error level usually indicates a problem in an application program. DOS returns an error level of 0 during normal program operation. You can also place a number in EXPN to set the DOS error level. When you return to DOS or another program, that program can check the DOS error level to see if any errors occurred during operation. You may also use error level information in batch (.BAT) files to change the execution path.

Table 99-1. DOS Extended Error Information

Code	Description	Code	Description
0	No Error	37-49	Reserved
1	Function Number Invalid	50	Unsupported Network Request
2	File Not Found	51	Remote Machine Not Listening
3	Path Not Found	52	Duplicate Name on Network
4	Too Many Open Files	53	Network Name Not Found
5	Access Denied	54	Network Busy
6	Handle Invalid	55	Device No Longer Exists on Network
7	Memory Control Block Destroyed	56	NetBIOS Command Limit Exceeded
8	Insufficient Memory	57	Error in Network Adapter Hardware
9	Memory Block Address Invalid	58	Incorrect Response From Network
10	Environment Invalid	59	Unexpected Network Error
11	Format Invalid	60	Remote Adapter Incompatible
12	Access Code Invalid	61	Print Queue Full
13	Data Invalid	62	Not Enough Space for Print File
14	Unknown Unit	63	Print File Canceled
15	Disk Drive Invalid	64	Network Name Deleted
16	Attempted to Remove Current Directory	65	Network Access Denied
17	Not Same Device	66	Incorrect Network Device Type
18	No More Files	67	Network Name Not Found
19	Disk Write-Protected	68	Network Name Limit Exceeded
20	Unknown Unit	69	NetBIOS Session Limit Exceeded
21	Drive Not Ready	70	File Sharing Temporarily Paused
22	Unknown Command	71	Network Request Not Accepted
23	Data Error (CRC)	72	Print or Disk Redirection Paused
24	Bad Request Structure Length	73-79	Reserved
25	Seek Error	80	File Already Exists
26	Unknown Media Type	81	Reserved
27	Sector Not Found	82	Cannot Make Directory
28	Printer Out of Paper	83	Fail on Int 24h
29	Write Fault	84	Too Many Redirections
30	Read Fault	85	Duplicate Redirection
31	General Failure	86	Invalid Password
32	Sharing Violation	87	Invalid Parameter
33	Lock Violation	88	Network Device Fault
34	Disk Change Invalid	89	Function Not Supported by Network
35	FCB Unavailable	90	Required System Component Not Installed
36	Sharing Buffer Exceeded		

The FKLabel( ) and FKMax( ) functions are provided for compatibility with dBASE III Plus. These two functions help you determine the number and status of the function keys on the current machine. FKLabel( ) returns a character string containing the name of the specified function key. If you supply a value greater than 40 or less than 1, then Clipper returns a null string (""). Originally, this function made porting dBASE programs to other machines easier. However, it currently serves no useful purpose. All Clipper functions accept a number between 1 and 40 as a function key argument. The FKMax( ) function returns the number of function keys on the current machine. Clipper always returns a value of 40 for this function.

The GetE( ) and GetEnv( ) functions return the information associated with a DOS environment variable. Use GetE( ) with the Summer 87 version of Clipper. Use the GetEnv( ) function with the 5.0 version of Clipper. (The GetE( ) variation is still acceptable in version 5.0.) You create and deallocate DOS environment variables using the DOS Set command (see your DOS manual for more information). In many ways the environment works like a permanent command line. Unlike command line parameters, environment variables remain available to programs executing under DOS. By setting the environment, you can configure a program without using special command line switches. EXPC contains the name of the environment variable you want to retrieve. If Clipper finds the variable, it returns it as a string. Otherwise, Clipper returns a null ("") string. Even though this function is not case sensitive, it is sensitive to the placement and number of spaces in the environment string. Make sure you provide a string that exactly matches the environment string you wish to find.

The OS( ) function returns a string with the current operating system name and version number. You use it by setting a variable equal to the function (for example, OS_STR := OS( )). You can also use this function by itself in a display or as an argument to another function.

The Version( ) function returns the version number of the Clipper EXTEND library. By knowing the version of this value you can determine if certain functions are available to your program. Clipper returns the version number as a string.

APPLICATIONS

Use the CurDir( ) function whenever you allow the user to change the directory using a configuration program, or the program initialization to ensure the program can find the appropriate database and associated files.

Use the DiskSpace( ) function to determine the amount of room left on a particular disk. This is convenient for several purposes. For instance, you could use it as part of a backup routine. By knowing the size of each record and the amount of space on the disk drive, you can compute the number of records the disk will hold. To restore the backup, simply use the APPEND command to retrieve records stored on separate disks. Another example of how to use this function is user warning messages. When the user is about to run out of data space on the current disk, you can suspend operations and display a warning message.

Use the DOSError( ) function to retrieve the DOS error number. Some DOS errors do not result in system crashes. In these cases you can post a message telling the user what to do to fix the problem. In cases where the system does crash, you can usually display an error message saying what error occurred.

Use the ErrorLevel( ) function when you want to tell a program at a higher level in the hierarchy about a program error. This allows the higher level program to recover from the error and try the low level procedure a second time.

Avoid using the FKLabel( ) and FKMax( ) functions whenever possible. Clipper provides them for compatibility with dBASE III Plus programs. There are other, more efficient methods of performing the tasks that these functions provide. For example, you could define a variable with a value of 40 in place of using the FKMax( ) function.

Use the GetE( ) or GetEnv( ) function to retrieve the value of an environment variable. You can use this information to configure the program dynamically.

Use the OS( ) function whenever you need to determine the operating system name and version number. In many cases the version number is the most important part of the return string. If your program uses the special features of one operating system over another or it requires a specific version of the operating system to perform a task, you can use this function to prevent program errors.

Use the Version( ) function when you need to determine if the Clipper EXTEND library contains a specific routine. Using the Version( ) function allows you take advantage of advanced features in new versions of Clipper and still provide alternate methods for older versions. This function is most useful in situations where you do not know what version of the library a person will use to compile their program. For example, if you sell a function library or program to another company in source code format.

TYPICAL OPERATION

In this example you create the first half of a disk backup routine using the CurDir( ), DiskSpace( ), DOSError( ), ErrorLevel( ), and GetE( ) functions described above. Begin this example in your word processor with MAINT.PRG loaded.

1. Add the following text to the maintenance program.

```
* Start a file backup if desired.
input 'Do you want to backup the data files? ' to ANSWER
ANSWER = upper(ANSWER)
if len(ANSWER) > 1
   ANSWER = substr(ANSWER, 1, 1)
endif
if ANSWER = 'Y'
   ? 'Place disk in drive A'
   SPACE = diskspace(1)
   if SPACE > 33553919
      ? chr(7) + 'Make sure you use a formatted disk.'
      ? 'Make sure you closed the drive door.'
      wait
   endif
   ? 'Copying files in ' + curdir() + ' to drive A.'
   if doserror() <> 0
      errorlevel(1)
      quit
   endif
endif
* Exit this utility
```

2. Save the document and exit your word processor. Type **CLD MAINT** at the DOS prompt. Press **Enter**.

3. Type **MAINT**. Press **Enter**. The program asks for a directory path and skeleton.

4. Type **'*.DBF'** and press **Enter**. The program displays a listing of files ending with .DBF. Then the program asks if you want to delete any files.

5. Type **'N'** and press **Enter**. The program asks if you want to rename any files.

6. Type **'N'** and press **Enter**. The program asks "Do you want to backup the data files?"

7. Place a blank, formatted disk in drive A. Do not close the drive door. Type **'Y'** and press **Enter**. The drive light on drive A illuminates, the program beeps, then displays an error message.

8. Close the drive door. Press **Enter**. The program displays a file copy message and exits normally.

```
Type directory path and skeleton
'*.DBF'
CHCKBOOK DBF       1035  07/15/89
MAILLIST DBF       1625  07/16/89
NOTEPAD  DBF        406  07/16/89
SUMMARY  DBF        550  07/11/89
NEWTEMP  DBF       1035  07/15/89
HELP     DBF        162  07/16/89

Do you want to delete any of the files? 'N'
Do you want to rename any of the files? 'N'
Do you want to backup the data files? 'Y'
Place disk in drive A
Make sure you use a formatted disk.
Make sure you closed the drive door.
Press any key to continue...
Copying files in CLIPPER\0022 to drive A.
C:\CLIPPER\0022>
```

9. Turn to Module 111 to continue the learning sequence.

Module 100
DBEDIT( ), BROWSE( ), DBCREATE( ), DBEVAL( )

DESCRIPTION

The Browse( ), DBCreate( ), DBEdit( ), and DBEval( ) functions help you perform maintenance on your database. Each function excels at a specific task. The following paragraphs explain the purpose of each function. The command line interface of the Browse( ), DBCreate( ), DBEdit( ), and DBEval( ) functions appears below.

```
BROWSE([<EXPN1>] [, <EXPN2>] [, <EXPN3>] [, <EXPN4>])
DBCREATE(<EXPC>, <ARRAY>)
DBEDIT([<EXPN1>] [, <EXPN2>] [, <EXPN3>] [, <EXPN4>] [, <ARRAY1>] ;
[, <EXPC1>] [, <ARRAY2/EXPC2>] [, <ARRAY3/EXPC3>] [, <ARRAY4/EXPC4>] ;
[, <ARRAY5/EXPC5>] [, <ARRAY6/EXPC6>] [, <ARRAY7/EXPC7>])
DBEVAL(<CODE BLOCK> [, <FOR CONDITION> [, <WHILE CONDITION> [, <EXPN1> ;
[, <EXPN2> [, <EXPL>]]]]])
```

BROWSE( ) The Browse( ) function provides a general purpose editor for the database in the current work area. This function works faster and requires less input than the DBEdit( ) function. However, it only allows you to browse, edit, or append records to the database in the current work area. It also limits your ability to define the appearance of the edit area. This function helps you duplicate the browse feature provided by dBASE III Plus. Table 100-1 provides a listing of the navigation keys used by this function.

Table 100-1. Standard Browse( ) or DBEdit( ) Keystrokes

Keystroke	Action
Up Arrow	The highlight goes up one record.
Down Arrow	The highlight goes down one record.
Left Arrow	The highlight goes left one field.
Right Arrow	The highlight goes right one field.
Ctrl-Left Arrow	The database pans left one field.
Ctrl-Right Arrow	The database pans right one field.
Home	The leftmost field in the current display appears highlighted.
End	The rightmost field in the current display appears highlighted.
Ctrl-Home	The leftmost field in the database appears highlighted.
Ctrl-End	The rightmost field in the database appears highlighted.
PgUp	Clipper advances the display by the number of records appearing in the window. The highlight appears in the same place. For example, if the current window contains five records (records 6 through 10) with record 8 highlighted, then pressing PgUp would display records 1 through 5 with record 3 highlighted.

Table 100-1. Standard Browse( ) or DBEdit( ) Keystrokes (Cont.)

Keystroke	Action
PgDn	Clipper shifts the display down the number of records appearing in the window. The highlight appears in the same place. For example, if the current window contains five records (records 1 through 5) with record 3 highlighted, then pressing PgDn would display records 6 through 10 with record 8 highlighted.
Ctrl-PgUp	The first record in the database appears highlighted.
Ctrl-PgDown	The last record in the database appears highlighted.
Enter	Terminate Browse( ) or DBEdit( ).
Esc	Terminate Browse( ) or DBEdit( ).

EXPN1 through EXPN4 contain the display coordinates used by the Browse( ) function. EXPN1 defines the top, EXPN2 defines the left side, EXPN3 defines the bottom, and EXPN4 defines the right side coordinates. Unlike other display functions, Browse( ) does not require you supply any of these coordinates. If you do not supply a coordinate, Browse( ) assumes the maximum value in the designated direction.

DBCREATE( ) The DBCreate( ) function allows you to duplicate the field structure of a current database or create a new one. This function allows you to use the multidimensional array feature of Clipper 5.0 to create databases. You can duplicate the field structure of a current database by creating an array with the DBStruct( ) function (Module 91). This array automatically contains all the information you need to duplicate the field structure of an existing database. To create a new database you must format the array by hand or change the format of an array created with the DBStruct( ) function. To use the DBCreate( ) function, you place the name of the new database in EXPC and the name of the specially designed array in ARRAY. In addition, you must include the DBSTRUCT.CH file in your program by typing #INCLUDE "DBSTRUCT.CH". This file provides some of the constructs you need to use the DBCreate( ) and DBStruct( ) functions.

Each element of the array refers to one field of the database. DBCreate creates the fields in the same order they appear in the array. There are four subarrays within each array element. These subarrays contain the field name, type, width, and decimals. You access each subarray using a special name. The name subarray uses DBS_NAME. The type subarray uses DBS_TYPE. The length subarray uses DBS_LEN, and decimals uses DBS_DEC. To use these special names you would place the name in brackets after the element number. For example, to add a name to the second field you would type SARRAY[2][DBS_NAME] := "SomeField".

DBEDIT( ) The DBEdit( ) function provides the means of creating table-style database editing screens. The DBU utility supplied with Clipper provides this type of display for browsing the database.

EXPN1 through EXPN4 contain the display coordinates used by the DBEdit( ) function. EXPN1 defines the top, EXPN2 defines the left side, EXPN3 defines the bottom, and EXPN4 defines the right side coordinates. Unlike other display functions, DBEdit( ) does not require that you supply any of these coordinates. If you do not supply a coordinate, DBEdit( ) assumes the maximum value in the designated direction.

NOTE

All the following DBEdit( ) clauses are optional. However, you must present any arguments you wish to make in the order shown at the beginning of this module. If you skip any arguments, place a dummy value consisting of a null string ("") in its place.

ARRAY1 contains a list of field names you want DBEdit( ) to display. If you do not include this parameter, DBEdit( ) displays all the fields for the database in the current work area.

EXPC1 contains the name of a function Clipper executes if the user presses a key not defined for use with the DBEdit( ) function. Table 100-1 contains a listing of standard DBEdit( ) keystrokes. A discussion of how to create advanced user-defined functions is not within the scope of this book. Refer to Module 44 for a discussion of how to create functions using the Function command.

ARRAY2 contains strings used to format the columns (fields). These strings work the same as the picture clause of the AT (@) Say/Get commands. If you specify a string (EXPC2) instead of an array, Clipper uses the same picture for all columns.

ARRAY3 contains strings displayed as headings. To display multi-line headings, use a semi-colon (;) between each line of the heading. If you specify a string (EXPC3) instead of an array, Clipper uses the same heading for all columns.

ARRAY4 contains strings used to draw horizontal lines separating the heading from the field area. By using the extended ASCII character set, you can create heading separators that remain constant throughout an editing session. If you specify a string (EXPC4) instead of an array, Clipper uses the same character sequence for all columns.

ARRAY5 contains strings used to draw vertical lines between the columns. Unlike most of the arrays described previously, you normally use a string for this array. If you specify a string (EXPC5) instead of an array, Clipper uses the same character sequence for all columns.

ARRAY6 contains strings used to draw horizontal lines separating the footer from the field area. By using the extended ASCII character set, you can create footer separators that remain constant throughout an editing session. If you specify a string (EXPC6) instead of an array, Clipper uses the same character sequence for all columns.

ARRAY7 contains strings displayed as footers. To display multi-line footers, use a semi-colon (;) between each line of the footer. If you specify a string (EXPC7) instead of an array, Clipper uses the same footer for all columns.

DBEVAL( ) The DBEval( ) function allows you to evaluate the contents of a database using a predefined procedure. CODE BLOCK contains these special procedures. A discussion of code blocks is outside the scope of this book. Refer to your Clipper manual if you need more information about the DBEval( ) function in particular and code blocks in general.

APPLICATIONS

Use the Browse( ) function when you want to allow the user to edit the database in the current work area without worrying about a lot of esoteric formatting features. This function allows you to create an easy-to-edit environment for single database programs. It also provides a convenient method of implementing a database maintenance function. Always use this function in place of DBEdit( ) where ease of implementation and speed are the primary considerations.

Use the DBCreate( ) function to create new databases quickly and easily. This is especially true when you want to duplicate or modify the structure of an existing database (see the DBStruct( ) function in Module 91). The multidimensional array approach used by Clipper 5.0 reduces the amount of work required to create a database. This function allows you to make full use of this feature.

Use the DBEdit( ) function when you want to create a full screen editor for a database. Instead of seeing a single record, DBEdit( ) allows you to see as many as your screen will hold. This particular display is especially useful in situations where a company used to store handwritten documents in tabular format. It allows the person using the database to make an easy transition from written to electronic format.

Use the DBEval( ) function when standard methods of checking the contents of a database are inappropriate or unusable. For example, if you wanted to use a weighted measure to find specific records. This function provides you access to the advanced features of Clipper 5.0. However, using code blocks is time consuming. Make certain you need these advanced features before using them.

TYPICAL OPERATION

In this example you create a full screen editor for the checkbook program. Begin this example in your word processor with CHCKBOOK.PRG loaded.

1. Add the following text to the EDIT_REC procedure.

```
* This procedure allows the user to edit the database.
set color to N/W,W+/N
dbedit(03, 03, 19, 76, FIELD_ARRAY, "CHOICE")   && Choice is a procedure for
set color to 'W/N,N/W,,,W+/N'                    && handling user input.

return
function CHOICE
* User Defined Function (UDF) for Database Edit Control.
* The edit control must handle every keystroke that the user might input.
* You only need to act on those keystrokes that perform an action you want
* the Database Edit Control to handle.
parameters STATUS, FLD   && Clipper passes these parameters automatically.
* Assign Variables
RET_TYPE = 0                && UDF Request Message
NEWREC = 'Y'               && Add a record to an empty database.
if STATUS = 0              && No key input or other action by user.
   RET_TYPE = 1
elseif STATUS = 1          && User moved cursor past beginning of file.
   ? chr(7)
   RET_TYPE = 1
elseif STATUS = 2          && User moved cursor past end of file.
   append blank            && Add a record.
   @ row()+1, col()        && Move the cursor.
   do EDITREC with FLD
   RET_TYPE = 2
elseif STATUS = 3          && Database is empty.
   @ 23, 03 say 'Database is empty. Add a record? ' get NEWREC picture '!'
   read
   if NEWREC = 'Y'
      append blank
      @ row()+1, col()
```

```
                do EDITREC with FLD
           endif
     * If the user pressed escape or answered no, then leave without
     * adding a record.
        if (lastkey() = 27) .or. NEWREC = 'N'
           RET_TYPE = 0
        else
           RET_TYPE = 2
        endif
     elseif STATUS = 4                        && User input an unknown keystroke.
        do case                               && Test for various keystrokes.
           case lastkey() = 13                && Carriage Return.
               do EDITREC with FLD
               RET_TYPE = 2
           case (lastkey() > 48) .and. (lastkey() < 57)     && Any Numeric Char.
               keyboard chr(lastkey())
               do EDITREC with FLD
               RET_TYPE = 2
           case (lastkey() > 65) .and. (lastkey() < 122)    && Any Alpha Char.
               keyboard chr(lastkey())
               do EDITREC with FLD
               RET_TYPE = 2
           case lastkey() = 27                && Escape
               RET_TYPE = 0
           case lastkey() = 7                 && Delete
               if deleted()
                  recall
               else
                  delete
               endif
               if deleted()                   && Show the record status.
                  @ 21, 04 say ' DELETED '
               else
                  @ 21, 04 say '           '
               endif
               RET_TYPE = 2
           otherwise                          && Unused keystroke, do nothing.
               RET_TYPE = 2
        endcase
     endif
     return RET_TYPE
     * Edit the selected record.
     procedure EDITREC
     parameters FLDNUM
     * Assign Variables
     FIELD_NAME = field(FLDNUM)
     * Edit the field.
     set cursor on
     @ row(), col() get &FIELD_NAME
     read
     set cursor off
     @ 01, 00 to 24, 79 double              && Refresh the border.
     return
```

2. Save the document and exit your word processor. Type **CL CHCKBOOK** at the DOS prompt. Press **Enter**.

3. Type **MAILLIST**. Press **Enter**.

4. Press **F4**. The checkbook program menu appears.

5. Type **E** then press **Enter**. The full screen database editor appears.

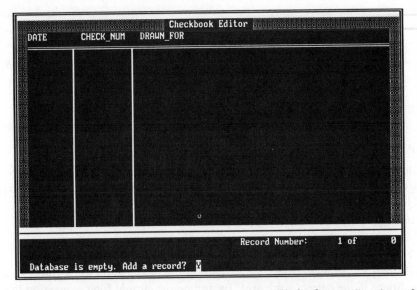

6. Press **Enter** to add a new record. Press **Enter**. Press **Right Arrow** five times. Notice the display scrolls to show the other database fields.

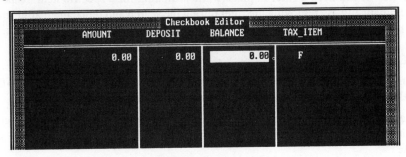

7. Press **Esc**. The checkbook program menu appears.

8. Type **Q** to select Quit. Press **Enter**. The DOS prompt appears.

9. Turn to Module 25 to continue the learning sequence.

Module 101
DBFILTER( )

DESCRIPTION

The DBFilter( ) function returns a string containing the filter expression for the current work area. If the current work area does not have a filter set, then DBFilter( ) returns a null string. The command line interface of the DBFilter( ) function appears below.

```
DBFILTER()
```

APPLICATIONS

Use the DBFilter( ) function to determine the current filter expression when you need to set up special conditions in the current work area. By storing the current filter expression in a string, you can restore it after performing a specialized task. This is especially convenient to use during search routines. If you keep a filter in place while searching for a specific item, response time increases dramatically. By removing the filter during the search and replacing it after finding the particular record, you can improve response time while maintaining the system status.

TYPICAL OPERATION

In this example you check for any filters set in the current work area by using the DBFilter( ) function. Begin this example in your word processor with CHCKBOOK.PRG loaded.

1. Change the following text in the DISP_SCRN5 procedure (use the same text created in Module 102).

```
endif
* Show any active filters.
if dbfilter() = ""
    @ 22, 04 say 'NO ACTIVE FILTERS   '
else
    @ 22, 04 say 'Filter set to: ' + dbfilter()
endif
set color to 'W/N,N/W,,,W+/N'
```

2. Save the document and exit your word processor. Type **CL CHCKBOOK** at the DOS prompt. Press **Enter**.

3. Type **MAILLIST**. Press **Enter**.

4. Press **F4**. The checkbook program menu appears. Notice the program accurately displays a message saying no filters currently exist.

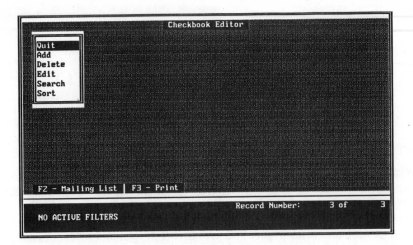

5. Type **Q** to select Quit. Press **Enter**. The DOS prompt appears.

6. Turn to Module 97 to continue the learning sequence.

Module 102
DBRELATION( ), DBRSELECT( )

DESCRIPTION

The DBRelation( ) and DBRSelect functions provide information about any relations created between the current work area and any other work areas using the Set Relation command. DBRelation( ) returns a string containing the linking expression for relation EXPN. If relation EXPN does not exist, DBRelation( ) returns a null string. DBRSelect( ) returns a number indicating which work area is the target of relation EXPN. If relation EXPN does not exist, then DBRSelect( ) returns a zero. The command line interface of the DBRelation( ) and DBRSelect functions appears below.

```
DBRELATION(<EXPN>)
DBRSELECT(<EXPN>)
```

APPLICATIONS

Use the DBRelation( ) and DBRSelect functions within generic routines to determine the effect of a given procedure on databases other than the one in the current work area. If a generic procedure produces adverse effects when the program uses certain relations, you can use the DBRelation( ) function to obtain the linking expression. Then, you can obtain the target work area by using the DBRSelect( ) function. All this allows you to terminate the relation temporarily while you perform the generic function. You can then restore the relation after completing the current task.

TYPICAL OPERATION

In this example you use the DBRelation( ) and DBRSelect( ) functions to determine if any relations exist when you enter the checkbook program. Begin this example in your word processor with CHCKBOOK.PRG loaded.

1. Add the following text to the DISP_SCRN5 procedure.
    ```
    endif
    * Show any active relations.
    if dbrelation(1) = ""
       @ 22, 04 say 'NO ACTIVE RELATIONS'
    else
       @ 22, 04 say 'Relation ' + dbrelation(1) +;
          ' set between current work area and ' + str(dbrselect(1), 1, 0)
    endif
    set color to 'W/N,N/W,,,W+/N'
    ```

2. Save the document and exit your word processor. Type **CL CHCKBOOK** at the DOS prompt. Press **Enter**. The Clipper batch file clears the screen, then compiles and links the program.

3. Type **MAILLIST**. Press **Enter**. The mailing list program menu appears.

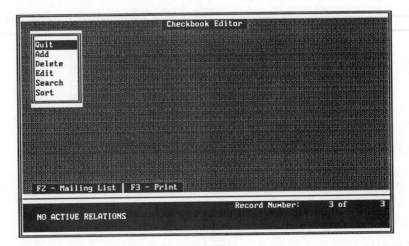

4. Press **F4**. The checkbook program menu appears. Notice the program accurately displays a message saying no relations currently exist.

5. Type **Q** to select Quit. Press **Enter**. The DOS prompt appears.

6. Turn to Module 101 to continue the learning sequence.

Module 103
DELETED( )

DESCRIPTION

The Deleted( ) command provides a method of determining deleted status of the current record. It usually appears as an argument in a control structure. The command line interface of the Deleted( ) function appears below.

```
DELETED( )
```

APPLICATIONS

Use the Deleted( ) function when you want to determine the deleted status of the current record.

TYPICAL OPERATION

In this example you add a message to the sample program showing the deleted status of the current record using the Deleted( ) function. Begin this example in your word processor with MAILLIST.PRG loaded.

1. Add the following text after the @ Say command shown below.

```
@ 02, 65 say reccount()
if deleted()
   @ 02, 04 say ' DELETED '
else
   @ 02, 04 say '  ▒▒▒▒▒▒▒▒  '  && Press Alt-177 (on numeric keypad) 9 times.
endif
if bof()
```

2. Save the document and exit your word processor. Type **CL MAILLIST** at the DOS prompt. Press **Enter**.

3. Type **MAILLIST**. Press **Enter**.

4. Type **D**. The DELETED message appears.

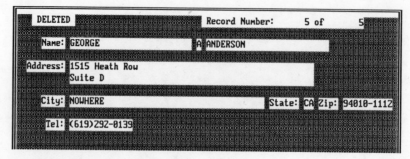

5. Type **Q**. The DOS prompt appears.

6. Turn to Module 105 to continue the learning sequence.

Module 104
DESCEND( )

DESCRIPTION

The Descend( ) function tells Clipper to sort, index, and search database files in descending rather than ascending order. Normally Clipper performs all sorts, indexes, and searches in ascending order. The command line interface of the Descend( ) function appears below.

```
DESCEND(<EXP>)
```

APPLICATIONS

Use the Descend( ) function whenever you need to index, sort, or search a database in descending order. One example of this is when you want the newest orders in an inventory database to appear first. This reduces the average search time required to find an order since you work on the newest orders most often.

Another example of when to use the Descend( ) function is financial databases. In some cases you want the largest sums of money displayed first, the least displayed last.

TYPICAL OPERATION

In this example you add the option of using ascending or descending order when reindexing the checkbook database. Begin this example in your word processor with CHCKBOOK.PRG loaded.

1. Add the following text to the variable section of the SORT_REC procedure.

```
private NAME_ARRAY, AVAIL_ARRAY, ORDER_ARRAY, SORT_STRING
private TEMP_STRING, SORT_SELECT, ORDER_SELECT, PREV_LEN
declare NAME_ARRAY[7]
NAME_ARRAY[1] = 'Quit'
NAME_ARRAY[2] = 'Date'
NAME_ARRAY[3] = 'Check Number'
NAME_ARRAY[4] = 'Drawn For'
NAME_ARRAY[5] = 'Check Amount'
NAME_ARRAY[6] = 'Deposit Amount'
NAME_ARRAY[7] = 'Tax Ded. Item'
declare AVAIL_ARRAY[7]
afill(AVAIL_ARRAY, .T.)
declare ORDER_ARRAY[2]
ORDER_ARRAY[1] = 'Ascending Order'
ORDER_ARRAY[2] = 'Descending Order'
SORT_STRING = ' '
TEMP_STRING = ' '
SORT_SELECT = 2
ORDER_SELECT = 1
PREV_LEN = 1
```

2. Add the following text to the SORT_REC procedure.

```
   endcase
* If the user selects quit, exit the loop.
   if NAME_ARRAY[SORT_SELECT] = 'Quit'
      exit
   endif
* Ask the user to select between ascending and descending
* order.
   save screen to TEMP_SCRN
   set color to 'W/N,N/W,,,W+/N'
   @ 12, 12 to 15, 29 double
   ORDER_SELECT = achoice(13, 13, 14, 28, ORDER_ARRAY)
* Change the SORT_STRING variable to match the descending
* order requirement.
   if ORDER_ARRAY[ORDER_SELECT] = 'Descending Order'
      TEMP_STRING = substr(SORT_STRING, PREV_LEN, len(SORT_STRING) - ;
        PREV_LEN - 2)
      if PREV_LEN = 1
         SORT_STRING = ''
      else
         SORT_STRING = substr(SORT_STRING, 1, PREV_LEN)
      endif
      SORT_STRING = SORT_STRING + 'DESCEND(' + TEMP_STRING + ') + '
   endif
   restore screen from TEMP_SCRN
   set color to 'N/W,W/N,,,W+/N'
* Set PREV_LEN to the new length of SORT_STRING for use with
* the descending order function.
   PREV_LEN = len(SORT_STRING)
enddo
```

3. Save the document and exit your word processor. Type **CL CHCKBOOK** at the DOS prompt. Press **Enter**.

4. Type **MAILLIST**. Press **Enter**. The mailing list program menu appears.

5. Press **F4**. The checkbook program menu appears.

6. Press **Down Arrow** until the Sort option of the menu appears.

7. Press **Enter**. The Sort menu appears.

8. Select Date by pressing **Down Arrow**. Press **Enter**. The program highlights the Date option and asks which order you want to sort in.

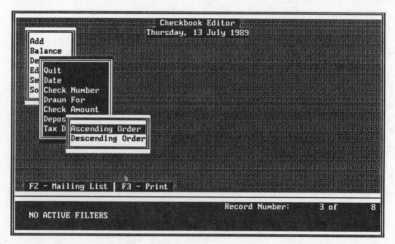

9. Select Descending by pressing **Down Arrow** then **Enter**. The program returns the selector to the Quit option on the first menu.

10. Select Drawn For by pressing **Down Arrow** twice. Press **Enter**. Select Descending by pressing **Down Arrow** then **Enter**. Select Quit by pressing **Enter**. The program displays an error message (which we fix in the next module).

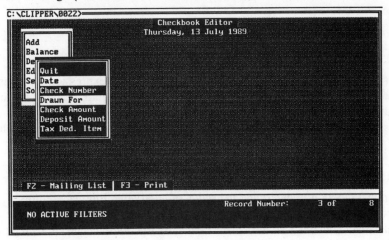

11. Turn to Module 41 to continue the learning sequence.

Module 105
EMPTY( )

DESCRIPTION

The Empty( ) function determines if a variable or any other expression contains nothing. Empty( ) returns true (.T.) when a character variable contains a null, spaces, tabs, or carriage returns; a numeric variable contains a zero; a date variable contains a null; or a logical variable contains false (.F.). The command line interface of the Empty( ) function appears below.

```
EMPTY(<EXP>)
```

APPLICATIONS

Use the Empty( ) function to determine the status of a variable. Empty( ) returns .T. when the variable contains a null value. You can use the Empty( ) function to ensure the key field of every record in a database contains a value. This is especially true for data entry screen input.

TYPICAL OPERATION

In this example you use the Empty( ) function to ensure the user fills all three fields used as a key in the sample database index. Begin this example in your word processor with MAILLIST.PRG loaded.

1. Add the following text to the get statements in the append elseif statement section.
   ```
   append blank
   @ 04, 12 get FIRST_NAME picture '@!' valid .not. empty(FIRST_NAME)
   @ 04, 38 get MIDDLE picture '!' valid .not. empty(MIDDLE)
   @ 04, 40 get LAST_NAME picture '@!' valid .not. empty (LAST_NAME)
   ```

2. Add the following text to the get statements in the edit elseif statement section.
   ```
   elseif ANSWER = 'E'
   @ 04, 12 get FIRST_NAME picture '@!' valid .not. empty(FIRST_NAME)
   @ 04, 38 get MIDDLE picture '!' valid .not. empty(MIDDLE)
   @ 04, 40 get LAST_NAME picture '@!' valid .not. empty (LAST_NAME)
   ```

3. Save the document and exit your word processor. Type **CL MAILLIST** at the DOS prompt. Press **Enter**.

4. Type **MAILLIST**. Press **Enter**.

5. Type **E** to execute the edit option. Press **Ctrl-T** to delete the contents of the first name field. Press **Enter**. The program will not allow you to exit the field without typing a name.

6. Type **GEORGE**. Press **Enter**. The cursor moves to the next field.

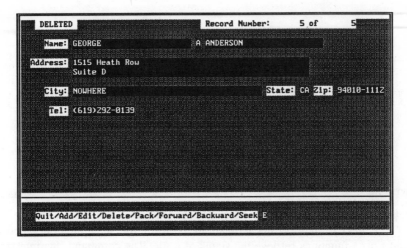

7. Press **PgDn** to exit the edit option. Type **Q**. The DOS prompt appears.
8. Turn to Module 139 to continue the learning sequence.

Module 106
FCLOSE( ), FCREATE( ), FERROR( ),
FILE( ), FOPEN( ), FREAD( ), FREADSTR( ),
FSEEK( ), FWRITE( )

DESCRIPTION

These functions all perform tasks on files. The FClose( ), FCreate( ), FOpen( ), FRead( ), FReadSTR( ), FSeek( ), and FWrite( ) functions perform file manipulation functions. The FError( ) and File( ) functions retrieve the status of a file. The command line interface of the FClose( ), FCreate( ), FError( ), File( ), FOpen( ), FRead( ), FReadSTR( ), FSeek( ), and FWrite( ) functions appears below.

NOTE
These functions all require an intimate knowledge of DOS as a minimum. In some cases you also need an understanding of the low level workings of DOS as well. Use these functions with great caution.

```
FCLOSE(<EXPN>)
FCREATE(<EXPC> [, <EXPN>])
FERROR( )
FILE(<EXPC>)
FOPEN(<EXPC> [, <EXPN>])
FREAD(<EXPN1>, @<MEMVARC>, <EXPN2>)
FREADSTR(<EXPN1>, <EXPN2>)
FSEEK(<EXPN1>, <EXPN2> [, <EXPN3>])
FWRITE(<EXPN1>, <EXPC> [, <EXPN2>])
```

The FClose( ) function closes a file previously opened using the FOpen( ) or FCreate( ) functions. When you open a file, DOS issues a name for it called a handle. When you close a file, you must give DOS the handle to close. EXPN contains the file handle.

The FCreate( ) function creates a new file. Once it creates the file, FCreate( ) returns the DOS file handle for the new file. EXPC contains the ASCII name you want to assign the file. You can also place a path in this variable as well. The option EXPN allows you to create a file with specific attributes. The attributes affect what you can do with the file. Table 106-1 contains a listing of the file attributes you can use.

Table 106-1. DOS File Attributes

Value	Attribute	Definition
0	Normal	Files with the normal attribute allow both reading and writing. They also appear on any directory searches you wish to perform.
1	Read Only	Files with the read only attribute allow file reading but not writing. You would not normally create a read only file within Clipper. However, you could create a read only file externally and open it in Clipper. These files also appear on any directory searches you want to perform.
2	Hidden	Files with the hidden attribute allow both reading and writing. They do not appear on any directory search using standard DOS commands. They will appear in directory searches using certain utility programs. You could use this attribute with Clipper to create files you do not want the user to find.
4	System	You must never use the system attribute with Clipper. DOS reserves this attribute for operating system specific files.

The FError( ) function retrieves the last DOS error code encountered during a file operation. This function allows you to tell the user what file error occurred. Table 106-2 provides a listing of DOS file error codes.

Table 106-2. Extended Error Information

Code	Description
0	No Error
2	File Not Found
3	Path Not Found
4	Too Many Open Files
5	Access Denied
6	Handle Invalid
11	Format Invalid
12	Access Code Invalid
13	Data Invalid
14	Unknown Unit
15	Disk Drive Invalid
16	Attempted to Remove Current Directory
17	Not Same Device
18	No More Files
19	Disk Write-Protected
20	Unknown Unit
21	Drive Not Ready
22	Unknown Command
23	Data Error (CRC)
24	Bad Request Structure Length
25	Seek Error
26	Unknown Media Type
27	Sector Not Found

Table 106-2. Extended Error Information (Cont.)

Code	Description
29	Write Fault
30	Read Fault
31	General Failure
32	Sharing Violation
33	Lock Violation
34	Disk Change Invalid
35	FCB Unavailable
36	Sharing Buffer Exceeded
50	Unsupported Network Request
51	Remote Machine Not Listening
52	Duplicate Name on Network
53	Network Name Not Found
54	Network Busy
55	Device No Longer Exists on Network
56	NetBIOS Command Limit Exceeded
57	Error in Network Adapter Hardware
58	Incorrect Response From Network
59	Unexpected Network Error
60	Remote Adapter Incompatible
64	Network Name Deleted
65	Network Access Denied
66	Incorrect Network Device Type
67	Network Name Not Found
68	Network Name Limit Exceeded
69	NetBIOS Session Limit Exceeded
71	Network Request Not Accepted
72	Print or Disk Redirection Paused
80	File Already Exists
82	Cannot Make Directory
83	Fail on Int 24h
84	Too Many Redirections
85	Duplicate Redirection
87	Invalid Parameter
88	Network Device Fault
89	Function Not Supported by Network
90	Required System Component Not Installed

The File( ) function returns the status of the filename contained in EXPC. If the file exists in the specified directory, then File( ) returns true. If you do not specify a file path, then Clipper uses the current directory.

The FOpen( ) function allows you to open a previously created file. EXPC contains the filename and file path. The optional EXPN clause allows you to designate how DOS opens the file. By limiting the range of the operations performed on a file, you can allow more than one person to access the file on a network. Table 106-3 contains a listing of the open codes allowed by Clipper.

Table 106-3. DOS File Open Attributes

Value	Attribute	Definition
1	Read Only	Files opened with the read only attribute allow file reading but not writing. You would not normally open a read only file on a non-network system. By opening a file as read only, you allow more than one person to view its contents.
2	Write Only	Files opened with the write only attribute allow file writing but not reading. You would not normally open a write only file on a non-network system. By opening a file as write only, you can change a file's contents without allowing the user to view it.
3	Read Write	Files opened with the read write attribute allow you to both read and write the file. Unfortunately, only one person on a network may open a file as read write without incurring damage to the file. This is the normal method of opening a file on non-network systems.

The FRead( ) function allows you to obtain information from a file opened using the FOpen( ) or FCreate( ) functions. You may also read information from a standard DOS file (for more information on standard DOS files, see your DOS manual). EXPN1 contains the file handle of the file you want to read (even DOS files have handles). The @MEMVARC clause contains the name of the memory variable used to hold the file input. EXPN2 contains the number of characters you want to read. There are three different returns from this function. If the value returned equals EXPN2, then the read was completely successful. If the value returned is less than EXPN2 but more than zero, then the read was successful. However, DOS found an end of file marker before it read all the characters you requested. Use the FError( ) function to make sure no other errors occurred. If the FRead( ) function returns zero, then the read was unsuccessful. Use the FError( ) function to find out what error occurred. Then, ask the user to correct the problem before attempting to read the file again.

The FReadSTR( ) function works much like the FRead( ) function. However, it differs in where you use it, the value returned, and the values input. EXPN1 contains the file handle. EXPN2 contains the number of characters to read. Instead of returning the number of characters read, this function returns the characters. You set the character string equal to the function instead of providing it as an input. Use this function when you do not need to know the number of characters actually read from the file.

The FSeek( ) function finds a particular place in the text file. For example, if the file contains fixed length records, you could find a particular record number using the FSeek( ) function. EXPN1 contains the file handle of the file you want to read. You may not use this function on standard DOS files in most cases (there are a limited number of special cases discussed in the DOS technical reference manual). EXPN2 contains the number of bytes to move from the current position in the specified direction. If you use a positive number, DOS moves the file pointer forward. If you use a negative number, DOS moves the file pointer backward. Clipper uses a default beginning point of the current pointer position and a default direction of forward. The optional clause EXPN3 contains a modifier for direction and starting position. Table 106-4 contains a listing of these modifiers. FSeek( ) returns the file pointer position from the beginning of the file.

Table 106-4. DOS File Pointer Direction and Starting Point Modifiers

Modifier	Description
0	Start at the beginning of the file. Move forward.
1	Start at the current file pointer position. Move forward.
2	Start at the end of the file. Move backward.

The FWrite( ) function outputs a character string to a file opened using the FOpen( ) or FCreate( ) functions. You may also write information to a standard DOS file (for more information on standard DOS files, see your DOS manual). EXPN1 contains the file handle of the file you want to write. EXPC contains the text string you want to write. The optional EXPN2 contains the number of bytes to write. If you do not include this parameter, DOS automatically writes the contents of the entire buffer (EXPC). This function returns the number of characters written. If this number does not equal EXPN2 (when specified) or the function returns 0, then the write failed. Use the FError( ) function to determine exactly what error occurred.

APPLICATIONS

Use these functions to manage text files output from word processors or other applications that do not produce system data files (SDF). You can also use these functions to create MODEM and other device interfaces to Clipper. Other uses include creating text files for export to other applications. For example, you can create formatted text files for your desktop publishing system. By using this technique, you can add formatting codes to the file so the user performs the minimum reformatting required. Finally, you can use these functions for error correction/ detection routines.

TYPICAL OPERATION

In this example you add file management routines to the print program using the functions listed above. Begin this example in your word processor with PRINT.PRG loaded.

1. Add the following variable to the beginning of the program.

```
PRNT_TEST = 'Y'
PRNT_FILE = space(74)
MENU_SEL = 2
ANSWER4 = 'Y'
```

2. Add the following code to the printer port selection section of the program.

```
@ 06, 04 say 'Enter the printer port you wish to use. ';
    get PRNT_PORT picture '@!'
read
* See if the user wants to print to a file.
if trim(PRNT_PORT) = 'FILE'
    @ 08, 04 say 'Enter the filename and path.'
    @ 09, 04 get PRNT_FILE picture '@!'
    read
    if .not. file(PRNT_FILE)
        PRNT_PORT = PRNT_FILE
    else
        @ 11, 04 say 'File already exists!  Do you want to overwrite it? ';
```

```
            get ANSWER4 picture '!'
        read
        if ANSWER4 = 'Y'
            PRNT_PORT = PRNT_FILE
        else
            @ 08, 04 say 'Enter the filename and path.'
            @ 09, 04 get PRNT_FILE picture '@!'
            read
            PRNT_PORT = PRNT_FILE
        endif
    endif
endif
do while .not. PRNT_ON (PRNT_PORT)
```

3. Add the following text to the PRNT_ON function.

```
set printer to &PORT_NAME
* Check the printer status if port is LPT1.
if trim(PRNT_PORT) = 'LPT1'
    if isprinter()
        IS_PORT = .T.
    else
        IS_PORT = .F.
    endif
else
    IS_PORT = .T.
endif
```

4. Save the document and exit your word processor. Type **CL PRINT** at the DOS prompt. Press **Enter**.

5. Type **PRINT**. Press **Enter**.

6. Type **FILE**. Press **Enter** to select file output instead of printer output. The program displays an entry asking for a filename.

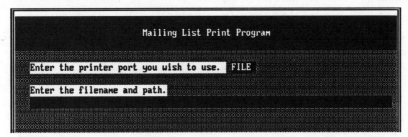

7. Type **EXAMPLE.TXT** and press **Enter**. Type **N** to forego running the printer test. The program displays a menu for selecting the database you want to print.

8. Select Notepad. The program displays another menu.

9. Select Category. The program asks if you want partial or complete notes.

10. Type **C**. The Main menu appears.

11. Select Quit. The DOS prompt appears.

12. Type **CLS** and press **Enter** to clear the display. Type **TYPE EXAMPLE.TXT**. Press **Enter**. The contents of the notepad printout appear.

```
C:\CLIPPER\0022>TYPE EXAMPLE.TXT
                    Notes Printout

       Note Number:3
       Subject: THIS IS THE THIRD NOTE.
       Priority Category: 1

       This is a high priority note. Notice the special category‌
                                            notation on
the printout.
       Note Number:1
       Subject: THIS IS THE FIRST NOTE.
       Category: GENERAL

       This is a note.
       Note Number:2
       Subject: THIS IS THE SECOND NOTE.
       Category: GENERAL

       This is a note too!
C:\CLIPPER\0022>
```

13. Type **PRINT**. Press **Enter**. The mailing list print program display appears.

14. Type **FILE**. Press **Enter** to select file output instead of printer output. The program displays an entry asking for a filename.

15. Type **EXAMPLE.TXT** and press **Enter**. The program displays a message saying the file already exists.

16. Type **Y** to overwrite the file. Type **N** to forego running the printer test. The program displays a menu for selecting the database you want to print.

17. Press **Enter** to select Check Book. The program displays another menu.

18. Select Check Date by pressing **Down Arrow**. Press **Enter**. The program prints the checkbook report. The Main menu appears.

19. Select Quit by pressing **Up Arrow**. Press **Enter**. The DOS prompt appears.

20. Type **CLS** and press **Enter** to clear the display. Type **TYPE EXAMPLE.TXT**. Press **Enter**. The contents of the checkbook printout appear.

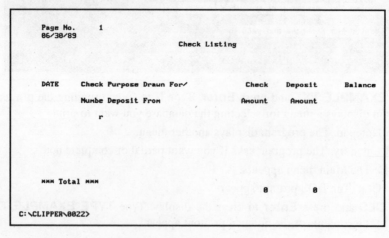

```
     Page No.      1
     06/30/89
                              Check Listing


     DATE      Check Purpose Drawn For/        Check       Deposit      Balance
               Numbe Deposit From              Amount      Amount
               r



     *** Total ***
                                                 0           0

C:\CLIPPER\0022>
```

21. Turn to Module 74 to continue the learning sequence.

Module 107
FCOUNT( ), FIELD( )/FIELDNAME( )

DESCRIPTION

The FCount( ) and Field( )/FieldName( ) functions assist you in determining the number of fields and the field names of a database. The FCount function returns the total number of database fields. The Field( )/FieldName( ) function returns the name of EXPN field. If you use a number higher than the total number of fields in the database, Clipper returns a null string (""). Clipper also returns a null string for field zero. The command line interface of the FCount( ) and Field( )/FieldName( ) functions appears below.

```
FCOUNT( )
FIELD(<EXPN>)
FIELDNAME(<EXPN>)
```

APPLICATIONS

Use the FCount( ) function when you want to know how many fields a database contains. This is especially useful when you want to create generic routines for handling arrays of database field names or create loops for working with the database fields.

Use the Field( )/FieldName( ) function when you want to know the name of a specific database field. By using the FCount( ) function, you can determine the maximum number of fields contained in the database in advance. These functions are especially useful for functions that use arrays of database fields as part of an argument.

TYPICAL OPERATION

In this example you create an array and initialize it with the names of the database fields for CHCKBOOK.DBF. You use the FCount( ) function to declare an array and create a loop. You also use the Field( )/FieldName( ) function to initialize the array declared using FCount( ). Begin this example in your word processor with CHCKBOOK.PRG loaded.

1. Add the following variable to the beginning of the program.
```
ANSWER = 0
FIELD_NUMBER = 1
* Create the menu array and place the menu values in it.
```

2. Add the following text after opening the database at the beginning of the program.
```
use CHCKBOOK index CHCKNUM, DATE
* Create an array containing the database field names for
* use with database editing routines.
declare FIELD_ARRAY[fcount()]
* Initialize the array with the field names.
for FIELD_NUMBER = 1 to fcount()
   FIELD_ARRAY[FIELD_NUMBER] = fieldname(FIELD_NUMBER)
next
* Temporarily display the field names so we can check them.
for FIELD_NUMBER = 1 to fcount()
```

```
        @ FIELD_NUMBER + 2, 04 say FIELD_ARRAY[FIELD_NUMBER]
next
wait
* Perform this procedure until the user selects quit.
```

3. Save the document and exit your word processor. Type **CL CHCKBOOK** at the DOS prompt. Press **Enter**.

4. Type **MAILLIST**. Press **Enter**.

5. Press **F4**. A list of database field names appears.

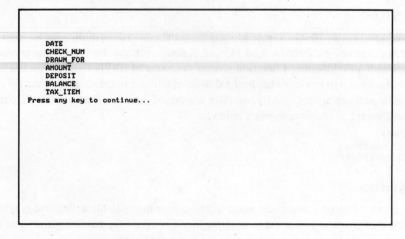

```
DATE
CHECK_NUM
DRAWN_FOR
AMOUNT
DEPOSIT
BALANCE
TAX_ITEM
Press any key to continue...
```

6. Press **Enter**. The checkbook program menu appears.

7. Type **Q** to select Quit. Press **Enter**. The DOS prompt appears.

8. Load CHCKBOOK.PRG into your word processor. Remove the temporary text which appears below.

```
* Temporarily display the field names so we can check them.
for FIELD_NUMBER = 1 to fcount()
    @ FIELD_NUMBER + 2, 04 say FIELD_ARRAY[FIELD_NUMBER]
next
wait
```

9. Save the document and exit your word processor.

10. Turn to Module 100 to continue the learning sequence.

Module 108
FLOCK( ), RLOCK( )/LOCK( )

DESCRIPTION

The FLock( ) and RLock( )/Lock( ) functions change the accessibility of a given portion of a database. You normally use these commands exclusively in a network environment. The FLock( ) function locks an entire database. The RLock( )/Lock( ) function locks a single record in a database. Both commands work only with shared databases. You open a database in the shared mode by setting the exclusive feature off and not using the exclusive clause of the Use command. Opening a database in the shared mode means more than one person can use it at once. The command line interface of the FLock( ) and RLock( )/Lock( ) functions appears below.

```
FLOCK( )
RLOCK( )
LOCK( )
```

When you create an application for use within a network, you also create a hazard to the database. If two people access and change a record in the database at the same time, which update does Clipper use to change the database? To prevent this situation, you use the FLock( ) and RLock( )/Lock( ) functions. Both functions return true if you successfully lock the database or record. If they return false, then Clipper will not allow you to change the affected database section.

APPLICATIONS

Use the FLock( ) and RLock( )/Lock( ) functions in a network environment to prevent more than one user from updating the same record at the same time. Each function has a distinct purpose. If you want to change the database globally, for example by using the Pack or Reindex command, then you need to lock the entire database using the FLock( ) function. If you want to change a single database record, for example by using the Append or Edit command, then you need to only lock a single record using the RLock( ) or Lock( ) function. If you need to open the database momentarily to perform a global operation, employ the Set Exclusive On (Module 77) or Use command with the exclusive feature active instead of these functions.

TYPICAL OPERATION

In this example you use the Clipper-supplied network program to see how the FLock( ) and RLock( )/Lock functions work. This example works on both network and single user machines. If you have a network, you can use the program at two or more machines to see the effects of trying to open a database with FLock( ) active. You can also see the result when you try to access a locked record. For DOS machines not operating on a network, you can see the change in file status. The LOCKS.PRG file contains the routines used to lock records and databases using Clipper. Begin this example in the Clipper directory at the DOS prompt.

1. Type **CLD NETWORK** and press **Enter** to compile the network program.

2. Type **CD \CLIPPER\0022** to get back to the sample program directory. Type **NETWORK** and press **Enter** after Clipper compiles and links the network program. The network menu appears.

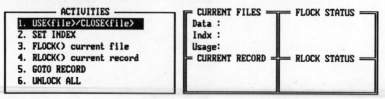

3. Type **1**. The program asks which file you want to use. Notice it automatically displays a list of database files to choose from.

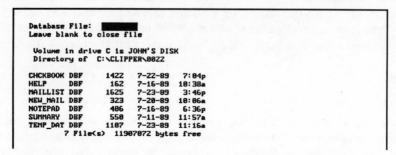

4. Type **MAILLIST**. The program asks if you want to open the file for exclusive use.

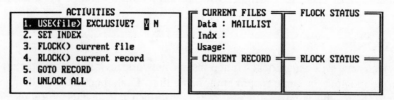

5. Type **Y**. The program opens the file for exclusive use. Notice it displays Not Applicable for FLock and RLock status.

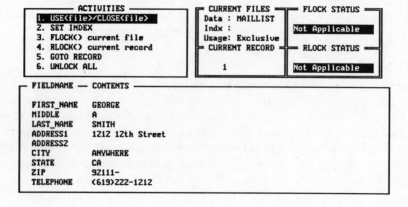

6. Type **1**. The program asks which file you want to use. Leave the filename blank (erase MAILLIST if necessary) and press **Enter**. The program closes the database.

7. Type **1**. The program asks which file you want to use.

8. Type **MAILLIST**. Type **N** when asked if you want to open the database for exclusive use. The program opens the file for shared use. Notice it displays Not FLOCKed for FLock status and Not RLOCKed for RLock status.

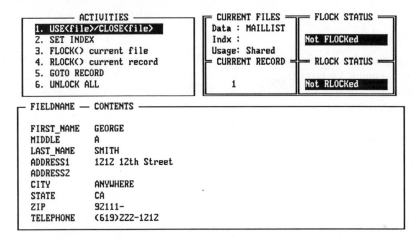

9. Type **3**. The program displays MAILLIST FLOCKed in the FLock status.

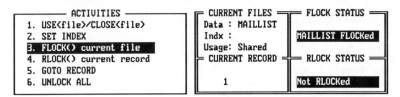

10. Type **4**. The program displays Not FLOCKed in the FLock status and Rec 1 RLOCKed in the RLock status.

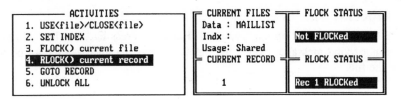

11. Press **Esc**. The DOS prompt appears.

12. Turn to Module 127 to continue the learning sequence.

Module 109
FOUND( )

DESCRIPTION

The Found( ) function returns the status of a Seek, Find, or Locate/Continue command. If the record exists, Found( ) returns true; otherwise, it returns false. The command line interface of the Found( ) function appears below.

```
FOUND( )
```

APPLICATIONS

Use the Found( ) function to determine the status of a record search using the Seek, Find, or Locate/Continue commands. When you determine the status, you can inform the user if the search succeeded or failed.

TYPICAL OPERATION

In this example you enhance the seek option of the sample program using the Found( ) function. Begin this example in your word processor with MAILLIST.PRG loaded.

1. Add the following text as shown below.
   ```
   if eof()
      @ 23,04 say ' End of File '
   endif
   if .not. found() .and. ANSWER = 'S'
      @ 23, 04 say ' Name not found. '
   endif
   if .not. (bof() .or. eof()) .or. found()
   ```

2. Save the document and exit your word processor. Type **CL MAILLIST** at the DOS prompt. Press **Enter**.

3. Type **MAILLIST**. Press **Enter**.

4. Type **S** to select the seek option. Type **NOTFOUND**. Press **Enter**. The program displays a name not found message. Notice the display shows the database record pointer at the end of the file.

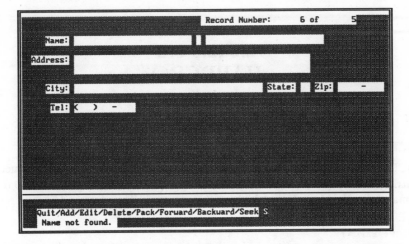

5. Type **S**, then **WILSON**. Press **Enter**. The program finds the name in the database and displays it.

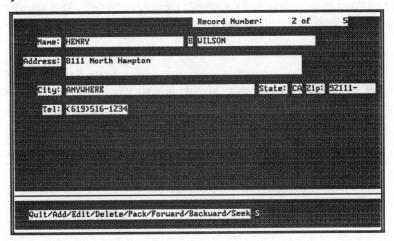

6. Type **Q**. The DOS prompt appears.
7. Turn to Module 103 to continue the learning sequence.

DESCRIPTION

The HardCR( ) function changes the soft carriage returns (carriage return only) in memo fields to hard carriage returns (carriage return and line feed). This lets you display a memo field using the same margins as the MemoEdit( ) function that created it. The command line interface of the HardCR( ) function appears below.

```
HARDCR(<EXPC>)
```

APPLICATIONS

Use the HardCR( ) function to display a previously created memo field. This allows you to show the contents of the memo field while eliminating the possibility of the user modifying it.

TYPICAL OPERATION

In this example you add the capability to display memo fields to the SHOW_RECS procedure using the HardCR( ) function. Begin this example in your word processor with DOSSHELL. PRG loaded.

1. Add the following text to the SHOW_RECS procedure.

```
            case type(FIELD_CONTENTS) = 'M'
               DISP_STR = hardcr(&FIELD_CONTENTS) + chr (13) + chr(10)
            case type(FIELD_CONTENTS) = 'L'
               if &FIELD_CONTENTS = .T.
                  DISP_STR = '.T.'
               else
                  DISP_STR = '.F.'
               endif
         endcase
      else
         FIELD_CONTENTS = FIELD_ARRAY[COUNTER]
         do case
            case type(FIELD_CONTENTS) = 'C'
               DISP_STR = DISP_STR + ' ' + &FIELD_CONTENTS
            case type(FIELD_CONTENTS) = 'D'
               DISP_STR = DISP_STR + ' ' + dtoc(&FIELD_CONTENTS)
            case type(FIELD_CONTENTS) = 'N'
               DISP_STR = DISP_STR + ' ' + str(&FIELD_CONTENTS)
            case type(FIELD_CONTENTS) = 'M'
               DISP_STR = DISP_STR + chr(10) + chr(13) +;
                  hardcr(&FIELD_CONTENTS) + chr(10) + chr(13)
```

2. Save the document and exit your word processor. Type **CL DOSSHELL** at the DOS prompt. Press **Enter**.

3. Type **MAILLIST** and press **Enter**. The mailing list program menu appears.

4. Press **F5** to select the notepad program. Press **F10** to activate the DOS shell menu. Type **S** and press **Enter**. The program displays the notepad database records. Notice the display now contains the memo field.

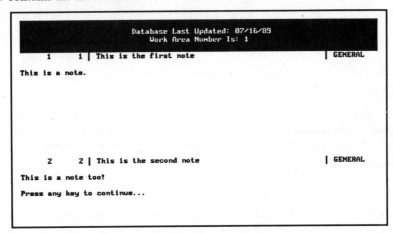

5. Press **Enter**. The second page of the notepad database appears. Notice the line breaks for the memo field appear in the same place as for the notepad edit display.

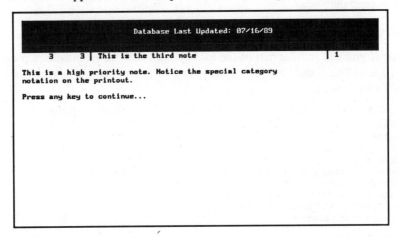

6. Press **Enter**. The DOS shell menu appears.
7. Type **Q** and press **Enter** to quit the DOS shell menu. Press **Enter** to select Quit. The DOS prompt appears.
8. Turn to Module 112 to continue the learning sequence.

Module 111
HEADER( )

DESCRIPTION

The Header( ) function returns the length of the header for the database in the selected work area. The header contains identifying information about the database. It appears before any records. The command line interface of the Header( ) function appears below.

```
HEADER( )
```

APPLICATIONS

Use the Header( ) function to obtain the length of the header area of a database. Use this function in conjunction with the LastRec( ) and RecSize( ) functions to determine the exact size of a database. By knowing this information you can check a target disk for the required space before attempting to copy the database to it. Or you can determine the number of files to copy to a set of disks for backup purposes.

TYPICAL OPERATION

In this example you add another part of the backup routine to the maintenance program using the Header( ), LastRec( ), and RecSize( ) functions. Begin this example in your word processor with MAINT.PRG loaded.

1. Add the following variables to the beginning of the maintenance program.
   ```
   DIR_SKEL = ' '
   DIR_SIZE = 0
   DIR_FILE = space(12)
   COUNTER = 0
   * Create a directory array to hold database filenames.
   DIR_SIZE = adir('*.DBF')
   declare DIR_ARRAY[DIR_SIZE]
   adir('*.DBF', DIR_ARRAY)
   * Display a directory.
   ```

2. Add the following text to the backup section of the maintenance program.
   ```
   ? 'Copying files in ' + curdir() + ' to drive A.'
   ?
   for COUNTER = 1 to DIR_SIZE
       ? 'Copying database ' + DIR_ARRAY[COUNTER] + ' to drive A. '
       DIR_FILE = DIR_ARRAY[COUNTER]
       use &DIR_FILE
       ?? ltrim(str(header() + (lastrec() * recsize()) + 1, 10, 0)) ;
           + ' bytes'
   next
   if doserror() <> 0
   ```

3. Save the document and exit your word processor. Type **CLD MAINT** at the DOS prompt. Press **Enter**.

4. Type **MAINT**. Press **Enter**. The program asks for a directory path and skeleton.

5. Type **'*.DBF'** and press **Enter**. The program displays a listing of files ending with .DBF. Notice the directory size of each file. Then the program asks if you want to delete any files.

6. Type **'N'** and press **Enter**. The program asks if you want to rename any files.

7. Type **'N'** and press **Enter**. The program asks if you want to perform a data file backup.

8. Place a blank, formatted disk in drive A. Type **'Y'** and press **Enter**. The drive light on drive A illuminates. The program displays a file copy message, the amount of memory required, and exits normally. Notice the amounts shown match the file sizes returned by DOS.

```
Type directory path and skeleton
'*.DBF'
CHCKBOOK DBF     1035   07/15/89
MAILLIST DBF     1625   07/16/89
NOTEPAD  DBF      406   07/16/89
SUMMARY  DBF      550   07/11/89
NEWTEMP  DBF     1035   07/15/89
HELP     DBF      162   07/16/89

Do you want to delete any of the files? 'N'
Do you want to rename any of the files? 'N'
Do you want to backup the data files? 'Y'
Place disk in drive A
Copying files in CLIPPER\0022 to drive A.
Copying database CHCKBOOK.DBF to drive A. 1035 bytes
Copying database MAILLIST.DBF to drive A. 1625 bytes
Copying database NOTEPAD.DBF to drive A. 406 bytes
Copying database SUMMARY.DBF to drive A. 550 bytes
Copying database NEWTEMP.DBF to drive A. 1035 bytes
Copying database HELP.DBF to drive A. 162 bytes
C:\CLIPPER\0022>
```

9. Turn to Module 28 to continue the learning sequence.

Module 112
IF( )/IIF( ), EVAL( )

DESCRIPTION

Both the If( )/IIf( ) and Eval( ) functions allow you to perform in-line analysis of an expression and perform some action based on the result. These two functions differ in their approach to analysis. The If( )/IIf( ) function performs a logical analysis of the condition. Either the condition is true or false. The result determines which of two paths that If( )/IIf( ) takes. The Eval( ) function performs a procedural analysis. It uses a program sequence and determines a result based on input to that sequence. The command line interface of the If( )/IIf( ) and Eval( ) functions appears below.

```
IF(<EXPL>, <EXP1>, <EXP2>)
IIF(<EXPL>, <EXP1>, <EXP2>)
EVAL(<CODE BLOCK> [, <CODE BLOCK ARGUMENT LIST>])
```

The If( )/IIf( ) function lets you perform in-line evaluations of a logical expression and perform one of two actions based on that evaluation. EXPL contains the logical statement to evaluate. EXP1 contains the expression, function, or command Clipper chooses if EXPL evaluates true. EXP2 contains the expression, function, or command Clipper chooses if EXPL evaluates false. The If( )/IIf( ) function lets you perform only one action for each condition.

The Eval( ) function consists of two parts: the evaluation section and the argument section. You declare a code block used to create the evaluation section prior to using Eval( ). Place its name in the CODE BLOCK variable. Eval( ) uses the values placed in CODE BLOCK ARGUMENT LIST as input to the code block in the evaluation section. Eval( ) reports only the final result (output) of the evaluation. The code block can store any intermediate results in an array or group of variables. A complete description of code blocks is out of the scope of this book. Refer to the Clipper manual for a thorough discussion of code blocks.

APPLICATIONS

Use the If( )/IIf( ) function in place of an IF THEN ELSE command when you want to perform one of two actions based on current conditions. This command executes faster and requires less memory than an equivalent IF THEN ELSE command. However, the IF THEN ELSE command provides greater flexibility. In most cases use the IIf( ) form of the function so you can perform searches for the command from within your word processor. Both forms of the function perform exactly the same.

This function provides the greatest functionality in display statements where you display one string if a condition exists and another string if it doesn't. This is especially useful on forms where you want to provide the user a reasonable choice based on current conditions. Another display type function is printouts. You can force a single print routine to perform multiple tasks based on user input. For example, you could toggle the report heading on or off based on user needs.

Use the Eval( ) function when you require a flexible assessment of a condition. While the Eval( ) function returns only the final result, you can use the code block to return intermediate results as well. This makes the Eval( ) function useful for statistical and other types of analysis. The only problem with using this function is the amount of time required to create the code block. You pay for the flexibility provided by Eval( ) with more complex programming requirements. The Eval( ) function works best when the flexibility required of the evaluation overrides the complexity of the solution.

TYPICAL OPERATION

In this example you compare the memory requirements of an IF THEN ELSE command versus an If( )/IIf( ) function. This example also shows how to typically use the If( )/IIf( ) function within a program to reduce memory requirements without reducing functionality. Begin this example at the DOS prompt.

1. Type **DIR MAILLIST.OBJ** and press **Enter**. DOS displays the mailing list object file size and other parameters. Type **DIR MAILLIST.EXE** and press **Enter**. DOS displays the mailing list executable file size and other parameters.

```
C:\CLIPPER\0022>DIR MAILLIST.OBJ

 Volume in drive C is JOHN'S DISK
 Directory of  C:\CLIPPER\0022

MAILLIST OBJ     5284    7-23-89   3:38p
          1 File(s)  12505088 bytes free

C:\CLIPPER\0022>DIR MAILLIST.EXE

 Volume in drive C is JOHN'S DISK
 Directory of  C:\CLIPPER\0022

MAILLIST EXE   244032    7-23-89   3:40p
          1 File(s)  12505088 bytes free

C:\CLIPPER\0022>
```

2. Load MAILLIST.PRG into your word processor. Remove the following text from the DISPLAY_STATUS procedure.
```
if deleted()
   @ 21, 04 say ' DELETED '
else
   @ 21, 04 say '           '
endif
```

3. Add the following text to the DISPLAY_STATUS procedure.
```
@ 21, 71 say reccount()
@ 21, 04 say iif(deleted(), ' DELETED ', '           ')
do case
```

4. Save the document and exit your word processor. Type **CL MAILLIST** at the DOS prompt. Press **Enter**.

5. Type **DIR MAILLIST.OBJ** and press **Enter**. DOS displays the mailing list object file size and other parameters. Type **DIR MAILLIST.EXE** and press **Enter**. DOS displays the mailing list executable file size and other parameters. Notice both files consume less space than before.

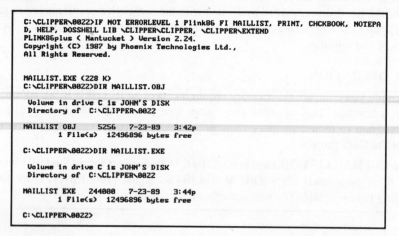

```
C:\CLIPPER\0022>IF NOT ERRORLEVEL 1 Plink86 FI MAILLIST, PRINT, CHCKBOOK, NOTEPA
D, HELP, DOSSHELL LIB \CLIPPER\CLIPPER, \CLIPPER\EXTEND
PLINK86plus ( Nantucket ) Version 2.24.
Copyright (C) 1987 by Phoenix Technologies Ltd.,
All Rights Reserved.


MAILLIST.EXE (228 K)
C:\CLIPPER\0022>DIR MAILLIST.OBJ

 Volume in drive C is JOHN'S DISK
 Directory of  C:\CLIPPER\0022

MAILLIST OBJ    5256   7-23-89   3:42p
        1 File(s)  12496896 bytes free

C:\CLIPPER\0022>DIR MAILLIST.EXE

 Volume in drive C is JOHN'S DISK
 Directory of  C:\CLIPPER\0022

MAILLIST EXE   244000   7-23-89   3:44p
        1 File(s)  12496896 bytes free

C:\CLIPPER\0022>
```

6. Type **MAILLIST** and press **Enter**. The mailing list program menu appears.
7. Type **D**. The program reacts as before and displays a deleted status for the record.

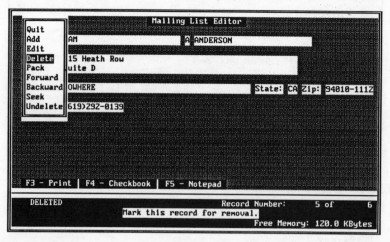

8. Type **U**. The program removes the deleted status for the record.

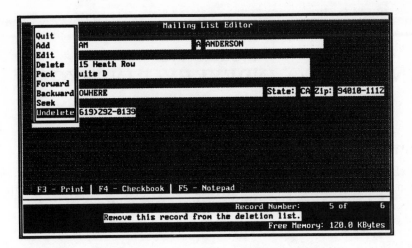

9. Type **Q** and press **Enter** to select Quit. The DOS prompt appears.
10. Turn to Module 113 to continue the learning sequence.

Module 113
INDEXEXT( ), INDEXKEY( ), INDEXORD( )

DESCRIPTION

The IndexEXT( ), IndexKey( ), and IndexORD( ) functions all provide different status information about the indexes used with Clipper programs. The command line interface of the IndexEXT( ), IndexKey( ), and IndexORD( ) functions appears below.

```
INDEXEXT( )
INDEXKEY(<EXPN>)
INDEXORD( )
```

The IndexEXT( ) function returns a character string containing the extension used for the index files. Clipper uses a NTX extension for its own special index files. These indexes allow you to perform searches and other index related functions faster than dBASE III indexes. Clipper also allows you to use the dBASE III NDX extension for compatibility reasons.

The IndexKey( ) function returns the key used for the specified index to a database in the current work area. EXPN contains the index number. When you specify 0, IndexKey( ) returns the key for the controlling index, no matter where it occurs in the index file list. You change the controlling index using the Set Order To command (Module 77).

The IndexORD( ) function returns the position of the controlling index within the list of current indexes. When you originally open the indexes using the index clause of the Use or Set Index To command, the controlling index appears first. You change the controlling index using the Set Order To command (Module 77). Although this changes the controlling index, it does not change the index order.

APPLICATIONS

Use the IndexEXT( ) function when you want to create a program or procedure that adjusts itself to the current index type. Since Clipper allows two different types of index, you need to know which type the current program uses to create generic procedures. For example, you could create a generic print routine which allows you to use either index type to order the printout. The NTX extension index file provides speed, while the NDX extension index file provides compatibility.

Use the IndexKey( ) function to retrieve the key used to create an index. You could use the key for an index status display to the user showing the order of the current database. By doing this, you allow the user to keep track of database status in complex program environments or in networks. This function also allows you to check if an index exists before creating a temporary index for print routines. By checking for the existence of the index first, you save valuable indexing time, especially when using larger database files.

Use the IndexORD( ) function to change the order of a database by changing the controlling index, then change the order back to its original state. By placing the current controlling order in a variable, you could change the order back once you perform a desired task. As with the

IndexEXT( ) function, this allows you to create generic functions that do not rely on a known program state. Instead, the program automatically compensates for any differences between calling procedures.

TYPICAL OPERATION

In this example you add an index status display to the DOS shell program using the IndexEXT( ), IndexKey( ), and IndexORD( ) functions. Begin this example in your word processor with DOSSHELL.PRG loaded.

1. Add the following text to the beginning of the DOS shell program.

```
declare MENU_ARRAY[6]
MENU_ARRAY[1] = 'Quit'
MENU_ARRAY[2] = 'Dos Shell'
MENU_ARRAY[3] = 'Show Records'
MENU_ARRAY[4] = 'Consolidate Checks'
MENU_ARRAY[5] = 'Type Text File'
MENU_ARRAY[6] = 'Index File Status'
SELECT = 2
* Save the display.
save screen to TEMP2
* Get the user selection.
do while MENU_ARRAY[SELECT] <> 'Quit'
    @ 03, 39 clear to 08, 58
    @ 03, 39 to 08, 58 double
    SELECT = achoice(04, 40, 07, 57, MENU_ARRAY)
    do case
        case MENU_ARRAY[SELECT] = 'Dos Shell'
            do DOS_SHELL
        case MENU_ARRAY[SELECT] = 'Show Records'
            do SHOW_RECS
        case MENU_ARRAY[SELECT] = 'Consolidate Checks'
            do CONSOLIDATE
        case MENU_ARRAY[SELECT] = 'Type Text File'
            do TYPE_FILE
        case MENU_ARRAY[SELECT] = 'Index File Status'
            do IFILE_STATS
```

2. Add the following procedure to the end of the procedure section of the DOS shell program.

```
procedure IFILE_STATS
* This procedure returns the current status of the
* controlling index file.
save screen to IFILE
* Display a frame then the status information.
set color to N/W,W+/N
@ 13, 02 clear to 19, 77
@ 13, 02 to 19, 77 double
@ 14, 04 say 'Index Extension Used:    ' + indexext()
@ 15, 04 say 'Controlling Index Order: ' + ltrim(str(indexord(),3,0))
@ 16, 04 say 'Controlling Index Key:   ' + indexkey(0)
@ 18, 04 say 'Press any key when ready...'
inkey(0)
set color to 'W/N,N/W,,,W+/N'
restore screen from IFILE
return
```

3. Save the document and exit your word processor. Type **CL DOSSHELL** at the DOS prompt. Press **Enter**.

4. Type **MAILLIST** and press **Enter**. The mailing list program menu appears.

5. Press **F10** to activate the DOS shell menu. Type **I**. A new menu entry appears.

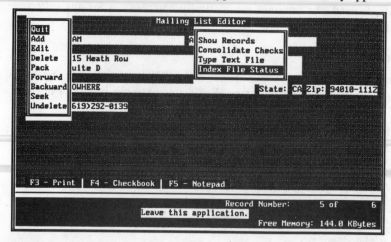

6. Press **Enter**. The program displays the status of the index files.

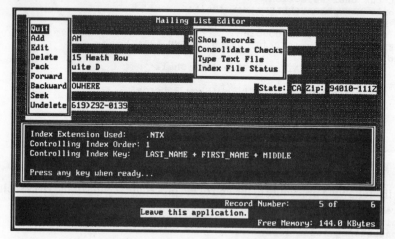

7. Press **Enter** to return to the DOS shell menu. Type **Q** and press **Enter** to quit the DOS shell menu. Press **Enter** to select Quit. The DOS prompt appears.

8. Turn to Module 132 to continue the learning sequence.

Module 114
INKEY( ), LASTKEY( ), NEXTKEY( ),
READKEY( ), SETKEY( )

DESCRIPTION

The InKey( ), LastKey( ), NextKey( ), ReadKey( ), and SetKey( ) functions let you directly interface your program with the keyboard. The command line interface of these functions appears below.

```
INKEY([<EXPN>])
LASTKEY()
NEXTKEY()
READKEY()
SETKEY(<EXPN> [, <CODE BLOCK>]
```

The Inkey( ) function places the value entered at the keyboard by the user in a variable. The optional EXPN clause allows you to designate the time duration in seconds that Inkey( ) waits for a response. If you select a response time of zero, Inkey( ) halts program execution until the user presses a key. If the time lapses and the user does not press a key, Inkey( ) returns a zero. If you use Inkey( ) without the time interval, it does not wait for the user to press a key; it returns the value of the keystroke instead. Inkey( ) returns the key value as a number.

The Lastkey( ) function works much like the Inkey function with no time interval specified. Instead of getting the key value currently in the keyboard buffer, Lastkey( ) returns the value of the last keystroke retrieved from the buffer. This is especially useful when two functions must know the value of the character in the keyboard buffer, but the first function actually removes the keystroke.

The Nextkey( ) function obtains the value of the keystroke currently in the keyboard buffer without removing it. This is useful when the function following the Nextkey( ) function must know the value of the keystroke as well.

The ReadKey( ) function allows you to determine what key the user pressed to end a Read command. These values allow you to take appropriate action to process the information entered by the user. The values returned by ReadKey( ) differ from the values returned by the InKey( ) function. Table 114-1 contains a listing of the return codes for different keystrokes.

Table 114-1. ReadKey( ) Return Values

Keystroke	Return Value	Keystroke	Return Value
Ctrl-PgDn	30	PgDn	7
Ctrl-PgUp	31	PgUp	6
Ctrl-End, Ctrl-W	14	Return (Enter)	15
Down Arrow	2	Type Past End	15
Esc	12	Up Arrow	5

The SetKey( ) function allows you to change or monitor the default action performed when a user presses a key. EXPN contains the InKey( ) value of a key. The optional CODE BLOCK contains code defining the action you want the key to perform. If you use SetKey without a code block, it returns the code block currently associated with the key. Clipper returns NIL if the key does not have a code block associated with it. The action you define for a key to perform takes effect during any wait state imposed by the AChoice( ), DBEdit( ), MemoEdit( ), Accept, Input, Read, or Wait functions. A thorough discussion of code blocks and how to implement them is outside the scope of this book. Refer to the Clipper manual for further details on this subject.

APPLICATIONS

Use the Inkey( ) function in place of an @ Get command when you need to obtain control characters from the user, the user does not actually need to enter a keystroke, or the program requires the numeric equivalent of a keystroke instead of the actual value. You can use the Inkey( ) function as part of the condition for a Do While command. This is useful for print routines and other time consuming procedures that the user may want to end before the computer finishes.

Use the Lastkey( ) function with commands or functions that remove the contents of the keyboard buffer; for example, if you wanted to get the actual keystroke entered by the user while using the Menu To command. You can use this function to determine the key used to end a Read command. By checking the value of the Updated( ) function, you can determine if the user entered anything. If not, the user probably ended the Read early.

Use the Nextkey( ) function to read the contents of the keyboard buffer before another function or command retrieves it. For example, if you wanted to validate a user entry before passing the input to another function, you could use the Nextkey( ) function to retrieve it. Since the Nextkey( ) function does not remove the keystroke from the keyboard buffer, it is exceptionally useful for keystroke validation.

Use the ReadKey( ) function whenever you want to take action based on the method used to exit a Read command; for example, if the user modified information on-screen, then decides that he or she wants to undo the edit. By providing a special procedure for the escape key, you could undo the edit. You could also use the enter key as the method of indicating acceptance of the current record. By using the ReadKey( ) function, you could build edit and browse routines that intelligently monitor user input.

Use the SetKey( ) function whenever you want to create an automatically executed function. For example, you could assign a help routine to the F1 key. Each time the user presses F1, they receive information about the task they want to perform. This allows you to create a function-key-driven environment for the user and makes your programs easier to use.

TYPICAL OPERATION

In this example you see the effects of using the Lastkey( ) function to determine actual user input to the Menu To command. Begin this example in your word processor with MAILLIST.PRG loaded.

1. Add the following text to the variable section at the beginning of the sample program.
   ```
   OLD_COLOR = ' '
   KEYPRESS = 0
   ```

2. Add the following text to the database edit menu section.

```
do DISPLAY_MENU
KEYPRESS = lastkey()
@ 23, 67 say KEYPRESS
```

3. Save the document and exit your word processor. Type **CL MAILLIST** at the DOS prompt. Press **Enter**.

4. Type **MAILLIST**. Make sure you use capital letters using the Caps Lock key instead of the Shift key. Press **Enter**.

5. Type **E**. The menu disappears and the edit screen appears as before. The program displays 69 in the lower right corner of the display.

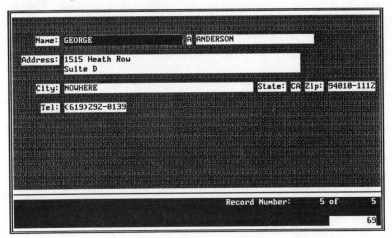

6. Press **Esc** to get back to the Main menu. Press **Caps Lock**. Type **E**. The program displays 101 in the lower right corner of the display.

7. Press **Esc** to get back to the Main menu. Press **Ctrl-Break** (located on the same key as Scroll Lock). The program displays 3 in the lower right corner of the display.

8. Press **Esc** to get back to the Main menu. Press **Enter**. The program displays 13 in the lower right corner of the display.

9. Press **Esc** to get back to the Main menu. Type **Q**. The DOS prompt appears.

10. Turn to Module 16 to continue the learning sequence.

Module 115
INT( ), ROUND( )

DESCRIPTION

The INT( ) and Round( ) functions change a number with a decimal portion (called a real number in programming terms) to an integer or less precise real. The INT( ) function does this by simply removing the decimal portion. In other words, this function always rounds down. The Round( ) function looks at the decimal portion of EXPN1 and rounds up or down based on the decimal value. EXPN2 determines where the Round( ) function rounds the number to. If you specify a positive number, Round( ) retains that number of digits after the decimal point. For example, Round(15.555, 2) produces the number 15.56. If you specify zero, Round( ) produces an integer. For example, Round(15.49, 0) produces the number 15. If you specify a negative number, Round( ) sets that number of digits to the left of the decimal point to 0. For example, Round(155, –1) produces the number 160. The command line interface of the INT( ) and Round( ) functions appears below.

```
INT(EXPN)
ROUND(<EXPN1>, <EXPN2>)
```

APPLICATIONS

Use the INT( ) function when you need to create integers from real numbers and the rounding up of decimal portions equal or greater than .5 is not important. This function produces smaller, faster code than the Round( ) function. While this time differential remains small for few conversions, it does create a large difference in loops or when performing a large number of conversions.

Use the Round( ) function when you need to reduce the precision of a number, but do not want to remove the entire decimal. This is convenient in cases where you want all the numbers in a printout to contain the same number of digits after the decimal point. You can also reduce the precision of whole numbers. This is convenient when the whole numbers are so large that it becomes cumbersome to view the entire number in a report. Finally, you can create integers using Round( ) when the fractional portion is important to the rounding process.

TYPICAL OPERATION

In this example you use the INT( ) function to reduce the precision of the averages produced by the sample program. Begin this example in your word processor with CHCKBOOK.PRG loaded.

1. Add/change the following text in the STATS procedure.

```
@ 15, 04 say 'Average Check Amount:                    $' +;
   ltrim(str(int(AVE_CHCK), 10, 0))
@ 16, 04 say 'Average Deposit Amount:                  $' +;
   ltrim(str(int(AVE_DEP), 10, 0))
```

2. Save the document and exit your word processor. Type **CL CHCKBOOK** at the DOS prompt. Press **Enter**.

3. Type **MAILLIST**. Press **Enter**. The mailing list program menu appears.

4. Press **F4**. The checkbook program menu appears.

5. Press **Down Arrow** until the Stats option of the menu appears.

6. Press **Enter**. The checkbook statistics appear. Notice the averages now appear in whole dollars. The dollar sign ($) tells the user that the number represents whole dollars.

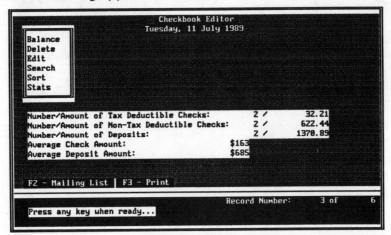

```
                              Checkbook Editor
                          Tuesday, 11 July 1989
 ┌────────────┐
 │ Balance    │
 │ Delete     │
 │ Edit       │
 │ Search     │
 │ Sort       │
 │ Stats      │
 └────────────┘

  Number/Amount of Tax Deductible Checks:        2 /        32.21
  Number/Amount of Non-Tax Deductible Checks:    2 /       622.44
  Number/Amount of Deposits:                     2 /      1370.89
  Average Check Amount:                    $163
  Average Deposit Amount:                  $685


 │ F2 - Mailing List │ F3 - Print │

                               Record Number:       3 of       6
  Press any key when ready...
```

7. Press **Enter** to erase the statistics and return to the menu. Type **A** and press **Enter**. Enter the following information at the fields indicated. Type **N** when asked if you want to add any more checks. The checkbook program menu appears.

   Date: 07/11/89
   Check: 0
   For: PAYCHECK
   Deposit: 1200.98
   Tax Item: N

8. Press **Down Arrow** to select Stats. Press **Enter**. The checkbook statistics appear. Notice the statistics correctly show the addition of a deposit and a different deposit average.

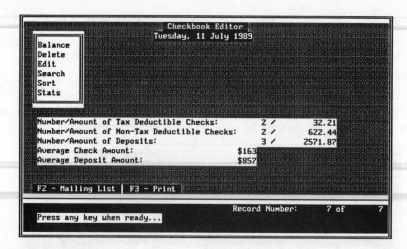

9. Press **Enter** to return to the checkbook program menu. Type **Q** to select Quit. Press **Enter**. The DOS prompt appears.

10. Turn to Module 90 to continue the learning sequence.

Module 116
ISALPHA( ), ISDIGIT( ), ISLOWER( ), ISUPPER( )

DESCRIPTION

The IsAlpha( ), IsDigit( ), IsLower( ), and IsUpper( ) functions all check the status of the beginning character of a character string. They all require a single character string entry as input. The IsAlpha( ) function determines if the beginning character in a string contains an alpha character (a-z or A-Z). The IsDigit( ) function determines if the beginning character is a number between zero and nine. The IsUpper( ) function determines if the beginning character in a string contains an uppercase letter. The IsLower( ) function determines if the beginning character in a string contains a lowercase letter. The command line interface of the IsAlpha( ), IsDigit( ), IsLower( ), and IsUpper( ) functions appears below.

```
ISALPHA(<EXPC>)
ISDIGIT(<EXPC>)
ISLOWER(<EXPC>)
ISUPPER(<EXPC>)
```

APPLICATIONS

Use these functions to check user or other input. In some cases, the first character input must contain a certain value. For example, you could use these functions to sort the values input using an ASCII file. Since you cannot always obtain delimited or other formatted input, these functions provide an excellent means of determining input type.

Another good use of these functions is determining user input when using the Inkey( ) function. Since Inkey( ) retrieves all characters from the keyboard, and you may need to sort that input, you could use these functions to perform that task.

TYPICAL OPERATION

In this example you use the IsAlpha( ), IsLower( ), and IsUpper( ) functions to sort through user input. Begin this example in your word processor with PRINT.PRG loaded.

1. Modify the print statement for CATEGORY in the NOTE_PRNT procedure as shown below.

```
@ ROW, COL say 'Subject: ' + upper(SHORT_SUBJ)
ROW = ROW + 1
* Determine the category type and print appropriately.
if .not. isalpha(CATEGORY)
    @ ROW, COL say 'Priority Category: ' + CATEGORY
else
    @ ROW, COL say 'Category: ' + CATEGORY
endif
ROW = ROW + 2
@ ROW, COL say NOTE
```

2. Save the document and exit your word processor. Type **CL PRINT** at the DOS prompt. Press **Enter**.

3. Type **DBU** and press **Enter**. The DBU Main menu appears.

4. Type **NOTEPAD** in the Files field. Press **Enter**. DBU opens the database file.

5. Press **Down Arrow**. Type **CATEGORY** in the Index field. Press **Enter**.

6. Press **Down Arrow**. Type **NOTENUM** in the Index field. Press **Enter**.

7. Press **Down Arrow**. Type **SUBJECT** in the Index field. Press **Enter**.

8. Press **F5** to select Browse. Select Database by pressing **Enter**. The database browse display appears.

9. Press **Down Arrow** twice to create a new record. Type **3** in the note number field. Press **Enter**. Type **This is the third note.**. Press **Enter**. Type **1**. Press **Enter** twice. The memo edit display appears.

10. Type **This is a high priority note. Notice the special category notation on the printout.** Press **Ctrl-W** to exit the memo edit display.

11. Press **Esc** twice. The DBU utility asks if you want to exit to DOS.

12. Type **Y**. The DOS prompt appears.

13. Type **PRINT**. Press **Enter**.

14. Type **LPT1**. Press **Enter** to select a printer. Type **N** to forego running the printer test.

15. Select Notepad.

16. Select Category. The program prints the three note entries in category then note number order. Notice note 3 contains a special category heading. The Main menu appears.

17. Select Quit by pressing **Up Arrow**. Press **Enter**. The DOS prompt appears.

18. Turn to Module 119 to continue the learning sequence.

Module 117
ISCOLOR( )/ISCOLOUR, SETCOLOR( )

DESCRIPTION

The IsColor( ) and SetColor( ) functions help you manage the colors used to paint the database display screens. The IsColor( ) function returns true when the display adapter currently in use can display color images. After you determine the display adapter type, you can change the display colors accordingly using the SetColor( ) function. In addition to changing the color, you can obtain the current display colors using the SetColor function. The command line interface of the IsColor( )/IsColour and SetColor( ) functions appears below

```
ISCOLOR()/ISCOLOUR()
SETCOLOR([<EXPC>])
```

The SetColor( ) function places the value of the current display adapter color settings in a variable or displays the colors on screen for you. EXPC contains the new display adapter color settings. If you use the SetColor( ) function with no new color assignments, Clipper retains the current settings. Table 117-1 contains a complete listing of the colors used by Clipper. Note that unlike the SET COLOR command, you may not use numeric color identifiers with the SetColor( ) function. EXPC must contain the colors in table 117-1 in the following order: standard foreground/ background, enhanced foreground/background, border, background, and unselected foreground/ background.

Table 117-1. Clipper Color Selection Table for SetColor( )

Color	Letter	Color	Letter
Black	N	White	W
Blue	B	Gray	N+
Green	G	Yellow	GR+
Cyan	BG	Blank	X
Red	R	Underline	U
Magenta	RB	Inverse Video	I
Brown	GR		

NOTE:
Clipper supports only underlining and inverse video on monochrome monitors. It does not support colors.

APPLICATIONS

Use the IsColor( ) and SetColor( ) functions combined to automatically save the original display adapter color selections, then reset them, taking the display adapter type into account. You could then use customized color settings even if the user runs the program on different machines.

Use the IsColor( ) function separately to ensure that user controlled color selections correspond to those allowed by the display adapter. By providing different menus for different display adapters, you could reduce user frustration in not seeing differences in color for a change in settings.

Use the SetColor( ) function separately to save and reset color settings when jumping between database displays. This is especially important when you want to display pop-up error messages or menus.

TYPICAL OPERATION

In this example you use the IsColor( ) and SetColor( ) functions to detect the display adapter type and set the colors accordingly. Begin this example in your word processor with MAILLIST.PRG loaded.

1. Add the following variables at the beginning of the program.

```
DB_NAME = 'Y'
NO_COLOR1 = 'W/N,N/W,,,W+/N'
COLOR1 = 'W/B,GR+/B,,,G/B'
OLD_COLOR = ' '
```

2. Add the following text before and after the first SET COLOR command.

```
if iscolor()
    set color to GR+/B,W+/G
else
    set color to N/W,W+/N
endif
```

3. Add the following text in place of the second SET COLOR command.

```
if iscolor()
    OLD_COLOR = setcolor(COLOR1)
else
    OLD_COLOR = setcolor(NO_COLOR1)
endif
```

4. Save the document and exit your word processor. Type **CL MAILLIST** at the DOS prompt. Press **Enter**.

5. Type **MAILLIST**. Press **Enter**. If you have a color monitor, the display colors are different.

NOTE

> The figures in this book will always show the black and white version of the database display. If you use a color monitor, your display will appear slightly different.

6. Type **Q**. The DOS prompt appears.

7. Turn to Module 60 to continue the learning sequence.

Module 118
ISPRINTER( )

DESCRIPTION

The IsPrinter( ) function determines the status of LPT1. It returns true if LPT1 is ready. This function only works on IBM BIOS compatible systems. What this means is that some clone machines may or may not produce inaccurate results. The command line interface of the IsPrinter( ) function appears below.

```
ISPRINTER( )
```

APPLICATIONS

Use this function to determine the status of LPT1 before printing. By using this function in advance, you can reduce the risk of errors. This function works well for print error handling routines for LPT1. Unfortunately, it does not work for other printer ports.

TYPICAL OPERATION

In this example you add error handling capabilities to the sample program. Begin this example in your word processor with PRINT.PRG loaded.

1. Add the following text to the print loop.

```
for PRNT_COUNT = 1 to reccount()
   do DISP_COUNT
   do REC_PRINT
next
```

2. Add the following text to the variable section.

```
PRNT_PORT = 'PRN  '
ANSWER = 'C'
```

3. Add the following text to the end of the sample program procedure section.

```
return IS_PORT
procedure REC_PRINT
* This procedure sends the contents of one record to the
* printer.
if PRNT_PORT = 'LPT1'
   do while .not. isprinter()
      set color to N/W,W+/N
      @ 22, 04 say 'Printer Is Not Ready To Receive The Next Record!'
      @ 23, 04 say 'Do you want to (C)heck the printer or (E)xit the ' +;
         'print procedure? ' get ANSWER picture '!'
      read
      set color to W/N,N/W
      if ANSWER = 'E'
         quit
      endif
   enddo
endif
return
```

4. Change the PRNT_ON function as shown below.

```
set printer to &PORT_NAME
if isprinter()
    IS_PORT = .T.
else
    IS_PORT = .F.
endif
```

5. Add the following text to the printer status check section of the program.

```
do while .not. PRNT_ON (PRNT_PORT)
    set color to N/W,W+/N
    @ 22, 04 say 'Printer Is Not Ready!'
    @ 23, 04 say 'Do you want to (C)heck the printer or (E)xit the ' +;
        'print procedure? ' get ANSWER picture '!'
    read
    set color to W/N,N/W
    if ANSWER = 'E'
        quit
    endif
    @ 06, 04 say 'Enter the printer port you wish to use. ';
        get PRNT_PORT picture '@!'
    read
```

6. Save the document and exit your word processor. Compile your program.

7. Type **PRINT**. Press **Enter**.

NOTE

This section of the procedure requires you have a printer connected to parallel port 1 (LPT1). If you have one parallel port, then it usually comes configured as LPT1. Make sure you set the printer power switch on.

8. Type **LPT1**. Press **Enter**. The record number counts from 1 through 5, then the DOS prompt appears.

9. Set the printer ON LINE switch to off. Type **PRINT**. Press **Enter**. Type **LPT1**. Press **Enter**. The program displays an error message.

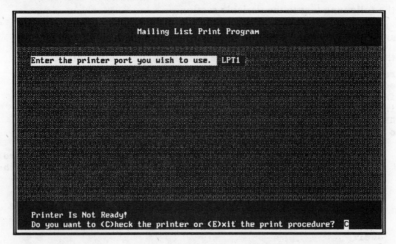

10. Set the printer ON LINE switch to on. Type **C**. Press **Enter**. Quickly set the printer ON LINE switch to off before the program prints all the records. The program displays an error message.

11. Type **E**. The DOS prompt appears.

12. Turn to Module 88 to continue the learning sequence.

Module 119
LEFT( ), RIGHT( )

DESCRIPTION

The Left( ) and Right( ) functions let you retrieve a specified number of characters from the source string and place them in a target. The Left( ) function retrieves characters starting from the left and working toward the right. The Right( ) function retrieves characters from the right, working toward the left. Both functions require a source string (EXPC) and the number of characters to retrieve (EXPN). The command line interface of the Left( ) and Right( ) functions appears below.

```
LEFT(<EXPC>, <EXPN>)
RIGHT(<EXPC>, <EXPN>)
```

APPLICATIONS

Use these functions to retrieve sections of a string for processing. For example, if the field contained in a custom report contains too many characters to fit on a single line, you could use the Left( ) or Right( ) functions to split the field into printable sections.

TYPICAL OPERATION

In this example you use the Left( ) and Right( ) functions to change the output of the sample program. Begin this example in your word processor with PRINT.PRG loaded.

1. Add the following text to the beginning of the NOTE_PRNT procedure.
```
private ROW, COL, CONV_STR
* Initialize variables.
ANSWER3 = 'C'
* Ask if user wants complete or partial notes.
set color to N/W,W+/N
@ 22, 04 say 'Do you want (C)omplete or (P)artial notes? ' get ANSWER3;
    picture '!' valid (ANSWER3 = 'P') .or. (ANSWER3 = 'C')
read
@ 22, 04 clear to 22, 77
set color to W/N,N/W
* Setup initial conditions.
```

2. Modify the print statement for NOTE in the NOTE_PRNT procedure as shown below.
```
    endif
* Print complete or partial note based on previous response.
    ROW = ROW + 2
    if ANSWER3 = 'P'
       @ ROW, COL say left(NOTE, 55)
    else
       @ ROW, COL say NOTE
    endif
    ROW = ROW + 1
* Show the number of records printed.
```

336

3. Save the document and exit your word processor. Type **CL PRINT** at the DOS prompt. Press **Enter**.
4. Type **PRINT**. Press **Enter**.
5. Type **LPT1**. Press **Enter** to select a printer. Type **N** to forego running the printer test.
6. Select Notepad. The program displays another menu.
7. Select Category. The program asks if you want partial or complete notes.

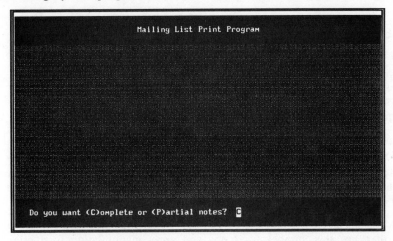

8. Type **P**. The program prints the three note entries in category then note number order. Notice note 3 contains a partial note since it exceeded the partial note size. The Main menu appears.
9. Select Quit. The DOS prompt appears.
10. Turn to Module 120 to continue the learning sequence.

Module 120
LEN( )

DESCRIPTION

The LEN( ) function returns the length of a character string or the declared number of elements in an array. The command line interface of the LEN( ) function appears below.

```
LEN(<EXPC>/<ARRAY>)
```

APPLICATIONS

Use this function whenever you need to know the length of a character string for formatting purposes. For example, if you wanted to center a heading on the display and you knew the length of the display, then you could use LEN( ) to determine the length of the heading. After you determine the heading length, subtract display length from heading length and divide by 2. This would produce the starting location of the heading.

You can also use the LEN( ) function to determine the declared number of elements in an array. You could then use this number for loops and array manipulation instructions. This is exceptionally effective in user-defined functions where the number of elements in an array passed to a function is not constant.

TYPICAL OPERATION

In this example you use the LEN( ) function to format various elements of the display and printout. Begin this example in your word processor with PRINT.PRG loaded.

1. Add the following function at the end of the procedure section of the sample program.

```
function CENTER_LINE
* This function centers a heading on the display.
parameters CSTRING
private CLENGTH
* Initialize variables.
CLENGTH = len(CSTRING)
START_SPOT = 0
* Find the center point.
START_SPOT = (80 - CLENGTH) / 2
return START_SPOT
```

2. Modify the DISP_SCRN procedure as shown below.

```
procedure DISP_SCRN
* This procedure displays a print screen.
private HEADING_CENTER
* Get the number required to center the heading.
HEADING_CENTER = center_line ('Mailing List Print Program')
clear
@ 01, 00, 24, 79 box DOUBLE_LINE
set color to N/W,W+/N
```

```
@ 02, 01 clear to 04, 78
@ 21, 01 clear to 23, 78
@ 03, HEADING_CENTER say 'Mailing List Print Program'
```

3. Modify the NOTE_PRNT procedure as shown below.

```
CONV_STR = space(1)
CENTER_PT = 0
* Print the heading.
CENTER_PT = center_line('Notes Printout')
@ ROW, CENTER_PT say 'Notes Printout'
ROW = ROW + 2
* Perform this procedure until we print all the records.
```

4. Save the document and exit your word processor. Type **CL PRINT** at the DOS prompt. Press **Enter**.

5. Type **PRINT**. Press **Enter**. Notice the CENTER_LINE function centers the heading perfectly.

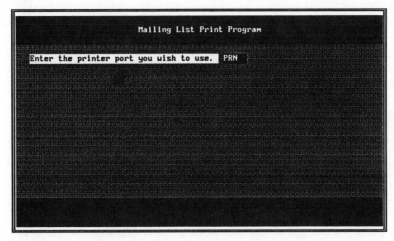

6. Type **LPT1**. Press **Enter** to select a printer. Type **N** to forego running the printer test. The program displays a menu for selecting the database you want to print.

7. Select Notepad. Press **Enter**. The program displays another menu.

8. Select Category. Press **Enter**. The program asks if you want partial or complete notes.

9. Type **P**. The program prints the three note entries in category then note number order. Notice the printout now contains a centered heading. The Main menu appears.

10. Select Quit. Press **Enter**. The DOS prompt appears.

11. Turn to Module 122 to continue the learning sequence.

Module 121
LOWER( ), PAD( ), QOUT( ), SPACE( ), STR( ), STRTRAN( ), STUFF( ), TRANSFORM( ), UPPER( ), VAL( )

DESCRIPTION

The Lower( ), Pad( ), QOut( ), Space( ), STR( ), STRTran( ), Stuff( ), Transform( ), Upper( ), and VAL( ) functions have a single trait in common, they all manipulate strings. In addition to character strings, the Pad( ) function manipulates dates and numbers as well. The command line interface of the Lower( ), Pad( ), QOut( ), Space( ), STR( ), STRTran( ), Stuff( ), Transform( ), Upper( ), and VAL( ) functions appears below.

```
LOWER(<EXPC>)
PADL(<EXP>, <EXPN> [, <EXPC>])
PADC(<EXP>, <EXPN> [, <EXPC>])
PADR(<EXP>, <EXPN> [, <EXPC>])
QOUT([<EXP>])
QQOUT([<EXP>])
SPACE(<EXPN>)
STR(<EXPN1> [, <EXPN2> [, <EXPN3>]])
STRTRAN(<EXPC1>, <EXPC2> [, <EXPC3>] [, <EXPN1>] [, <EXPN2>])
STUFF(<EXPC1>, <EXPN1>, <EXPN2>, <EXPC2>)
TRANSFORM(<EXP>, <EXPC>)
UPPER(<EXPC>)
VAL(<EXPC>)
```

The Lower( ) function changes all uppercase characters in EXPC to lowercase characters. The Upper( ) function performs exactly the opposite task. It converts lowercase characters to uppercase.

The Pad( ) function is actually split into three subfunctions. Each function reacts differently to the expression you input. All three versions output a character string. The fourth digit identifies the justification provided by the Pad( ) function. For example, PadL( ) left-justifies the expression you provide. The other two justification methods are: right (R) and center (C). EXP contains a character, numeric, or date expression. EXPN contains the final length of the character string. The optional EXPC contains a fill character. If you do not specify a fill character, Clipper uses spaces.

The QOut( ) and QQOut( ) functions are the routines used to create the ? and ?? commands. The functions allow you to output strings directly to the screen. Each function starts the string at the current cursor position. The QOut( ) function includes a carriage return and line feed as part of its output. The QQOut( ) function leaves the cursor at the position next to the final character of the output string. Both functions automatically update Row( ), Col( ), PRow( ), PCol( ) as appropriate. EXP contains the expression you want to send to the display. You may use both these functions within other functions or code blocks, which is an advantage over the ? and ?? commands.

The Space( ) function returns a string of spaces the length specified by EXPN. By using this function you reduce the size of the data space for your code.

The STR( ) function converts a numeric to a character string. EXPN1 contains the number to convert. EXPN2 contains the overall length of the string after conversion. This number does not necessarily match the actual length of the variable or field. EXPN3 contains the number of characters after the decimal point. For example, if you used the expression SOMESTR = str(SOMENUM, 10, 3), then SOMESTR would contain a ten-digit number composed of six characters before the decimal point, the decimal point, and three characters after the decimal point. The VAL( ) function performs exactly the opposite task. It converts a character string of numbers to an actual numeric. VAL( ) requires only the character string as input. It automatically adjusts the decimal point and number of characters.

The STRTran( ) function performs a search and replace on the target string. EXPC1 contains the target string. EXPC2 contains the search value. EXPC3 contains the replace value. EXPN1 contains the number of the first occurrence to replace. EXPN2 contains the number of occurrences to replace. STRTran( ) requires you supply only EXPC1 and EXPC2. If you do not specify EXPC3, STRTran( ) automatically replaces all occurrences of the search string with null strings in the target string. STRTran( ) uses a default of one for the first occurrence to replace. It uses a default of all for the number of occurrences to replace.

The Stuff( ) function performs a task similar to STRTran( ). Instead of searching for a character string, you specify a starting position within the target string. EXPC1 contains the target string. EXPN1 contains the number of the character to start replacing the string at. EXPN2 contains the number of characters to replace. EXPC2 contains the replacement string. For example, if you wrote the expression SOMESTR = stuff('ABCDEF', 4, 3, 'CBA'), then SOMESTR would contain 'ABCCBA'.

The Transform( ) function converts any data type to a character string. In addition, it formats the string according to the rules you specify. EXP contains the variable or database field to convert. EXPC contains the conversion to perform. Clipper allows you to specify the format of each character in the output string to form a template, or you can use a function to determine the format of the entire string. In this way Transform( ) works much like the picture clause of an AT (@) SAY/GET command. Table 121-1 contains a complete listing of Transform( ) functions. Table 121-2 contains a complete listing of Transform( ) templates.

Table 121-1. Transform( ) Functions

Function	Action
B	This function displays strings left justified.
C	This function works with numbers only. It places CR after all positive numbers.
D	This function works with dates only. It converts a date to the Set Date format instead of the standard format.
E	This function works with dates only. It converts a date to the British format.
R	This function allows you to insert non-template characters.
X	This function works with numbers only. It places DB after all negative numbers.
Z	This function uses blanks in place of leading zeros.
(	This function works with numbers only. It places parentheses around all negative numbers.
!	This function converts all lowercase alphabetic characters to uppercase.

Table 121-2. Transform( ) Templates

Template	Action
A	Converts only alphabetic characters. No symbols or numbers allowed.
N	Converts only alphabetic characters or numbers. No symbols allowed.
X	Converts any character.
9	Converts numbers and negative/positive sign symbols only. No alphabetic characters or other symbols allowed.
#	Converts numbers, negative/positive signs, and spaces for any data type. No alphabetic characters or other symbols allowed.
L	Converts only logical operators .T. and .F. No alphabetic characters, numbers, or symbols allowed.
Y	Converts only logical operators Y and N. No alphabetic characters, numbers, or symbols allowed.
!	Converts alphabetic characters to uppercase.
$	Uses a dollar sign in place of leading spaces in a numeric variable.
*	Uses an asterisk in place of leading spaces in a numeric variable.
.	Marks the position of a decimal point in numeric variables.
,	Marks the position of a comma in numeric variables.
Symbol	Any symbol other than those described above.

APPLICATIONS

Use these functions to manipulate text strings. (You can use the Pad( ) function on numeric and date expressions as well.) By using these functions you can create print and other routines that output consistent data even when the input is inconsistent. You can also use these functions as described above as part of the argument for report/label forms and indexes.

TYPICAL OPERATION

In this example, you add to the consistency of printed output by using the functions described above. Module 7 contains examples of how to use these functions as part of report and label definitions. Modules 5, 6, and 98 contain examples of how to use these functions as part of an index key description. Begin this example in your word processor with PRINT.PRG loaded.

1. Change the NOTE_PRNT procedure as follows.

```
* This is a customized print routine for the notepad.
private ROW, COL, CONV_STR
* Setup initial conditions.
set console off
set print on
set device to print
setprc (5, 10) && Set the margins.
PRNT_COUNT = 1
ROW = prow()
COL = pcol()
CONV_STR = space(1)
* Perform this procedure until we print all the records.
do while .not. eof()
* Convert the Note Number to a string.
   CONV_STR = strtran(str(NOTE_NUM, 5, 0), ' ')
```

```
* Print the information
    @ ROW, COL say chr(13) && Place print head at beginning.
    @ ROW, COL say 'Note Number: ' + CONV_STR
    ROW = ROW + 1
    @ ROW, COL say 'Subject: ' + upper(SHORT_SUBJ)
    ROW = ROW + 1
```

2. Save the document and exit your word processor. Type **CL PRINT** at the DOS prompt. Press **Enter**.

3. Type **PRINT**. Press **Enter**.

4. Type **LPT1**. Press **Enter** to select a printer. Type **N** to forego running the printer test. The program displays a menu for selecting the database you want to print.

5. Select Notepad by pressing **Down Arrow** twice. Press **Enter**. The program displays another menu.

6. Select Category by pressing **Down Arrow** twice. Press **Enter**. The program prints the two note entries in note number order. Notice the program now prints the note number without an excess of leading spaces. It also prints the subject in uppercase letters.

7. Select Quit by pressing **Up Arrow** three times. Press **Enter**. The DOS prompt appears.

8. Turn to Module 116 to continue the learning sequence.

Module 122
LTRIM( ), SUBSTR( ),
TRIM( )/RTRIM( ), ALLTRIM( )

DESCRIPTION

The AllTrim( ), LTrim( ), SubSTR( ), and Trim( )/RTrim( ) functions format text prior to display or printing. The AllTrim( ) function removes both leading and trailing spaces from a string. In effect, the AllTrim( ) function performs the tasks of both the LTrim( ) and RTrim( ) functions in a single step. The LTrim( ) function removes leading spaces from a string of characters. The Trim( )/RTrim( ) function removes trailing spaces from a string of characters. The SubSTR( ) function places a subset of the source string starting at character EXPN1 in the destination string. EXPN2 specifies how many characters to place in the destination string. If you do not include this optional parameter, Clipper automatically places all the source string from the starting point to the end of the string in the destination string. The command line interface of the AllTrim( ), LTrim( ), SubSTR( ), and Trim( )/RTrim( ) functions appears below.

```
ALLTRIM(<EXPC>)
LTRIM(<EXPC>)
SUBSTR(<EXPC>, <EXPN1> [, <EXPN2>])
TRIM(<EXPC>)/RTRIM(<EXPC>)
```

APPLICATIONS

Use the AllTrim( ), LTrim( ) and Trim( )/RTrim( ) functions to remove excess spaces from a string. For example, when you convert a number to a character string, the resulting string normally contains leading spaces. When you output the contents of a partially filled database field, it contains trailing spaces. If you use the field in a form letter, removing the excess spaces enhances the letter's appearance.

Use the SubSTR( ) function when you need only part of the contents of a field or variable. For example, if you wanted only the numeric part of a field containing a number and a unit of measure, you could use this function to separate them.

TYPICAL OPERATION

Begin this example in your word processor with PRINT.PRG loaded.

1. Change the following text in the NOTE_PRNT procedure.
   ```
   * Convert the Note Number to a string.
     CONV_STR = ltrim(str(NOTE_NUM, 5, 0))
   * Print the information
   ```

2. Save the document and exit your word processor. Type **CL PRINT** at the DOS prompt. Press **Enter**.

3. Type **PRINT**. Press **Enter**.

4. Type **LPT1**. Press **Enter** to select a printer. Type **N** to forego running the printer test. The program displays a menu for selecting the database you want to print.

5. Select Notepad. The program displays another menu.

6. Select Category. The program asks if you want partial or complete notes.

7. Type **P**. The program prints the three note entries in category, then note number order. Notice the note number appears without extra spaces between the heading and the actual number. The Main menu appears.

8. Select Quit. The DOS prompt appears.

9. Turn to Module 106 to continue the learning sequence.

Module 123
LUPDATE( )

DESCRIPTION

The LUpdate( ) function returns the last date someone updated the database in the current work area. Clipper does not change the date until you close the file. If you use LUpdate on a new database (one never closed before) or a work area with no database in use, Clipper returns a blank date. The command line interface of the LUpdate( ) function appears below.

```
LUPDATE( )
```

APPLICATIONS

Use the LUpdate( ) function in displays when you want the user to know the last date of database modification. You can also use the LUpdate( ) function to help determine when to modify a database. For example, some accounting practices require aging of accounts. You could place all the accounts due on the same date in a single database, then check the database on a daily basis to see if that set of accounts requires reconciliation.

TYPICAL OPERATION

In this example you add the last date of database modification by using the LUpdate( ) function to the sample program. Begin this example in your word processor with DOSSHELL.PRG loaded.

1. Add the following text to the beginning of the SHOW_RECS procedure.

```
clear screen
set color to N/W,W+/N
@ 00, 00 clear to 02, 79
@ 01, 25 say 'Database Last Updated: ' + dtoc(lupdate())
@ 03, 00  && This sets the cursor to a new position.
set color to 'W/N,N/W,,,W+/N'
do while .not. eof()
```

2. Add the following text to the end of the SHOW_RECS procedure.

```
      clear screen
      set color to N/W,W+/N
      @ 00, 00 clear to 02, 79
      @ 01, 25 say 'Database Last Updated: ' + dtoc(lupdate())
      @ 03, 00  && This sets the cursor to a new position.
      set color to 'W/N,N/W,,,W+/N'
   endif
```

3. Save the document and exit your word processor. Type **CL DOSSHELL** at the DOS prompt. Press **Enter**.

4. Type **MAILLIST** and press **Enter**. The mailing list program menu appears.

5. Press **F10**. The DOS shell menu appears.

6. Select Show Records by typing **S** and pressing **Enter**. The program lists a complete listing of the mailing list records. Notice the program displays the date of last update at the top of the screen.

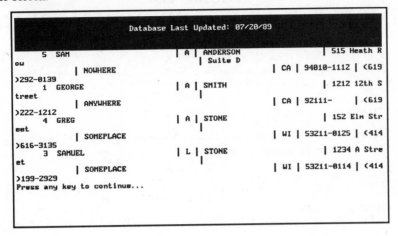

7. Press **Enter** twice. The DOS shell menu appears.
8. Type **Q** and press **Enter** to quit the DOS shell menu.
9. Select Quit by pressing **Enter**. The DOS prompt appears.
10. Turn to Module 76 to continue the learning sequence.

Module 124
MEMOEDIT( ), MEMOLINE( ), MEMOREAD( ),
MEMOTRAN( ), MEMOWRIT( )

DESCRIPTION

The MemoEdit( ), MemoLine( ), MemoRead( ), MemoTran( ), and MemoWrit( ) functions manipulate data resident in memo fields. The command line interface of the MemoEdit( ), MemoLine( ), MemoRead( ), MemoTran( ), and MemoWrit( ) functions appears below.

```
MEMOEDIT([<EXPC1>] [, <EXPN1>] [, <EXPN2>] [, <EXPN3>] [, <EXPN4>]
[, <EXPL1>] [, <EXPC2>] [, <EXPN5>] [, <EXPN6>] [, <EXPN7>] [, <EXPN8>]
[, <EXPN9>] [, <EXPN10>]
MEMOLINE(<EXPC> [, <EXPN1>] [, <EXPN2>] [, <EXPN3>] [, <EXPL>])
MEMOREAD(<EXPC>)
MEMOTRAN(<EXPC1> [, <EXPC2> [, <EXPC3>]])
MEMOWRIT(<EPXC1>, <EXPC2>)
```

The MemoEdit( ) function lets you place formatted memo field strings on screen and edit them. EXPC1 contains the name of a character string or memo field to edit. EXPN1 through EXPN4 contain the window coordinates for the edit area. EXPN1 contains the top, EXPN2 contains the left, EXPN3 contains the bottom, and EXPN4 contains the right screen coordinate. EXPL1 contains a .T. if you want to edit the memo field, .F. if you do not. The default condition is true. EXPC2 contains the name of a user-defined function for handling unexpected keystrokes. EXPN5 contains the line length. EXPN6 contains the tab length. EXPN7 contains the initial memo row, EXPN8 contains the initial memo column to begin editing. EXPN9 contains an offset for cursor row placement relative to the window position. Normally, Clipper places the cursor at position 0 in the window. EXPN10 contains an offset for cursor column placement relative to the window position. Normally, Clipper places the cursor at position 0 in the window. As with all full screen editing commands, you must specify these arguments in order. If you do not want to use a particular element, you must place a dummy argument in its stead. You do not have to specify any parameters when using this command.

The MemoLine( ) function lets you extract a single line of a memo field and place it on screen. EXPC contains the name of a memo field to use. EXPN1 contains the number of characters to place on one line. The standard number of characters is 79. You must not specify a number larger than 254. EXPN2 contains the line number to extract. EXPN3 contains the tab width in characters. EXPL contains .T. to turn word wrap on. This is the default condition.

The MemoRead( ) function lets you read a memo field disk file or a text file and place its contents in a character string. EXPC contains the name of the file to read. This includes the path and extension (if any).

The MemoTran( ) function replaces the carriage return, line feed pairs found in memo fields with other characters. EXPC1 contains the memo field or character string variable name. EXPC2 contains the character you want in place of hard carriage returns (both the carriage return and line feed). EXPC3 contains the character you want in place of soft carriage returns (carriage return only).

The MemoWrite( ) function lets you place the contents of a character string in a memo field. EXPC1 contains the name of the disk file you want to send data to. EXPC2 contains the memo field name or character string variable you want used as a source.

APPLICATIONS

Use these functions as described above to manipulate character strings and memo fields. Normally, you use these functions exclusively for memo fields. Text manipulation from other sources is a secondary function.

Use the MemoRead( ) and MemoWrite( ) functions to perform input/output to the disk drive. These functions allow you to read the memo file without actually using the database. It also lets you import text created using a word processor. One use for this imported text is as a free form or text-based database.

Use the MemoTran( ) function to remove unreadable hard and soft carriage returns from your file before displaying them.

Use the MemoEdit( ) and MemoLine( ) functions to provide full screen displays of memo field contents. In addition, you can use the MemoEdit( ) function to change the contents of a memo field. Since the MemoLine( ) function contains fewer arguments, use it in place of the MemoEdit( ) function whenever possible.

TYPICAL OPERATION

In this example you start completing the help program and begin a note editing program using the MemoEdit( ), MemoLine( ), MemoRead( ), MemoTran( ), and MemoWrit( ) functions. You complete the help program and test it first. Then start the new note editing program. Begin this example in your word processor with HELP.PRG loaded.

1. Add the following text in the help program. Remove the line @ 04, 04 say HELP_DATA as shown.

```
LINE_COUNT = 13
COUNTER = 0
LINE_DATA = space(74)
* Display screen.
save screen to TEMP
clear screen
@ 01, 00, 24, 79 box DOUBLE_LINE
@ 20, 01 to 20, 78
set color to N/W,W+/N
@ 02, 01 clear to 03, 78
@ 02, 37 say ' Help '
set color to 'W/N,N/W,,,W+/N'
if readinsert()
    @ 00, 60 say 'INSERT ON'
else
    @ 00, 60 say 'OVERTYPE ON'
endif
readexit(.T.)
* Find, then display the help information.
use HELP index HELP
seek PROGRAM + VARIABLE
for COUNTER = 1 to LINE_COUNT
```

```
LINE_DATA = memoline (HELP_DATA, 74, COUNTER)
@ 04 + COUNTER, 04 say LINE_DATA
next
@ 22, 04 say 'Press any key when finished...' get DONE
read
```

2. Save the document and exit your word processor. Type **CL HELP** at the DOS prompt. Press **Enter**.

3. Add the following text to the help database using the DBU utility (do not create a new record, add this to the memo field of the existing one).

```
Quit      - Leave this application.
Add       - Place another name in the database.
Edit      - Change the information for the current record.
Delete    - Remove the name from the database.
Pack      - Remove all deleted records.
Forward   - Advance one name.
Backward  - Go back one name.
Seek      - Find a name in the database.
Undelete  - Restore a deleted name to the database (if not packed).
```

4. Press **Ctrl-W** to save the text. Press **Esc** twice and type **Y** to exit to DOS. Type **MAILLIST**. Press **Enter**. The mailing list program menu appears.

5. Press **F1** to select the help program. The program clears the screen and displays the help screen. Notice the help screen displays the help information formatted.

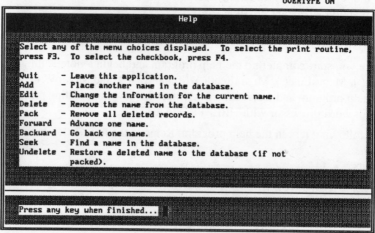

6. Press **Enter**. The mailing list program display reappears.

7. Press **Q** to select Quit. The DOS prompt appears.

8. Load CL.BAT into your word processor and add/change the following text.

```
IF NOT ERRORLEVEL 1 Plink86 FI MAILLIST, PRINT, CHCKBOOK, NOTEPAD, HELP LIB
\CLIPPER\CLIPPER, \CLIPPER\EXTEND
```

9. Save the changes. Load MAILLIST.PRG into your word processor and add the following text to the program defaults section.

```
set key -3 to CHCKBOOK    && Point F4 to the checkbook program.
set key -4 to NOTEPAD     && Point F5 to the notepad.
```

10. Add the following text to the DISPLAY_STATUS procedure.

```
@ 19, 03 say ' F3 - Print ' + chr(179) + ' F4 - Checkbook ' +;
   chr(179) + ' F5 - Notepad '
```

11. Save the document and exit your word processor. Type **CLIPPER MAILLIST** at the DOS prompt. Press **Enter**. Clipper compiles the program.

12. Load PRINT.PRG into your word processor and add the following text to the program defaults section.

```
set key -3 to CHCKBOOK && Point F3 to checkbook program.
set key -4 to NOTEPAD  && Point F5 to the notepad.
```

13. Add the following text to the DISP_SCRN procedure.

```
@ 20, 04 say ' F2 - Mailing List ' + chr(179) + ' F4 - Checkbook ' +;
   chr(179) + ' F5 - Notepad '
```

14. Save the document and exit your word processor. Type **CLIPPER PRINT** at the DOS prompt. Press **Enter**. Clipper compiles the program.

15. Load CHCKBOOK.PRG into your word processor and add the following text to the program defaults section.

```
set key -3 to          && Make sure F4 is clear.
set key -4 to NOTEPAD   && Point F5 to the notepad.
```

16. Add the following text to the DISP_SCRN5 procedure.

```
@ 19, 03 say ' F2 - Mailing List ' + chr(179) + ' F3 - Print ' +;
   chr(179) + ' F5 - Notepad '
```

17. Save the document and exit your word processor. Type **CLIPPER CHCKBOOK** at the DOS prompt. Press **Enter**. Clipper compiles the program.

18. Create a new program, NOTEPAD.PRG, using the following text.

```
* NOTEPAD.PRG
* This program manages a notepad.
* YOUR NAME
* TODAY'S DATE
* Perform program setup.
set key -1 to MAILLIST    && Point F2 to mailing list program.
set key -2 to PRINT       && Point F3 to print program.
set key -3 to CHCKBOOK    && Point F4 to checkbook program.
set key -4 to             && Make sure F5 points to nothing.
* Create the menu array and place the menu values in it.
declare MENU_ITEM[6]
MENU_ITEM[1] = 'Quit'
MENU_ITEM[2] = 'Add'
MENU_ITEM[3] = 'Delete'
MENU_ITEM[4] = 'Sort'
MENU_ITEM[5] = 'Edit'
MENU_ITEM[6] = 'Search'
* Initialize the variables.
ANSWER = 2
DOUBLE_LINE = chr(201) + chr(205) + chr(187) + chr(186) + chr(188) + ;
   chr(205) + chr(200) + chr(186) + chr(177)
DATE_STR = cdow(date()) + ', ' + substr(dtoc(date()), 4, 2) + ' ' + ;
   cmonth(date()) + ' ' + ltrim(str(year(date())))
* Open the database and associated indexes.
use NOTEPAD index NOTENUM, CATEGORY, SUBJECT
* Perform this procedure until the user selects quit.
do while MENU_ITEM[ANSWER] <> 'Quit'
* Display the screen.
   do DISP_SCRN6
* Perform the user requested function.
```

```
        do case
            case MENU_ITEM[ANSWER] = 'Add'
                do ADD_REC2
            case MENU_ITEM[ANSWER] = 'Delete'
                do DEL_REC2
            case MENU_ITEM[ANSWER] = 'Sort'
                do SORT_REC2
            case MENU_ITEM[ANSWER] = 'Edit'
                do EDIT_REC2
            case MENU_ITEM[ANSWER] = 'Search'
                do SRCH_REC2
        endcase
    enddo
* Restore the cursor.
set cursor on
* Close the databases and return.
quit
* Begin Procedure Section
procedure DISP_SCRN6
* This procedure displays the screen.
@ 01, 00, 24, 79 box DOUBLE_LINE
@ 20, 01 to 20, 78
set color to N/W,W+/N
@ 02, 32 say ' Notepad Editor '
@ 03, 40 - (len(DATE_STR)/2) say DATE_STR
@ 19, 03 say ' F2 - Mailing List ' + chr(179) + ' F3 - Print ' + ;
    chr(179) + ' F4 - Checkbook '
@ 21, 01 clear to 23, 78
set color to 'W/N,N/W,,,W+/N'
* Obtain the user selection.
@ 03, 03, 10, 13 box DOUBLE_LINE
ANSWER = achoice(04, 04, 09, 12, MENU_ITEM)
return
procedure ADD_REC2
* This procedure adds new records to the notepad.
return
procedure DEL_REC2
* This procedure removes notes.
return
procedure SORT_REC2
* This procedure places the notes in order.
return
procedure EDIT_REC2
* This procedure changes the contents of the notes.
* Restore the cursor.
set cursor on
*  Display the non-memo data first.
save screen to EDIT_SAVE
@ 03, 01 clear to 23, 78
@ 04, 04 say 'Memo Number: ' get NOTE_NUM picture '@9'
@ 05, 04 say 'Subject:     ' get SHORT_SUBJ picture '@!'
@ 06, 04 say 'Category:    ' get CATEGORY picture '@!'
read
* Now display the actual note.
set color to N/W,W+/N
memoedit(NOTE, 08, 01, 23, 78)
set color to 'W/N,N/W,,,W+/N'
restore screen from EDIT_SAVE
set cursor off  && Turn the cursor off.
return
procedure SRCH_REC2
* This procedure looks for a particular note.
return
```

19. Save the document and exit your word processor. Type **CL NOTEPAD** at the DOS prompt. Press **Enter**.

20. Type **MAILLIST**. Press **Enter**. The mailing list program menu appears. Notice the new function key entry.

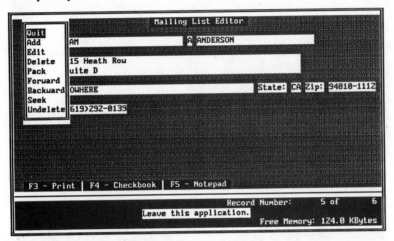

21. Press **F5**. The notepad menu appears.

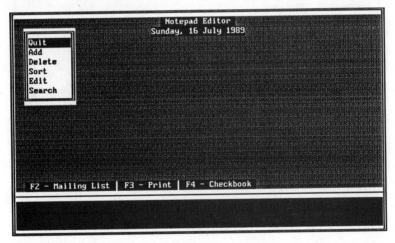

22. Type **E** and press **Enter**. The note edit display appears.

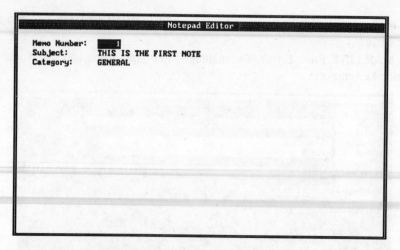

23. Press **PgDn**. The note section of the display highlights. Notice you can move freely inside the note area, but not outside.

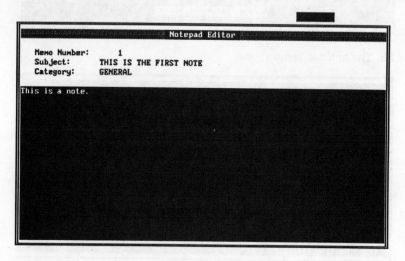

24. Press **Esc**. The notepad menu appears.
25. Press **Q** to quit. Press **Enter**. The DOS prompt appears.
26. Turn to Module 126 to continue the learning sequence.

Module 125
MEMORY( )

DESCRIPTION

The Memory( ) function returns the free memory left for your program to perform sorts, indexes, and other memory consuming tasks. It also shows the space left for variables and other dynamically allocated data. The command line interface of the Memory( ) function appears below.

```
MEMORY(0)
MEMORY(1)
MEMORY(2)
```

The Memory(0) function returns the total amount of free space left on your machine for character values. Since this command returns only total space free, you do not know the addresses of the free RAM or if the free RAM appears in contiguous sections. Therefore, a task that allocates a large memory block could fail even if the Memory( ) function says enough RAM exists.

The Memory(1) function returns the largest contiguous block of memory available for character values. This version of the function allows you to determine if a specific function or command will fail. It does not tell you the total amount of memory left for character values.

The Memory(2) function returns the amount of memory left for RUN commands. This tells you if you can execute a program from within the current program. It provides the same basic information as the CHKDSK and MEM commands provided by DOS. However, it does not tell you how much memory Clipper set aside for character values. Therefore, the actual total memory available in your machine consists of the RUN free space plus the character value free space.

APPLICATIONS

Use the Memory( ) function to allocate RAM based on system resources rather than maximum need. By allocating memory based on resources, you can allow a machine with a large amount of RAM to perform a task quicker than a machine with little RAM. Each machine uses buffers and other memory areas as large as system capabilities allow. You can also reduce the risk of your program running out of memory during critical operations. Running out of memory during critical operations could corrupt data or index files. Worse, it could take a much needed file server off-line in network applications. Finally, you can show the user the memory usage of a particular program. This helps the user understand how the program uses memory and the need for more RAM for certain applications.

TYPICAL OPERATION

In this example you add a memory display to both the print and mailing list programs. Begin this example in your word processor with PRINT.PRG loaded.

1. Add the following text to the DISP_SCRN procedure.

```
@ 03, HEADING_CENTER say 'Mailing List Print Program'
@ 21, 04 say 'Free Memory: ' + ltrim(str(memory(0), 12, 1)) + ' KBytes'
set color to W/N,N/W
```

2. Save the document and exit your word processor. Type **CL PRINT** at the DOS prompt. Press **Enter**.

NOTE

The memory amounts displayed in these screen shots may not match those shown on your display. This is due to differences between individual machine configurations.

3. Type **PRINT**. Press **Enter**. Notice the program displays the free memory left in KBytes.

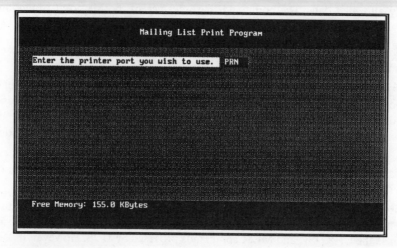

4. Type **LPT1** and press **Enter** to select printer output. Type **N** to forego the printer test. The program displays a menu.

5. Select Quit by pressing **Enter**. The DOS prompt appears.

6. Load MAILLIST.PRG into your word processor. Add the following text to the DISPLAY_STATUS procedure.

```
endcase
@ 23, 53 say 'Free Memory: ' + ltrim(str(memory(0), 5, 1)) + ' KBytes'
if iscolor()
```

7. Save the document and exit your word processor. Type **CL MAILLIST** at the DOS prompt. Press **Enter**.

8. Type **MAILLIST**. Press **Enter**. Notice the program displays the free memory left in KBytes.

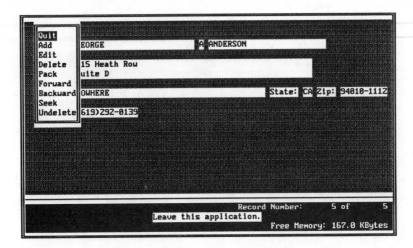

9. Select Quit by pressing **Enter**. The DOS prompt appears.

10. Load CL.BAT into your word processor. Change the second line as shown below. This allows you to add print to the mailing list program during linking.

```
IF NOT ERRORLEVEL 1 Plink86 FI %1, %2 LIB \CLIPPER\CLIPPER, \CLIPPER\EXTEND
```

11. Save the changes. Load PRINT.PRG into your word processor. Add the following text to the beginning of the program.

```
* Perform program setup.
set key -1 to MAILLIST && Point F2 to mailing list program.
set key -2 to          && Make sure F3 points to nothing.
* Declare standard variables public.
```

12. Add the following text to the DISP_SCRN procedure.

```
@ 03, HEADING_CENTER say 'Mailing List Print Program'
@ 20, 04 say 'F2 - Mailing List'
@ 21, 04 say 'Free Memory: ' + ltrim(str(memory(0), 12, 1)) + ' KBytes'
```

13. Save the document and exit your word processor. Type **CLIPPER PRINT** at the DOS prompt. Press **Enter**. Clipper compiles the print program.

14. Load MAILLIST.PRG into your word processor. Add the following text to the setup section at the beginning of the program.

```
set wrap on
set key -1 to           && Make sure F2 is clear.
set key -2 to PRINT      && Point F3 to the print program.
* Clear the display and prepare database for use.
```

15. Add the following text to the DISPLAY_STATUS procedure.

```
endif
@ 19, 04 say 'F3 - Print'
@ 21, 01 clear to 23, 78
```

16. Save the document and exit your word processor. Type **CL MAILLIST PRINT** at the DOS prompt. Press **Enter**. The Clipper batch file clears the screen, then compiles and links the program. Notice the batch file compiles MAILLIST.PRG only.

17. Type **MAILLIST**. Press **Enter**. The mailing list program menu appears. Notice the program displays the free memory left in KBytes. Notice the program shows less memory than the first loading of the mailing program.

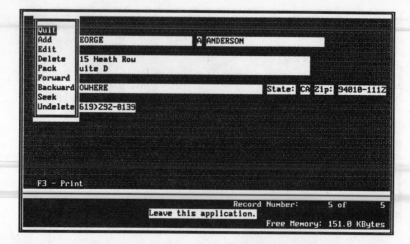

18. Press **F3**. The print program appears. Notice it displays less memory than the mailing list program.

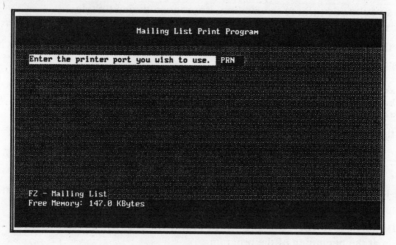

19. Press **F2**. The mailing list program appears. Notice it now displays the same amount of memory as the print program.

20. Select Quit by pressing **Enter**. The DOS prompt appears.

21. Turn to Module 65 to continue the learning sequence.

Module 126
MLCOUNT( ), MLPOS( )

DESCRIPTION

The MLCount( ) and MLPos( ) functions provide statistical information about a text string or memo field. MLCount( ) returns the number of word-wrapped sentences a text string or memo field contains. MLPos( ) returns the position within the string of the start of the specified sentence. The command line interface of the MLCount( ) and MLPos( ) functions appears below.

```
MLCOUNT(<EXPC> [, <EXPN1>] [, <EXPN2>] [, <EXPL>])
MLPOS(<EXPC>, <EXPN1>, <EXPN2> [, <EXPN3>] [, <EXPL>])
```

The only required parameter for MLCount( ) is EXPC, which contains the memo field or text string variable name. EXPN1 contains the number of characters per line. EXPN2 contains the tab size in characters. EXPL allows you to toggle word wrap on or off. Clipper uses a default condition of on. When you turn word wrap off, Clipper breaks sentences exactly at the end of line, even if the end of line splits a word.

The MLPos( ) function requires three inputs. EXPC contains the memo field or text string variable name. EXPN1 contains the number of characters per line. EXPN2 contains the sentence number you wish to find. The optional parameter, EXPN3, contains the tab size in characters. EXPL allows you to toggle word wrap on or off.

APPLICATIONS

Use the MLCount( ) function when you need to know how many sentences worth of information a text string variable or memo field contains. This is especially important when you use the MemoLine( ) function. By knowing in advance exactly how many lines to expect, you can use MemoLine( ) with greater efficiency.

Use the MLPos( ) function when you need to know the starting point of a new sentence within a text string variable or memo field. By knowing the total length of a string and the current position within it, you can provide the user complete information for memo field related tasks.

TYPICAL OPERATION

In this example you complete the help program using the MLCount( ) function. Begin this example in your word processor with HELP.PRG loaded.

1. Add the following text to the help program.
```
seek PROGRAM + VARIABLE
LINE_COUNT = mlcount(HELP_DATA, 74)
for COUNTER = 1 to LINE_COUNT
```

2. Save the document and exit your word processor. Type **CL HELP** at the DOS prompt. Press **Enter**.

3. Type **MAILLIST**. Press **Enter**. The mailing list program menu appears.

4. Press **F1** to select the help program. The program clears the screen and displays the help screen. Notice the help screen displays only the number of lines of information required by the memo field size.

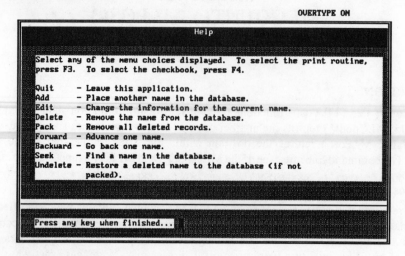

5. Press **Enter**. The mailing list program display reappears.
6. Press **Q** to select Quit. The DOS prompt appears.
7. Turn to Module 130 to continue the learning sequence.

Module 127
NETERR( ), NETNAME( )

DESCRIPTION

The NetERR( ) and NetName( ) functions provide information about the network you use with Clipper. The NetName( ) function returns a string containing the identification for the current workstation. When the network is non-functional or on a machine not connected to a network, Clipper returns a null string. The NetERR( ) function returns true when an error occurs on the network rather than the current workstation. If there is no error or the current workstation does not connect to a network, Clipper returns false. The command line interface of the NetERR( ) and NetName( ) functions appears below.

```
NETERR( )
NETNAME( )
```

APPLICATIONS

Use the NetName( ) function to determine the name or identification of the current workstation. This is especially convenient when you want to determine if the workstation connects to a network. As shown in Module 108, you need to lock and unlock various portions of a database when using it in a network environment. However, you can increase program execution speed by not performing these procedures in a non-network environment. This function also provides the identification information needed by low-level routines written to interface with the network. You can execute manufacturer supplied routines using the Run command.

Use the NetERR( ) function when you want to determine the source of an error. If the error appears on the network, you can temporarily suspend network operation and still operate locally. This provides much needed flexibility and error recovery for your application. You can then use the DOSError( ) function (Module 99) to retrieve the error number and display an appropriate message to the user.

TYPICAL OPERATION

These functions require a network. Since each network operates differently and most machines do not have a network connection, this module does not contain a typical operation. However, you can experiment with network operation using the network program discussed in Module 108. Turn to Module 85 to continue the learning sequence.

Module 128
PCOUNT( )

DESCRIPTION

The PCount( ) function returns the number of parameters passed to the current procedure or function by another procedure, function, or DOS command line. PCount( ) returns 0 if no parameters exist. The command line interface of the PCount( ) function appears below.

```
PCOUNT( )
```

APPLICATIONS

Use the PCount( ) function to determine the number of parameters passed to a function or procedure. This is especially useful when the receiving function or procedure may receive an arbitrary number of parameters. By allowing different parameters for various occasions, you can make a procedure more generic, reducing the time spent recoding for different applications.

TYPICAL OPERATION

In this example you begin creating a help routine for the sample program using the PCount( ) function. Begin this example in your word processor with HELP.PRG loaded.

NOTE
Since Clipper automatically assigns the F1 key to a procedure named help, you do not need to add anything to the other modules. This is completely different from program starts shown in the previous modules in the learning sequence.

1. Create and save the main HELP procedure using the following text.
   ```
   * HELP.PRG
   * This program manages a mailing list.
   * YOUR NAME
   * TODAY'S DATE
   * Begin by declaring parameters.
   parameters PROGRAM, LINE_NUM, VARIABLE
   save screen to TEMP
   clear screen
   @ 02, 04 say pcount()
   wait
   restore screen from TEMP
   return
   ```

2. Load CL.BAT into your word processor and change it as shown below.
   ```
   IF NOT ERRORLEVEL 1 Plink86 FI MAILLIST, PRINT, CHCKBOOK, HELP LIB
   \CLIPPER\CLIPPER, \CLIPPER\EXTEND
   ```

3. Save the document and exit your word processor. Type **CL HELP** at the DOS prompt. Press **Enter**. The Clipper batch file clears the screen, then compiles and links the program.

4. Type **MAILLIST**. Press **Enter**. The mailing list program menu appears.

5. Press **F1** to select the help program. The program clears the screen and displays the number of parameters passed by Clipper. Clipper always passes three parameters to the help routine consisting of the procedure name, procedure line number, and procedure variable name of the calling procedure.

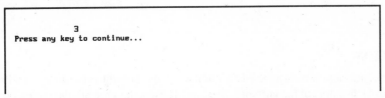

6. Press **Enter**. The mailing list program display reappears.

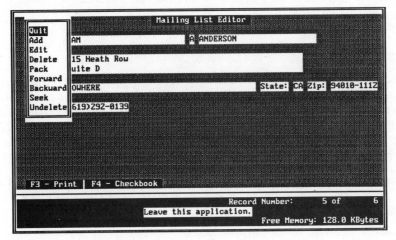

7. Press **Q** to select Quit. The DOS prompt appears.

8. Turn to Module 138 to continue the learning sequence.

Module 129
PROCLINE( ), PROCNAME( )

DESCRIPTION

The ProcLine( ) function returns the line number of the current procedure. The ProcName( ) function returns the name of the current procedure. These names are not the same as those passed to the help program by Clipper, which contain the name of the calling procedure and line number. The command line interface of the ProcLine( ) and ProcName( ) functions appears below.

```
PROCLINE()
PROCNAME()
```

APPLICATIONS

Use the ProcLine( ) and ProcName( ) functions to determine the current procedure name and line number. In most cases error handling or debugging routines require this information to determine a correct course of action. You may also use these functions to make sure a procedure does not call itself recursively, potentially locking the user out of the program.

TYPICAL OPERATION

In this example you add an error handling routine to the help program using the ProcLine( ) and ProcName( ) functions. Begin this example in your word processor with HELP.PRG loaded.

1. Add the following text to the help program.

```
parameters PROGRAM, LINE_NUM, VARIABLE
* Check for error condition.
if procname() = PROGRAM
    save screen to TEMP2
    clear typeahead
    @ 22, 04 say 'ERROR! Do not press F1 from within Help!'
    wait
    restore screen from TEMP2
    return
endif
* Declare Program Variables
DOUBLE_LINE = chr(201) + chr(205) + chr(187) + chr(186) + chr(188) +;
    chr(205) + chr(200) + chr(186) + chr(177)
* Display screen.
save screen to TEMP
clear screen
@ 01, 00, 24, 79 box DOUBLE_LINE
@ 20, 01 to 20, 78
set color to N/W,W+/N
@ 02, 02 clear to 03, 78
@ 02, 37 say ' Help '
set color to 'W/N,N/W,,,W+/N'
@ 02, 04 say pcount()
```

2. Save the document and exit your word processor. Type **CL HELP** at the DOS prompt. Press **Enter**. The Clipper batch file clears the screen, then compiles and links the program.

3. Type **MAILLIST**. Press **Enter**. The mailing list program menu appears.

4. Press **F1** to select the help program. The program clears the screen and displays the types of parameters passed by Clipper.

5. Press **F1** a second time. The program displays an error message.

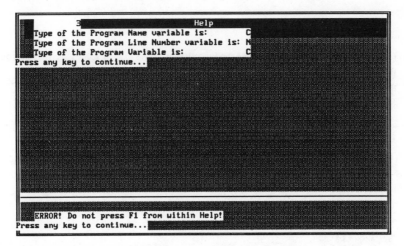

6. Press **Enter**. The error message disappears and the original help display reappears.

7. Press **Enter**. The mailing list program display reappears.

8. Press **Q** to select Quit. The DOS prompt appears.

9. Turn to Module 131 to continue the learning sequence.

Module 130
RAT( )

DESCRIPTION

The RAT( ) function searches for the last occurrence of EXPC1 in EXPC2. It lets you perform searches within character strings and memo fields. The command line interface of the RAT( ) command appears below.

```
RAT(<EXPC1>, <EXPC2>)
```

APPLICATIONS

Use the RAT( ) command when you want to find the last occurrence of a search string in a target string. This is especially useful in conducting searches of text-based databases. You can also use it in conjunction with other functions to separate component parts of a string used for control purposes. For example, you could use it to separate the path of a file from the filename.

TYPICAL OPERATION

In this example you use the RAT( ) function to build a text search function for the notepad database. Begin this example in your word processor with NOTEPAD.PRG loaded.

1. Add the following to the SRCH_REC2 procedure at the end of the procedure section.

```
* Initialize Variables.
private SEARCH_TYPE, NOTE_TEXT, BUFFER, FOUND_IT, NUM_CHECKS
private CURR_CHCK
SEARCH_TYPE = 'N'
M->NOTE_NUM = A->NOTE_NUM
M->CATEGORY = A->CATEGORY
M->SHORT_SUBJ = A->SHORT_SUBJ
NOTE_TEXT = space(50)
BUFFER = space(80)
FOUND_IT = .F.
NUM_CHECKS = 0
CURR_CHCK = 0
* Get the user preference of search type and perform the search.
@ 15, 04 say 'Search for a note by Note number, Category, ;
Subject, or note Text? ' get SEARCH_TYPE picture '!'
read
do case
   case SEARCH_TYPE = 'N'
      @ 16, 04 say 'Enter note number: ' get M->NOTE_NUM picture '@9'
      read
      seek M->NOTE_NUM
   case SEARCH_TYPE = 'C'
      @ 16, 04 say 'Enter note category: ' get M->CATEGORY picture '@!'
      read
      set index to CATEGORY, NOTENUM, SUBJECT
      seek M->CATEGORY
   case SEARCH_TYPE = 'S'
      @ 16, 04 say 'Enter note subject: ' get M->SHORT_SUBJ picture '@!'
```

```
      read
      set index to SUBJECT, NOTENUM, CATEGORY
      seek M->SHORT_SUBJ
   case SEARCH_TYPE = 'T'
      @ 16, 04 say 'Enter note text: ' get NOTE_TEXT
      read
      NOTE_TEXT = trim(NOTE_TEXT)
      goto top
      do while (.not. eof()) .and. (.not. FOUND_IT)
         NUM_CHECKS = mlcount(NOTE, 80)
         for CURR_CHCK = 1 to NUM_CHECKS
            BUFFER = memoline(NOTE, 80, CURR_CHCK)
            FOUND_IT = rat(NOTE_TEXT, BUFFER) <> 0
            if FOUND_IT = .T.
               exit
            endif
         next
         if .not. FOUND_IT
            skip
         endif
      enddo
endcase
* Display the record.
do EDIT_REC2
* Restore the indexes to normal.
set index to NOTENUM, CATEGORY, SUBJECT
return
```

2. Save the document and exit your word processor. Type **CL NOTEPAD** at the DOS prompt. Press **Enter**.

3. Type **MAILLIST**. Press **Enter**. The mailing list program menu appears.

4. Press **F5**. The notepad menu appears.

5. Select Search by pressing **Down Arrow**. Press **Enter**. The program asks what type of search you want to conduct.

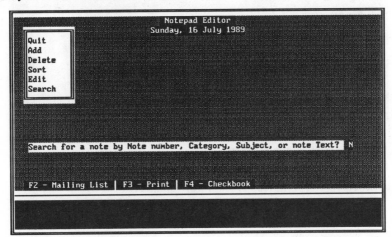

6. Type **T** to select note text. The program asks "Enter note text:"

7. Type **special**. Press **Enter**. The program displays note number 3.

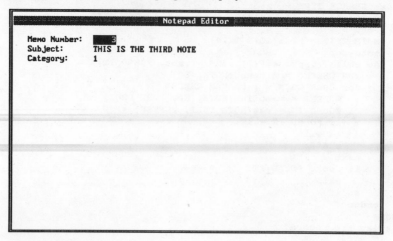

8. Press **PgDn**. The program reveals the note text containing the word special.

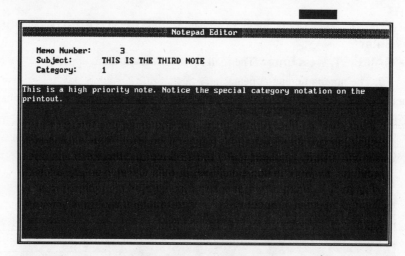

9. Press **Esc**. The notepad menu appears.

10. Press **Q** to quit. Press **Enter**. The DOS prompt appears.

11. Turn to Module 94 to continue the learning sequence.

Module 131
READEXIT( ), READINSERT( ), READVAR( )

DESCRIPTION

The ReadExit( ), ReadInsert( ), and ReadVar( ) functions retrieve/change the read state of the keyboard. The ReadExit( ) function toggles the Up and Down Arrows as exit keys for a read within an At (@) Get command. The ReadInsert( ) function changes the insert state to the desired setting. If you select .T., then Clipper sets insert on. Otherwise Clipper sets overtype on. If you use either of these functions with or without an argument in EXPL, you obtain the keyboard current state. The ReadVar( ) function returns the name of the current get or menu variable. It returns a null string (" ") for all other types of input command. The command line interface of the ReadExit( ), ReadInsert( ), and ReadVar( ) functions appears below.

```
READEXIT([<EXPL>])
READINSERT([<EXPL>])
READVAR()
```

APPLICATIONS

Use the ReadExit( ), ReadInsert( ), and ReadVar( ) functions to monitor and change the keyboard status. In most cases you use these functions as part of a debugging or error control routine. In some cases, you use the ReadInsert( ) and ReadExit( ) functions within normal routines to temporarily change the keyboard status while performing a customized routine. For example, you may want to change the status of ReadExit( ) during a routine using a checklist. In this way the user could use the arrow keys to get around the checklist, then exit. Or, if you wanted to control how Clipper displayed the state of the insert key, you could use the ReadInsert( ) function for monitoring purposes.

TYPICAL OPERATION

In this example you use the ReadExit( ), ReadInsert( ), and ReadVar( ) functions to monitor and change the keyboard status. Begin this example in your word processor with HELP.PRG loaded.

1. Remove the following text from the help program.

```
@ 02, 04 say pcount()
@ 03, 04 say 'Type of the Program Name variable is:        ' + ;
   type('PROGRAM')
@ 04, 04 SAY 'Type of the Program Line Number variable is: ' + ;
   type('LINE_NUM')
@ 05, 04 say 'Type of the Program Variable is:             ' + ;
   type('VARIABLE')
wait
```

2. Add the following text to the help program.

```
* Set program environment
set scoreboard off
* Declare Program Variables
```

```
DOUBLE_LINE = chr(201) + chr(205) + chr(187) + chr(186) + chr(188) +;
    chr(205) + chr(200) + chr(186) + chr(177)
DONE = ' '
* Display screen.
save screen to TEMP
clear screen
@ 01, 00, 24, 79 box DOUBLE_LINE
@ 20, 01 to 20, 78
set color to N/W,W+/N
@ 02, 02 clear to 03, 78
@ 02, 37 say ' Help '
set color to 'W/N,N/W,,,W+/N'
if readinsert()
    @ 00, 60 say 'INSERT ON'
else
    @ 00, 60 say 'OVERTYPE ON'
endif
readexit(.T.)
@ 22, 04 say 'Press any key when finished...' get DONE
read
readexit(.F.)
* Prepare to exit.
restore screen from TEMP
set scoreboard on
```

3. Save the document and exit your word processor. Type **CL HELP** at the DOS prompt. Press **Enter**.

4. Type **MAILLIST**. Press **Enter**. The mailing list program menu appears.

5. Press **E**. The edit display appears.

6. Press **Ins** to display Ins in the upper right corner of the display. Press **Down Arrow** ten times. Notice Clipper does not allow you to exit the edit display using the Down Arrow.

7. Press **Enter**. The mailing list menu appears.

8. Press **F1** to select the help program. The program clears the screen and displays the help screen. Notice the help screen displays INSERT ON in the upper right corner of the display.

9. Press **Ins** then **Down Arrow**. The help program allows you to use the Down Arrow to exit. The mailing list menu appears.

10. Press **F1**. The program clears the screen and displays the help screen. Notice the help screen displays OVERTYPE ON in the upper right corner of the display.

11. Press **Enter**. The mailing list program display reappears.

12. Press **Q** to select Quit. The DOS prompt appears.

13. Turn to Module 133 to continue the learning sequence.

Module 132
REPLICATE( )

DESCRIPTION

The Replicate( ) function performs a function very similar to the Space( ) function. Instead of returning spaces only, this function can return a sequence of any character or string. When used with an At (@) Say command, this function works much like an At (@) To Double command (when used to draw lines). Instead of only drawing lines, you can use any character or string. The Replicate( ) function uses memory equalling that of the Space( ) function. EXPC contains the character or string to repeat. EXPN contains the number of times you want the character or string repeated. The command line interface of the Replicate( ) function appears below.

```
REPLICATE(<EXPC>, <EXPN>)
```

APPLICATIONS

Use the Replicate( ) function when you need to create a series of characters not obtainable using other methods. For example, you can use this function to create special effects on displays. By using different line drawing characters than the normal single- or double-line, you reduce the boredom normally associated with data entry.

TYPICAL OPERATION

In this example you replace the single line rule in the mailing list program with a triple line rule using the Replicate( ) function. Begin this example in your word processor with MAILLIST .PRG loaded.

1. Replace the following text in the DISPLAY_STATUS procedure of the sample program.
   ```
   @ 01, 00, 24, 79 box DOUBLE_LINE
   @ 20, 01 say replicate(chr(240), 78)
   if iscolor() = .F.
   ```

2. Save the document and exit your word processor. Type **CL MAILLIST** at the DOS prompt. Press **Enter**.

3. Type **MAILLIST** and press **Enter**. The mailing list program menu appears. Notice a triple line rule appears instead of the usual single line rule.

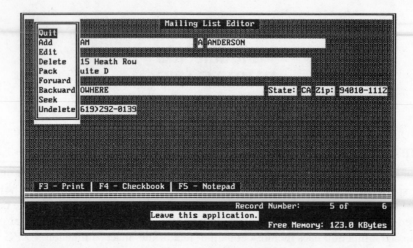

4. Press **Enter** to select Quit. The DOS prompt appears.
5. Turn to Module 135 to continue the learning sequence.

Module 133
RESTSCREEN( ), SAVESCREEN( ), SCROLL( )

DESCRIPTION

The RestScreen( ), SaveScreen( ), and Scroll( ) functions manipulate the display. The SaveScreen( ) function places a copy of the desired display section in a memory variable for later display. The RestScreen( ) function restores a previously saved screen section to the display. The Scroll( ) function moves a section of the display up or down without disturbing the entire display. The command line interface of the RestScreen( ), SaveScreen( ), and Scroll( ) functions appears below.

```
RESTSCREEN(<EXPN1>, <EXPN2>, <EXPN3>, <EXPN4>, <EXPC>)
SAVESCREEN(<EXPN1>, <EXPN2>, <EXPN3>, <EXPN4>)
SCROLL(<EXPN1>, <EXPN2>, <EXPN3>, <EXPN4>, <EXPN5>)
```

The RestScreen( ) function uses five variables. The first four variables EXPN1 through EXPN4 describe the area of the screen to restore the screen section to. EXPN1 contains the top, EXPN2 contains the left, EXPN3 contains the bottom, and EXPN4 contains the right screen coordinate. EXPC contains the name of a variable holding the screen section.

The SaveScreen( ) function uses four variables. They consist of the same screen coordinates used in the RestScreen( ) function described above.

The Scroll( ) function uses five variables. The first four variables match the screen coordinates used by the RestScreen( ) function described above. The fifth variable, EXPN5 contains the number of lines to scroll. If EXPN5 contains a number greater than 0, Clipper scrolls the display up. Otherwise, Clipper scrolls the display down.

APPLICATIONS

Use the RestScreen( ), SaveScreen( ), and Scroll( ) functions when you want to create windows rather than using full screen displays. For example, you could display the contents of two database files at once. Or, you could show a browse view of a database in one window and a single record editor in a second. These functions also work when you want to create pop-up windows, dialogue boxes, and messages.

TYPICAL OPERATION

In this example you begin enhancing the help display using the RestScreen( ), SaveScreen( ), and Scroll( ) functions. Begin this example in your word processor with HELP.PRG loaded.

1. Add/Change the following text in the help program.

```
* Check for error condition.
if procname() = PROGRAM
    TEMP2 = savescreen(22, 00, 23, 79)
    clear typeahead
    @ 22, 04 say 'ERROR! Do not press F1 from within Help!'
    wait
```

```
        restscreen(22, 00, 23, 79, TEMP2)
        return
endif
* Set program environment
set scoreboard off
* Declare Program Variables
DOUBLE_LINE = chr(201) + chr(205) + chr(187) + chr(186) + chr(188) +;
  chr(205) + chr(200) + chr(186) + chr(177)
DONE = ' '
* Display screen.
save screen to TEMP
clear screen
@ 01, 00, 24, 79 box DOUBLE_LINE
@ 20, 01 to 20, 78
set color to N/W,W+/N
@ 02, 01 clear to 03, 78
@ 02, 37 say ' Help '
set color to 'W/N,N/W,,,W+/N'
if readinsert()
    @ 00, 60 say 'INSERT ON'
else
    @ 00, 60 say 'OVERTYPE ON'
endif
readexit(.T.)
* Find, then display the help information.
use HELP index HELP
seek PROGRAM + VARIABLE
@ 04, 04 say HELP_DATA
```

2. Save the document and exit your word processor. Type **CL HELP** at the DOS prompt. Press **Enter**.

3. Create the help database with the following fields using DBU.

```
Structure of HELP.DBF    Field 1

Field Name    Type       Width   Dec

PROGRAM       Character     10
VARIABLE      Character     10
HELP_DATA     Memo          10
```

4. Create an index to the help database using PROGRAM and VARIABLE as key fields. (Type PROGRAM + VARIABLE in the key field of the index file, HELP).

5. Type the following information into the database. Press **Esc** twice and type **Y** to exit to DOS.

```
PROGRAM: DISPLAY_ME
VARIABLE: ANSWER
HELP_DATA: Select any of the menu choices displayed.  To select the
print routine, press F3.  To select the checkbook, press F4.
```

6. Type **MAILLIST**. Press **Enter**. The mailing list program menu appears.

7. Press **F1** to select the help program. The program clears the screen and displays the help screen. Notice the help screen displays the help information typed into the database.

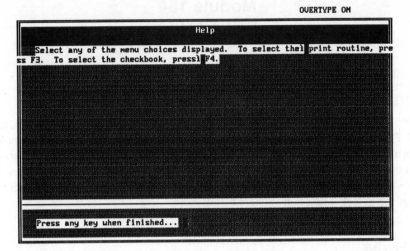

8. Press **Enter**. The mailing list program display reappears.
9. Press **Q** to select Quit. The DOS prompt appears.
10. Turn to Module 124 to continue the learning sequence.

Module 134
SELECT( )

DESCRIPTION

The Select( ) function returns the number of the current work area or the work area expressed by EXPC. EXPC contains the alias of the database whose work area you wish to know. If you provide an alias that does not exist, Select( ) returns zero. The Select( ) function differs from the SELECT command by the task it performs. The Select( ) function reports the number of the work area, while the SELECT command changes the number of the work area. The command line interface of the Select( ) function appears below.

```
SELECT([<EXPC>])
```

APPLICATIONS

Use the Select( ) function when you need to know the current work area. This is especially convenient when calling a procedure. The called procedure may not know the current work area when called. By using Select( ) within the called procedure, you can compensate for any variations between databases in different work areas.

You can also use the Select( ) function when you need to know which work area a database appears in. This is especially useful in multi-tasking, multi-user, or network situations. The work area for a particular database may change from one session to the next based on which workstation logged on first. This function also allows you to check if the database is open.

TYPICAL OPERATION

In this example you check which work area is open and display the number on screen. Begin this example in your word processor with DOSSHELL.PRG loaded.

1. Add the following text to the SHOW_RECS procedure.
   ```
   @ 01, 25 say 'Database Last Updated: ' + dtoc(lupdate())
   @ 02, 29 say 'Work Area Number Is: ' + ltrim(str(select(),3,0))
   @ 03, 00  && This sets the cursor to a new position.
   ```

2. Save the document and exit your word processor. Type **CL DOSSHELL** at the DOS prompt. Press **Enter**.

3. Type **MAILLIST** and press **Enter**. The mailing list program menu appears.

4. Press **F10**. The DOS shell menu appears.

5. Select Consolidate Checks by typing **C** and pressing **Enter**. The program displays the contents of the mailing list database. Notice the work area number appears at the top of the display.

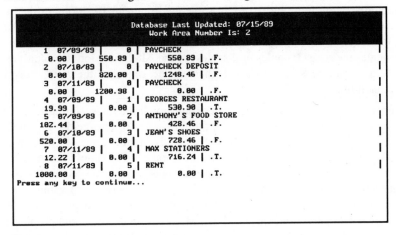

6. Press **Enter** twice. The program displays the contents of the checkbook database. Notice the work area number changes to reflect the change in database.

```
          Database Last Updated: 07/15/89
               Work Area Number Is: 2

    1  07/09/89 |      0 | PAYCHECK
    0.00 |    550.89 |    550.89 | .F.                    |
    2  07/10/89 |      0 | PAYCHECK DEPOSIT              |
    0.00 |    820.00 |   1248.46 | .F.                    |
    3  07/11/89 |      0 | PAYCHECK                      |
    0.00 |   1200.98 |      0.00 | .F.                    |
    4  07/09/89 |      1 | GEORGES RESTAURANT            |
   19.99 |      0.00 |    530.90 | .T.                    |
    5  07/09/89 |      2 | ANTHONY'S FOOD STORE          |
  102.44 |      0.00 |    428.46 | .F.                    |
    6  07/10/89 |      3 | JEAN'S SHOES                  |
  520.00 |      0.00 |    728.46 | .F.                    |
    7  07/11/89 |      4 | MAX STATIONERS                |
   12.22 |      0.00 |    716.24 | .T.                    |
    8  07/11/89 |      5 | RENT                          |
 1000.00 |      0.00 |      0.00 | .T.                    |
Press any key to continue...
```

7. Press **Enter**. The DOS shell menu appears.

8. Type **Q** and press **Enter** to quit the DOS shell menu.

9. Select Quit by pressing **Enter**. The DOS prompt appears.

10. Turn to Module 49 to continue the learning sequence.

Module 135
SETCANCEL( ), SET( )

DESCRIPTION

The SetCancel( ) and Set( ) functions let you retrieve and set the condition flags used by Clipper to control program execution. The command line interface of the SetCancel( ) and Set( ) functions appears below.

```
SETCANCEL([<EXPL>])
SET(<EXPN> [, <EXP>])
```

The SetCancel( ) function lets you change the status of the cancel program execution key (Alt-C). Normally, Clipper lets you stop program execution permanently or pause program execution temporarily by pressing Alt-C. In some environments or during critical sections of program execution, this feature becomes undesirable since it can corrupt the database. The SetCancel( ) function returns a logical value indicating the current status. If you use SetCancel by itself, it toggles the status (enables or disables) of the Alt-C function. By supplying a logical value, EXPL, you can be sure SetCancel changes the status of the Alt-C function to the appropriate condition.

The Set( ) function lets you control a variety of system condition flags (settings). EXPN contains a number which determines the setting you want to examine or change. EXP contains the new value of the setting. The value you place in EXP depends on the setting you want to change. For example, if the setting requires a logical value, then you need to supply either .T. or .F. to the Set( ) function. To make this function easier to use, Clipper provides a header file (SET.CH) with the constant values you need to use. To use this header file, assign the value of the constant specifier to a variable. For example, N := _SET_EXACT. Table 135-1 provides a listing of the constant specifiers and the settings they change. Module 77 tells you about each of the settings and the program parameters they affect. Once you place the constant value into a variable, you initiate the Set( ) function. For example, SET(N, .T.) sets the exact setting to true.

Table 135-1. Set Command Values Defined in SET.CH

Constant	Value Type	Set Command (Module 77)
_SET_DEBUG	Logical	AltD( )
_SET_EXIT	Logical	ReadExit( )
_SET_INSERT	Logical	ReadInsert( )
_SET_ALTERNATE	Logical	Set Alternate
_SET_ATFILE	Character	Set Alternate To
_SET_BELL	Logical	Set Bell
_SET_CONFIRM	Logical	Set Confirm
_SET_CONSOLE	Logical	Set Console
_SET_DATEFORMAT	Character	Set Date
_SET_DECIMALS	Numeric	Set Decimals
_SET_DEFAULT	Character	Set Default
_SET_DELETED	Logical	Set Deleted

Table 135-1. Set Command Values Defined in SET.CH (Cont.)

Constant	Value Type	Set Command (Module 77)
_SET_DELIMITERS	Logical	Set Delimiters
_SET_DELIMCHARS	Character	Set Delimiters To
_SET_DEVICE	Character	Set Device
_SET_EPOCH	Numeric	Set Epoch
_SET_ESCAPE	Logical	Set Escape
_SET_EXACT	Logical	Set Exact
_SET_EXCLUSIVE	Logical	Set Exclusive
_SET_FIXED	Logical	Set Fixed
_SET_INTENSITY	Logical	Set Intensity
_SET_MARGIN	Numeric	Set Margin
_SET_MESSAGE	Numeric	Set Message
_SET_MCENTER	Logical	Set Message
_SET_PATH	Character	Set Path
_SET_PRINTER	Logical	Set Printer
_SET_PRINTFILE	Character	Set Printer To
_SET_SCOREBOARD	Logical	Set Scoreboard
_SET_SOFTSEEK	Logical	Set Softseek
_SET_UNIQUE	Logical	Set Unique
_SET_WRAP	Logical	Set Wrap
_SET_CANCEL	Logical	SetCancel( )
_SET_COLOR	Character	SetColor( )
_SET_CURSOR	Numeric	SetCursor( )

APPLICATIONS

Use the SetCancel( ) function to enable or disable the Alt-C function. You may also use this function to retrieve the current status of the function. By using the SetCancel( ) function to disable the Alt-C function, you prevent one source of accidental database corruption. By keeping the SetCancel( ) function active, you provide the means of escaping from program errors during program debugging.

Use the Set( ) function to dynamically store, retrieve, and change your program settings. Since you can use this function within other functions, it lets you perform tasks that you cannot normally perform using the Set commands. In addition, you cannot read the status of the Set commands. This function lets you read these settings before you change them. You can then store them, change the setting as desired, then return the settings to their original state after you complete a specific task.

TYPICAL OPERATION

In this example you examine the results of pressing Alt-C with the SetCancel( ) function active and inactive. Begin this example at the DOS prompt.

1. Type **MAILLIST** and press **Enter**. The mailing list program menu appears.
2. Press **Alt-C**. The program asks if you want to continue program execution.

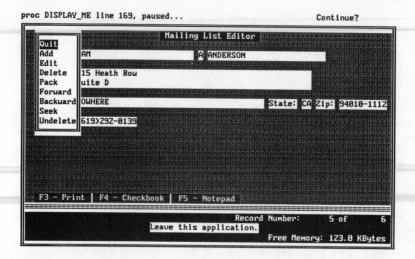

proc DISPLAY_ME line 169, paused...   Continue?

3. Type **N**. The DOS prompt appears. Notice the cursor is missing.

4. Type **MODE BW80, MODE CO80,** or **MODE MONO** depending on your display adapter type. Press **Enter**. The cursor reappears.

5. Load MAILLIST.PRG into your word processor. Add the following text to the beginning of the program.

```
clear all
setcancel(.F.)
* Program Variables
```

6. Save the document and exit your word processor. Type **CL MAILLIST** at the DOS prompt. Press **Enter**.

7. Type **MAILLIST** and press **Enter**. The mailing list program menu appears.

8. Press **Alt-C**. The program does not display a termination message.

9. Press **Enter** to select Quit. The DOS prompt appears.

10. Turn to Module 108 to continue the learning sequence.

Module 136
SOUNDEX( )

DESCRIPTION

The SoundEx( ) function adds flexibility to searches of indexed and non-indexed databases. SoundEx( ) works by creating a phonetic representation of the search string, EXPC. You may also use it to perform database indexing. While this technique saves the user frustration in finding an item in the database, it does increase search times. The command line interface of the SoundEx( ) function appears below.

```
SOUNDEX(<EXPC>)
```

APPLICATIONS

Use the SoundEx( ) function when you need to increase the flexibility of the database search technique. For example, if you have a database of names, then using the SoundEx( ) function to find the name will allow you to find the desired information more often. However, using the SoundEx( ) function to find a monetary amount increases access time with no discernable benefit to the user in terms of flexibility.

TYPICAL OPERATION

In this example you increase the flexibility of the locate function created in previous modules using the SoundEx( ) function. Begin this example in your word processor with CHCKBOOK.PRG loaded.

1. Change the LOCATE procedure at the end of the program as follows.

```
private FIND_NAME, FIND_AGAIN, S_TYPE
FIND_NAME = space(50)
FIND_AGAIN = 'Y'
S_TYPE = 'S'
@ 12, 04 say 'Which check entry name do you want to find? '
@ 13, 04 get FIND_NAME picture '@!'
read
@ 14, 04 say 'Use Standard or Phonetic search? ' get S_TYPE picture '!'
read
if S_TYPE = 'S'
    locate for DRAWN_FOR = FIND_NAME
else
    index on soundex(DRAWN_FOR) to TEMP_IND
    seek soundex(FIND_NAME)
endif
* Display the record.
do EDIT_REC
do while FIND_AGAIN = 'Y'
    @ 22, 04 clear to 22, 76
    @ 22, 04 say 'Find the next occurrence of ' + trim(FIND_NAME) + '? ' ;
        get FIND_AGAIN picture '!'
    read
```

```
if FIND_AGAIN = 'Y'
    if S_TYPE = 'S'
        continue
    else
        skip
    endif
    do EDIT_REC
else
    set index to CHCKNUM, DATE
endif
```

2. Save the document and exit your word processor. Type **CL CHCKBOOK** at the DOS prompt. Press **Enter**.

3. Type **MAILLIST**. Press **Enter**. The mailing list program menu appears.

4. Press **F4** to select the checkbook program. Press **Down Arrow** until the Locate option of the menu appears. Press **Enter**. The program asks which entry name you want to locate.

5. Type **PAYCHCK** and press **Enter**. The program asks if you want a standard or phonetic search.

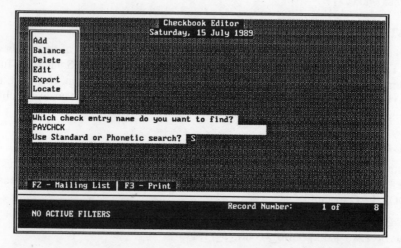

6. Type **P**. The program displays the edit screen with PAYCHECK highlighted. Notice the program does not require you type the exact field contents. It locates the contents phonetically.

7. Press **Esc**. The program asks if you want to find the next occurrence of PAYCHCK.

8. Type **Y**. The program displays the edit screen with the second occurrence of PAYCHECK highlighted.

9. Press **Esc**. The program asks if you want to find the next occurrence of PAYCHCK.

10. Type **Y**. The program displays the edit screen with the third occurrence of PAYCHECK highlighted.

11. Press **Esc** then type **N** to return to the checkbook menu. Type **Q** to select Quit. Press **Enter**. The DOS prompt appears.

12. Turn to Module 128 to continue the learning sequence.

Module 137
TONE( )

DESCRIPTION

The Tone( ) function sounds a tone using the computer speaker for a specified duration. This function works only on 100%-IBM-compatible computers. EXPN1 contains the tone frequency. EXPN2 contains the tone duration in $1/18^{ths}$ of a second. In other words, to create a tone lasting 1 second EXPN2 must equal 18. The command line interface of the Tone( ) function appears below.

```
TONE (<EXPN1>, <EXPN2>)
```

APPLICATIONS

Use the Tone( ) function to add sound to your program. One common example of this is a beep or other tone when the user commits an error. You could use different tones for different error types, cueing the user to the error type instantly. There are other uses for sound as well. For example, many programs use sound for music during the program introductory screen (usually not appropriate for serious business applications).

TYPICAL OPERATION

In this example you use the Tone( ) function to tell the user an input error occurred. Begin this example in your word processor with MAILLIST.PRG loaded.

1. Add the following text to the menu display section at the beginning of the program (after the Ctrl-Break check).
   ```
   if KEYPRESS = 27          && If the user pressed Esc
      @ 22, 06 say 'Press a menu item letter, function key, Enter, ' +;
         or Ctrl-Break only!'
      tone(1200, 3)
      tone(600, 3)
      inkey(1)               && Wait 1 second.
   ```

2. Save the document and exit your word processor. Type **CL MAILLIST PRINT** at the DOS prompt. Press **Enter**.

3. Type **MAILLIST**. Press **Enter**.

4. Press **Esc**. The program sounds two tones. The first tone is higher than the second. Then the program displays an error message, waits one second, and redisplays the menu.

5. Select Quit by pressing **Enter**. The DOS prompt appears.

6. Turn to Module 32 to continue the learning sequence.

Module 138
TYPE( ), VALTYPE( )

DESCRIPTION

Both the Type( ) and ValType( ) functions tell you about the information contained in a variable. However, they differ in their approach to this task. The command line interface of the Type( ) and ValType( ) functions appears below.

```
TYPE(<EXPC>)
VALTYPE(<EXP>)
```

The Type( ) function returns the type of information contained in a variable, parameter, or database field. It uses macro substitution to determine the type of a variable name that you supply.

The ValType( ) function returns the type of information contained in a variable, parameter, local/static variable, user-defined function, EXTEND.LIB function, or database field. It uses the actual variable to make its evaluation of variable type. Table 138-1 provides a listing of the letters returned for different types.

Table 138-1. Values Returned by the Type( ) and ValType( ) Functions

Value	Description
A	Array
B	Block (Clipper 5.0 Only)
C	Character
D	Date
L	Logical
M	Memo Field
N	Numeric
O	Object (Clipper 5.0 Only)
U	Undefined (Summer of 87 Version)
	NIL, Local, or Static (Clipper 5.0 Only)
UE	Expression is a syntactical (language) error.
UI	Expression is an indeterminate (Clipper cannot identify it) error.

APPLICATIONS

Use the Type( ) function to determine if a procedure passed the correct type of information. You can also use the Type( ) function when you do not know what type of data a procedure passes or a database contains. This function normally appears in user-defined functions of a generic nature.

Use the ValType( ) function when you need to know the type of local or static variables, user-defined functions, or EXTEND.LIB functions. Since the ValType( ) function uses the actual variable in place of macro substitution, it provides you with greater flexibility in determining variable type. This function is available with Clipper 5.0 only.

TYPICAL OPERATION

In this example you see what type of variables Clipper passes to the help program using the Type( ) function. Begin this example in your word processor with HELP.PRG loaded.

1. Add the following text to the help program.

```
@ 02, 04 say pcount( )
@ 03, 04 say 'Type of the Program Name variable is:        ' + ;
   type('PROGRAM')
@ 04, 04 say 'Type of the Program Line Number variable is: ' + ;
   type('LINE_NUM')
@ 05, 04 say 'Type of the Program Variable is:             ' + ;
   type('VARIABLE')
wait
```

2. Save the document and exit your word processor. Type **CL HELP** at the DOS prompt. Press **Enter**.

3. Type **MAILLIST**. Press **Enter**. The mailing list program menu appears.

4. Press **F1** to select the help program. The program clears the screen and displays the types of parameters passed by Clipper. Clipper always passes the same type parameters to the help program.

```
        3
   Type of the Program Name variable is:        C
   Type of the Program Line Number variable is: N
   Type of the Program Variable is:             C
Press any key to continue...
```

5. Press **Enter**. The mailing list program display reappears.

6. Press **Q** to select Quit. The DOS prompt appears.

7. Turn to Module 129 to continue the learning sequence.

Module 139
UPDATED( )

DESCRIPTION

The Updated( ) function returns true when Clipper detects a change in any of the pending gets during or after the current read. The command line interface of the Updated( ) function appears below.

```
UPDATED( )
```

APPLICATIONS

Use the Updated( ) function to determine if any of the fields of a data entry form changed during the last read. By using this command, you save valuable user entry time. If no changes occurred, then the program automatically goes to the next procedure without updating the database.

TYPICAL OPERATION

In this example you use the Updated( ) function to tell the user when the program does not need to update the current record. Begin this example in your word processor with MAILLIST.PRG loaded.

1. Add the following text after the name not found message.

```
   @ 23, 04 say ' Name not found. '
endif
if .not. updated() .and. ANSWER = 'E'
   @ 23, 04 say ' Record not updated '
endif
if .not. (bof() .or. eof()) .and. found() .and. updated()
   @ 23, 04 say ' ▮▮▮▮▮▮▮▮▮▮▮▮ '        && Press Alt-177 on the numeric;
   *       keypad 20 times.
```

2. Save the document and exit your word processor. Type **CL MAILLIST** at the DOS prompt. Press **Enter**.

3. Type **MAILLIST**. Press **Enter**.

4. Type **E** to execute the edit option. Press **PgDn**. The message "Record not updated" appears.

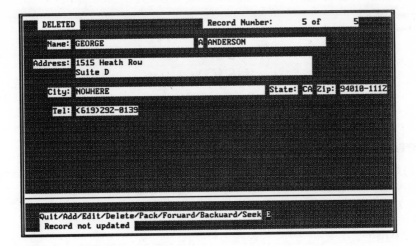

5. Type **F**. The error message disappears.

6. Type **Q**. The DOS prompt appears.

7. Turn to Module 140 to continue the learning sequence.

Module 140
USED( )

DESCRIPTION

The Used( ) function returns true when the current work area contains a database. The command line interface of the Used( ) function appears below.

```
USED()
```

APPLICATIONS

The Used( ) function lets you determine if a database appears in the current work area. One exceptionally good use of this function is in error trapping your program. If the user inadvertently erases the database file, you can post a message on the display and create another copy. Of course, the user loses the data contained in the database unless a backup copy exists (you cannot recover information that doesn't exist).

TYPICAL OPERATION

In this example you add an error trapping routine to the sample program using the Used( ) function. Begin this example in your word processor with MAILLIST.PRG loaded.

1. Add the following text after the Use command at the beginning of the example program.
```
use MAILLIST index LASTNAME
if used()
   @ 23, 04 say 'Database opened.'
else
   @ 23, 04 say 'Database not found in current directory.'
   quit
endif
```

2. Save the document and exit your word processor. Type **CL MAILLIST** at the DOS prompt. Press **Enter**.

NOTE
Some computers operate at speeds which do not allow you to see the message referenced in the next step. If your computer is in this category, type wait at the end of the say 'Database opened' command. During program execution, a prompt appears to press any key to continue.

3. Type **MAILLIST**. Press **Enter**. The message "Database opened." appears. Notice the program displays this message before performing any other tasks.

4. Type **Q**. The DOS prompt appears.

5. Turn to Module 63 to continue the learning sequence.

Module 141
BREAK

DESCRIPTION

The Break dialogue on the Debug Break menu lets you pause program execution at a certain point automatically. The debug program lets you set two types of break point.

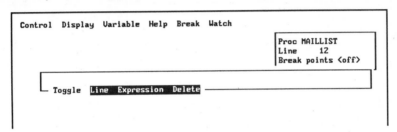

The first break point type, Line, pauses program execution at an absolute point. Debug asks you for the procedure name and the line number within that procedure. If the program reaches that point (in other words no error occurs and the break point does not appear in a non-executable portion of code), debug pauses program execution.

The second break point type, Expression, pauses program execution when the expression you provide becomes true. For example, if you wanted to pause each time the database reached the end of file mark, you would use the expression eof( ). This is a conditional break point since it does not stop at an absolute point in the program.

The opposite of setting break points is removing them. The Delete option of the Break dialogue box lets you remove unneeded break points. When you use this option, debug asks which break to remove. You enter the break number.

APPLICATIONS

Use the Break dialogue box to enter a break point. Using break points lets you reach a problem area in a program quickly, without using the Go (Animation) or Single Step command. The program executes at full speed until it reaches the absolute or conditional break point.

Use absolute break points to reach a specific procedure. This lets you perform localized fault isolation.

Use conditional break points when you know which variable or expression causes an error, but not which procedure. This lets you perform generalized fault isolation.

Use the Break Delete command to remove unneeded break points. By keeping only required break points you reduce the possibility of pausing at the wrong place in program execution. This in turn reduces the time required to fault isolate a program.

TYPICAL OPERATION

In this example you set an absolute break point using the Break dialogue box. After the program pauses, you set a conditional break point using the Break dialogue box. You then remove the break points using the Break Delete command. Begin this example at the Debug Control menu.

1. Select the Break menu option by pressing **Right Arrow** four times. Press **Enter**. The Break dialogue box appears.

2. Select Line by pressing **Right Arrow**. Press **Enter**. The program asks for a procedure name and line number.

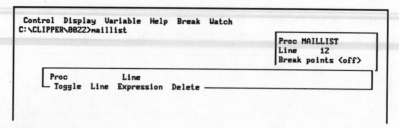

3. Type **DISPLAY_ME**. Type **170** and press **Enter**. The new break point appears in the Break dialogue box.

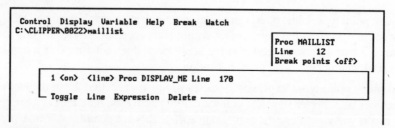

4. Press **Esc** to leave the Break dialogue box. Type **C** to select Control. Press **Enter** twice to select Go. The program pauses at procedure DISPLAY_ME line 170.

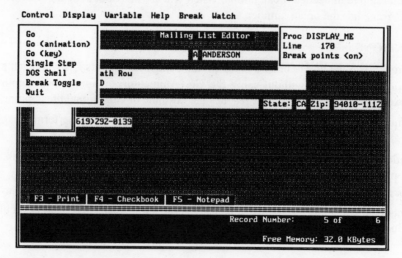

5. Select the Break menu option by pressing **Right Arrow**. Press **Enter**. The Break dialogue box appears.

6. Select Expression by pressing **Right Arrow**. Press **Enter**. The program asks you to enter a procedure name and expression.

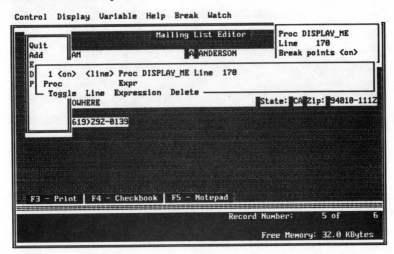

7. Type **MAILLIST** and press **Enter**. Type **eof( )** and press **Enter**. The new break point appears in the Break dialogue box.

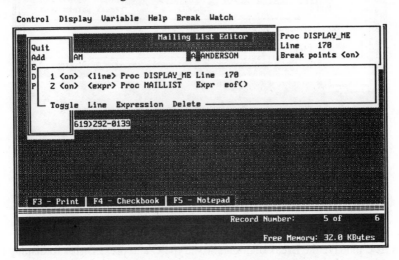

8. Press **Esc** to leave the Break dialogue box. Type **C** to select Control. Press **Enter** twice to select Go. Select Seek by typing **S**. Press **Ctrl-T** to clear the last name field. Press **PgDn**. The program pauses since it reaches the end of file.

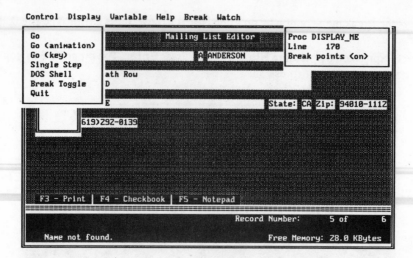

9. Select the Break menu option by pressing **Right Arrow**. Press **Enter**. The Break dialogue box appears.

10. Select Delete by pressing **Right Arrow**. Press **Enter**. The program asks which break point to delete.

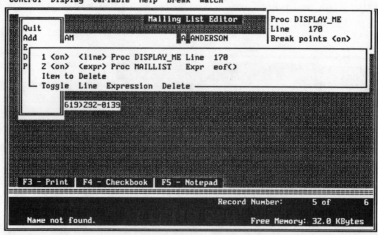

11. Type **1** and press **Enter**. The program removes the break point.

12. Press **Esc** to leave the Break dialogue box. Type **C** and press **Enter** to display the Debug Control menu. Type **Q** and press **Enter** to end the program. The DOS prompt appears.

13. Turn to Module 142 to continue the learning sequence.

Module 142
BREAK TOGGLE

DESCRIPTION

The Break Toggle command on the Break dialogue box provides a convenient method of turning break points on and off. When you select the Break Toggle command, the debug program asks which item to toggle. The Break Toggle command then sets the item to the opposite state. Each break point entry contains a status indicator. When you set a break point off, Clipper ignores it.

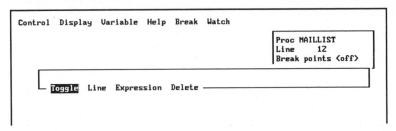

APPLICATIONS

Use the Break Toggle command to temporarily disable a break point. You also use this command to enable a break point after disabling it. By using this command you can retain break points needed during some parts of the program, but not others.

TYPICAL OPERATION

In this example you set a conditional break point, execute a command that activates it, then toggle the break point off using the Break Toggle command. Begin this example at the Debug Control menu.

1. Select the Break menu option by pressing **Right Arrow**. Press **Enter**. The Break dialogue box appears.

2. Select Expression by pressing **Right Arrow**. Press **Enter**. The program asks you to enter a procedure name and expression.

3. Type **MAILLIST** and press **Enter**. Type **eof( )** and press **Enter**. The new break point appears in the Break dialogue box.

4. Press **Esc** to leave the Break dialogue box. Type **C** to select Control. Press **Enter** twice to select Go. Notice the program stops immediately. This occurs because eof( ) remains true until you open a file.

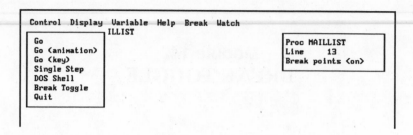

5. Select the Break menu option by pressing **Right Arrow**. Press **Enter**. The Break dialogue box appears.

6. Select Toggle by pressing **Enter**. The program asks which entry to toggle.

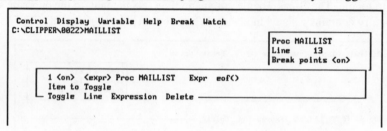

7. Type **1** and press **Enter**. The program changes the status of break point entry 1 to off.

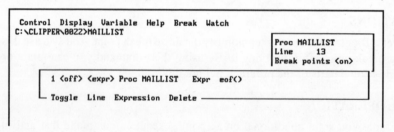

8. Press **Esc** to leave the Break dialogue box. Type **C** to select Control. Press **Enter** twice to select Go. Notice the program executes normally since the debug program ignores disabled break points. Type **Alt-D** to return to the debug program. Select Break and press **Enter**.

9. Select Toggle by pressing **Enter**. The program asks which entry to toggle.

10. Type **1** and press **Enter**. The program changes the status of break point entry 1 to on.

11. Press **Esc** to leave the Break dialogue box. Type **C** to select Control. Press **Enter** twice to select Go. Select Seek by typing **S**. Press **Ctrl-T** to clear the last name field. Press **PgDn**. The program pauses since it reaches the end of file.

12. Type **Q** to exit the program. The DOS prompt appears.

13. Turn to Module 151 to continue the learning sequence.

Module 143
DISPLAY EXPRESSION, DISPLAY TRACE, DISPLAY STATUS, DISPLAY DATABASE

DESCRIPTION

The Display Expression, Display Trace, Display Status, and Display Database commands provide information about various aspects of program operation. All four commands appear on the Display menu.

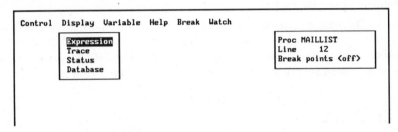

The Display Expression command lets you test the result of an expression. When you use this command, debug provides a blank area within a dialogue box to type the expression. The result appears in a blank below the expression.

The Display Trace command shows the sequence of procedures followed to reach the current point in program execution. Debug displays the procedure names and line numbers. The newest procedure appears at the top and the oldest procedure appears at the bottom.

The Display Status command shows the current condition of the Clipper configuration parameters established using the Set commands (Module 77). The various settings appear in two displays. To look at the second group of settings press PgDn.

The Display Database command displays various types of information about the current database. This includes indexes and their keys, relations, filters, and the overall database structure. Since all this information cannot appear on a single display, debug uses four displays. The first display (F1) presents an overview of database status information. It includes information about the locked status of records and files. The second display (F2) contains information about any relations set for the selected database. The third display (F3) contains information about the indexes associated with the selected database. The fourth display (F4) contains information about the database structure.

APPLICATIONS

Use the Display Expression command to check the outcome of various expressions during program execution. This command is particularly useful when you want to create complex conditional statements. By testing the expression during actual program execution, you reduce the time required to find the correct conditional statement using trial and error. You can also use the Display expression command to check the condition of the database or any program status. The Display Expression command also provides a convenient means of testing data conversion functions using actual data.

Use the Display Trace command to check your current position in the program and how you got there. Some program faults consist of errors in calling the wrong procedure or not calling the procedure in the correct sequence. Some program memory faults also result from the way you call procedures. The Display Trace command can provide useful information in determining the effect of a particular calling sequence.

Use the Display Status command to check the status of various Clipper settings. Many program errors occur because Clipper was not set up to execute the command properly. This type of error is especially frustrating since you cannot find any error in the procedure code. By checking the conditions required to execute a command against the actual program conditions, you can reduce the time required to find many errors.

Use the Display Database command to monitor the condition of the selected database. This is especially useful when creating search or indexing routines. It is also effective when creating network programs. By monitoring the lock and unlock condition of the database, you can reduce the chances of possible network errors caused by more than one person updating the database at once.

TYPICAL OPERATION

In this example you find a program fault and use the Display Expression, Display Trace, Display Status, and Display Database commands to fault isolate it. Begin this example at the Debug Control menu.

1. Press **Enter** to restart the program. The mailing list menu appears.

NOTE
The displays shown throughout this typical operation represent average screens. Your display may not appear exactly as shown. However, your display should show a message or trend similar to the one described in the text.

2. Press **F2**, **F3**, **F4**, and **F5** about 20 times (the number of times varies with the memory installed on your machine). The DOS prompt appears and the program displays an open error message.

```
Proc CHCKBOOK line 60, open error CHCKNUM (2)                    Retry? (Y/N)
```

3. Type **N** when the program asks if you want to retry opening the file. Type **MODE BW80**, **MODE CO80**, or **MODE MONO** at the DOS prompt if your cursor disappears.

4. Type **MAILLIST** and press **Enter**. The Debug menu appears.

5. Press **Enter** to restart program operation. Press **Alt-D** when the mailing list display appears. Select Display by pressing **Right Arrow**. The Display menu appears.

6. Select Database by pressing **Down Arrow**. Press **Enter**. The Database Overview display appears.

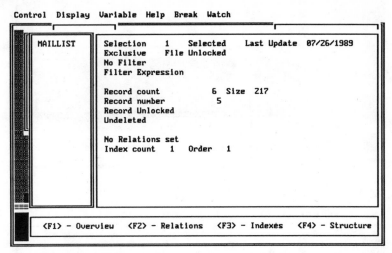

7. Press **F3**. The Database Index display appears. Notice the dialogue box shows the correct index for the current database.

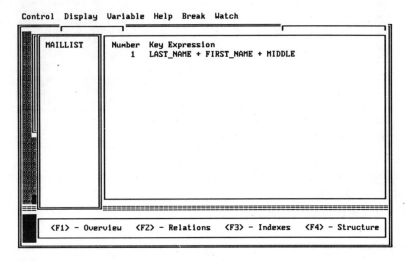

8. Press **F2**. The Database Relation display appears. Notice that the relation dialogue box appears empty since the program does not set any relations.

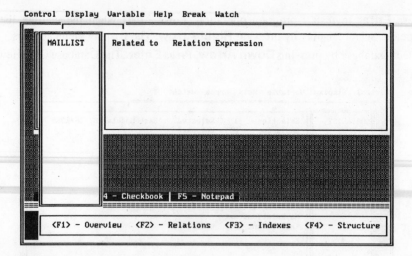

9. Press **F4**. The Database Structure display appears.

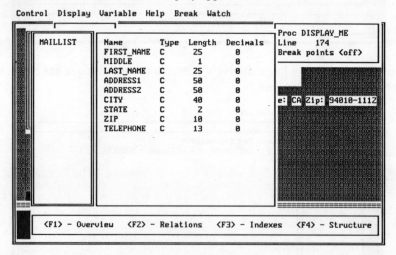

10. Press **Esc** twice to exit the Display menu. Type **C** to select Control. Press **Enter** twice to restart program execution.

11. Press **F3**. The print display appears.

12. Press **Alt-D** to activate the Debug menu. Select Display by pressing **Right Arrow**. The Display menu appears.

13. Select Status by pressing **Down Arrow**. Press **Enter**. The Status display appears.

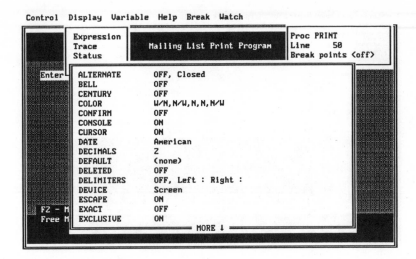

14. Press **Esc** twice to exit the Display menu. Type **C** to select Control. Press **Enter** twice to restart program execution.

15. Press **F4**. The Checkbook menu appears.

16. Press **Alt-D** to activate the Debug menu. Select Display by pressing **Right Arrow**. The Display menu appears.

17. Select Expression by pressing **Enter**. The Expression dialogue box appears.

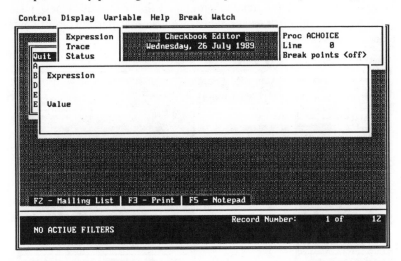

18. Type **ALIAS( )** and press **Enter**. The program erases the expression and displays the results of the Alias( ) function.

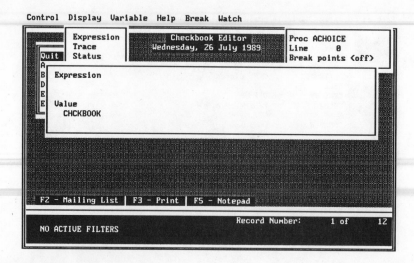

19. Press **Esc** twice to exit the Display menu. Type **C** to select Control. Press **Enter** twice to restart program execution.

20. Press **F5**. The Notepad menu appears.

21. Press **Alt-D** to activate the Debug menu. Select Display by pressing **Right Arrow**. The Display menu appears.

22. Select Trace by pressing **Down Arrow**. Press **Enter**. The Trace display appears. Notice that as you moved from program to program Clipper created a new instance of the program. Therefore, the error occurred because your machine ran out of memory to hold all the occurrences of each program.

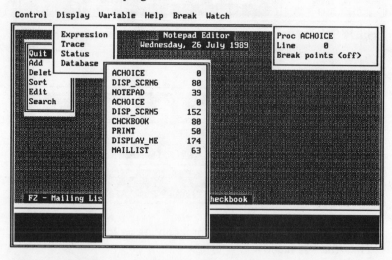

23. Press **Esc** twice to exit the Display menu. Type **C** and press **Enter** to select Control. Type **Q** and press **Enter** to quit.

24. Turn to Module 150 to continue the learning sequence.

Module 144
DOS SHELL

DESCRIPTION

The DOS Shell command on the Control menu lets you temporarily exit Clipper and perform another task using DOS. When you want to return to Clipper, type EXIT and press Enter. The memory Clipper provides to execute DOS commands is a combination of program size and available memory in the machine. You can increase the memory provided for DOS by using some of Clipper's unused buffer space. You do this by typing SET CLIPPER=R and the amount of buffer space to use in KBytes at the DOS prompt. If you use an R value that exceeds the buffer space Clipper can allocate, the program will not execute. In some cases Clipper will still not execute the DOS shell even if enough memory exists. This happens when Clipper cannot find COMMAND.COM even if the environment contains the correct COMSPEC statement (see your DOS manual). In these cases copying COMMAND.COM to the current directory will allow you to run the DOS shell.

APPLICATIONS

Use the DOS Shell command whenever you need to exit your application program to perform some other task in DOS. For example, if you forget to change the display mode before entering the program, you can quickly leave and change it using the DOS shell. You can also use the DOS shell to check the status of a file or any other task. The only limiting factor to what you can do is the amount of memory left by Clipper to perform the task.

TYPICAL OPERATION

In this example you use the DOS shell command to leave Clipper and execute a directory command. Begin this example at the Debug Control menu.

1. Type **D** and press **Enter**. The DOS prompt appears.

2. Type **DIR /W** and press **Enter**. DOS displays the contents of the current directory.

```
The IBM Personal Computer DOS
Version 3.10 (C)Copyright International Business Machines Corp 1981, 1985
              (C)Copyright Microsoft Corp 1981, 1985

C:\CLIPPER\0022>DIR/W

 Volume in drive C is JOHN'S DISK
 Directory of   C:\CLIPPER\0022

                               CL       BAK    CLD      BAK    CHCKBOOK DBF
 .          DBF   MAILLIST DBF  NEW_MAIL DBF    NOTEPAD  DBF    SUMMARY  DBF
 HELP       DBF   HELP     DBT  NOTEPAD  DBT    DOSSHELL PRG    MAILLIST EXE
 TEMP_DAT DBF  CL       BAT  CHCKLIST FRM    MAILLABL LBL    PRNTPORT MEM
 MAINT    EXE  CHCKNUM  NTX  DATE     NTX    HELP     NTX    LASTNAME NTX
 CATEGORY NTX  SUBJECT  NTX  CHCKBOOK OBJ    DOSSHELL OBJ    HELP     OBJ
 NOTENUM  NTX  MAINT    OBJ  NOTEPAD  OBJ    PRINT    OBJ    CHCKBOOK PRG
 MAILLIST OBJ  HELP     PRG  MAILLIST BAK    MAINT    PRG    NOTEPAD  PRG
 DOSSHELL BAK  EXAMPLE  SDF  PRINTER  TST    TEMP     NTX    TEMP     TXT
 PRINT    PRG  HEADER   PRG  HEADER   BAK    CLD      BAT    COMMAND  COM
 MAILLIST PRG  HEADER   OBJ  CLZ      BAT    CLZ      BAK
 HEADER   EXE
        54 File(s)  11513856 bytes free

C:\CLIPPER\0022>
```

3. Type **EXIT** and press **Enter**. The Debug Control menu reappears.

4. Type **Q** and press **Enter** to leave the program. The DOS prompt appears.

5. Turn to Module 145 to continue the learning sequence.

Module 145
GO, GO (ANIMATION), GO (KEY)

DESCRIPTION

The Go, Go (Animation), and Go (Key) commands on the Debug Control menu perform the same task but with different functionality. All three commands tell the debug program to restart the program. In addition to restarting the program, The Go (Animation) command controls the program execution speed. By slowing the sequence of events, you can see why a program fails or what events lead to its failure. The Go (Key) command does not immediately restart the program. Instead, it waits until you press a key on the keyboard. It places whatever keystroke you use to start the program in the keyboard buffer. The program reads the keystroke and uses it as if you entered it before entering debug.

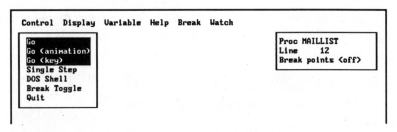

APPLICATIONS

Use the Go, Go (Animation), and Go (Key) commands when you want to restart program execution after entering Debug. Normally you use the Go command since you want the program to execute normally. The Go (Animation) command is especially convenient when you don't know what section of a program causes a certain failure. By watching the program execute at reduced speed and monitoring the contents of variables, you can determine what area causes the fault. You can then use other techniques to find the exact error. The Go (Key) command provides a convenient manner of placing a keystroke in the keyboard buffer before exiting debug. For example, if you started debug at a menu prompt, then placing a keystroke in the keyboard buffer will make the selection as soon as you exit debug.

TYPICAL OPERATION

In this exercise you see how the Go, Go (Animation), and Go (Key) commands perform the same task but in different ways. Begin this example at the Debug Control menu.

1. Type **G** and press **Enter**. The debug menu disappears and the mailing list menu appears.

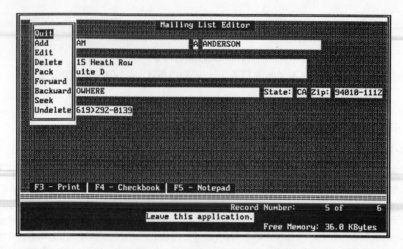

2. Press **Alt-D**. Press **Down Arrow** to select the Go (Animation) command. Press **Enter**. Type **E**. Notice the program pauses between each step of execution and displays the Debug menu.

3. Press **PgDn** to leave the edit display. Press **Alt-D**. Press **Down Arrow** to select the Go (Key) command. Press **Enter**. The program asks you to press any key.

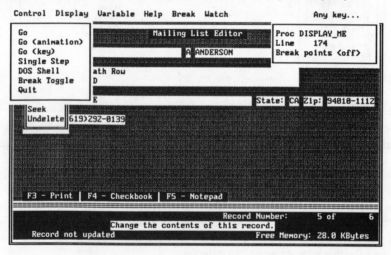

4. Type **S**. The seek display appears.

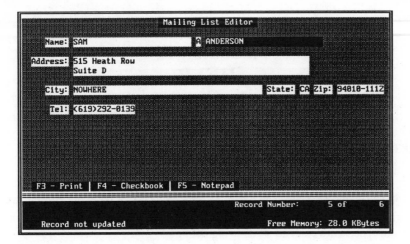

5. Press **PgDn** to exit the seek display. Type **Q** to select Quit. The DOS prompt appears.
6. Turn to Module 148 to continue the learning sequence.

Module 146
HELP

DESCRIPTION

The Help menu provides assistance whenever you need information about a debug menu selection. To access the Help menu simply highlight Help on the Main menu. To access the Help menu selections, highlight the appropriate selection and press Enter. The Help menu contains one selection for each of the Main menu selections. It also contains a selection with information about help and speed keys enabled when using debug.

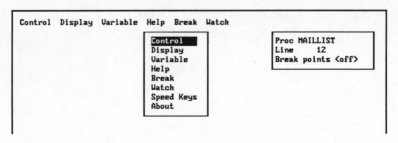

APPLICATIONS

Use the Help menu whenever you need information about a specific menu selection. This allows you to use the debugger without constantly referencing the Clipper manual.

TYPICAL OPERATION

In this example you invoke the Debug Help menu and display one of the help screens. Begin this example at the DOS prompt.

1. Type **MAILLIST** and press **Enter**. The Debug Control menu appears.
2. Press **Right Arrow** three times to select Help. The Debug Help menu appears.
3. Type **H** and press **Enter**. The Help information screen appears.

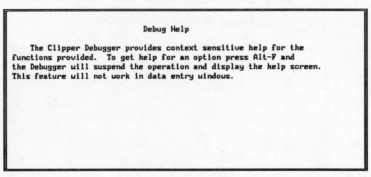

4. Press **Esc** to exit the Help information screen. Press **Left Arrow** three times to select Control. Type **Q** and press **Enter** to select Quit. The DOS prompt appears.

5. Turn to Module 144 to continue the learning sequence.

Module 147
QUIT

DESCRIPTION

The Quit command lets you close any open databases and associated indexes, terminate program execution, and exit to the DOS prompt. It does not set any of the display settings back to their original state. This includes the cursor. In some cases you need to use the DOS Mode command to restore the cursor.

APPLICATIONS

Use the Quit command whenever the normal exit routine for a program does not work or you do not wish to continue program execution. Normally you use this command as a means of escaping partially debugged routines that may cause file damage. You can also use the Quit command to exit from loops that contain logic errors that prevent a normal exit.

TYPICAL OPERATION

Begin this example in your word processor with CLD.BAT loaded.

1. Add the following text to CLD.BAT.

   ```
   IF NOT ERRORLEVEL 1 Plink86 FI MAILLIST, PRINT, CHCKBOOK, NOTEPAD, HELP, ;
   DOSSHELL, DEBUG LIB \CLIPPER\CLIPPER, \CLIPPER\EXTEND
   ```

2. Save the batch file and exit your word processor. Type **CLD MAILLIST** and press **Enter**. The Clipper batch file clears the screen, then compiles and links the program.

3. Type **MAILLIST** and press **Enter**. The mailing list menu appears.

4. Press **Alt-D**. The Debug Control menu appears.

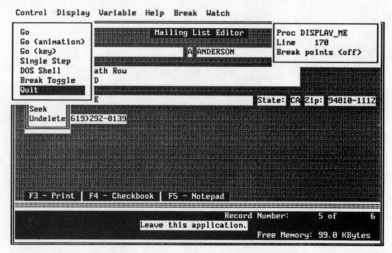

5. Type **Q** and press **Enter**. The DOS prompt appears.

6. Type **MODE BW80, MODE CO80,** or **MODE MONO** and press **Enter** to restore the cursor.

7. Turn to Module 92 to continue the learning sequence.

Module 148
SINGLE STEP

DESCRIPTION

The Single Step command on the Debug Control menu lets you observe program execution one step at a time. The debug program stops program execution after each command. It then displays the Debug menu and associated status displays. You monitor program execution by observing screen results, variable contents, database status, and program controls.

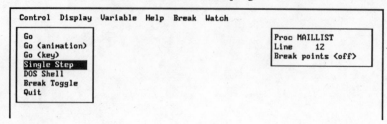

APPLICATIONS

Use the Single Step command to find problem areas in your code. Once you localize a fault, you can find the exact error by executing a command and observing screen results, variable contents, database status, and program controls.

TYPICAL OPERATION

In this example you use the Single Step command to execute one program command at a time. Begin this example at the Debug Control menu.

1. Type **S** and press **Enter**. The program counter in the display window increments to the next command.

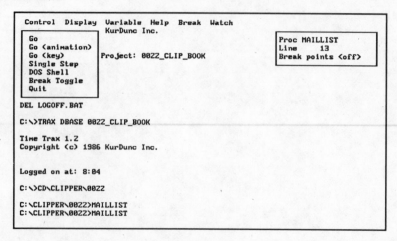

2. Press **Enter** twelve times. The program display shows the program entering a new procedure. Notice a new procedure always starts at line 0.

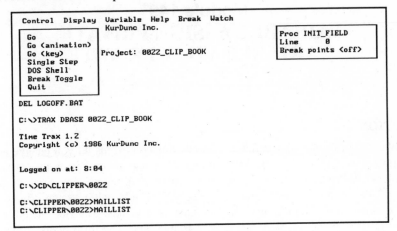

```
Control  Display  Variable  Help  Break  Watch
                  KurDunc Inc.                        Proc INIT_FIELD
Go                                                    Line      0
Go (animation)                                        Break points <off>
Go (key)          Project: 0022_CLIP_BOOK
Single Step
DOS Shell
Break Toggle
Quit

DEL LOGOFF.BAT

C:\>TRAX DBASE 0022_CLIP_BOOK

Time Trax 1.2
Copyright (c) 1986 KurDunc Inc.


Logged on at: 8:04

C:\>CD\CLIPPER\0022

C:\CLIPPER\0022>MAILLIST
C:\CLIPPER\0022>MAILLIST
```

3. Type **G** and press **Enter**. The mailing list menu appears.

4. Type **Q** to select Quit. The DOS prompt appears.

5. Turn to Module 141 to continue the learning sequence.

Module 149
VARIABLE ASSIGN PRIVATE,
VARIABLE VIEW PRIVATE

DESCRIPTION

The Variable Assign Private and Variable View Private commands let you change and see the private variables used in a program. Both commands appear as options on the Variable menu. The Variable View Private command presents a display of all the private variables declared in the program. The variables appear in the order declared. The Variable Assign Private command presents a dialogue box. The dialogue box contains four blanks. The first blank contains the variable name. The second blank contains the variable type. The third blank contains the old variable value. The fourth blank contains the new variable value. Debug automatically supplies the variable type and value after you supply the name.

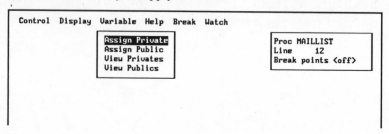

APPLICATIONS

Use the Variable View Private command to monitor the values of private variables. By making sure the variable always contains the value you expected, you can find known or potential failures. Unlike public variables, you can isolate the problem area for a private variable to a specific procedure. However, always make sure you observe the procedure indication in the Watch Status display since private variables with the same name in two different procedures may contain two different values.

Use the Variable Assign Private command to change the value of a variable. Once you discover a variable containing an unexpected value, you can change it to match what you expected it to contain. In some cases this lets you continue program execution to see if the program contains any other potential problems.

TYPICAL OPERATION

In this example you check the value of a private variable using the Variable View Private command. You then change its value using the Variable Assign Private command. Begin this example at the Debug Control menu.

1. Press **Enter** to restart program execution. Press **Alt-D** when the mailing list menu appears. Select Variable by pressing **Right Arrow**. The Variable menu appears.

2. Select View Privates by pressing **Down Arrow**. Press **Enter**. The Variable View Private display appears. Notice the DISPLAY_ME procedure does not contain any private variables.

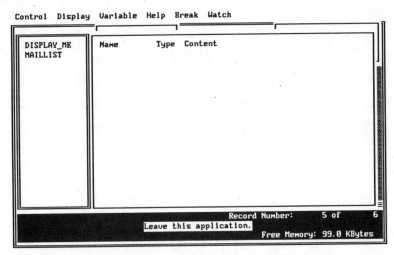

3. Press **Down Arrow** to select the MAILLIST procedure. Notice the Variable View Private display now contains variables.

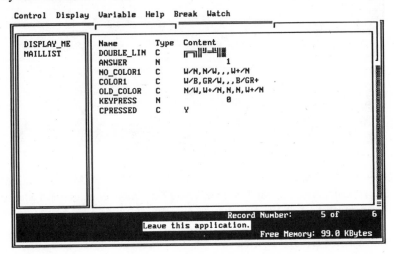

4. Press **Esc**. Select Assign Private by pressing **Up Arrow**. Press **Enter**. The Variable Assign Private dialogue box appears.

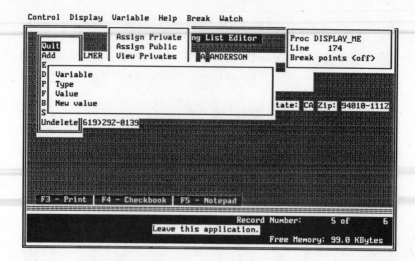

5. Type **DOUBLE_LIN**. Debug automatically fills in the type and value fields of the dialogue box.

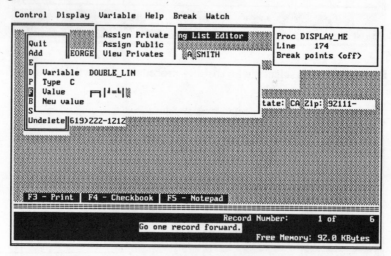

6. Type ' ' (use the numeric keypad to press Alt-213, Alt-205, Alt-184, Alt-179, Alt-190, Alt-205, Alt-212, Alt-179, and Alt-177) in the new value field and press **Enter**. Press **Esc** twice to exit the Variable menu. Type **C** and press **Enter** twice to restart program execution. Type **F** to redisplay the screen. Notice the display changes to reflect the new value for DOUBLE_LIN.

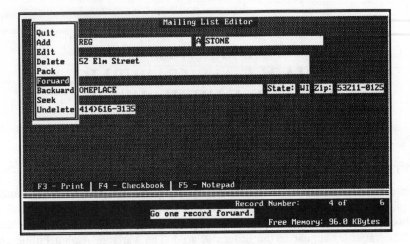

7. Press **Q** to quit the mailing list program. The DOS prompt appears.

   Congratulations, you just completed the entire learning sequence!

Module 150
VARIABLE ASSIGN PUBLIC,
VARIABLE VIEW PUBLIC

DESCRIPTION

The Variable Assign Public and Variable View Public commands let you change and see the public variables used in a program. Both commands appear as options on the Variable menu. The Variable View Public command presents a display of all the public variables declared in the program. The variables appear in the order declared. The Variable Assign Public command presents a dialogue box. The dialogue box contains four blanks. The first blank contains the variable name. The second blank contains the variable type. The third blank contains the old variable value. The fourth blank contains the new variable value. Debug automatically supplies the variable type and value after you supply the name.

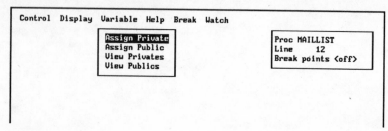

APPLICATIONS

Use the Variable View Public command to monitor the values of public variables. By making sure the variable always contains the value you expected, you can find known or potential failures.

Use the Variable Assign Public command to change the value of a variable. Once you discover a variable containing an unexpected value, you can change it to match what you expected it to contain. In some cases this lets you continue program execution to see if the program contains any other potential problems.

TYPICAL OPERATION

In this example you check the value of a public variable using the Variable View Public command. You then change its value using the Variable Assign Public command. Begin this example at the Debug Control menu.

1. Press **Enter** to restart program execution. Type **E** to select Edit, then press **Alt-D** when the mailing list menu appears. Select Variable by pressing **Right Arrow**. The Variable menu appears.

416

2. Select View Publics by pressing **Down Arrow**. Press **Enter**. The Variable View Public display appears.

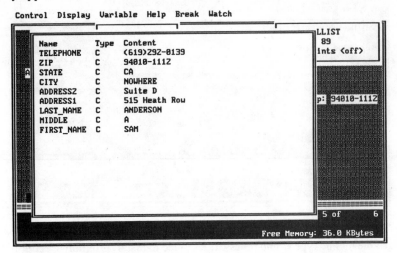

3. Press **Esc**. Select Assign Public by pressing **Up Arrow**. Press **Enter**. The Variable Assign Public dialogue box appears.

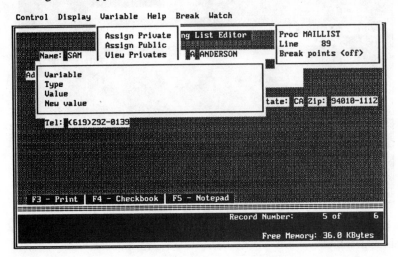

4. Type **FIRST_NAME**. Debug automatically fills in the type and value fields of the dialogue box.

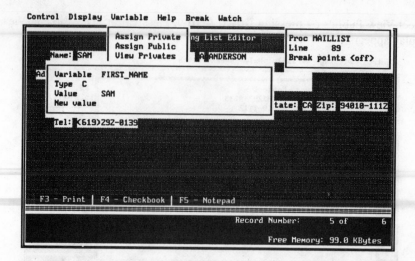

5. Type **'Elmer** ' in the new value field and press **Enter**. Press **Esc** twice to exit the Variable menu. Type **C** and press **Enter** twice to restart program execution. Notice the first name field contains Elmer.

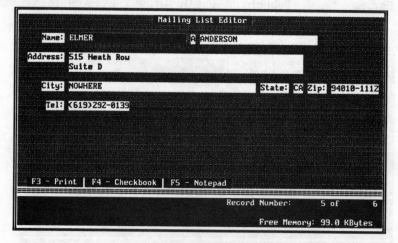

6. Press **PgDn** to exit the edit display. Press **Q** to quit the mailing list program. The DOS prompt appears.

7. Turn to Module 149 to continue the learning sequence.

Module 151
WATCH

DESCRIPTION

The Watch menu contains three entries. The Watch Toggle command lets you turn the Watch Status display on or off. The Watch Status display contains the name of the current procedure, the line number, and the values of any variables or expressions you want to watch. The Watch Status display provides a means of observing the contents of a variable or the results of an expression as a program executes.

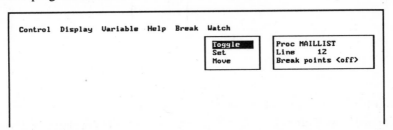

The Watch Set command lets you tell the debug program which variables or expressions to watch. When you select this option, the debug program displays a dialogue box with three options. The dialogue box also contains a listing of any other watch values. The Toggle option temporarily disables selected variables or expressions. You use the same command to enable disabled commands. The Add option displays a cursor at the first available position in the dialogue box. To enter a variable or expression, type the variable name or expression in the blank and press Enter. The Delete option lets you remove any unneeded variables or expressions from the Watch Status display.

The Watch Move command lets you change the position of the Watch Status display from one side of the screen to the other. This lets you observe the watch values from a position that does not interfere with the display.

APPLICATIONS

Use the Watch Toggle command to temporarily remove the Watch Status display from the screen. You use this same command to place the Watch Status display back on the screen. This command is especially convenient when you want to see most of the display without exiting the debug routine.

Use the Watch Set command to add or delete variables and expressions to/from the Watch Status display. This command gives you complete control over when the debug displays the contents of variables or expressions you select.

Use the Watch Move command when you want to see the portion of the display covered by the Watch Status display. This is especially important when you create new displays. By moving the display from one side of the screen to the other, you can observe the entire display while staying in the debug routine.

TYPICAL OPERATION

In this example you observe the effects of the three Watch menu entries on the Watch Status display. Begin this example at the Debug Control menu.

1. Select the Watch option of the Debug menu by pressing **Right Arrow**. The Watch menu appears.

2. Press **Enter** to select the Watch Toggle command. The Watch Status display disappears.

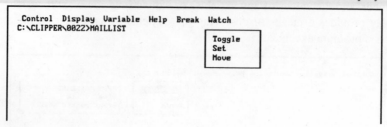

3. Press **Enter** a second time. The Watch Status display reappears.

4. Type **M** and press **Enter**. The Watch Status display moves to the left side of the display.

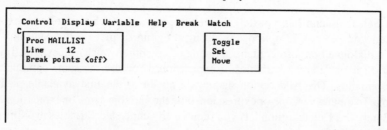

5. Type **M** and press **Enter**. The Watch Status display moves back to the right side of the display.

6. Type **S** and press **Enter**. The Watch Set dialogue box appears.

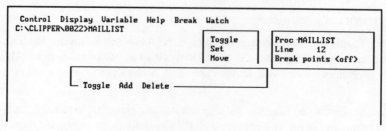

7. Type **A** and press **Enter**. The program moves the cursor to the first entry position in the dialogue box.

8. Type **ANSWER** and press **Enter**. The Watch Status display enters the word <UNDEFINED> as the contents of ANSWER.

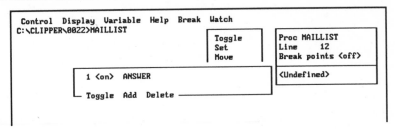

9. Press **Esc** twice to exit the Watch menu. Type **C** and press **Enter** twice to begin program execution. When the mailing list menu appears, press **Alt-D**. Notice the value of ANSWER now contains 1.

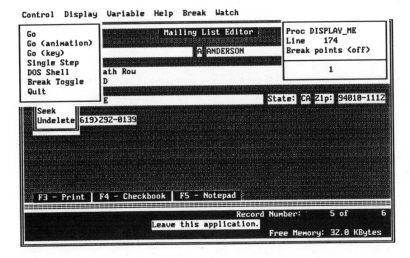

10. Press **Enter** to restart the program. Type **E** to select Edit. When the Edit display appears, press **Alt-D**. Notice the value of ANSWER changed to 3.

11. Press **Enter** to restart the program. Press **PgDn** to exit the Edit display. Type **Q** to select Quit. The DOS prompt appears.

12. Turn to Module 143 to continue the learning sequence.

Appendix A
TERMS AND DEFINITIONS

Term	Definition
Alias	The name given to a work area containing an open database. You can assign an alias to the database when opening it with the Use command. Clipper automatically uses the database filename if you do not specify an alias.
Application	The complete program or group of programs. An application is a complete environment for performing one or more related tasks.
Argument	A value you pass to a procedure or function. The procedure or function recognizes the value by using the Parameters command to retrieve it.
Array	A freeform structure that acts much like a database with a single field. An array lets you randomly or sequentially access each element by number.
ASCII	(American Standard Code for Information Interchange) Clipper uses this code when creating database and associated files. You can also use ASCII codes within the program to create special effects on screen or during printing.
Assignment	An expression that places a value into a variable using the equals (=) sign. You may also make an assignment using the Store or any other command/function that directly places a value within a variable.
Attribute	An attribute expresses some feature peculiar to an object. When referring to a database, each field has an attribute that expresses what type of information it contains, the length of the field, the field name, and the number of decimals. When referring to a display, the attribute expresses pixel color, intensity, and position.
Beginning-of-File	The very first record in a database. This does not include the header which appears before the beginning of the database file. dBASE III compatible files do not use an actual beginning-of-file record. Instead, the program maintains a variable to indicate the beginning-of-file.
Buffer	The area in memory where Clipper stores program variable and database information. For example, instead of reading or writing each record to/from the database individually, Clipper reads a group of records. It stores these records in a buffer for quick access.
Clause	An optional or required part of a Clipper command that appears separately from the actual command word. In most cases a clause contains a key word followed by a variable. However, a clause can consist of a key word alone or a variable alone.

Term	Definition
Comment	Text that describes some aspect of program execution or logic. A programmer adds comments to a program as notes. The compiler ignores these comments when creating the program.
Compiler	A program that converts English-like statements into machine instructions in an executable or intermediate form. Intermediate files normally use an OBJ extension. These files require linking before you can use them. Executable files normally use an EXE extension. You can use these files immediately.
Concatenate	Creating a single string from two or more strings. The new string contains all the elements of the individual strings. These elements appear in the same order as the individual strings in the concatenation expression. You use the plus (+) sign to show that you want two or more strings combined into one.
Condition	The expression part of a for or while clause. The expression normally contains a field name, followed by a relational operator (<, >, <>, or =), and ending with a value.
Conditional Statement	A command that determines if a defined condition exists. If the condition exists, then the command executes the commands following it. Otherwise, it skips the command and restarts program execution at the first command following the conditional commands.
Constant	A value that does not change during the course of program execution. You may use variables to hold constants or use the constants themselves within commands and functions.
Control Structure	A programming tool that alters the flow of program execution. A control structure normally contains one or more conditional statements used to determine how program execution continues.
Controlling Index	The index that Clipper uses to order the associated database. Clipper updates and maintains all open indexes attached to a database. However, only one index controls the order used for database searches and other organizational activities.
Data Type	The nature of the information contained in a variable or database field. Clipper recognizes five data types. The date type contains a number representing a date. The character type contains ASCII characters that Clipper interprets literally. The numeric type contains numbers. The logic type is a single bit. If the bit equals 0 then the value of the variable equals false. The memo type is a special instance of the character type. Clipper limits the length of variables and database fields using the character type. Clipper does not limit the length of database fields using the memo type. Variables may not use the memo type.
Database	A file structure consisting of a file header and fixed length records. Each record contains one or more fields. Each field contains a specific type of information.

Term	Definition
DBMS	(Database Management System) A program or group of programs used to manage information. A DBMS includes the application, database and associated files, and any other software required to manage the information found in the database.
Delimiter	A boundary between two different objects. The boundary normally consists of a special symbol or group of symbols. A delimited file contains variable length records. Each field normally uses a comma as a delimiter. Each record normally uses a carriage return as a delimiter.
Element	A single component of an array.
End-of-File	The very last record in a database. This record does not really exist. In actuality, the record pointer points past the last physical record in the database. Clipper maintains a special variable to keep track of the end-of-file status.
EXPC	A variable containing a character or string.
EXPD	A variable containing a date value.
EXPL	A variable containing a logical value.
EXPN	A variable containing a number.
Expression	A group of variables, database fields, relational operators, and functions that evaluate to a value.
EXT/Extension	The extension or last three characters of a filename. In most cases the extension indicates what type of information the file contains.
Field	The smallest component of a database. It contains a single instance of a value of one specific type. Each field has four attributes: name, type, length, and decimals.
Filename	The up-to-eight-digit name identifying a file. The filename may include the drive and path where the file appears. It does not include the extension.
Function	A set of commands placed in a separate control structure. A function always returns a value. Functions normally manipulate or evaluate data.
Identifier	The name used to reference a function, procedure, or variable. An identifier always begins with a character. Clipper recognizes only the first ten characters of an identifier. However, identifiers may contain any number of characters.
Index	A field, group of fields, or field expression used to organize a database. An index orders the database without actually sorting it. Clipper uses the index, when available, for all search and other reference functions.
Initialize	The act of assigning a known value to a variable before using it.
Integer	A number with no decimal portion. Clipper does not use integers. All fields and variables contain real numbers.
Interpreter	A program that converts English-like statements into machine instructions but does not write these instructions to disk. An interpreter reads each command and executes it before reading the next command.

Term	Definition
Key Expression	A field, group of fields, or field expression used to index a database. A key expression may contain functions that change the value of the field. For example, you may want to change a date field to a character string for indexing purposes.
Linker	A program that converts intermediate (OBJ) files into executable form. You normally use a linker to combine compiled program files with library files.
Literal	The actual value instead of a variable representing the actual value. A literal normally appears in conditional statements with unchanging conditions.
Macro	A shorthand method of representing a value or expression by placing the representation in a variable. Clipper substitutes the contents of the variable for the variable. The macro function appears as an ampersand (&) in front of the variable.
Master Index	The index that Clipper uses to order the associated database. Clipper updates and maintains all open indexes attached to a database. However, only one index controls the order used for database searches and other organizational activities.
Memvar	A memory variable name.
Natural Order	The order the database received information in. Clipper uses the natural order of the database when you open it without using an index.
Operand	The variable, field, function, or expression that appears on either side of an equals (=) sign. Clipper usually requires two operators to perform an evaluation.
Operator	A symbol that modifies or evaluates one or more operands. For example, the greater-than (>) sign in the following expression forms the basis for an evaluation: a > b.
Parameter	A value received by a function or procedure from another function or procedure, the DOS command line, or some other source.
Procedure	A set of commands placed in a separate control structure. A procedure usually performs a task and returns to the calling procedure or function. Procedures do not return values directly.
Procedure File	An ASCII file containing one or more procedures or functions.
Real Number	A number that contains both an integer and a decimal portion. All Clipper numeric fields and variables use real numbers (even if you don't use the decimal portion).
Record	One instance of all the fields composing a database.
Relational Operator	A symbol that forms the basis for an evaluation of two operands. For example, in the statement a > b, the greater-than sign forms the basis for an evaluation.
Runtime Error	An error that occurs while a program executes.

Term	Definition
Scope (Database)	An expression defining the database section covered by a command or function. The all scope tells Clipper to perform a task on all the records in the database. The next <n> scope tells Clipper to perform the task on the next n records beginning with the current record. The record <n> scope tells Clipper to perform the task only on record n. The rest scope tells Clipper to perform the task on the rest of the database including the current record.
Scope (Variable)	Clipper provides two different scopes for variables, private and public. Only the current and lower procedures may use a private variable. All procedures may use a public variable.
Skeleton	A mask consisting of a filename and extension. The mask may include the wildcard characters * and ?. The asterisk represents any characters required to fill the space remaining in a filename or extension. A filename contains eight characters. An extension contains three characters. The question mark represents a single instance of any character.
String	Two or more characters connected to form a word or other character-based information.
Variable	An identifier used to point to an area of memory containing a value.
Wait State	A processor loop where the program keeps checking the keyboard buffer for a character. The wait state ends when the user presses a key and the procedure retrieves it from the buffer.

Appendix B
PRINTING YOUR PROGRAM USING THE LINE PROGRAM

INTRODUCTION

The line program supplied on the Clipper disk lets you create on-screen displays or printer output of your programs with line numbers. Both the error system and the debugger supplied with Clipper refer to the procedure name and line number when providing you with fault isolation information. To adequately use this information, you need a method of quickly referring to the correct line number. The line program provides the method of doing this.

TYPICAL OPERATION

In this example you use the Line program to create an on-screen display and a printout of the HELP.PRG created during the learning sequence. Begin this example at the DOS prompt.

1. Type **LINE HELP.PRG | MORE** and press **Enter**. The Line program displays one full screen of the program with line number information.

```
00001 : * HELP.PRG
00002 : * This program manages a mailing list.
00003 : * YOUR NAME
00004 : * TODAY'S DATE
00005 :
00006 : * Begin by declaring parameters.
00007 :
00008 : parameters PROGRAM, LINE_NUM, VARIABLE
00009 :
00010 : * Check for error condition.
00011 :
00012 : if procname() = PROGRAM
00013 :     TEMP2 = savescreen(22, 00, 23, 79)
00014 :     clear typeahead
00015 :     @ 22, 04 say 'ERROR! Do not press F1 from within Help!'
00016 :     wait
00017 :     restscreen(22, 00, 23, 79, TEMP2)
00018 :     return
00019 : endif
00020 :
00021 : * Set program environment
00022 :
00023 : set scoreboard off
00024 :
-- More --
```

2. Press **Enter** three times. The DOS prompt reappears.

3. Type **LINE HELP.PRG > PRN** and press **Enter**. The Line program outputs the program with line information to the printer.

Appendix C
INCREASING YOUR PRODUCTIVITY USING MAKE AND PRE-PROCESSOR/ COMPILER DIRECTIVES

INTRODUCTION

Clipper provides you with several methods of reducing the work required to create a program. Each of these methods uses a different technique to reduce the work required in different areas of your program. The following paragraphs help you understand these timesaving methods and the basics of using them. Unlike many other programming situations, using these timesaving techniques is not a straightforward task. You must learn how to use them with regard to your personal preferences, the needs of your organization, and the programming task at hand.

MAKE

The Make utility lets you decrease the time required to compile your programs after each change. Each time you edit your program file and save it, DOS changes the date and time to reflect the current system time. Make looks at the date and time markers for each program file as compared to the date and time marker on the dependent object file. It compiles only those programs containing changed information. The linking process works the same way. The command line interface for Make appears below.

```
MAKE <DESCRIPTION FILE> /N
```

Make needs to know which program files belong to which object files, and which object files belong to which executable files. To give Make this information, you must create a description file. This file contains rules of dependency. It provides Make with a set of commands to execute if it sees any discrepancies. Make takes these commands, places them in a batch file, then executes the batch file before terminating. The rules may also contain comments to help you remember why certain dependencies exist. Every comment appears preceded by a number sign (#). The format of a Make dependency rule appears below.

```
<TARGET_FILE : <DEPENDANT_FILE> ... >
    <COMMANDS> ...
    # <COMMENTS> ...
```

Besides the dependency rules contained within a Make description file, another dependency exists. The orders must appear in their own order of dependency. In other words, all of the rules of dependency for object modules must appear first, executable files second. If one rule depends on the results of another, then the dependant rule appears after the rule it requires input from.

The /N command option lets you execute Make and test a description file without actually performing the command. When you specify the /N option, Make outputs the same commands that it would if you actually generated a batch file.

MAKE MACROS

Clipper lets you use specialized macros within a description file to reduce the amount of typing required. The first macro operator is the dollar sign ($). To use the $ operator, you set an identifier equal to some expression, then refer to the identifier as part of a dependency rule. An example of this macro appears below.

```
FILENAME = SOME.OBJ, ANOTHER.OBJ
FINAL.EXE : $(FILENAME)
     COMMANDS ...
```

Another macro, $*, works with a special rule of dependency known as an inference rule. Some commands appear more than one time within a description file. For example, you probably compile all the program files using the same options. It becomes tedious to type the same command for each file. Inference rules provide a method of reducing the amount of typing required. The format of an inference rule appears below.

```
<DEPENDENT EXTENSION><TARGET EXTENSION>:
     <COMMANDS> ...
     # <COMMENTS> ...
```

You use the $* macro to add the filename without an extension to the commands appearing in an inference rule. The example below shows how you could use both the inference rule and the $* macro within a description file. Notice that you no longer need to type the command for each dependency. Make automatically knows which commands to execute.

```
     CLIPPER $* -1
FILE1.OBJ : FILE1.PRG
FILE2.OBJ : FILE2.PRG
FILE3.OBJ : FILE3.PRG
```

Make lets you use two other macros within description files. The first macro, $@, provides the name and extension of the target file as output. The second macro, $**, provides a complete list of all the dependencies for the target in question. You use both macros like the $* macro explained above.

PRE-PROCESSOR AND COMPILER DIRECTIVES

Clipper 5.0 provides you with an additional tool besides Make for reducing your work load. The pre-processor and compiler directives allow you to add or delete pieces of code depending on the conditions at a certain time. For example, you could add conditional statements before and after debugging code. When you finished debugging a program you could remove the associated code by removing the condition that adds it. The following paragraphs describe the pre-processor and compiler directives and how to use them.

#COMMAND/#TRANSLATE The #Command and #Translate directives allow you to change a piece of code to match the current condition. Both directives do this by matching a piece of input text to the MATCH PATTERN provided on the command line. If the MATCH PATTERN and the text match, then Clipper outputs the RESULT PATTERN. The command line parameters for these two directives are as follows.

```
#COMMAND <MATCH PATTERN> => <RESULT PATTERN>
#TRANSLATE <MATCH PATTERN> => <RESULT PATTERN>
```

The #Command and #Translate directives differ in how they match a pattern. The #Command directive matches the input text for complete statements only. The #Translate directive matches incomplete statements. Therefore, you use the #Command directive for command line syntax and the #Translate directive for clauses and psuedo-functions.

There are four match pattern components: literal tokens, words, match markers, and optional clauses. A match pattern consists of one or more of these components. Literal tokens are characters that appear in the match pattern. Clipper takes these characters at face value. The input text must match them exactly. Words are keywords or identifiers that Clipper compares according to standard dBASE conventions (case-insensitive, first four letters mandatory). Match markers are identifiers that Clipper assigns to a portion of the input text. There are three types of match markers. You must enclose them in angle brackets as shown. <Id Markers> match the next legal expression in the input text. <Id Markers,...> match a comma-separated legal expression. <*Id Markers*> match any input text from the current position to the end of the statement. Use this match marker to match illegal statements. Optional clauses are surrounded by brackets ([ ]). Use them to identify optional portions of the match pattern.

There are four result pattern components: literal tokens, words, result markers, and repeating clauses. Output from a #Command or #Translate directive is the result of one or more of these components. Literals are characters that Clipper outputs directly to the result text. Words are identifiers that Clipper outputs directly to the result text. There are six types of result markers. Each of these markers appear in angle brackets as shown. <Id Markers> write the input text to the result text if Clipper found a match. Otherwise, Clipper writes nothing. <#Id Markers> write the input text to the result text and enclose it in quotes if Clipper found a match. Otherwise, Clipper writes a null string (""). <"Id Markers"> write the input text to the result text and enclose it in quotes if Clipper found a match. Otherwise, Clipper writes the NIL keyword enclosed in quotes. <(Id Markers)> write the input text to the result text and enclose it in quotes if Clipper found a match and the statement does not already constitute a complex statement. If the statement does constitute a complex statement and Clipper matched the input, then the output gets written without quotes. Otherwise, Clipper writes the NIL keyword enclosed in quotes. <{Id Marker}> writes the input text to the result text as a code block if Clipper found a match. Otherwise, Clipper writes the NIL keyword enclosed in quotes. <.Id Marker.> writes .T. to the result if Clipper matched the text. Otherwise, Clipper writes .F. Repeating clauses appear surrounded in brackets. Clipper repeats the text within the brackets for the number of times it has input text.

#DEFINE The #Define directive tells the compiler to substitute a value or psuedo-function each time it sees an identifier in the program. For example, if you see #Define CR 13, then Clipper replaces CR with 13 each time it appears in the program. The command line parameters for this directive appear below.

```
#DEFINE <CONSTANT> [<RESULT TEXT>]
#DEFINE <FUNCTION> [(<ARGUMENT LIST>)] [<EXP>]
```

The CONSTANT refers to a constant value you want to replace or define. If you want to replace the text, then you must supply a RESULT TEXT value. The FUNCTION refers to a psuedo-function you want to identify or replace. ARGUMENT LIST is a set of arguments the calling procedure must supply to the function. You must place this argument list within parentheses and separate each argument with a comma. EXP contains the functional code that forms the psuedo-function.

#IFDEF The #IfDef directive tells the compiler to look for a specific definition. A definition could consist of a function, procedure, or variable. You can tell the compiler to perform one procedure if it finds the definition, and another procedure if it does not find the definition. The command line syntax for #IfDef appears below.

```
#IFDEF <IDENTIFIER> <STATEMENTS> ... [#ELSE] <STATEMENTS> ... #ENDIF
```

Each #IfDef directive provides an identifier to check for, a set of steps to perform, and an #EndIf as a minimum. You may want to add the #Else clause as well. In this case, the #IfDef directive adds text to the program whether or not it finds the definition. The definition only determines which text gets added.

#IFNDEF The #IfNDef directive is similar to the #IfDef directive. However, it adds the text if it does not find the prescribed definition. This is exactly opposite of the #IfDef directive. The command line syntax for #IfNDef appears below.

```
#IFNDEF <IDENTIFIER> <STATEMENTS> ... [#ELSE] <STATEMENTS> ... #ENDIF
```

#INCLUDE The #Include directive allows you to include Clipper header files in your program. Clipper substitutes the text it finds in the header file for the #Include directive in your program. Header files provide a convenient method of defining external programs, psuedo-functions, variables, and other programming constructs. The command line syntax for the #Include directive appears below.

```
#INCLUDE "<HEADER FILE>"
```

#UNDEF The #UnDef directive removes a specific variable or psuedo-function from memory. It deactivates a variable or psuedo-function you created using the #Define directive.

TYPICAL OPERATION

In this example you build a description file and recreate the sample programs described throughout the learning sequence in this book. Begin this example in your word processor with nothing loaded.

1. Type the following text.

```
# This is a sample description file showing how to use Make
# and all its associated macros.

FILES =  MAILLIST.OBJ PRINT.OBJ CHCKBOOK.OBJ NOTEPAD.OBJ ;
   HELP.OBJ DOSSHELL.OBJ

# Command for program files. J:
     REM *** $@
     CLIPPER $* -1

# Program file dependencies.
MAILLIST.OBJ : MAILLIST.PRG

PRINT.OBJ    : PRINT.PRG

CHCKBOOK.OBJ : CHCKBOOK.PRG

NOTEPAD.OBJ  : NOTEPAD.PRG

HELP.OBJ     : HELP.PRG
```

```
DOSSHELL.OBJ : DOSSHELL.PRG

# Dependencies for executable file.
MAILLIST.EXE : $(FILES)
   Plink86 FI MAILLIST, PRINT, CHCKBOOK, NOTEPAD, HELP, ;
      DOSSHELL LIB \CLIPPER\CLIPPER, \CLIPPER\EXTEND
```

2. Save the document as MAILLIST.MAK. Load MAILLIST.PRG into your word processor. Save the document and exit your word processor. Type **MAKE MAILLIST.MAK** at the DOS prompt. Press **Enter**. Make clears the screen, compiles, then links the appropriate files.

```
C:\CLIPPER\0022>REM *** MAILLIST.OBJ

C:\CLIPPER\0022>CLIPPER MAILLIST -l
The Clipper Compiler, Summer '87
Copyright (c) Nantucket Corp 1985-1987.  All Rights Reserved.
Microsoft C Runtime Library Routines,
Copyright (c) Microsoft Corp 1984-1987.  All Rights Reserved.

Compiling MAILLIST.PRG
Code Pass 1
Code Pass 2
Code size 1803, Symbols 608, Constants 1205

C:\CLIPPER\0022>Plink86 FI MAILLIST, PRINT, CHCKBOOK, NOTEPAD, HELP, DOSSHELL LI
B \CLIPPER\CLIPPER, \CLIPPER\EXTEND
PLINK86plus ( Nantucket ) Version 2.24.
Copyright (C) 1987 by Phoenix Technologies Ltd.,
All Rights Reserved.


MAILLIST.EXE (225 K)
C:\CLIPPER\0022>

C:\CLIPPER\0022>
```

Appendix D
DBASE III PLUS COMMANDS AND
FUNCTIONS CLIPPER DOESN'T SUPPORT

Clipper supports all dBASE III Plus commands and functions not used in the interactive mode. Clipper is a compiler and does not provide an interactive mode. Since dBASE III Plus is an interpreter designed to work in the interactive mode, it requires the additional commands listed in Table D-1.

Table D-1. dBASE III Plus Commands and Functions Not Supported by Clipper

Append	Assist	Browse
Change	Clear Field	Create Label
Create Report	Create Query	Create Screen
Create View	Display Files	Display Memory
Display Status	Display Structure	DIsplay Users
Edit	Error( )	Export To
Help	Import From	Insert
List Files	List History	List Memory
List Status	List Structure	Load
Logout	Message	Modify Command
Modify Label	Modify Query	Modify Report
Modify Screen	Modify Structure	Modify View
On Error/Escape/Key	Resume	Retry
Return to Master	Set	Set Carry
Set Catalog	Set Color On/Off	Set Debug
Set Do History	Set Echo	Set Encryption
Set Fields	Set Heading	Set Help
Set History	Set Memo Width	Set Menus
Set Safety	Set Status	Set Step
Set Talk	Set Title	Set Typeahead
Set View		

Appendix E
CLIPPER COMPILER ERROR MESSAGES

Clipper provides error messages telling you what syntax or other errors it found in your program file. A syntax error occurs when you use a command or function incorrectly, without the correct number of paramenters, or with incorrect clauses. Clipper always supplies the procedure name and line number of the offending command or function. Table E-1 lists all the Clipper syntax and other errors. It also provides a recommended approach to correcting the error.

Table E-1. Clipper Compiler Error Messages

Error	Possible Solution
Accept/Input ERROR	Syntax error, check the command for correct clause spelling and the correct number of parameters.
Append ERROR	Syntax error, check the command for correct clause spelling and the correct number of parameters.
Assignment ERROR	Syntax error, check the command for correct clause spelling and the correct number of parameters.
Average ERROR	Syntax error, check the command for correct clause spelling and the correct number of parameters.
Average NUMBER OF EXPRESSIONS AND VARIABLES	Syntax error, check the command for the correct number and type of parameters. Make sure your expression contains relevant information.
Call ERROR	Syntax error, check the command for correct clause spelling and the correct number of parameters.
Clear ERROR	Syntax error, check the command for correct clause spelling and the correct number of parameters.
Close ERROR	Syntax error, check the command for correct clause spelling and the correct number of parameters.
Copy ERROR	Syntax error, check the command for correct clause spelling and the correct number of parameters.
Count ERROR	Syntax error, check the command for correct clause spelling and the correct number of parameters.
Create ERROR	Syntax error, check the command for correct clause spelling and the correct number of parameters.
Delete ERROR	Syntax error, check the command for correct clause spelling and the correct number of parameters.
Do ERROR	Syntax error, check the command for correct clause spelling and the correct number of parameters.
Filter ERROR	Syntax error, check the command for correct clause spelling and the correct number of parameters. Make sure any macro substitutions contain relevant information.
For ERROR	Syntax error, check the command for correct clause spelling and the correct number of parameters. Make sure the for loop ends with a next statement.
Label ERROR	Syntax error, check the command for correct clause spelling and the correct number of parameters.

Error	Possible Solution
List ERROR	Syntax error, check the command for correct clause spelling and the correct number of parameters.
Locate ERROR	Syntax error, check the command for correct clause spelling and the correct number of parameters.
Parameter ERROR	Syntax error, check the command for correct clause spelling. Make sure you use the correct number and type of parameters.
Recall ERROR	Syntax error, check the command for correct clause spelling and the correct number of parameters.
Relation ERROR	Syntax error, check the command for correct clause spelling and the correct number of parameters.
Release ERROR	Syntax error, check the command for correct clause spelling and the correct number of parameters.
Replace ERROR	Syntax error, check the command for correct clause spelling and the correct number of parameters. Make sure the variable you want to replace the database field with actually exists.
Restore ERROR	Syntax error, check the command for correct clause spelling and the correct number of parameters.
Save ERROR	Syntax error, check the command for correct clause spelling and the correct number and type of parameters.
Set ERROR	Syntax error, check the command for correct clause spelling and the correct number of parameters.
Set NOT RECOGNIZED	Syntax error, check the command for correct spelling.
Set SWITCH ERROR	Syntax error, check the command for correct clause spelling. Make sure the Set command lets you use the specified and/or variables.
Sum ERROR	Syntax error, check the command for correct clause spelling and the correct number of parameters.
Use ERROR	Syntax error, check the command for correct clause spelling and the correct number of parameters. Make sure any macro substitutions contain relevant information.
Wait ERROR	Syntax error, check the command for correct clause spelling and the correct number of parameters.
Case w/o Do Case	Make sure the case statement appears between a do case and endcase statement. Ensure each statement appears on a separate line.
Else w/o If	Make sure each if statement ends with an endif statement. Check to see if an if statement appears before the else clause in question.
Endcase w/o Do Case	Make sure each case statement ends with an endcase statement.
Enddo w/o Do While	Make sure each do while statement ends with an enddo statement.
Endif w/o If	Make sure each if statement ends with an endif statement.
Exit w/o Do While	Make sure each do while statement ends with an enddo statement. Check to see if the exit statement appears between a do while and enddo statement.

NOTE

Clipper displays this error message on the screen only. If you normally redirect
error messages to a file, Clipper will not redirect this error to it.

Fatal at <n> - Invalid Procedure Mode	Two procedures use the same name. Check all of your program files for duplicate procedures. Some code generation programs create duplicate procedures in the course of helping you create an application.
Illegal Device	Clipper does not recognize the device you used as an argument for a Set Device To command.

Error	Possible Solution
Illegal LValue	Syntax error, check the command for correct clause spelling and the correct number of parameters. Check the assignment to make sure you place a value into a variable. For example, Store <VALUE> To <VARIABLE>.
Loop w/o Do While	Make sure each do while statement ends with an enddo statement. Check to see if the loop statement appears between a do while and enddo statement.
Missing 2nd Quote	Check any strings or literals appearing within the offending command. Make sure each string or literal begins and ends with a quote.
Next w/o For	Make sure each for statement ends with a next statement.
Otherwise w/o Do Case	Make sure the otherwise statement appears between a do case and endcase statement. Ensure each statement appears on a separate line.
Rest of Line Ignored	Clipper did not recognize the information at the end of a line. Check the command and clause spelling. Make sure any comments appearing at the end of the line begin with a double ampersand (&&).
Symbol Redefinition Error	Clipper requires all files and procedures to use different names. During compilation Clipper found a procedure and file with the same name. Check the names of your procedures against the names of the files used to store them.
Too Many Constants	Clipper found too many constants in your program. Compile the procedure files separately. Link them together using the linker.
Too Many Symbols	Clipper found too many symbols in your program. Compile the procedure files separately. Link them together using the linker.
Unbalanced Do Case	Make sure each case statement ends with an endcase statement.
Unbalanced Do While	Make sure each do while statement ends with an enddo statement.
Unbalanced For/Next	Make sure each for statement ends with a next statement.
Unbalanced If/Else	Make sure each if statement ends with an endif statement.
Vert Not Recognized	Syntax error, check the command for correct spelling. Check the command clauses for correct spelling and the correct number of parameters.

Appendix F
LINKER WARNING AND ERROR MESSAGES

When you link object modules together using a linker you actually perform a final assembly of your program. The linker makes sure that every procedure, command, and function reference has an associated routine. The linker also resolves any memory conflicts and assigns permanent locations to variables and routines. When the linker flashes an error message on the display, there are normally three causes.

1. You referenced a procedure, command, or function that doesn't exist. To fix this problem, carefully check your code for any misspellings. Also make sure every procedure, command, and function call uses the correct number of parameters of the correct type. Check the batch file you used to create the executable file. Make sure you included all of the object and library files. When all else fails, another person may see an error you overlooked. Seek assistance from a fellow programmer.

2. You ran out of memory. Most linkers require a minimum of 256 KBytes of memory in theory. In reality you need at least 512 KBytes to make sure a program links properly. If you load your machine's memory with TSR (terminate and stay resident) programs, the linker could run out of memory. A linker seldom displays an error message stating it ran out of memory. Normally the linker displays a message saying some type of obscure problem exists.

3. The linker file became corrupted. For some reason the linker executable file contains errors. Any number of disk failures can cause these errors. Reload the linker from your master disk onto the hard disk drive. This should fix any errors resulting from a corrupted file.

If you try all three of these solutions and none of them work, then find the error code in the Clipper manual and try the suggested remedy. If you still can't find the problem, call Nantucket's help line for assistance.

Appendix G
ERROR MESSAGES DISPLAYED
DURING PROGRAM EXECUTION

INTRODUCTION

Errors that appear while running a program usually involve problems in the logic used to derive a program function or a macro expansion or other indeterminate data. Clipper provides several different runtime error handling routines. The ERRORSYS.PRG file contains the source code for the standard error handling routine. The ALTERROR.PRG file contains the source code for a specialized debug error handling routine. This routine provides a little more information about the error than the standard error handling routine. You can alter either file to meet your own needs.

FINDING A RUNTIME ERROR

When a runtime error occurs, Clipper displays a message stating approximately what type of error occurred, the procedure name and line number, and some ancillary information. The most important information to observe is the error type, procedure name, and line number. With these three pieces of information you can find most runtime problems. Table G-1 contains a listing of runtime error types and some suggested remedies.

Table G-1. Runtime Error Messages

Runtime Error	Suggested Remedy
DATABASE ERRORS	
Database Required	This error occurs when you attempt to perform a database operation without opening a database in the current work area first. Look for errors in a Select or Use command.
Lock Required	This error occurs on networked applications only. When you attempt to change the contents of a database without locking the record or database first, Clipper displays this error message. Use the functions in the LOCKS program or create your own functions to lock the database or record before changing it. Also, Debug provides lock and exclusive status information as part of the Database Overview display.
Exclusive Required	This error occurs on networked applications only. You must open a database for exclusive use when performing global functions like Pack or Reindex. Check the Use command for this database. Also, Debug provides lock and exclusive status information as part of the Database Overview display.
Field Numeric Overflow	The defined size of a numeric field limits the size number Clipper allows you to place in it. Use Debug to monitor the value of the variable. This allows you to find the error more quickly.

Runtime Error	Suggested Remedy
Index File Corrupted	This problem occurs from many different sources, both hardware and software. To initially recover from this fault, use DBU or Index to reindex the database. If the problem occurs again, and you have expanded memory installed, use the command SET CLIPPER=E000 to display the expanded memory. If this still doesn't correct the problem, use Debug to monitor the fault.

EXPRESSION ERRORS

Type Mismatch	This error occurs frequently when you use macro expansions as part of a command. It also occurs frequently when you fail to convert the output of a function to a format suitable with a particular command. Finally, this error can occur when you try to mix text and numeric information on the same line of an At (@) Say/Get command (for example). In all cases, check your code to make sure the data used matches the requirements of the command. If the code appears correct, use Debug to monitor the values of variables used for macro expansion.
Subscript Range	This error normally occurs when you do not provide enough safeguards for input to menus and other control structures using arrays. The program tried to access a value outside the normal range of the array. By checking how the error occurs, you can determine what type of safeguards to add. In some cases a logic error also causes this problem.
Zero Divide	This error always occurs as the result of a math error. This error is hard to find at times because many commands and functions use math as part of their operation. For example, all the screen positioning commands use math to find the correct screen location. Try to narrow the math error down to user code by using debug. If no math errors occur in user code, then check the parameters input to commands and functions in the problem area.
Expression Error	This error always occurs as a result of flawed logic. First check the flow of program code to make sure no errors appear in loops or other control structures. Then use Debug to check the contents of variables, especially those used in macro expansions.

MISCELLANEOUS ERRORS

RUN Error	This error occurs when you execute a nonexistent DOS command, do not have enough memory, or Clipper cannot find COMMAND.COM. As a first step to correcting the problem type SET CLIPPER=R100 and press Enter at the DOS prompt. If this does not correct the problem, then try copying COMMAND.COM into the current directory. If this still doesn't correct the problem, monitor the DOS command the program tries to run using Debug.
Open Error	This error occurs when you try to open a nonexistent file or CONFIG.SYS does not allocate enough files. To fix this problem, check the filename you want to open. Make sure you specify the correct path and drive (if required). If this doesn't solve the problem, try increasing the number of files allocated using CONFIG.SYS. Make sure you reboot your machine after changing CONFIG.SYS.
Print Error	This error occurs if your printer is off-line (turned off or the ready light not lit) or you try to use a nonexistent printer port. Check the status of your printer. If the printer is on-line and connected to the computer, check the port specified as the destination within your code.

Runtime Error	*Suggested Remedy*

UNDEFINED ERRORS

Undefined Identifier This error occurs when you try to use a variable that doesn't exist as an argument to a command or function. Check your code and make sure you initialize all variables before using them.

Not An Array This error occurs when you try to use a non-array variable with array functions. If you started with an array, monitor the variable type using Debug. Some commands and functions change variable type.

Missing EXTERNAL This error occurs when you conceal an external routine from both the compiler and linker using a macro expansion. You can correct this problem by declaring the external procedure using the External command.

OTHER ERRORS

Internal Error This error usually results from a bad index file. However, any bad file or other Clipper internal error can cause this fault as well. If you reindex the file and the error still occurs, try compiling and linking the program again.

Disk Full This error occurs when the disk is full or a disk failure develops. In either case, exit the program and check the status of your hard disk drive.

Multiple Error This error occurs when a Clipper error function fails. To fix this problem, compile and link the program again.

Out of Memory This error occurs when Clipper runs out of buffer space. You can remedy this problem using the Release command to deallocate unneeded variables. You can also use some of the memory saving commands, functions, and techniques discussed throughout the learning sequence in this book.

Not Enough Memory This error occurs when your machine does not contain enough memory to perform a task. This error also appears if you set the R value in the SET CLIPPER=RXXX command too high. In either case, use memory conservation techniques to fix the problem.

Appendix H
PROGRAM SOURCE CODE LISTINGS

To assist you in finding errors, this appendix contains a complete listing of the source code for each program file. These are the completed, not intermediate, versions of the source code. This means that your code may not match the source code presented here as you go through the learning sequence. Your code should match this code when you complete the learning sequence. The source code appears in alphabetical order. All of the following programs are available on disk for $10.00 plus $2.00 shipping and handling. Order from Wordware Publishing, Inc. at 1506 Captial Ave., Plano, TX 75074 or call the order line 1-800-229-4949.

CHECKBOOK.PRG

```
* CHCKBOOK.PRG
* This program manages a checkbook.
* YOUR NAME
* TODAY'S DATE

* Program Variables

DOUBLE_LINE = chr(201) + chr(205) + chr(187) + chr(186) + chr(188) + chr(205) + chr(200) + chr(186) + chr(177)
ANSWER = 0
FIELD_NUMBER = 1
DATE_STR = cdow(date()) + ', ' + substr(dtoc(date()), 4, 2) + ' ' + cmonth(date()) + ' ' + ltrim(str(year(date())))

* Create the database variables.

DATE = date()
CHECK_NUM = 0
DRAWN_FOR = space(50)
AMOUNT = 0.00
DEPOSIT = 0.00
BALANCE = 0.00
TAX_ITEM = .F.

* Create the menu array and place the menu values in it.

declare MENU_ITEM[11]
MENU_ITEM[1] = 'Quit'
MENU_ITEM[2] = 'Add'
MENU_ITEM[3] = 'Delete'
MENU_ITEM[4] = 'Sort'
MENU_ITEM[5] = 'Edit'
MENU_ITEM[6] = 'Search'
MENU_ITEM[7] = 'Stats'
MENU_ITEM[8] = 'Balance'
MENU_ITEM[9] = 'Reindex'
MENU_ITEM[10] = 'Export'
MENU_ITEM[11] = 'Locate'

* Sort the menu items then place Quit at the top.

asort(MENU_ITEM)
ANSWER = ascan(MENU_ITEM, 'Quit')
adel(MENU_ITEM, ANSWER)
ains(MENU_ITEM, 1)
MENU_ITEM[1] = 'Quit'

* Setup program defaults.

set softseek on
```

```
set wrap on
set key -1 to MAILLIST                    && Point F2 to the mailing list program.
set key -2 to PRINT                       && Point F3 to the print program.
set key -3 to                             && Make sure F4 is clear.
set key -4 to NOTEPAD                      && Point F5 to the notepad.


* Declare external procedures.

external DESCEND

* Clear the display and prepare the database for use.

clear screen
use CHCKBOOK index CHCKNUM, DATE

* Create an array containing the database field names for use with database editing routines.

declare FIELD_ARRAY[fcount()]

* Initialize the array with the field names.

for FIELD_NUMBER = 1 to fcount()
   FIELD_ARRAY[FIELD_NUMBER] = fieldname(FIELD_NUMBER)
next

* Perform this procedure until the user selects quit.

ANSWER = 2
do while MENU_ITEM[ANSWER] <> 'Quit'

* Display the screen.

   do DISP_SCRN5

* Perform the user requested function.

   do case
      case MENU_ITEM[ANSWER] = 'Add'
         do ADD_REC
      case MENU_ITEM[ANSWER] = 'Delete'
         do DEL_REC
      case MENU_ITEM[ANSWER] = 'Sort'
         do SORT_REC
      case MENU_ITEM[ANSWER] = 'Edit'
         do EDIT_REC
      case MENU_ITEM[ANSWER] = 'Search'
         do SEARCH_REC
      case MENU_ITEM[ANSWER] = 'Stats'
         do STATS
      case MENU_ITEM[ANSWER] = 'Balance'
         do BALANCE
      case MENU_ITEM[ANSWER] = 'Reindex'
         do REINDEX
      case MENU_ITEM[ANSWER] = 'Export'
         do EXPORT
      case MENU_ITEM[ANSWER] = 'Locate'
         do LOCATE
   endcase

enddo

* Close the databases and return.

quit

* Begin procedures here.

procedure DISP_SCRN5

* This procedure displays the screen and status information.

@ 01, 00, 24, 79 box DOUBLE_LINE
@ 20, 01 to 20, 78
set color to N/W,W+/N
@ 02, 31 say ' Checkbook Editor '
@ 03, 40 - (len(DATE_STR)/2) say DATE_STR
@ 19, 03 say ' F2 - Mailing List ' + chr(179) + ' F3 - Print ' + chr(179) + ' F5 - Notepad '
@ 21, 01 clear to 23, 78
@ 21, 45 say ' Record Number: '
```

```
@ 21, 60 say recno()
@ 21, 67 say ' of '
@ 21, 71 say reccount()

* Show the record status.

if deleted()
   @ 21, 04 say ' DELETED '
else
   @ 21, 04 say '          '
endif

* Show any active filters.

if dbfilter() = ""
   @ 22, 04 say 'NO ACTIVE FILTERS'
else
   @ 22, 04 say 'Filter set to: ' + dbfilter()
endif

set color to 'W/N,N/W,,,W+/N'

* Obtain the user selection.

@ 03, 03, 10, 13 box DOUBLE_LINE
ANSWER = achoice(04, 04, 09, 12, MENU_ITEM)

return

procedure ADD_REC

* This procedure adds records to the database.

* Set the Shift-F2 key to output the date.

set key -11 to DATE_OUT

* Create procedure variables.

private MORE
MORE = 'Y'

* Create a screen area.

@ 03, 15, 12, 78 box DOUBLE_LINE
@ 04, 16 clear to 11, 77
@ 10, 16 to 10, 77

* Get the new check information.

do while MORE = 'Y'
   @ 04, 16 say 'Date:     ' get M->DATE picture '@D'
   @ 05, 16 say 'Check:    ' get M->CHECK_NUM picture '99999'
   @ 06, 16 say 'For:      ' get M->DRAWN_FOR picture '@K@!'
   @ 07, 16 say 'Amount:   ' get M->AMOUNT picture '9999999.99'
   @ 08, 16 say 'Deposit:  ' get M->DEPOSIT picture '9999999.99'
   @ 09, 16 say 'Tax Item: ' get M->TAX_ITEM picture 'Y'
   read

* If the user added a check, put it in the database.

   if (M->AMOUNT <> 0) .or. (M->DEPOSIT <> 0)
      append blank
      replace A->DATE with M->DATE
      replace A->CHECK_NUM with M->CHECK_NUM
      replace A->DRAWN_FOR with M->DRAWN_FOR
      replace A->AMOUNT with M->AMOUNT
      replace A->DEPOSIT with M->DEPOSIT
      replace A->TAX_ITEM with M->TAX_ITEM
      commit
   endif

   @ 11, 16 say 'Add another check? ' get MORE picture '!'
   read
enddo

* Release the Shift-F2 key.

set key -11 to
```

```
return

procedure DATE_OUT

* This procedure outputs the date using the Keyboard command.

keyboard dtoc(date())

return

procedure DEL_REC

* This procedure removes records from the database.

* Get user input for record deletions.

set color to N/W,W+/N
dbedit(03, 01, 23, 78, FIELD_ARRAY, 'REMOVE_REC')
set color to 'W/N,N/W,,,W+/N'

* Remove the deleted records from the database.

pack

return

function REMOVE_REC

* This function marks the records for deletion. It does not actually remove them.

* Declare variables.

private STATUS
STATUS = 1                                        && Continue with DBEdit() function.

* Check if user wants record deleted.

if lastkey() = 7 .and. .not. deleted()
   delete
   commit
elseif lastkey() = 7 .and. deleted()
   recall
   commit
endif

* Display record status.

if deleted()
   @ 02, 70 say 'DELETED'
else
   @ 02, 70 say '        '
endif

* Display time and date.

@ 02, 04 say dtoc(date()) + '    ' + time()

* Check if user wants to exit DBEdit()

if lastkey() = 27
   STATUS = 0                                     && Exit DBEdit() function.
endif

return STATUS

procedure SORT_REC

* This procedure changes the index used by the database.

* Initialize Variables.

private NAME_ARRAY, AVAIL_ARRAY, ORDER_ARRAY, SORT_STRING
private TEMP_STRING, SORT_SELECT, ORDER_SELECT, PREV_LEN
private VARA, VARB, VARC, VARD, VARE, VARF, NUM

declare NAME_ARRAY[7]
NAME_ARRAY[1] = 'Quit'
NAME_ARRAY[2] = 'Date'
```

```
NAME_ARRAY[3] = 'Check Number'
NAME_ARRAY[4] = 'Drawn For'
NAME_ARRAY[5] = 'Check Amount'
NAME_ARRAY[6] = 'Deposit Amount'
NAME_ARRAY[7] = 'Tax Ded. Item'

declare AVAIL_ARRAY[7]
afill(AVAIL_ARRAY, .T.)

declare ORDER_ARRAY[2]
ORDER_ARRAY[1] = 'Ascending Order'
ORDER_ARRAY[2] = 'Descending Order'

SORT_STRING = ' '
TEMP_STRING = ' '
SORT_SELECT = 2
ORDER_SELECT = 1
PREV_LEN = 1

VARA = ' '
VARB = ' '
VARC = ' '
VARD = ' '
VARE = ' '
VARF = ' '
NUM = 'A'

* Keep adding parameters to the sort string until the user quits the sort menu.

set color to 'N/W,W/N,,,W+/N'
do while .not. NAME_ARRAY[SORT_SELECT] = 'Quit'
   @ 06, 06 to 14, 21 double
   SORT_SELECT = achoice(07, 07, 13, 20, NAME_ARRAY, AVAIL_ARRAY)
   do case
      case NAME_ARRAY[SORT_SELECT] = 'Date'
         SORT_STRING = ltrim(SORT_STRING) + 'DTOS(DATE) + '
         VAR&NUM = 'DATE'
         NUM = chr(asc(NUM) + 1)
         AVAIL_ARRAY[SORT_SELECT] = .F.
      case NAME_ARRAY[SORT_SELECT] = 'Check Number'
         SORT_STRING = ltrim(SORT_STRING) + 'STR(CHECK_NUM,5,0) + '
         VAR&NUM = 'CHECK_NUM'
         NUM = chr(asc(NUM) + 1)
         AVAIL_ARRAY[SORT_SELECT] = .F.
      case NAME_ARRAY[SORT_SELECT] = 'Drawn For'
         SORT_STRING = ltrim(SORT_STRING) + 'DRAWN_FOR + '
         VAR&NUM = 'DRAWN_FOR'
         NUM = chr(asc(NUM) + 1)
         AVAIL_ARRAY[SORT_SELECT] = .F.
      case NAME_ARRAY[SORT_SELECT] = 'Check Amount'
         SORT_STRING = ltrim(SORT_STRING) + 'STR(AMOUNT,10,2) + '
         VAR&NUM = 'AMOUNT'
         NUM = chr(asc(NUM) + 1)
         AVAIL_ARRAY[SORT_SELECT] = .F.
      case NAME_ARRAY[SORT_SELECT] = 'Deposit Amount'
         SORT_STRING = ltrim(SORT_STRING) + 'STR(DEPOSIT,10,2) + '
         VAR&NUM = 'DEPOSIT'
         NUM = chr(asc(NUM) + 1)
         AVAIL_ARRAY[SORT_SELECT] = .F.
      case NAME_ARRAY[SORT_SELECT] = 'Tax Ded. Item'
         SORT_STRING = ltrim(SORT_STRING) + 'TAX_ITEM + '
         VAR&NUM = 'TAX_ITEM'
         NUM = chr(asc(NUM) + 1)
         AVAIL_ARRAY[SORT_SELECT] = .F.
   endcase

* If the user selects quit, exit the loop.

   if NAME_ARRAY[SORT_SELECT] = 'Quit'
      exit
   endif

* Ask the user to select between ascending and descending order.

   save screen to TEMP_SCRN
   set color to 'W/N,N/W,,,W+/N'
   @ 12, 12 to 15, 29 double
   ORDER_SELECT = achoice(13, 13, 14, 28, ORDER_ARRAY)
```

```
* Change the SORT_STRING variable to match the descending order requirement.

    if ORDER_ARRAY[ORDER_SELECT] = 'Descending Order'
        TEMP_STRING = substr(SORT_STRING, PREV_LEN, len(SORT_STRING) - PREV_LEN - 2)
        if PREV_LEN = 1
            SORT_STRING = ''
        else
            SORT_STRING = substr(SORT_STRING, 1, PREV_LEN)
        endif
        SORT_STRING = SORT_STRING + 'DESCEND(' + TEMP_STRING + ') + '
    endif
    restore screen from TEMP_SCRN
    set color to 'N/W,W/N,,,W+/N'

* Set PREV_LEN to the new length of SORT_STRING for use with the descending order function.

    PREV_LEN = len(SORT_STRING)

enddo

* Trim the last plus sign from the end of SORT_STRING.

SORT_STRING = substr(SORT_STRING, 1, len(SORT_STRING) - 3)

* Sort the database.

do case
    case NUM = 'B'
        sort on &VARA to TEMPDATA
    case NUM = 'C'
        sort on &VARA, &VARB to TEMPDATA
    case NUM = 'D'
        sort on &VARA, &VARB, &VARC to TEMPDATA
    case NUM = 'E'
        sort on &VARA, &VARB, &VARC, &VARD to TEMPDATA
    case NUM = 'F'
        sort on &VARA, &VARB, &VARC, &VARD, &VARE to TEMPDATA
    case NUM = 'G'
        sort on &VARA, &VARB, &VARC, &VARD, &VARE, &VARF to TEMPDATA
endcase

* Create then look at index.

index on &SORT_STRING to TEMP_IND
do EDIT_REC
set index to CHCKNUM, DATE
set color to 'W/N,N/W,,,W+/N'

return

procedure EDIT_REC

* This procedure allows the user to edit the database.

set color to N/W,W+/N
dbedit(03, 01, 23, 78, FIELD_ARRAY)
set color to 'W/N,N/W,,,W+/N'

return

procedure SEARCH_REC

* This procedure allows the user to search the database.

private CHECK_VALUE, DATE_VALUE, SEARCH_TYPE, WAIT_VAR
CHECK_VALUE = 0
DATE_VALUE = date()
SEARCH_TYPE = 'C'
WAIT_VAR = ' '

* Get the search type.

@ 14, 04 say 'Search for (C)heck Number or (D)ate? ' get SEARCH_TYPE picture '!'
read

* Setup the index.

do case
    case SEARCH_TYPE = 'C'
```

```
          set index to CHCKNUM
     case SEARCH_TYPE = 'D'
          set index to DATE
endcase

* Get the search information.

do case
   case SEARCH_TYPE = 'C'
      @ 15, 04 say 'Which check do you want? ' get CHECK_VALUE picture '99999'
   case SEARCH_TYPE = 'D'
      @ 15, 04 say 'Which date do you want? ' get DATE_VALUE picture '99/99/99'
endcase
read

* Convert the information to an acceptable format.

CHECK_VALUE = conv_num(CHECK_VALUE)
DATE_VALUE = conv_date(DATE_VALUE)

* Find the check.

do case
   case SEARCH_TYPE = 'C'
      find &CHECK_VALUE
   case SEARCH_TYPE = 'D'
      find &DATE_VALUE
endcase

if .not. found()
   @ 17, 04 say 'Check not found! Press any key.' get WAIT_VAR
   read
else
   do EDIT_REC
endif

set index to CHCKNUM, DATE

return

function CONV_NUM

* Convert CONV_VALUE to a string with leading zeros.

parameters CONV_VALUE

CONV_VALUE = str(CONV_VALUE, 5, 0)
CONV_VALUE = strtran(CONV_VALUE, ' ', '0')

return CONV_VALUE

function CONV_DATE

* Convert CONV_VALUE to a string.

parameters CONV_VALUE

CONV_VALUE = dtoc(CONV_VALUE)

return CONV_VALUE

procedure STATS

* This procedure produces a list of statistics about the checkbook database.

private TCHECKS, NTCHECKS, DEPOSITS, READY
private MIN_CHCK, AVE_CHCK, MAX_CHCK, MIN_DEP, AVE_DEP, MAX_DEP
MIN_CHCK = 9999999.99
AVE_CHCK = 0
MAX_CHCK = 0
MIN_DEP = 9999999.99
AVE_DEP = 0
MAX_DEP = 0
TCHECKS = 0
NTCHECKS = 0
DEPOSITS = 0
CHCKAMT1 = 0
CHCKAMT2 = 0
DEPOSITT = 0
```

```
READY = ' '

* Get the statistics.

count to TCHECKS for (TAX_ITEM = .T.) .and. (DEPOSIT = 0)
count to NTCHECKS for (TAX_ITEM = .F.) .and. (DEPOSIT = 0)
count to DEPOSITS for DEPOSIT <> 0
average AMOUNT to AVE_CHCK for AMOUNT <> 0
average DEPOSIT to AVE_DEP for DEPOSIT <> 0
sum DEPOSIT, AMOUNT to DEPOSITT, CHCKAMT1 for TAX_ITEM = .F.
sum AMOUNT to CHCKAMT2 for TAX_ITEM = .T.
goto top
do while .not. eof()
   if AMOUNT <> 0
      MIN_CHCK = MIN(MIN_CHCK, AMOUNT)
      MAX_CHCK = MAX(MAX_CHCK, AMOUNT)
   else
      MIN_DEP = MIN(MIN_DEP, DEPOSIT)
      MAX_DEP = MAX(MAX_DEP, DEPOSIT)
   endif
   skip
enddo

* Display the statistics.

@ 12, 04 say 'Number/Amount of Tax Deductable Checks:       ' + str(TCHECKS, 5, 0) + ' / ' + str(CHCKAMT2, 12, 2)
@ 13, 04 say 'Number/Amount of Non-Tax Deductable Checks: ' + str(NTCHECKS, 5, 0) + ' / ' + str(CHCKAMT1, 12, 2)
@ 14, 04 say 'Number/Amount of Deposits:                   ' + str(DEPOSITS, 5, 0) + ' / ' + str(DEPOSITT, 12, 2)
@ 15, 04 say 'Average Check Amount:                       $' + ltrim(str(int(AVE_CHCK), 10, 0))
@ 16, 04 say 'Average Deposit Amount:                     $' + ltrim(str(int(AVE_DEP), 10, 0))
@ 17, 04 say 'Minimum/Maximum Check Amount:                ' + ltrim(str(MIN_CHCK, 10, 2)) + '/' + ltrim(str(MAX_CHCK, 10, 2))
@ 18, 04 SAY 'Minimum/Maximum Deposit Amount:              ' + ltrim(str(MIN_DEP, 10, 2)) + '/' + ltrim(str(MAX_DEP, 10, 2))
@ 22, 04 say 'Press any key when ready...' get READY
read

return

procedure BALANCE

* This procedure balances the checkbook database using the Sum command.

* Initialize variables.

private PREV_TOTAL, NEW_TOTAL
PREV_TOTAL = 0
NEW_TOTAL = 0

* Initialize the database. Place the database in date order first, then check number within that date.

set index to DATE, CHCKNUM
goto top

* Perform this procedure on all records.

do while .not. eof()
   sum next 1 PREV_TOTAL + A->DEPOSIT - A->AMOUNT to NEW_TOTAL
   replace A->BALANCE with NEW_TOTAL
   PREV_TOTAL = NEW_TOTAL
   skip
enddo

* Create a summary report.

total on DATE fields DEPOSIT, AMOUNT to SUMMARY
use SUMMARY
replace all DRAWN_FOR with 'DATE TOTALS'
goto top
PREV_TOTAL = 0
do while .not. eof()
   replace BALANCE with PREV_TOTAL + DEPOSIT - AMOUNT
   PREV_TOTAL = BALANCE
   skip
enddo

* Set database back to its original status.

use CHCKBOOK index CHCKNUM, DATE

return
```

```
procedure REINDEX

* This procedure sorts and reindexes the database.

set color to N/W,W+/N
@ 22, 04 say 'Sorting Database, Please Wait...'
sort on CHECK_NUM, DATE to TEMPDATA
use TEMPDATA
copy to CHCKBOOK all
@ 22, 04 say 'Reindexing Database, Please Wait...'
use CHCKBOOK index CHCKNUM, DATE
reindex
set color to 'W/N,N/W,,,W+/N'

return

procedure EXPORT

* This procedure exports the database to a SDF formatted file.

* Initialize Variables.

EXP_FILE = space(60)

@ 12, 04 say 'What file do you want to export to? '
@ 13, 04 get EXP_FILE picture '@!'
read
copy to &EXP_FILE all SDF

return

procedure LOCATE

* This procedure locates the desired checkbook entry name without changing the index.

* Set softseek on so we can find names that are close to the correct name.

set softseek on

* Initialize Variables

private FIND_NAME, FIND_AGAIN, S_TYPE
FIND_NAME = space(50)
FIND_AGAIN = 'Y'
S_TYPE = 'S'

@ 12, 04 say 'Which check entry name do you want to find? '
@ 13, 04 get FIND_NAME picture '@!'
read
@ 14, 04 say 'Use Standard or Phonetic search? ' get S_TYPE picture '!'
read
if S_TYPE = 'S'
   locate for DRAWN_FOR = FIND_NAME
else
   index on soundex(DRAWN_FOR) to TEMP_IND
   seek soundex(FIND_NAME)
endif

* Display the record.

do EDIT_REC

do while FIND_AGAIN = 'Y'
   @ 22, 04 clear to 22, 76
   @ 22, 04 say 'Find the next occurrence of ' + trim(FIND_NAME) + '? ' get FIND_AGAIN picture '!'
   read
   if FIND_AGAIN = 'Y'
      if S_TYPE = 'S'
         continue
      else
         skip
      endif
      do EDIT_REC
   else
      set index to CHCKNUM, DATE
   endif
enddo

return
```

DOSSHELL.PRG

```
* DOSSHELL.PRG
* This program allows the user to exit to DOS from within Clipper.
* YOUR NAME
* TODAY'S DATE

* Declare the local variables.

declare MENU_ARRAY[7]
MENU_ARRAY[1] = 'Quit'
MENU_ARRAY[2] = 'Dos Shell'
MENU_ARRAY[3] = 'Show Records'
MENU_ARRAY[4] = 'Consolidate Checks'
MENU_ARRAY[5] = 'Type Text File'
MENU_ARRAY[6] = 'Index File Status'
MENU_ARRAY[7] = 'Copy Database'

SELECT = 2

* Save the display.

save screen to TEMP2

* Get the user selection.

do while MENU_ARRAY[SELECT] <> 'Quit'

    @ 03, 39 clear to 08, 58
    @ 03, 39 to 08, 58 double
    SELECT = achoice(04, 40, 07, 57, MENU_ARRAY)

    do case
       case MENU_ARRAY[SELECT] = 'Dos Shell'
          do DOS_SHELL
       case MENU_ARRAY[SELECT] = 'Show Records'
          do SHOW_RECS
       case MENU_ARRAY[SELECT] = 'Consolidate Checks'
          do CONSOLIDATE
       case MENU_ARRAY[SELECT] = 'Type Text File'
          do TYPE_FILE
       case MENU_ARRAY[SELECT] = 'Index File Status'
          do IFILE_STATS
       case MENU_ARRAY[SELECT] = 'Copy Database'
          do COPY_DB
    endcase

enddo

* Restore the display.

restore screen from TEMP2

return

* Begin the procedures.

procedure SHOW_RECS

* This procedure displays the database records on screen.

* Initialize the variables.

NUM_FIELDS = 0
DISP_STR = ''
COUNTER = 0
FIELD_CONTENTS = ''

* Save the screen and position the record pointer.

save screen to TEMP
goto top

* Obtain the number of fields, get the field names, place the contents of the fields in a string, then display
* the string. Cycle the display every 20 names.

NUM_FIELDS = fcount()
declare FIELD_ARRAY[NUM_FIELDS]
afields(FIELD_ARRAY)
```

```
clear screen
set color to N/W,W+/N
@ 00, 00 clear to 02, 79
@ 01, 25 say 'Database Last Updated: ' + dtoc(lupdate())
@ 02, 29 say 'Work Area Number Is: ' + ltrim(str(select(),3,0))
@ 03, 00  && This sets the cursor to a new position.
set color to 'W/N,N/W,,,W+/N'
do while .not. eof()
   for COUNTER = 1 to NUM_FIELDS
      if COUNTER = 1
         FIELD_CONTENTS = FIELD_ARRAY[1]
         do case
            case type(FIELD_CONTENTS) = 'C'
               DISP_STR = &FIELD_CONTENTS
            case type(FIELD_CONTENTS) = 'D'
               DISP_STR = dtoc(&FIELD_CONTENTS)
            case type(FIELD_CONTENTS) = 'N'
               DISP_STR = str(&FIELD_CONTENTS)
            case type(FIELD_CONTENTS) = 'M'
               DISP_STR = hardcr(&FIELD_CONTENTS) + chr (13) + chr(10)
            case type(FIELD_CONTENTS) = 'L'
               if &FIELD_CONTENTS = .T.
                  DISP_STR = '.T.'
               else
                  DISP_STR = '.F.'
               endif
         endcase
      else
         FIELD_CONTENTS = FIELD_ARRAY[COUNTER]
         do case
            case type(FIELD_CONTENTS) = 'C'
               DISP_STR = DISP_STR + ' 3 ' + &FIELD_CONTENTS
            case type(FIELD_CONTENTS) = 'D'
               DISP_STR = DISP_STR + ' 3 ' + dtoc(&FIELD_CONTENTS)
            case type(FIELD_CONTENTS) = 'N'
               DISP_STR = DISP_STR + ' 3 ' + str(&FIELD_CONTENTS)
            case type(FIELD_CONTENTS) = 'M'
               DISP_STR = DISP_STR + chr(10) + chr(13) + hardcr(&FIELD_CONTENTS) + chr(10) + chr(13)
            case type(FIELD_CONTENTS) = 'L'
               if &FIELD_CONTENTS = .T.
                  DISP_STR = DISP_STR + ' 3 .T.'
               else
                  DISP_STR = DISP_STR + ' 3 .F.'
               endif
         endcase
      endif
   next
   list next 1 DISP_STR
   if .not. eof()
      skip
   endif
   if (row() > 18) .or. (eof())
      wait
      clear screen
      set color to N/W,W+/N
      @ 00, 00 clear to 02, 79
      @ 01, 25 say 'Database Last Updated: ' + dtoc(lupdate())
      @ 03, 00  && This sets the cursor to a new position.
      set color to 'W/N,N/W,,,W+/N'
   endif
enddo

restore screen from TEMP

return

procedure DOS_SHELL

* Execute DOS command processor.  This example assumes the command processor is in the root directory of drive C.

save screen to TEMP
clear screen
set cursor on
run C:\COMMAND
restore screen from TEMP

return

procedure CONSOLIDATE
```

```
* This procedure creates a new database by using the contents of two previously created databases.

* Open the databases.

select A
use MAILLIST index LASTNAME
select B
use CHCKBOOK index CHCKNUM, DATE

* Create the new database. Note the use of the semicolon at the end of each line. This allows you to create extended commands.

join with MAILLIST to TEMP_DAT for trim(B->DRAWN_FOR) = ;
upper(trim(A->FIRST_NAME) + ' ' + A->MIDDLE + ' ' + ;
trim(A->LAST_NAME)) fields B->DATE, B->CHECK_NUM, ;
B->DRAWN_FOR, B->AMOUNT, B->TAX_ITEM, A->ADDRESS1, ;
A->ADDRESS2, A->CITY, A->STATE, A->ZIP, A->TELEPHONE

* Eliminate any redundant records.

select A
use TEMP_DAT
index on DRAWN_FOR to TEMP
goto top
do while .not. eof()
   OLD_NAME = DRAWN_FOR
   skip
   if OLD_NAME = DRAWN_FOR
      delete
   endif
enddo
pack

* Update the composite database using CHCKBOOK.

goto top
replace all AMOUNT with 0
update on DRAWN_FOR from CHCKBOOK replace A->AMOUNT with A->AMOUNT + B-> AMOUNT random

return

procedure TYPE_FILE

* This procedure accepts any filename as input and sends contents to the display, printer, a file, or any its
* combination of the three as output.

* Declare the variables.

DIR_ENTRIES = 0
DIR_CHOICE = 2
FILE_NAME = space(12)
OUT_SELECT = 2
OUT_FILE = space(12)
DO_SCREEN = .F.
DO_PRINT = .F.
DO_FILE = .F.

save screen to TYPE1

* Get the user's text file selection.

DIR_ENTRIES = adir('*.*')
declare DIR_ARRAY[DIR_ENTRIES]
adir('*.*', DIR_ARRAY)
asort(DIR_ARRAY)
@ 05, 47 CLEAR = 13, 61
@ 05, 47 TO 13 = 1 double
DIR_CHOICE = achoice(06, 48, 12, 60, DIR_ARRAY)
FILE_NAME = DIR_ARRAY[DIR_CHOICE]

* Get the user's output selection

declare OUT_ARRAY[4]
OUT_ARRAY[1] = 'Quit'
OUT_ARRAY[2] = 'Display'
OUT_ARRAY[3] = 'Printer'
OUT_ARRAY[4] = 'File'

do while OUT_ARRAY[OUT_SELECT] <> 'Quit'
```

```
      @ 09, 54 clear to 14, 62
      @ 09, 54 to 14, 62 double
      OUT_SELECT = achoice(10, 55, 13, 61, OUT_ARRAY)
      do case
         case OUT_ARRAY[OUT_SELECT] = 'Display'
            DO_SCREEN = .T.
         case OUT_ARRAY[OUT_SELECT] = 'Printer'
            DO_PRINT = .T.
         case OUT_ARRAY[OUT_SELECT] = 'File'
            DO_FILE = .T.
            @ 17, 40 say 'Output Filename: ' get OUT_FILE
            read
         endcase
enddo

* Output the file.

if .not. DO_SCREEN
   set console off
endif

clear screen

do case
   case DO_PRINT .and. .not. DO_FILE
      type &FILE_NAME to print
   case .not. DO_PRINT .and. DO_FILE
      type &FILE_NAME to file &OUT_FILE
   case DO_PRINT .and. DO_FILE
      type &FILE_NAME to print
   otherwise
      type &FILE_NAME
endcase

set console on

if DO_SCREEN
   wait
endif

restore screen from TYPE1

return

procedure IFILE_STATS

* This procedure returns the current status of the controlling index file.

save screen to IFILE

* Display a frame then the status information.

set color to N/W,W+/N
@ 13, 02 CLEAR = 19, 77
@ 13, 02 TO 19 = 7 double
@ 14, 04 SAY ' = ex Extension Used:     ' + indexext()
@ 15, 04 SAY ' = trolling Index Order: ' + ltrim(str(indexord(),3,0))
@ 16, 04 SAY ' = trolling Index Key:   ' + indexkey(0)
@ 18, 04 SAY ' = ss any key when ready...'
inkey(0)
set color to 'W/N,N/W,,,W+/N'

restore screen from IFILE

return

procedure COPY_DB

* This procedure copies the current database to a new database, then removes the records from the new database.

private OLD_NAME

* Store the current database name.

OLD_NAME = alias()

* Copy the database to a new one, then zap the new one.

copy to TEMP_DAT
```

```
zap

* Restore the database.

use &OLD_NAME
do case
   case OLD_NAME = 'MAILLIST'
      set index to LASTNAME
   case OLD_NAME = 'CHCKBOOK'
      set index to CHCKNUM, DATE
   case OLD_NAME = 'NOTEPAD'
      set index to NOTENUM, CATEGORY, SUBJECT
endcase

return
```

HEADER.PRG

```
* HEADER.PRG
* This program allows you to display and edit the header of a database.
* YOUR NAME
* TODAY'S DATE

* Initialize the variables.

DB_NAME = space(12)
HANDLE = 0
YEAR = 0
MONTH = 0
DAY = 0
NUM_RECS = space(4)
REC_SIZE = space(2)
DATE_STR = space(8)

* Get the filename and open the file.

clear screen
@ 01, 00 to 24, 79 double
@ 02, 02 say 'Enter a database filename: ' get DB_NAME picture '@!'
read

if at('DBF', DB_NAME) = 0
   DB_NAME = trim(DB_NAME) + '.DBF'
endif

if .not. file(DB_NAME)
   @ 03, 02 say 'File not found!'
   quit
endif

HANDLE = fopen(DB_NAME, 2)

* Get the date.

fseek(HANDLE, 1, 0)
YEAR = bin2i(freadstr(HANDLE, 1))
MONTH = bin2i(freadstr(HANDLE, 1))
DAY = bin2i(freadstr(HANDLE, 1))

* Get the number of records.

fseek(HANDLE, 4, 0)
fread(HANDLE, @NUM_RECS, 4)
NUM_RECS = bin2l(NUM_RECS)

* Get the record size.

fseek(HANDLE, 10, 0)
fread(HANDLE, @REC_SIZE, 2)
REC_SIZE = bin2w(REC_SIZE)

* Display the information.

DATE_STR = str(MONTH, 2) + '/' + str(DAY, 2) + '/' + str(YEAR, 2)
@ 04, 02 say 'File Date: ' get DATE_STR picture '99/99/99'
@ 05, 02 say 'Number of Records: ' get NUM_RECS picture '@9'
```

```
@ 06, 02 say 'Record Size: ' get REC_SIZE picture '@9'
read

* Place the new information in the database header.

* Replace the date.

MONTH = i2bin(val(substr(DATE_STR, 1, 2)))
DAY = i2bin(val(substr(DATE_STR, 4, 2)))
YEAR = i2bin(val(substr(DATE_STR, 7, 2)))
fseek(HANDLE, 1, 0)
fwrite(HANDLE, YEAR, 1)
fwrite(HANDLE, MONTH, 1)
fwrite(HANDLE, DAY, 1)

* Replace the number of records.

NUM_RECS = l2bin(NUM_RECS)
fseek(HANDLE, 4, 0)
fwrite(HANDLE, NUM_RECS, 4)

* Replace the record size.

REC_SIZE = l2bin(REC_SIZE)
fseek(HANDLE, 10, 0)
fwrite(HANDLE, REC_SIZE, 2)

fclose(HANDLE)
clear screen
return
```

HELP.PRG

```
* HELP.PRG
* This program manages a mailing list.
* YOUR NAME
* TODAY'S DATE

* Begin by declaring parameters.

parameters PROGRAM, LINE_NUM, VARIABLE

* Check for error condition.

if procname() = PROGRAM
    TEMP2 = savescreen(22, 00, 23, 79)
    clear typeahead
    @ 22, 04 say 'ERROR! Do not press F1 from within Help!'
    wait
    restscreen(22, 00, 23, 79, TEMP2)
    return
endif

* Set program environment

set scoreboard off

* Declare Program Variables

DOUBLE_LINE = chr(201) + chr(205) + chr(187) + chr(186) + chr(188) + chr(205) + chr(200) + chr(186) + chr(177)
DONE = ' '
LINE_COUNT = 13
COUNTER = 0
LINE_DATA = space(74)

* Display screen.

save screen to TEMP
clear screen
@ 01, 00, 24, 79 box DOUBLE_LINE
@ 20, 01 to 20, 78
set color to N/W,W+/N
@ 02, 01 clear to 03, 78
@ 02, 37 say ' Help '
set color to 'W/N,N/W,,,W+/N'
if readinsert()
```

```
    @ 00, 60 say 'INSERT ON'
else
    @ 00, 60 say 'OVERTYPE ON'
endif
readexit(.T.)

* Find, then display the help information.

use HELP index HELP
seek PROGRAM + VARIABLE
LINE_COUNT = mlcount(HELP_DATA, 74)
for COUNTER = 1 to LINE_COUNT
    LINE_DATA = memoline (HELP_DATA, 74, COUNTER)
    @ 04 + COUNTER, 04 say LINE_DATA
next

* Ask the user to signal when done.

@ 22, 04 say 'Press any key when finished...' get DONE
read
readexit(.F.)

* Prepare to exit.

restore screen from TEMP
set scoreboard on

return
```

MAILLIST.PRG

```
* MAILLIST.PRG
* This program manages a mailing list.
* YOUR NAME
* TODAY'S DATE

* Invoke the debugger.

altd()

* Make sure the environment is clear.

clear gets
clear memory
clear all
setcancel(.F.)

* Program Variables

DOUBLE_LINE = chr(201) + chr(205) + chr(187) + chr(186) + chr(188) + chr(205) + chr(200) + chr(186) + chr(177)
ANSWER = 0
NO_COLOR1 = 'W/N,N/W,,,W+/N'
COLOR1 = 'W/B,GR/W,,,B/GR+'
OLD_COLOR = ' '
KEYPRESS = 0
CPRESSED = 'Y'

* Database Variables

public FIRST_NAME, MIDDLE, LAST_NAME, ADDRESS1, ADDRESS2, CITY, STATE, ZIP, TELEPHONE
do INIT_FIELDS

* Setup program defaults.
set softseek on
set wrap on
set key -1 to                && Make sure F2 is clear.
set key -2 to PRINT          && Point F3 to the print program.
set key -3 to CHCKBOOK       && Point F4 to the checkbook program.
set key -4 to NOTEPAD        && Point F5 to the notepad.
set key -9 to DOSSHELL       && Point F10 to the DOS Shell.

* Clear the display and prepare the database for use.
clear screen
use MAILLIST index LASTNAME

* Begin processing loop.
```

```
        do while ANSWER <> 1

        * If the user presses Ctrl-C, then ask if they really want  to exit.

        begin sequence

        * Display the message area.

        do DISPLAY_STATUS with ANSWER

        * Display the edit area.

        do DISPLAY_SCRN
        do DISPLAY_DATA

        * Display the database edit menu.

        do DISPLAY_MENU
        KEYPRESS = lastkey()
        if KEYPRESS = 3                              && If the user pressed Ctrl-C
           break                                     && then exit.
        endif
        if KEYPRESS = 27                             && If the user pressed Esc
           @ 22, 06 say 'Press a menu item letter, function key, Enter, or Ctrl-Break only!'
           tone(1200, 3)
           tone(600, 3)
           inkey(1)                                  && wait 1 second,
           clear typeahead                           && clear the buffer, and
           loop                                      && go back to the beginning.
        endif

        * Append a blank record.
        do case
        case ANSWER = 2
           goto bottom
           do GET_DATA
           read
           append blank
           do SET_FIELDS

        * Display the database information and the editing screen.
        case ANSWER = 3
           do GET_DATA
           read
           do SET_FIELDS

        * Delete the current record.
        case ANSWER = 4
           delete

        * Remove the deleted records.
        case ANSWER = 5
           pack

        * Move forward one record.
        case ANSWER = 6
           skip

        * Move backward one record.
        case ANSWER = 7
           skip -1

        * Search for the desired last name.
        case ANSWER = 8
           SEARCH_NAME = LAST_NAME
           @ 04, 40 get SEARCH_NAME picture '@K@!'
           read
           seek SEARCH_NAME

        * Undelete a previously deleted record.
        case ANSWER = 9
           recall
        endcase

        if ANSWER <> 1
           loop                                      && Back to beginning if no errors occur.
        endif

        * Close the database and exit to DOS.
```

```
IF ANSWER = 1
quit
ENDIF
end                                                    && Begin Sequence.
IF ANSWER <> 1 ; loop; ENDIF
* If the user presses Ctrl-C follow this routine.

@ 23, 04 say 'Are you sure you want to exit? ' get CPRESSED picture '!'
read
if CPRESSED = 'Y'
   quit
endif                                                  && Otherwise go back up and get another menu selection.
store 0 to ANSWER
enddo


* Begin Procedures

procedure DISPLAY_DATA

* This procedure displays the data in the current record.

@ 04, 12 say FIRST_NAME picture '@!'
@ 04, 38 say MIDDLE picture '!'
@ 04, 40 say LAST_NAME picture '@!'
@ 06, 12 say ADDRESS1
@ 07, 12 say ADDRESS2
@ 09, 12 say CITY picture '@!'
@ 09, 60 say STATE picture '!!'
@ 09, 68 say ZIP picture '99999-9999'
@ 11, 12 say TELEPHONE picture '(999)999-9999'
return

procedure DISPLAY_MENU

* This procedure displays the program menu.

save screen
set message to 22 center
@ 03, 04 clear to 11, 11
@ 02, 03 to 12, 12 double
@ 03, 04 prompt 'Quit' message 'Leave this application.'
@ 04, 04 prompt 'Add' message 'Add a new record.'
@ 05, 04 prompt 'Edit' message 'Change the contents of this record.'
@ 06, 04 prompt 'Delete' message 'Mark this record for removal.'
@ 07, 04 prompt 'Pack' message 'Remove all marked records.'
@ 08, 04 prompt 'Forward' message 'Go one record forward.'
@ 09, 04 prompt 'Backward' message 'Go one record back.'
@ 10, 04 prompt 'Seek' message 'Find a particular last name.'
@ 11, 04 prompt 'Undelete' message 'Remove this record from the deletion list.'
menu to ANSWER
restore screen
return

procedure DISPLAY_SCRN

* This procedure displays the edit area of the database display. It does not display the data.

@ 04, 06 say 'Name:'
@ 06, 03 say 'Address:'
@ 09, 06 say 'City:'
@ 09, 53 say 'State:'
@ 09, 63 say 'Zip:'
@ 11, 07 say 'Tel:'
return

procedure DISPLAY_STATUS

parameters MENU_VAR                                    && Contains the current menu selection.

* This procedure displays status information including the current record number, file status
* messages, and menu entry prompts.

@ 01, 00, 24, 79 box DOUBLE_LINE
@ 20, 01 say replicate(chr(240), 78)
if iscolor() = .F.
   set color to GR/W,W+/GR
else
   set color to N/W,W+/N
endif
@ 02, 30 say ' Mailing List Editor '
```

```
@ 19, 03 say ' F3 - Print ' + chr(179) + ' F4 - Checkbook ' + chr(179) + ' F5 - Notepad '
@ 21, 01 clear to 23, 78
@ 21, 45 say ' Record Number: '
@ 21, 60 say recno()
@ 21, 67 say ' of '
@ 21, 71 say reccount()
@ 21, 04 say iif(deleted(), ' DELETED ', '           ')
do case
case bof() .and. MENU_VAR = 7
   @ 23,04 say ' Beginning of File '
case eof() .and. .not. MENU_VAR = 8
   @ 23,04 say ' End of File '
case .not. found() .and. MENU_VAR = 8
   @ 23,04 say ' Name not found. '
case .not. updated() .and. MENU_VAR = 3
   @ 23,04 say ' Record not updated '
otherwise
   @ 23,04 clear to 23,78
endcase
@ 23, 53 say 'Free Memory: ' + ltrim(str(memory(0), 5, 1)) + ' KBytes'
if iscolor() = .F.
   OLD_COLOR = setcolor(COLOR1)
else
   OLD_COLOR = setcolor(NO_COLOR1)
endif
return


procedure GET_DATA

* This procedure gets the data from the current record.

   do SET_VARIABLES
   @ 04, 12 get M->FIRST_NAME picture '@!' valid .not. empty(M->FIRST_NAME)
   @ 04, 38 get M->MIDDLE picture '!' valid .not. empty(M->MIDDLE)
   @ 04, 40 get M->LAST_NAME picture '@!' valid .not. empty (M->LAST_NAME)
   @ 06, 12 get M->ADDRESS1
   @ 07, 12 get M->ADDRESS2
   @ 09, 12 get M->CITY picture '@!'
   @ 09, 60 get M->STATE picture '!!'
   @ 09, 68 get M->ZIP picture '99999-9999'
   @ 11, 12 get M->TELEPHONE picture '(999)999-9999'
return


procedure INIT_FIELDS

* This procedure initializes the memory variables used in place of actual database fields.

M->FIRST_NAME = space(25)
M->MIDDLE = ' '
M->LAST_NAME = space(25)
M->ADDRESS1 = space(50)
M->ADDRESS2 = space(50)
M->CITY = space(40)
M->STATE = space(2)
M->ZIP = space(10)
M->TELEPHONE = space(13)


return


procedure SET_VARIABLES

* This procedure gets the contents of the current database record and places it in the database variables.

M->FIRST_NAME = A->FIRST_NAME
M->MIDDLE = A->MIDDLE
M->LAST_NAME = A->LAST_NAME
M->ADDRESS1 = A->ADDRESS1
M->ADDRESS2 = A->ADDRESS2
M->CITY = A->CITY
M->STATE = A->STATE
M->ZIP = A->ZIP
M->TELEPHONE = A->TELEPHONE


return


procedure SET_FIELDS

* This procedure gets the contents of the database variables and places it in the current database record.
```

```
replace A->FIRST_NAME with M->FIRST_NAME
replace A->MIDDLE with M->MIDDLE
replace A->LAST_NAME with M->LAST_NAME
replace A->ADDRESS1 with M->ADDRESS1
replace A->ADDRESS2 with M->ADDRESS2
replace A->CITY with M->CITY
replace A->STATE with M->STATE
replace A->ZIP with M->ZIP
replace A->TELEPHONE with M->TELEPHONE

return
```

MAINT.PRG

```
* MAINT.PRG
* This program is the beginning of a programmer's toolbox for Clipper.
* YOUR NAME
* TODAY'S DATE

* Initialize variables.

DIR_SKEL = ' '
DIR_SIZE = 0
DIR_FILE = space(12)
COUNTER = 0
DATA_NAME = space(8)
NDAT_NAME = space(8)

* Create a directory array to hold database filenames.

DIR_SIZE = adir('*.DBF')
declare DIR_ARRAY[DIR_SIZE]
adir('*.DBF', DIR_ARRAY)

* Display a directory.

clear screen
input 'Type directory path and skeleton' + chr(13) + chr(10) to DIR_SKEL
if len(DIR_SKEL) < 2
   dir
else
   dir &DIR_SKEL
endif

* Ask if any files require deletion.

input 'Do you want to delete any of the files? ' to ANSWER
ANSWER = upper(ANSWER)
if len(ANSWER) > 1
   ANSWER = substr(ANSWER, 1, 1)
endif
if ANSWER = 'Y'
   input 'Which file(s) do you want deleted?' + chr(13) + chr(10) to DEL_FILE
   delete file &DEL_FILE
endif

* Ask if any files require renaming.

input 'Do you want to rename any of the files? ' to ANSWER
ANSWER = upper(ANSWER)
if len(ANSWER) > 1
   ANSWER = substr(ANSWER, 1, 1)
endif
if ANSWER = 'Y'
   input 'Which file do you want renamed?' + chr(13) + chr(10) to REN_FILE
   if file(REN_FILE)
      input 'Enter a new filename.' + chr(13) + chr(10) to RENTO_FILE
      rename &REN_FILE to &RENTO_FILE
   endif
endif

* Start a file backup if desired.

input 'Do you want to backup the data files? ' to ANSWER
ANSWER = upper(ANSWER)
if len(ANSWER) > 1
```

```
        ANSWER = substr(ANSWER, 1, 1)
    endif
if ANSWER = 'Y'
    ? 'Place disk in drive A'
    SPACE = diskspace(1)
    if SPACE > 33553919
        ? chr(7) + 'Make sure you use a formatted disk.'
        ? 'Make sure you closed the drive door.'
        wait
    endif
    ? 'Copying files in ' + curdir() + ' to drive A.'
    ?
    for COUNTER = 1 to DIR_SIZE
        ? 'Copying database ' + DIR_ARRAY[COUNTER] + ' to drive A. '
        DIR_FILE = DIR_ARRAY[COUNTER]
        use &DIR_FILE
        ?? ltrim(str(header() + (lastrec() * recsize()) + 1, 10, 0)) + ' bytes'
        ?? ' Header size: ' + ltrim(str(header() + 1, 10, 0)) + ' bytes.'
        copy file &DIR_FILE to a:&DIR_FILE
    next
    if doserror() <> 0
        errorlevel(1)
        quit
    endif
endif

* Create and extended structure database, show the contents on screen, then create a new instance
* of the database, if desired.

input 'Do you want to create a new database? ' to ANSWER
ANSWER = upper(ANSWER)
if len(ANSWER) > 1
    ANSWER = substr(ANSWER, 1, 1)
endif
if ANSWER = 'Y'
    input 'Enter old the database file name. ' to DATA_NAME
    DATA_NAME = upper(DATA_NAME)
    if len(DATA_NAME) > 8
        DATA_NAME = substr(DATA_NAME, 1, 8)
    endif
    use &DATA_NAME
    copy structure extended to TEMP_DAT
    use TEMP_DAT
    ?
    ? 'Database Contains the Following Fields:'
    ?
    ? 'Name        Type Length Decimals'
    do while .not. eof()
        ? FIELD_NAME + ' ' + FIELD_TYPE + '    '
        ?? str (FIELD_LEN,3,0) + '    ' + str(FIELD_DEC,3,0)
        skip
    enddo
    ?
    input 'Enter the new database name. ' to NDAT_NAME
    NDAT_NAME = upper(NDAT_NAME)
    if len(NDAT_NAME) > 8
        NDAT_NAME = substr(NDAT_NAME, 1, 8)
    endif
    create &NDAT_NAME from TEMP_DAT
endif

* Exit this utility.

quit
```

NOTEPAD.PRG
```
* NOTEPAD.PRG
* This program manages a notepad.
* YOUR NAME
* TODAY'S DATE

* Perform program setup.

set key -1 to MAILLIST            && Point F2 to mailing list program.
set key -2 to PRINT               && Point F3 to print program.
set key -3 to CHCKBOOK            && Point F3 to checkbook program.
set key -4 to                     && Make sure F5 points to nothing.

* Create the menu array and place the menu values in it.

declare MENU_ITEM[6]
MENU_ITEM[1] = 'Quit'
MENU_ITEM[2] = 'Add'
MENU_ITEM[3] = 'Delete'
MENU_ITEM[4] = 'Sort'
MENU_ITEM[5] = 'Edit'
MENU_ITEM[6] = 'Search'

* Initialize the variables.

ANSWER = 2
DOUBLE_LINE = chr(201) + chr(205) + chr(187) + chr(186) + chr(188) + chr(205) + chr(200) + chr(186) + chr(177)
DATE_STR = cdow(date()) + ', ' + substr(dtoc(date()), 4, 2) + ' ' + cmonth(date()) + ' ' + ltrim(str(year(date())))

* Open the database and associated indexes.

use NOTEPAD index NOTENUM, CATEGORY, SUBJECT

* Perform this procedure until the user selects quit.

do while MENU_ITEM[ANSWER] <> 'Quit'

* Display the screen.

   do DISP_SCRN6

* Perform the user requested function.

   do case
      case MENU_ITEM[ANSWER] = 'Add'
         do ADD_REC2
      case MENU_ITEM[ANSWER] = 'Delete'
         do DEL_REC2
      case MENU_ITEM[ANSWER] = 'Sort'
         do SORT_REC2
      case MENU_ITEM[ANSWER] = 'Edit'
         do EDIT_REC2
      case MENU_ITEM[ANSWER] = 'Search'
         do SRCH_REC2
   endcase

enddo

* Close the databases and return.

quit

* Begin Procedure Section

procedure DISP_SCRN6

* This procedure displays the screen.

@ 01, 00, 24, 79 box DOUBLE_LINE
@ 20, 01 to 20, 78
set color to N/W,W+/N
@ 02, 32 say ' Notepad Editor '
@ 03, 40 - (len(DATE_STR)/2) say DATE_STR
@ 19, 03 say ' F2 - Mailing List ' + chr(179) + ' F3 - Print ' + chr(179) + ' F4 - Checkbook '
@ 21, 01 clear to 23, 78
set color to 'W/N,N/W,,,W+/N'

* Obtain the user selection.
```

```
@ 03, 03, 10, 13 box DOUBLE_LINE
ANSWER = achoice(04, 04, 09, 12, MENU_ITEM)

return

procedure ADD_REC2

* This procedure adds new records to the notepad.

return

procedure DEL_REC2

* This procedure removes notes.

return

procedure SORT_REC2

* This procedure places the notes in order.

return

procedure EDIT_REC2

* This procedure changes the contents of the notes.
* Display the non-memo data first.

save screen to EDIT_SAVE
@ 03, 01 clear to 23, 78
@ 04, 04 say 'Memo Number: ' get NOTE_NUM picture '@9'
@ 05, 04 say 'Subject:    ' get SHORT_SUBJ picture '@!'
@ 06, 04 say 'Category:   ' get CATEGORY picture '@!'
read

* Now display the actual note.

set color to N/W,W+/N
memoedit(NOTE, 08, 01, 23, 78)
set color to 'W/N,N/W,,,W+/N'
restore screen from EDIT_SAVE

return

procedure SRCH_REC2

* This procedure looks for a particular note.
* Initialize Variables.

private SEARCH_TYPE, NOTE_TEXT, BUFFER, FOUND_IT, NUM_CHECKS
private CURR_CHCK

SEARCH_TYPE = 'N'
M->NOTE_NUM = A->NOTE_NUM
M->CATEGORY = A->CATEGORY
M->SHORT_SUBJ = A->SHORT_SUBJ
NOTE_TEXT = space(50)
BUFFER = space(80)
FOUND_IT = .F.
NUM_CHECKS = 0
CURR_CHCK = 0

* Get the user preference of search type and perform the search.

@ 15, 04 say 'Search for a note by Note number, Category, Subject, or note Text? ' get SEARCH_TYPE picture '!'
read
do case
   case SEARCH_TYPE = 'N'
      @ 16, 04 say 'Enter note number: ' get M->NOTE_NUM picture '@9'
      read
      seek M->NOTE_NUM
   case SEARCH_TYPE = 'C'
      @ 16, 04 say 'Enter note category: ' get M->CATEGORY picture '@!'
      read
      set index to CATEGORY, NOTENUM, SUBJECT
      seek M->CATEGORY
   case SEARCH_TYPE = 'S'
      @ 16, 04 say 'Enter note subject: ' get M->SHORT_SUBJ picture '@!'
```

```
        read
        set index to SUBJECT, NOTENUM, CATEGORY
        seek M->SHORT_SUBJ
    case SEARCH_TYPE = 'T'
        @ 16, 04 say 'Enter note text: ' get NOTE_TEXT
        read
        NOTE_TEXT = trim(NOTE_TEXT)
        goto top
        do while (.not. eof()) .and. (.not. FOUND_IT)
            NUM_CHECKS = mlcount(NOTE, 80)
            for CURR_CHCK = 1 to NUM_CHECKS
                BUFFER = memoline(NOTE, 80, CURR_CHCK)
                FOUND_IT = at(NOTE_TEXT, BUFFER) <> 0
                if FOUND_IT = .T.
                    exit
                endif
            next
            if .not. FOUND_IT
                skip
            endif
        enddo
endcase

* Display the record.

do EDIT_REC2

* Restore the indexes to normal.

set index to NOTENUM, CATEGORY, SUBJECT

return
```

PRINT.PRG

```
* PRINT.PRG
* This program manages a mailing list.
* YOUR NAME
* TODAY'S DATE

* Make sure the environment is clear.

clear gets
clear memory
clear all

* Perform program setup.

set key -1 to MAILLIST          && Point F2 to mailing list program.
set key -2 to                   && Make sure F3 points to nothing.
set key -3 to CHCKBOOK          && Point F3 to checkbook program.
set key -4 to NOTEPAD           && Point F5 to the notepad.

* Declare standard variables public.

public DOUBLE_LINE, PRNT_PORT

* Restore the previous printer configuration information.

restore from PRNTPORT additive

* Check variable length, if too long use default setting.

if len(PRNT_PORT) > 6
    PRNT_PORT = 'PRN  '
endif

* Program Variables

DOUBLE_LINE = chr(201) + chr(205) + chr(187) + chr(186) + chr(188) + chr(205) + chr(200) + chr(186) + chr(177)
PRNT_COUNT = 0
ANSWER = 'C'
PRNT_TEST = 'Y'
MENU_SEL = 2
PRNT_FILE = space(74)
ANSWER4 = 'Y'
```

```
* Display a print screen

do DISP_SCRN

* Check the printer status.

@ 06, 04 say 'Enter the printer port you wish to use. ' get PRNT_PORT picture '@!'
read

* See if the user wants to print to a file.

if trim(PRNT_PORT) = 'FILE'
   @ 08, 04 say 'Enter the filename and path.'
   @ 09, 04 get PRNT_FILE picture '@!'
   read
   if .not. file(PRNT_FILE)
      PRNT_PORT = PRNT_FILE
   else
      @ 11, 04 say 'File already exists!  Do you want to overwrite it? ' get ANSWER4 picture '!'
      read
      if ANSWER4 = 'Y'
         PRNT_PORT = PRNT_FILE
      else
         @ 08, 04 say 'Enter the filename and path.'
         @ 09, 04 get PRNT_FILE picture '@!'
         read
         PRNT_PORT = PRNT_FILE
      endif
   endif
endif
do while .not. PRNT_ON (PRNT_PORT)
   set color to N/W,W+/N
   @ 22, 04 say 'Printer Is Not Ready!'
   @ 23, 04 say 'Do you want to (C)heck the printer or (E)xit the print procedure? ' get ANSWER picture '!'
   read
   set color to W/N,N/W
   if ANSWER = 'E'
      quit
   endif
   @ 06, 04 say 'Enter the printer port you wish to use. ' get PRNT_PORT picture '@!'
   read
enddo

* Perform the printer test, if desired.

set color to N/W,W+/N
@ 22, 04 say 'Do you want to perform the printer test? ' get PRNT_TEST picture '!'
read
set color to W/N,N/W
if PRNT_TEST = 'Y'
   clear
   text to print
   abcdefghijklmnopqrstuvwxyz
   ABCDEFGHIJKLMNOPQRSTUVWXYZ
   1234567890
   !@#$%^&*()
   endtext
   eject
   wait
endif

* Perform this procedure until the user wants to stop.

do while MENU_SEL <> 1

* Display the print menu.

do DISP_SCRN
do DISP_MENU2

* Check the user selection.

do case
   case MENU_SEL = 2
      use CHCKBOOK
      do DISP_MENU3
      set console off
      report form CHCKLIST to print
      set console on
```

```
   case MENU_SEL = 3
      use MAILLIST index LASTNAME
      set console off
      @ 22, 04
      label form MAILLABL sample to print
      label form MAILLABL to print
      set console on
   case MENU_SEL = 4
      use NOTEPAD
      do DISP_MENU4
      do NOTE_PRNT
endcase

enddo

* Save the user printer port selection.

save to PRNTPORT all like PRNT_PORT

* Close the database and exit.

quit

* Begin Procedures

procedure DISP_SCRN

* This procedure displays a print screen.

private HEADING_CENTER

* Get the number required to center the heading.

HEADING_CENTER = center_line ('Mailing List Print Program')

clear
@ 01, 00, 24, 79 box DOUBLE_LINE
set color to N/W,W+/N
@ 02, 01 clear to 04, 78
@ 21, 01 clear to 23, 78
@ 03, HEADING_CENTER say 'Mailing List Print Program'
@ 20, 03 say ' F2 - Mailing List ' + chr(179) + ' F4 - Checkbook ' + chr(179) + ' F5 - Notepad '
@ 21, 04 say 'Free Memory: ' + ltrim(str(memory(0), 12, 1)) + ' KBytes'
set color to W/N,N/W

* Deallocate all variables used in this procedure.

release all

return

procedure DISP_COUNT

* This procedure displays the current record being printed and the total number to print.

set console on
set print off
set device to screen
set color to N/W,W+/N
@ 22, 04 say 'Printing record'
@ 22, 20 say PRNT_COUNT
@ 22, 31 say 'of'
@ 22, 34 say reccount()
set device to print
set console off
set print on
set color to W/N,N/W
return

function PRNT_ON

* This function checks the status of the printer port and returns true if the port exists and the printer is on.

private PORT_NAME, IS_PORT

parameters PORT_NAME

* Initialize the return variable.
```

```
IS_PORT = .F.

set printer to &PORT_NAME

* Check the printer status if port is LPT1.

if trim(PRNT_PORT) = 'LPT1'
   if isprinter()
      IS_PORT = .T.
   else
      IS_PORT = .F.
   endif
else
   IS_PORT = .T.
endif

* Deallocate only non-essential variables used in this procedure.

release all like PORT_NAME

return IS_PORT

procedure REC_PRINT

* This procedure sends the contents of one record to the printer.

if PRNT_PORT = 'LPT1'
   do while .not. isprinter()
      set color to N/W,W+/N
      @ 22, 04 say 'Printer Is Not Ready To Receive The Next Record!'
      @ 23, 04 say 'Do you want to (C)heck the printer or (E)xit the print procedure? ' get ANSWER picture '!'
      read
      set color to W/N,N/W
      if ANSWER = 'E'
         quit
      endif
   enddo

endif

return

procedure DISP_MENU2

* This procedure displays the program menu.

save screen
set message to 22 center
@ 06, 02 clear to 09, 15
@ 05, 01 to 10, 16 double
@ 06, 03 prompt 'Quit' message 'Leave this application.'
@ 07, 03 prompt 'Check Book' message 'Print the Check Book Database.'
@ 08, 03 prompt 'Mailing List' message 'Print the Mailing List Database.'
@ 09, 03 prompt 'Note Pad' message 'Print the contents of the Note Pad Database.'
menu to MENU_SEL
restore screen
return

procedure DISP_MENU3

* This procedure displays a menu for selecting an index for printing the check book.

private ANSWER2

save screen
set message to 22 center
@ 06, 02 clear to 07, 15
@ 05, 01 to 08, 16 double
@ 06, 03 prompt 'Check Number' message 'Print in Check Number Order.'
@ 07, 03 prompt 'Check Date' message 'Print in Check Date Order.'
menu to ANSWER2
restore screen

* Set the index to match user response.

if ANSWER2 = 1
   set index to CHCKNUM
else
   set index to DATE
```

```
endif

* Deallocate all variables used in this procedure.

release all

return

procedure DISP_MENU4

* This procedure displays a menu for selecting an index for printing the note pad.

private ANSWER2

save screen
set message to 22 center
@ 06, 02 clear to 08, 14
@ 05, 01 to 09, 15 double
@ 06, 03 prompt 'Note Number' message 'Print in Note Number Order.'
@ 07, 03 prompt 'Subject' message 'Print in Subject then Note Number Order.'
@ 08, 03 prompt 'Category' message 'Print in Category then Note Number Order.'
menu to ANSWER2
restore screen

* Set the index to match user response.

do case
   case ANSWER2 = 1
      set index to NOTENUM
   case ANSWER2 = 2
      set index to SUBJECT
   case ANSWER2 = 3
      set index to CATEGORY
endcase

* Deallocate all variables used in this procedure.

release all

return

procedure NOTE_PRNT

* This is a customized print routine for the notepad.

private ROW, COL, CONV_STR

* Intialize variables.

ANSWER3 = 'C'

* Ask if user wants complete or partial notes.

   set color to N/W,W+/N
   @ 22, 04 say 'Do you want (C)omplete or (P)artial notes? ' get ANSWER3 picture '!' valid (ANSWER3 = 'P');
    .or. (ANSWER3 = 'C')
   read
   @ 22, 04 clear to 22, 77
   set color to W/N,N/W

* Setup initial conditions.

set console off
set print on
set device to print
setprc (5, 10) && Set the margins.
PRNT_COUNT = 1
ROW = prow()
COL = pcol()
CONV_STR = space(1)
CENTER_PT = 0

* Print the heading.

CENTER_PT = center_line('Notes Printout')
@ ROW, CENTER_PT say 'Notes Printout'
ROW = ROW + 2

* Perform this procedure until all we print all the records.
```

```
   do while .not. eof()

* Convert the Note Number to a string.

   CONV_STR = ltrim(str(NOTE_NUM, 5, 0))

* Print the information

   @ ROW, COL say chr(13) && Place print head at beginning.
   @ ROW, COL say 'Note Number: ' && + ltrim( str(NOTE, 5, 0))
   ROW = ROW + 1
   @ ROW, COL say 'Subject: ' + upper(SHORT_SUBJ)
   ROW = ROW + 1

* Determine the category type and print appropriately.

   if .not. isalpha(CATEGORY)
      @ ROW, COL say 'Priority Category: ' + CATEGORY
   else
      @ ROW, COL say 'Category: ' + CATEGORY
   endif

* Print complete or partial note based on previous response.

   ROW = ROW + 2
   if ANSWER3 = 'P'
      @ ROW, COL say left(NOTE, 55)
   else
      @ ROW, COL say NOTE
   endif

   ROW = ROW + 1

* Show the number of records printed.

   do DISP_COUNT

* See if we need a new page.

   if ROW > 55
      eject
      setprc (5, 10)
      ROW = prow()
      COL = pcol()
   endif

* Go to the next record.

   skip
   PRNT_COUNT = PRNT_COUNT + 1

enddo

* Return the setup to normal.

set print off
set console on
set device to screen

* Deallocate all variables used in this procedure.

release all

return

function CENTER_LINE

* This function centers a heading on the display.

parameters CSTRING

private CLENGTH

* Intialize variables.

CLENGTH = len(CSTRING)
START_SPOT = 0
```

```
* Find the center point.
START_SPOT = (80 - CLENGTH) / 2
* Deallocate the non-essential variables used in this procedure.
release all except START_SPOT
return START_SPOT
```

Appendix I
ADVANCED TOPICS FOR CLIPPER 5.0 AND 5.01

INTRODUCTION

Clipper versions starting with 5.0 allow you to increase the functionality of your programs using three different tools. First, you can modify the way that the compiler preprocessor interprets your code. You can essentially change a command from the standard Clipper interpretation to any interpretation you deem necessary to the operation of your program. This means that you are no longer hindered by someone else's interpretation of your programming needs.

Second, code blocks allow you to create self-modifying code. This doesn't mean that you can modify the code block code, but by assigning a code block to a variable and passing that variable to a procedure or function, you can modify the behavior of the procedure or function. Code blocks represent the natural progression of the macro operator used in past versions of the compiler. In many instances in the past you had to create very complex coding routines to handle every programming situation that might occur during program execution. Using code blocks you can now create code that changes to meet the demands of the current operation. Code blocks can help you compensate for changes in hardware and operating environment. They can also increase the functionality of some existing functions.

Finally, Clipper objects allow you to implement, to a very small degree, some of the concepts of object oriented programming (OOP). While this book cannot act as a tutorial on all the dynamics of OOP, it can show you what this means in the Clipper environment. For the purposes of this book, OOP is a technique used to reduce the work required to manipulate data. Information and program code become objects that the programmer defines and manages. The objects themselves determine the procedure required to fulfill the programmer's wishes. This difference essentially determines how OOP is different from standard procedural languages.

The examples used in this section of the book were created using Clipper version 5.01. This means that some examples may or may not work exactly as stated with Clipper 5.0. The reason that we used Clipper 5.01 is the stability presented by that version of the program. This version also includes some enhanced features over the previous version. We made every effort to point out any enhanced features that might appear in the programming examples.

MANAGING THE COMPILER PREPROCESSOR

The compiler preprocessor is the means used to initialize various Clipper commands and functions prior to use. You can look at the preprocessor as the device used to read the introduction to the program before the compiler reads the main section of code and all its procedures. The preprocessor code is normally found in header files that use a CH extension in place of the PRG extension used on programs. You can also use preprocessor directives in your program files, but it is normally more convenient to use the header files.

There are seven preprocessor directives: #command, #translate, #define, #ifdef, #ifndef, #include, and #undef. You will probably never use these directives in simple programs. However, these directives become essential tools as the complexity of your program increases or the need to use external procedures written in C or assembler becomes evident. Each directive performs a different task as documented below.

NOTE

The format used for preprocessor directives in Clipper 5.0 is very different from the format used in version 5.01. While the formats are different, the techniques and theory are the same. Users of 5.0 can use the following definitions as examples, but should refer to the Nantucket documentation for actual formatting instructions.

#COMMAND/#XCOMMAND   The #command and #xcommand directives are used to translate a Clipper command or function into the appropriate syntax for accessing the library routines. You use the #command or #xcommand directive to translate complete statements. For example, the USE command with all its parameters defined is a complete statement; the USE command with only the database filename parameter defined is not. Every #command directive statement takes the form: #command <match pattern> => <result pattern>. An #xcommand directive follows the same format with #xcommand substituted for the #command directive. The match pattern contains the statement as it appears in your program. The result pattern contains the list of internal Clipper statements the compiler must produce to execute the program statement. The => symbol is required and could be defined as "translates to" when reading the directive. The biggest difference between the #command and the #xcommand directives is that the #command directive will accept the four-letter command abbreviations accepted by dBASE III. You use the #xcommand directive if you need to differentiate between two commands with the same four-letter abbreviation. The #xcommand directive is new to Clipper version 5.01. Table I-1 contains a list of the #command directive translation match patterns and their meaning.

TABLE I-1. #Command/#Translate Directive Match Patterns

Match Pattern	Definition
Literal Values	Literal values are characters which appear in the input text exactly the same way they appear in the output text. For example, in the directive:

```
#command TEXT TO PRINTER          ;
       =>  __TextSave("PRINTER")    ;
       ; text QOut, __TextRestore
```

the word PRINTER is a literal value.

Words	Every match pattern begins with a word. The word is compared using the dBASE convention (i.e., case insensitive and first four letters mandatory). This is how Clipper differentiates one command or function from another. For example, in the directive:

```
#command TEXT TO PRINTER          ;
       =>  __TextSave("PRINTER")    ;
       ; text QOut, __TextRestore
```

the words TEXT TO are word match patterns.

TABLE I-1. #Command/#Translate Directive Match Patterns (Cont.)

Match Pattern	Definition
Match Markers	There are four types of match markers. Clipper uses them to create variable entries. Each type of match marker is used to match the input text in a different way. Clipper substitutes the input text for the variable name in the output text using the rules defined by the match marker. All match markers appear within angle brackets (<>).
Regular Match Marker <idMarker>	A regular match expression places the next legal expression in the input text into a variable. For example, in the directive:

```
#command TEXT TO FILE <(file)>        ;
        => __TextSave( <(file)> )     ;
        ; text QOut, __TextRestore
```

the variable (file) contains the name of the output text file. As you can see in the output text, the variable appears a second time. Clipper substitutes the filename in the input text for the variable in the output string.

List Match Marker <idMarker,...>	The list match marker appears in places where the compiler needs to process zero or more expressions that appear as a list in the command. For example, in the directive:

```
#command @ <row>, <col> SAY <sayxpr>        ;
                        [<sayClauses,...>] ;
                        GET <var>           ;
                        [<getClauses,...>] ;
                                            ;
        => @ <row>, <col> SAY <sayxpr> [<sayClauses>]    ;
        ; @ Row(), Col()+1 GET <var> [<getClauses>]
```

both the sayClauses and getClauses variables are looking for a list of expressions.

Restricted Match Marker <idMarker:word list>	You use the restricted match marker when looking for specific words as input text. For example, in the directive:

```
.#command SET EXCLUSIVE <x:ON,OFF,&>     ;
        => Set( _SET_EXCLUSIVE, <(x)> )
```

the variable x, can accept one of three values as input: ON, OFF, or & (macro). If the input text does not contain one of these three values, then the match fails and the variable doesn't contain anything.

Wild Match Marker <*idMarker*>	The wild match marker accepts any input text, even expressions which are normally not legal in Clipper. For example, in the directive:

```
#command FIND <*text*>        ;
        => dbSeek( <(text)> )
```

text can be anything. It could contain numbers or characters.

Optional Match Clauses	In some cases a command will execute properly even if the program statement doesn't contain all the available parameters. An example is the while and for clauses used by some commands. In other cases it is possible to specify more than one parameter, but at least one parameter must be specified. For example, in the directive:

```
#command REPLACE <f1> WITH <v1> [, <fN> WITH <vN> ]     ;
        => _FIELD-><f1> := <v1> [; _FIELD- ><fN> := <vN>]
```

the programmer must supply one set of parameters (f1 and v1), while the other parameters (fN and vN) are optional. As you can see, optional parameters are always placed between two brackets ([]).

Every command or function you use in your program is defined in a header file (in most cases STD.CH) using the #command directive. When the preprocessor finds a match for the input string you provide as part of your PRG file, it translates it into something the compiler can understand. The output string for a #command directive is called a result. Like the match patterns used for the input string, the result patterns affect how the output string appears. Table I-2 contains a list of the #command directive translation result patterns and their meaning. All example code in both Table I-1 and Table I-2 uses the #command directive.

TABLE I-2. #Command/#Translate Directive Result Patterns

Match Pattern	Definition
Literal Tokens	This result pattern performs the same function on output text as the match pattern performs on the input string.
Words	This result pattern performs the same function on output text as the match pattern performs on the input string.
Result Markers	There are six types of result markers. Clipper uses them to create variable output. Each type of result marker is used to change the output text in a different way. Clipper substitutes the input text for the variable name in the output text using the rules defined by the result marker. All result markers appear within angle brackets (<>).
Regular Result Marker <idMarker>	A regular result marker places the value found in the specified variable in the output text. For example, in the directive:

```
#command TEXT TO FILE <(file)>       ;
    =>  __TextSave( <(file)> )      ;
    ; text QOut, __TextRestore
```

the variable (file) contains the name of the output text file. As you can see in the output text, the variable appears a second time. Clipper substitutes the filename in the input text for the variable in the output text.

Dumb Stringify Result Marker #<idMarker>	The dumb stringify result marker works much like the regular result marker. The main difference between the two is that the dumb stringify result marker places quotes ("") around the input text before placing it in the output text. For example, in the directive:

```
#command SET COLOR TO [<*spec*>]       ;
    => SetColor( #<spec> )
```

the wild match marker is converted to a string. Therefore, if the input text contained N/W, then the output text would be "N/W." If the input text is blank, then the output text contains a null string (""). List markers produce a single quoted string. For example, A, B, C produces "A, B, C" in the output text.

Normal Stringify Result Marker <"idMarker">	Like the dumb stringify result marker, the normal stringify result marker places the input text into quotes. However, there are two differences. First, if the input text contains nothing, the normal stringify result marker doesn't place anything in the output text. Second, when processing list markers, the output contains separately stringified elements. For example, A, B, C produces "A", "B", "C" in the output text.
Smart Stringify Result Marker <(idMarker)>	The smart stringify result marker matches input text enclosed in parentheses (). Like the normal stringify marker, if no match is found, the output text remains blank. In addition, each element of a list input is stringified. For example, (A, B, C) produces "A", "B", "C" in the output text. The smart stringify result marker also ignores expressions in the input text. For example, the expression (A + B) remains unchanged.

TABLE I-2. #Command/#Translate Directive Result Patterns (Cont.)

Match Pattern	Definition
Blockify Result Marker <{idMarker}>	The blockify result marker converts the input text to a code block. Many functions use code blocks for recursive calls to changing data like indexes. For example, in the directive:

```
#command INDEX ON <key> TO <(file)> [<u: UNIQUE>]   ;
    => dbCreateIndex(                                ;
                        <(file)>, <"key">, <{key}>,  ;
                        if( <.u.>, .t., NIL )         ;
                      )
```

the field name is passed as a string and a code block. The string provides the field name to the function. The code block evaluates the data at the record pointed to by that field. Lists elements are evaluated one at a time and converted to individual code blocks.

Match Pattern	Definition
Logify Result Marker <.idMarker.>	This result marker evaluates the input text and creates output based on that input. If the input text is matched, then the logify result marker writes true to the output text; otherwise, it writes false. For example, in the directive:

```
#command INDEX ON <key> TO <(file)> [<u: UNIQUE>]   ;
    => dbCreateIndex(                                ;
                        <(file)>, <"key">, <{key}>,  ;
                        if( <.u.>, .t., NIL )         ;
                      )
```

if the command line contains the word UNIQUE as the final entry on the line, then the variable u is matched. This results in the logify result marker .u. writing .T. to the output text. Otherwise, the logify result marker writes .F. to the output text.

#TRANSLATE/#XTRANSLATE   The #translate directive uses the same constructs as the #command directive. Like the #command directive, a #translate directive appears in the form #translate <match pattern> => <result pattern>. The translate directive uses the match patterns found in Table I-1 and the result patterns found in Table I-2. The biggest difference between the #translate directive and the #command directive is that the #translate directive operates on clauses. For example:

```
#xtranslate CenterText (<cString>, <nWidth>, <nRow>) => ;
    @ <nRow>, (<nWidth>/2)-(len(<cString>)/2) say <cString>
```

is an example of a #translate directive used to create a text centering pseudofunction. Notice that in this example you use standard Clipper commands and functions on both sides of the directive. Unlike a #command directive, the #translate directive does not require an in-depth knowledge of Clipper internal commands and functions. The difference between the #translate and the #xtranslate directives is that the #translate directive will accept the four-letter translate abbreviations accepted by dBASE III. You use the #xtranslate directive if you need to differentiate between two commands with the same four-letter abbreviation. The #xtranslate directive is new to Clipper version 5.01.

#DEFINE   In many cases you need to create a global variable that retains its meaning throughout a program. The escape key (character 27) is an example of just such a variable. Since the variable never changes its value, even from program to program, it would be a waste of valuable variable space to create it in every program module. A far more space and speed efficient method is to declare it as a "manifest constant" using the #define directive. For example:

```
#define K_LineFeed 10
#define K_CarriageRet 13
? "Hello World!" + chr(K_CarriageRet) + chr(K_LineFeed)
```

is an example of how you can create and use a manifest constant for two common control characters, line feed and carriage return.

Another use for the #define directive is as part of the preprocessing environment. You can use this technique to remove debugging code from a program without actually removing it from your source code. In the following example:

```
#ifdef Debug
    ? "Hello World Again!" + chr(K_CarriageRet) + chr(K_LineFeed)
#endif
```

the "Hello World Again" string gets compiled into the program only if the constant, Debug, is defined. You can define the constant in one of three ways. First, you can create a header file and use the /U parameter of the compiler to add it to the program. If you use this method, you must also add a statement at the beginning of your program to include STD.CH. Otherwise, Clipper generates a list of errors as it tries to find the standard definitions for the commands and functions in your program. Another way to define the constant is to use the /D parameter of the compiler. In this example you would simply type /DDebug as one of the command line switches to add debugging code to your application. Finally, you can use the #define directive within the program itself. When you no longer need debugging code, simply remove the #define from the program. Remember that in this case debugging code does not refer to the Clipper debugger, but debugging code you added to your program. You still need to add the /B switch to your code to be able to invoke the debugger.

A final use for the #define directive is as an easy method for creating pseudofunctions. In the following example:

```
#define CentConvert(Temp) ((Temp * 9 / 5) + 32)
? CentConvert(100)
```

the #define directive creates a pseudofunction to convert temperature in centigrade to degrees Fahrenheit. Unlike the #translate directive, the pseudofunction cannot consist of multiple steps. You may only use a single step function as shown in the example. However, the pseudofunction can contain multiple variables. While pseudofunctions created using the #define directive execute quicker than a user defined function, there are some things that you may need to consider. First, you cannot skip arguments in a pseudofunction. You must provide a value for each argument in the definition. Second, pseudofunctions are case sensitive. This means that you must use the full name of the function and use the same case as used in the #define directive. A pseudofunction defined as CENTCONVERT is different from one defined as CentConvert.

#ERROR The #error directive generates a compiler error and displays a specific message. You can use this directive to provide safeguards in user defined commands and manifest constants. Another good use is in enhancing existing Clipper error messages during compilation. Normally, the #error directive appears within a conditional statement that defines when the error condition exists. The #error directive is new to Clipper version 5.01. An example of the #error directive follows.

```
#ifndef SOME_CONDITION
    #error You failed to specify the correct conditions!
#endif
```

#IFDEF/#IFNDEF The #ifdef/#ifndef directives allow you to add conditional code, directives, and constructs to your code. You can use them in either a header file or within your code. The paragraphs describing the #define directive explain one use for the #ifdef directive. There are similar uses for the #ifndef directive. You can use either directive to remove the debugging code from a program without modifying the source code. A second use might be to differentiate between two versions of an application. For example, if you had a client that used PCs for some workstations and ATs for others, you could create a program that would run fast on a PC, but make use of the capabilities on an AT. One way you could do this is to provide enhanced graphics on the AT, but minimal graphics on the PC. Every #ifdef/#ifndef directive takes the form:

```
#ifdef <identifier>
    <statements>...
[#else]
    <statements>...
[#endif]
```

Notice that the #else and #endif clauses are conditional. You use the #else clause when you want to do one thing if the identifier exists and something else if it doesn't. Notice that you can't use multiple #else clauses and that there is no #elseif clause provided. The #endif clause appears whenever there is more than one statement after the #ifdef/#ifndef clause. Since the compiler never generates an error if you use the #endif clause, it is usually better to include it even if you only follow the #ifdef/#ifndef clause with a single statement. The main difference between the #ifdef and #ifndef directives is that the #ifdef directive is true when the constant exists, while the #ifndef is true when the constant does not exist.

#INCLUDE The #include directive can appear in a header file; although, it appears in source code files as a general rule. This directive instructs the preprocessor to include the definitions contained in a Clipper header file (CH extension) into your code. Header files are not limited to sets of definitions and other preprocessor directives. They can contain executable code as well. The only exception to this rule is STD.CH which contains only external declarations and preprocessor directives. This special file is automatically included into your program unless you use the /U compiler directive. It contains the directives that define the commands and functions supported by Clipper. Never modify the STD.CH header file unless you want to specifically change the behavior of a standard Clipper command or function. Of course, doing this makes your source code incompatible with the source code created for the standard definitions. When using the #include directive, the filename always appears in quotes as follows:

```
#include "SOMEFILE.CH."
```

#UNDEF The #undef directive removes an identifier created with the #define directive. There are two uses for this directive. First, you can undefine a directive before you redefine it. This prevents the redefinition warning message from appearing when you compile your program. You can also use it in conjunction with the #ifdef and #ifndef directives to make those directives specific to a certain area of the program. The #undef directive uses the following format:

```
#undef <IDENTIFIER>.
```

USING CODE BLOCKS

Code blocks are not found in any other X-Base dialect nor are they found in any other programming language. They are a construct unique to Clipper versions 5.0 and above. The mere fact that they are not to be found anywhere else causes some programmers concern. They feel that code blocks are overly complex and hard to use. The following paragraphs will show you that code blocks are a powerful tool in the hands of the Clipper programmer and that they can be used in ways undreamed of in other programming languages.

First, we must discuss what code blocks are. You can think of them as the predecessor to macro definitions and the ultimate function declaration. In many ways code blocks have all the advantages of macros, without any of the disadvantage. Like a macro, you can assign a code block to a variable. You can use the code block wherever and whenever necessary to perform a specific task. However, macros have a distinct disadvantage when you consider program execution speed. Every time your program sees a macro, it must interpret what the macro means before it can execute the instruction contained in the macro. Code blocks, on the other hand, are interpreted at compile time, greatly increasing program execution speed. Macros also have another distinct disadvantage. You cannot dynamically alter the values of the arguments in a macro. The program must reassign the value each time you need it changed. Code blocks accept variable input; therefore, you can modify them dynamically.

Many people also compare code blocks to assignable unnamed functions. In essence, they are functions that you can assign to a variable. But, unlike functions, you can use a code block to dynamically alter the output of another function. This places code blocks in a different category than a mere function. That is why it is more accurate to look at code blocks as the means to creating self-modifying code.

Every code block takes the form of an argument and an expression as follows.

```
{ | [<Argument List>] | <Expression List> }
```

The curly braces surrounding the entire code block identify it as such to the compiler. The first bar (|) identifies the beginning of the argument list. This list may contain variables or constants. You separate each argument with a comma. Clipper does not require that you supply any arguments to the code block. You must include the bar as part of the code block. The second bar identifies the beginning of expression list. This list contains executable code. You separate each expression with a comma. Clipper compiles each expression in turn, so the order in which you place the expressions is important. Unlike the argument list, you must supply the argument list. You must also supply the second bar. A simple code block that increments a numeric variable appears below.

```
{ |nVar| nVar + 1}
```

There are four ways in which to use a code block. You may evaluate the code block by itself, evaluate an array, evaluate a database, or supply it as an argument to a function. The first three uses always accept a code block as input. You must check the Clipper manual and Norton Guides before passing a code block as an argument to a function. In some cases you can use the Eval( ) function to provide the means of passing a code block to a function not expecting one. For example, if you wanted to create a function that returned the day of the week but weren't sure if the user would input a true date or a character date, you could use the following code block.

```
cDate1 := "01/01/91"
dDate2 := ctod("01/02/91")
bConvDate := { |CDate| iif(valtype(CDate)=='D', CDate, ctod(CDate))}
cls
? cdow(eval(bConvDate, cDate1))
? cdow(eval(bConvDate, dDate2))
```

Notice that the code block makes the determination whether or not it needs to convert the input variable, then turns control over to the cdow( ) function. The code block in this example expands the types of input that the cdow( ) function can accept. Of course, we could just as easily place this translation into a header file and redefine the way the cdow( ) function works in all our programs. As you can see, code blocks can extend the functionality of Clipper commands and functions in ways that are almost impossible in other languages.

We can use code blocks to greatly reduce the work required to display information in a database. In many cases, not only is the code shorter and more efficient, but easier to read as well. For example, the following code block and associated code prints out the debit, credit, and running balance from the CHCKBOOK file used for many examples in this book.

```
Local nCount := 0
Local bAddAmount := {| | qout( str(Amount)+"  "+str(Deposit) ),;
                    nCount := nCount + Deposit - Amount,;
                    qqout ( "  "+str(nCount) ) }
cls
use CHCKBOOK index CHCKNUM, DATE
dbeval (bAddAmount)
```

Notice how each expression in the code block occupies one line in the code block. This greatly enhances readability. Also observe that every expression is separated from the next with a comma and that each line is separated from the next with a semicolon. Using standard X-Base code, this same procedure would have occupied a minimum of ten lines of code, twice as many as in this example. In essence, the code block in this example displays the debit and credit values in the current record, adds the credit and deducts the debit value from a counter variable, then displays the counter value. The dbeval function automatically takes care of looping and moving of the database record pointer.

Arrays are equally easy to use with code blocks. In this case you use the aeval( ) function to evaluate the code block in relation to the contents of an array. For example, the following code reads the contents of your directory and displays it on screen.

```
#include "DIRECTRY.CH"
Procedure DDIR (cDirSkel)
local aDirect := directory (cDirSkel, "HSD")
local bDirDisp := { |aName| qout(padl(aName[F_NAME], 12)),;
                        qqout(padl(aName[F_SIZE], 12)),;
                        qqout(padl(aName[F_DATE], 10)),;
                        qqout(padl(aName[F_TIME], 10)),;
                        qqout(padl(aName[F_ATTR], 8)),;
                        nCount := nCount + 1,;
                        nFSize := nFSize + aName[F_SIZE] }
static nCount := 0
static nFSize := 0
cls
```

```
aeval(aDirect, bDirDisp)
?  ltrim(str(nCount)) + " Files      "
?? ltrim(str(nFSize)) + " Total Bytes"
return
```

NOTE

You must compile the preceding code with the /N switch. Failure to use this switch results in an immediate return to the DOS prompt each time you run the program. You execute the program by typing PROGRAM_ NAME [<DIR_SKELETON>]. If you do not specify file parameters the program assumes you want to see all files. If you do not specify a directory path, the program assumes you want to use the current directory.

As you can see by this example, the array evaluation example displays the filename, size, date, time, and attributes on the screen. In addition, nCount tracks the number of files and nFSize totals the files sizes of the files matching the prescribed directory skeleton. Since we use a static variable declaration, we can display these totals after aeval( ) exits. Notice that the example includes the directory header so we can use the easier-to-read array offsets shown in the program. Also notice that the Clipper manual incorrectly identifies F_ATT as the attribute declaration. F_ATTR is the declaration which appears in DIRECTORY.CH.

UNDERSTANDING THE TBROWSE CLASS

While the TBrowse class requires a better understanding of object oriented programming techniques than the other classes presented in this appendix, it is also provides the most utility. There are three types of objects that you need to consider when using the TBrowse class: functions, instance variables, and methods. Each of these objects performs a specific task as outlined in the following paragraphs.

A function in TBrowse does not vary much from a function used in a procedural sense. Like standard functions, you supply a set of parameters as input and the function provides some type of output. Unlike standard functions, you need to perform other tasks before the results of a TBrowse function can be seen. Table I-3 provides a listing and description of the TBrowse functions and the tasks you need to perform to use them.

TABLE I-3. TBrowse Class Functions

Function	*Description*
TBrowseNew (<nTop>, <nLeft>, <nBottom>, <nRight>)	This function creates a new, uninitialized TBrowse object that uses the specified screen coordinates. You must create the columns required to contain data and the data positioning code blocks. Use this function when you need to create an object that allows maximum flexibility. The command line format for creating an object that uses the entire display is as follows. `oBrowseDB := TBrowseNew (0, 0, 24, 79)`
TBrowseDB (<nTop>, <nLeft>, <nBottom>, <nRight>)	This function creates a new, initialized TBrowse object that uses the specified screen coordinates. You must create the columns required to contain data. However, this function automatically creates data positioning code blocks which use default values. These positioning blocks include: Go Top, Go Bottom, and Skip. Use this function when you need to create an object that requires a minimum of programming effort. The command line format for creating an object that uses the entire display is as follows. `oBrowseDB := TBrowseDB (0, 0, 24, 79)`

TBrowse supports exported instance variables that the programmer can modify as required to produce a specific result. An instance variable is different from the variables created by functions and procedures. When you create a variable in a function, that variable retains a specific value. Calling the function a second time (a process known as recursion) does not necessarily produce a new variable. The new instance of the function may retain the value produced by the first instance of the function. In addition, you can't retrieve a value contained in the first instance until the second instance of the function ends.

This problem does not exist with the object oriented approach. You can create multiple copies of an object and retrieve the value contained in the variables for each instance. In other words, each instance of the object creates an entirely new and independent set of variables. Some of the variables in an object are modifiable. These variables are called exported instance variables because you can retrieve and change their value. The programmer can only read the values of other variables. And a third set are for internal use only. The programmer doesn't even know they exist. Table I-4 contains a description of the exported instance variables supported by TBrowse.

TABLE I-4. TBrowse Class Exported Instance Variables

Variable	Description
Cargo	This variable contains the value of any data type as a user definable slot. You can think of cargo as a place to store information that doesn't belong anywhere else. It usually contains information specific to that instance of a TBrowse object. You use the cargo variable as follows. `oTObject:Cargo := "Some Value"`
colCount	This variable contains a number representing the total number of columns in the browse. There is one TBColumn object for each column in the browse. You use the colCount variable as follows. `nCol := oTObject:colCount`

colorSpec	The colorSpec variable contains the colors used by the TBrowse object to display data on screen. It contains the colors defined by Setcolor( ) when you initialize the TBrowse object. You use the colorSpec variable as follows to save the current color.
	`cColors := oTObject:colorSpec`
	You use the colorSpec variable as follows to change the current color.
	`oTObject:colorSpec := cColors`
	`colPos`
	Use this variable to determine the current position of the browse cursor. The columns are numbered starting at 1 from the leftmost column. You use the colPos variable as follows.
	`nCol := oTObject:colPos`

colSep	This variable determines what TBrowse uses as a separator between columns that do not have a separator defined. You use colSep variable as follows. `oTObject:colSep := chr(186)`
freeze	Use this variable to define the number of columns that are visible on the display at all times. The number of columns always begin at the left side of the display starting with column 1. You use the freeze variable as follows to freeze the first column in place. `oTObject:freeze := 1`

TABLE I-4. TBrowse Class Exported Instance Variables (Cont.)

Variable	Description
goBottomBlock	This variable contains the code block executed whenever the program issues a goBottom( ) message.
goTopBlock	This variable contains the code block executed whenever the program issues a goTop( ) message.
headSep	This variable determines what TBrowse uses as a separator between headers and detail that do not have a separator defined. You use colSep variable as follows. `oTObject:headSep := chr(196)`
hitBottom	This variable returns true whenever the user makes an attempt to navigate past the bottom of the file. Many programs use this as a signal to append a new record.
hitTop	This variable returns true whenever the user makes an attempt to navigate past the top of the file. Many programs use the tone( ) function to signal the user that they are at the beginning of the file.
LeftVisible( )	Use this variable to determine the leftmost unfrozen column visible on the browse display. This variable is available in Clipper version 5.01 and above. You use the LeftVisible( ) variable as follows. `nCol := oTObject:LeftVisible()`
nBottom	Use this variable to define the bottom of the display area. TBrowse automatically sets it as part of defining the original object. You use the nBottom variable as follows. `oTObject:nBottom := 24`
nLeft	Use this variable to define the left side of the display area. TBrowse automatically sets it as part of defining the original object. You use the nLeft variable as follows. `oTObject:nLeft := 0`
nRight	Use this variable to define the right side of the display area. TBrowse automatically sets it as part of defining the original object. You use the nRight variable as follows. `oTObject:nRight := 78`
nTop	Use this variable to define the top of the display area. TBrowse automatically sets it as part of defining the original object. You use the nTop variable as follows. `oTObject:nTop := 0`
RightVisible( )	Use this variable to determine the rightmost unfrozen column visible on the browse display. This variable is available in Clipper version 5.01 and above. You use the RightVisible( ) variable as follows. `nCol := oTObject:RightVisible()`
rowCount	This variable contains the number of detail rows visible on the screen. It does not include rows occupied by headers, footers, or separators. You use the rowCount variable as follows. `nRow := oTObject:rowCount`
rowPos	This variable contains a number which indicates the current browse cursor position in the detail rows. It does not include rows occupied by headers, footers, or separators. Do not confuse this number with the record number or any other database positioning information. It only indicates screen rows. You use the rowPos variable as follows. `nRow := oTObject:rowPos`

TABLE I-4. TBrowse Class Exported Instance Variables (Cont.)

Variable	Description
skipBlock	This variable contains a code block which defines the method used to skip records. TBrowse provides a default skipBlock entry when you initialize the object, which is sufficient for most purposes.
stable	Use this variable to determine if the TBrowse object is in a stable state. It returns true if the object is stable and false when it isn't. Most screen repositioning and data editing commands place the TBrowse object in an unstable state. Therefore, your program must monitor this variable and use the stabilize( ) method as appropriate to restabilize the object.

Once you configure an object using exported instance variables, you need to make it perform useful work. Unlike procedural languages, the programmer does not necessarily need to know all the details of how a task gets performed when using object oriented programming techniques. All the programmer does need to know is what method the object will use to perform the work and what it needs to do it. In many ways you can look at a method as you would look at a function or procedure. The major differences, of course, are the levels at which they operate. A method makes the programmer more like a foreman directing the flow of work, rather than a worker trying to perform all the required tasks at once. The use of methods also allows the language vendor to improve the inner workings of the language without changing the interface. Table I-5 contains a description of all the methods provided by the TBrowse class. The following source code shows one implementation of a TBrowse object. Notice that it includes examples on how to use the TBColumn and Get classes as well.

TABLE I-5. TBrowse Class Methods

Method	Description
Cursor Movement Methods	
delColumn(nPos)	Use this method to remove a column object from the middle of a browse. It returns a reference to the column. This method is available in Clipper version 5.01 and above.
down( )	This method moves the browse cursor down one row. If the cursor is already at the bottom of the display, the method scrolls the screen up one row and places the browse cursor on the new value displayed at the bottom of the display. When a user tries to move the cursor past the last record in the database, the method retains the current cursor position and sets the hitBottom variable true.
end( )	This method moves the browse cursor to the rightmost column in the browse object and redraws the screen.
goBottom( )	This method moves the browse cursor to the last record in the database and redraws the screen.
goTop( )	This method moves the browse cursor to the first record in the database and redraws the screen.
home( )	This method moves the browse cursor to the rightmost column in the browse object and redraws the screen.
insColumn(nPos,o Column)	Use this method to insert a column object into the middle of a browse. It returns a reference to the column. This method is available in Clipper version 5.01 and above.

TABLE I-5. TBrowse Class Methods (Cont.)

Method	Description
invalidate( )	Use this method to invalidate the entire browse display. TBrowse redraws the entire screen, including headers, footers, and separators during the next stabilize. The invalidate( ) method will not refresh the data displayed on the screen. In other words, it uses the current data values. Use the refresh( ) method if you need to refresh the data values in a column. This method is available in Clipper version 5.01 and above.
left( )	This method moves the browse cursor one column left in the browse object. If the cursor is already at the leftmost position on the display, the method pans the display one column to the left. If the cursor is on the last column, the browse cursor position remains unchanged.
pageDown( )	Use this method to skip down the number of records appearing in one display. The method automatically places the browse cursor on the first record in the new display. If the cursor is already on the last display page of records, the method simply places the browse cursor on the last record in the database. When a user tries to move the cursor past the last record in the database, the method retains the current cursor position and sets the hitBottom variable true.
pageUp( )	Use this method to skip up the number of records appearing in one display. The method automatically places the browse cursor on the first record in the new display. If the cursor is already on the first display page of records, the method simply places the browse cursor on the first record in the database. When a user tries to move the cursor past the first record in the database, the method retains the current cursor position and sets the hitTop variable true.
panEnd( )	This method moves the browse cursor to the rightmost data column. This pans the display completely to the right.
panHome( )	This method moves the browse cursor to the leftmost data column. This pans the display completely to the left.
panLeft( )	Use this method to pan the display one screen to the left without changing the position of the browse cursor. If the leftmost column is already in view, the position of the browse cursor remains unchanged.
panRight( )	Use this method to pan the display one screen to the right without changing the position of the browse cursor. If the rightmost column is already in view, the position of the browse cursor remains unchanged.
right( )	This method moves the browse cursor one column right in the browse object. If the cursor is already at the rightmost position on the display, the method pans the display one column to the right. If the cursor is on the last column, the browse cursor position remains unchanged.
up( )	This method moves the browse cursor up one row. If the cursor is already at the top of the display, the method scrolls the screen down one row and places the browse cursor on the new value displayed at the top of the display. When a user tries to move the cursor past the first record in the database, the method retains the current cursor position and sets the hitTop variable true.

Miscellaneous Methods

Method	Description
addColumn (<oColumn>)	Use this method to add a new column to the TBrowse object. The method automatically increments the colCount variable.
configure( )	This method forces TBrowse to re-examine all instance variables and TBColumn objects. The object then reconfigures its internal settings as required. Use this method after you modify the TBrowse instance variables manually.

TABLE I-5. TBrowse Class Methods (Cont.)

Method	Description
getColumn (<nColumn>)	The getColumn method returns the TBColumn object specified by nColumn.
refreshAll( )	This method marks all data rows invalid. The next stabilize( ) method call refreshes all the values displayed on screen from the database.
refreshCurrent( )	This method marks the current data row invalid. The next stabilize( ) method call refreshes the current data row values displayed on screen from the database.
setColumn (<nColumn>,<oColumn>	Use this method to replace the column object used by the column pointed to by nColumn with the object contained in oColumn.
stabilize( )	This method stabilizes the current TBrowse object and displays the results on screen. You must call the stabilize( ) method until the stabilize variable returns true since this method is incremental. An incremental stabilize allows asynchronous events such as keystrokes to occur. The method returns false until the TBrowse object is stable.

```
**********************************************************************
* TDEMO.PRG                                                          *
*                                                                    *
* TBrowse Demonstration Program for Clipper 5.01.  This program      *
* shows a specific example of how to use the TBrowse object in       *
* relation to one of the examples shown in the book.  Refer to the   *
* TBDemo program supplied with your Clipper disks for a generic      *
* example.  Together, the programs demonstrate some of the           *
* techniques you will need to use when creating TBrowse programs      *
* with Clipper 5.0x.                                                 *
*                                                                    *
* Written by: John Mueller                                           *
* 4/29/91                                                            *
**********************************************************************

// Include the standard key definitions.

#include "STD_DEFS.CH"

// Create the local variables.
local nInput := 0

// Open the database and index file.
use MAILLIST index LASTNAME

// Create a new TBrowse object.
oNewBrowse := TBrowseDB(02, 01, 23, 78)

// Define the columns we want displayed on screen.
oNewBrowse:addColumn(TBColumnNew("First",;
                     fieldwblock(field(1), select())))
oNewBrowse:addColumn(TBColumnNew("M",;
                     fieldwblock(field(2), select())))
oNewBrowse:addColumn(TBColumnNew("Last",;
                     fieldwblock(field(3), select())))
oNewBrowse:addColumn(TBColumnNew("Address 1",;
                     fieldwblock(field(4), select())))
oNewBrowse:addColumn(TBColumnNew("Address 2",;
                     fieldwblock(field(5), select())))
```

```
oNewBrowse:addColumn(TBColumnNew("City",;
                      fieldwblock(field(6), select()))))
oNewBrowse:addColumn(TBColumnNew("State",;
                      fieldwblock(field(7), select()))))
oNewBrowse:addColumn(TBColumnNew("Zip",;
                      fieldwblock(field(8), select()))))
oNewBrowse:addColumn(TBColumnNew("Telephone",;
                      fieldwblock(field(9), select()))))

// Define the on screen separators and other graphics.

oNewBrowse:colSep := "   "
oNewBrowse:headSep := "-"
@ 01, 00 to 24, 79 double

// Follow this procedure until the user presses escape.
do while .not. nInput == _esc_

// Wait until the display is stabilized before proceeding.
   do while .not. oNewBrowse:stabilize()
   enddo

// Get input from the user.
   nInput := inkey(0)

// Test the input against the movement key definitions.
// Move the cursor if necessary.
   do case
      case nInput == _left_
         oNewBrowse:left()
      case nInput == _right_
         oNewBrowse:right()
      case nInput == _up_
         oNewBrowse:up()
      case nInput == _down_
         oNewBrowse:down()
      case nInput == _home_
         oNewBrowse:panHome()
      case nInput == _end_
         oNewBrowse:panEnd()
      case nInput == _pgup_
         oNewBrowse:pageUp()
      case nInput == _pgdn_
         oNewBrowse:pageDown()
      case nInput == _enter_
         changeData(oNewBrowse)
   endcase
enddo

// Clear the display and close the database before leaving
// the program.
cls
close MAILLIST

*********************************************************************
* This procedure allows the program to change the contents of the  *
* highlighted entry.  Notice that it uses the new get object to    *
* perform the work.                                                *
*********************************************************************
```

```
static procedure ChangeData (oBrowseOBJ)

local nCol, oGet, cColorS

static cColorN := "W/N,W+/N,N/N,N/N,N/W"

// Save the current color set and change it to a new one.
cColorS := oBrowseOBJ:colorSpec
oBrowseOBJ:colorSpec := cColorN

// Get the current column object from TBrowse object.
oCol := oBrowseOBJ:getColumn(oBrowseOBJ:colPos)

// Create a corresponding GET object.
oGet := GetNew(Row(), Col(), oCol:block, oCol:heading,, oBrowseOBJ:colorSpec)

// Read it using the standard reader.
ReadModal( {oGet} )

// Restore the old color set.
oBrowseOBJ:colorSpec := cColorS

// Refresh the information on the display.
oBrowseOBJ:refreshAll()

// Wait until the display is stabilized before proceeding.
do while .not. oNewBrowse:stabilize()
enddo

return
```

As you can see, using the TBrowse Class allows you to create programs that provide greater flexibility and functionality with a minimum of effort. The resulting code is easier to read and requires less documentation as well. More importantly, using objects in your programs allows you to concentrate on the task at hand rather than how to perform that task.

ADDING THE TBCOLUMN CLASS

The TBColumn class is actually an adjunct to the TBrowse class. You must create a TBrowse object before you can create a TBColumn object. As its name suggests, a TBColumn object defines one column of a TBrowse object. You must create one TBColumn object for every column (field) you intend to display. Clipper provides many exported instance variables and methods to manipulate the columns as individual entities. For example, with the DBEdit() function, every column on the display used the same color. Using a TBColumn object every column can use a different color. Unlike DBEdit( ) you can move the columns around, add new ones, and delete old ones without recreating the TBrowse object. Everything you do with TBColumn is done while the TBrowse object is active.

There is only one function supplied with the TBColumn class. The TBColumnNew function adds new columns to a TBrowse object. It only requires two variables: a column heading and a code block defining how the column reacts to requests for data. The source code example in the TBrowse section of this appendix shows you how to create a standard column that allows editing. The Nantucket manual provides an example of how to create a standard column that does not allow editing.

As with the TBrowse class, the TBColumn class provides many exported instance variables. Unlike the TBrowse exported instance variables, these variables only modify the parameters of a single column. You would use these instance variables when you wanted to set one column apart from another. For example, you could change the color or the column separator. Some reasons that you might want to do this include highlighting a totals column or offsetting derived data. Table I-6 contains a complete listing and description of all the TBColumn exported instance variables. Notice that some variables are the same as those found in the TBrowse class. Remember that these variables only affect a single column.

TABLE I-6. TBColumn Class Exported Instance Variables

Variable	Description
block	You use this variable to define the code block that retrieves data for the column. This code block can contain any code required to perform the task. The TBColumn object does not supply any input. The block must supply data of the appropriate type for the column as output. You can create a noneditable code block as follows. ``` bNewBlock := { | | MAILLIST->FIRST_NAME} oTBObj := oNewBrowse:getColumn(1) oTBObj:block := bNewBlock oNewBrowse:setColumn(1, oTBObj) ```
Cargo	This variable contains the value of any data type as a user definable slot. You can think of cargo as a place to store information that doesn't belong anywhere else. It usually contains information specific to that instance of a TBrowse object. You use the cargo variable as follows. ``` oTBObj := oNewBrowse:getColumn(1) oTBObj:Cargo := "Some Value" oNewBrowse:setColumn(1, oTBObj) ```
colorBlock	Use this variable if you want to create a code block that determines the color of a row in a column by the value of the data. The code block must return a two-element array. The array contains numbers which are an index into the color table for the TBrowse object. This is very useful if, for example, you wanted to display positive numbers in black and negative numbers in red. You use the colorBlock variable as shown below. ``` local aClr1 := {1, 2} local aClr2 := {2, 3} local bColBlock := {| cFld |; iif(len(alltrim(cFld)) == 0, aClr2, aClr1)} oTBObj := oNewBrowse:getColumn(5) oTBObj:colorBlock := bColBlock oNewBrowse:setColumn(5, oTBObj) ```
colSep	This variable determines what TBrowse uses as a separator between columns that do not have a separator defined. You use colSep variable as follows. ``` oTBObj := oNewBrowse:getColumn(1) oTBObj:colSep := chr(186) oNewBrowse:setColumn(1, oTBObj) ```
defColor	The defColor variable lets you redefine the color of a column. As with the colorBlock variable, the defColor variable uses a two-element array. The array contains numbers which are an index into the color table for the TBrowse object. You use the defColor variable as shown below.

TABLE I-6. TBColumn Class Exported Instance Variables (Cont.)

Variable	Description
| defColor (Cont.) | ```
local aColor := {2, 3}
 oTBObj := oNewBrowse:getColumn(5)
 oTBObj:defColor := aColor
 oNewBrowse:setColumn(5, oTBObj)
``` |
| footing | This variable contains text that the TBColumn object displays at the bottom of the display area. You use the footing variable as follows.<br>```
oTBObj := oNewBrowse:getColumn(1)
oTBObj:footing := "Some Text"
oNewBrowse:setColumn(1, oTBObj)
``` |
| footSep | This variable determines what TBrowse uses as a separator between footers and detail. You use footSep variable as follows.<br>```
oTBObj := oNewBrowse:getColumn(1)
oTBObj:footSep := chr(196)
oNewBrowse:setColumn(1, oTBObj)
``` |
| heading | This variable contains text that the TBColumn object displays at the top of the display area. You use the heading variable as follows.<br>```
oTBObj := oNewBrowse:getColumn(1)
oTBObj:heading := "Some Text"
oNewBrowse:setColumn(1, oTBObj)
``` |
| headSep | This variable determines what TBrowse uses as a separator between headers and detail. You use headSep variable as follows.<br>```
oTBObj := oNewBrowse:getColumn(1)
oTBObj:headSep := chr(196)
oNewBrowse:setColumn(1, oTBObj)
``` |
| width | Use this variable to define the width of a column. If this variable is left blank, the TBColumn object uses the width of the input returned by TBColumn:block. You use the width variable as follows.<br>```
oTBObj := oNewBrowse:getColumn(1)
oTBObj:width := 20
oNewBrowse:setColumn(1, oTBObj)
``` |

USING THE GET CLASS

In many ways you have already used the Get class in every program created in this manual. Every @ Get command is translated by the preprocessor into a get object. So the question that many programmer's ask is why use the Get class at all. The major reason is flexibility. The @ Get command exercises, at most, a few of the methods available to you if you use the Get class. One example of how to use the Get class was demonstrated in the source code found in the TBrowse section. You would be unable to perform this same task using the @ Get command. However, this is only one way of using the get class. The following paragraphs provide descriptions of how to use the get class, while the tables provide detailed explanations of get class elements and provide examples of usage.

As with the previous two classes, the Get class possesses three elements: functions, exported instance variables, and methods. Like the TBColumn class, the Get class uses a single function to perform its work. This function uses the format:

```
GetNew ([<nRow>], [<nCol>], [<bBlock>], [<cPicture>], [<cColorSpec>]).
```

As you can see, you can call GetNew without any parameters. The Get class will create a get object which uses all default parameters.

Of course, most people will use some or all of the parameters supplied with the function. The nRow parameter inputs a value to the row exported instance variable and determines which row the get object appears on. The nCol parameter inputs a value to the col exported instance variable and determines the get object column position. You use the bBlock parameter to specify which variable the get object should operate on. This is the same as the block exported instance variable. Of course, the cPicture parameter fulfills the same function as the picture clause of the @ Get command. This parameter determines the value of the picture exported instance variable. Finally, the cColorSpec parameter determines the color of the get object. There are two colors required, one for when the object has the input focus (selected) and one when it doesn't. This parameter fills the colorspec exported instance variable.

The Get class uses a wide range of exported instance variables to modify the way it operates on variables. As with the other classes described so far, each exported instance variable performs a specific task. Table I-7 contains a complete listing and description of each exported instance variable.

TABLE I-7. Get Class Exported Instance Variables

Variable	Description
badDate	This variable returns true when the date entered by the user is invalid. It returns false for a good date entry. You use the badDate variable as follows. `lDateChk := oGetOBJ:badDate`
block	Use this variable to specify which variable you want the get object to operate on. The block variable may contain any valid code block which returns a legal value for the variable. You use the block variable as follows. `bGetVar := {| cInVal	if(pcount() > 0,;` ` cVar := cInVal,;` ` cVar) }` `oGetOBJ:block := bGetVar` `ReadModal ({oGetVar})`
buffer	The buffer variable contains the name of a buffer used while editing a get object. Normally, this variable contains a value of NIL. Attempts to assign a name to the buffer are futile until the get object has input focus.
cargo	This variable contains the value of any data type not used by the get system. You can use this variable to keep track of data that does not have a standard slot in the get object. For example, some programmers use this variable to track the edit status of the get object. You use the cargo variable as follows. `oGetOBJ:cargo := "Some Value"`
changed	Use this variable to determine if the user changed the contents of a get object during a read (when the get object had the input focus). If the buffer changed, then the changed variable contains true; otherwise, it contains false. You use the changed variable as follows. `lDChanged := oGetOBJ:changed`

TABLE I-7. Get Class Exported Instance Variables (Cont.)

Variable	Description
col	The col variable determines the column where the get object appears on the display. You use the col variable as follows. `oGetOBJ:col := 4`
colorSpec	This variable contains a character string which defines the colors used to display the get object. The string contains two sets of color specifications. The first set is the unselected color for the get. The second color is the selected color for the get. A get is selected when it has the input focus. Clipper automatically uses the colors defined with Setcolor( ) for the get object. You use the colorSpec variable as follows. `oGetOBJ:colorSpec := "N/W, W/N"`
decPos	The decPos variable contains the position of the decimal point within a get object. For example, if the decimal point is on the eighth position of a ten-digit number, then this variable returns 8. The contents of this variable are meaningful only when the get object has input focus. Otherwise, the variable contains NIL. You use the decPos variable as follows. `nSomeVar := oGetOBJ:decPos`
exitState	The Readmodal( ) function updates the exitState variable to show how a get object was exited when last read. There are nine potential exit states:

```
GE_NOEXIT     0     No Exit Attempted
GE_UP         1     Up Arrow Pressed
GE_DOWN       2     Down Arrow Pressed
GE_TOP        3     User Went Past First Get
GE_BOTTOM     4     User Went Past Last Get
GE_ENTER      5     Enter Pressed
GE_WRITE      6     Get Written
GE_ESCAPE     7     Escape Pressed
GE_WHEN       8     When Condition Not Satisfied
```

The variable returns a number which you may match to a text expression if you include GETEXIT.CH in your program. This method is available in Clipper version 5.01 and above. You use the exitState variable as follows.

`nSomeVar := oGetOBJ:exitState`

Variable	Description
hasFocus	The hasFocus variable returns true if the get object has the input focus (is selected for editing); otherwise, it returns false. You use the hasFocus variable as follows. `lGFocus := oGetOBJ:hasFocus`
name	The Readmodal( ) and Readvar( ) functions use this variable to determine the name of the get variable. You do not need to define this variable. The get object ignores the value contained in this variable. It was added for Summer 87 compatibility purposes. You use the name variable as follows. `oGetOBJ:name := "Some Value"`
original	The get object stores the original value of the get variable in the original variable when the object receives input focus. This allows the get system to undo user input using the undo( ) method. Never modify this variable.
picture	Use this variable to define a picture string for the get variable. The @ Get module of this manual contains a complete description of the pictures available for the get object. You use the picture variable as follows. `oGetOBJ:picture := "999.99"`

TABLE I-7. Get Class Exported Instance Variables (Cont.)

Variable	Description
pos	The pos variable contains the position of the cursor within a get object. For example, if the cursor is on the last position of a ten-character string, then this variable returns 10. The contents of this variable are meaningful only when the get object has input focus. Otherwise, the variable contains NIL. You use the pos variable as follows. `nSomeVar := oGetOBJ:pos`
postBlock	This variable contains a code block used to validate the contents of a get object after editing. If the get object contains a legal value, then the code block should return true. The get object ignores the code block contained in this variable. It is used by the standard Read command, replacing the Valid clause. This allows the Valid clause to verify the get variable without directly looking at it.
preBlock	This variable contains a code block which determines when the user can edit the get variable. If the code block returns true, then the user can edit the get variable. The get object ignores the code block. It is used by the standard Read command, replacing the When clause. This allows the When clause to verify that the get is open for editing without looking directly at the get variable.
reader	Use this variable to create special effects using a standard Get command. You supply a code block as input to the variable, which modifies the behavior of the specified get object. The code block may include calls to specialized procedures and functions. If the reader variable does not contain a code block, Readmodal( ) automatically uses the standard get routine. This method is available in Clipper version 5.01 and above.
rejected	Use the rejected variable to determine if the last character specified by an insert( ) or overstrike( ) method was rejected. If the get object rejected the input, then the rejected variable returns true. Any subsequent entry resets this variable. You use the rejected variable as follows. `lWasRej := oGetOBJ:rejected`
row	The row variable determines the row where the get object appears on the display. You use the row variable as follows. `oGetOBJ:row := 4`

subscript	Use this variable to determine the array element subscripts contained in a get object. The variable returns an array of numeric values relating to the subscripts used in the @ Get statement. There is one array element for each dimension of the get variable. If the get variable contains three dimensions, the subscript variable returns a one-dimensional array with three elements. If the get object contains a regular variable, the subscript variable returns NIL. This method is available in Clipper version 5.01 and above. You use the subscript variable as follows.
	
	`local a := "John "`
	`local b := "Mary "`
	`local c := "David "`
	`local aVar := {{a, b, c}, {c, b, a}}`
	`@ 01, 01 get aVar[1, 3]`
	`oGetVar := GetList [ Len(GetList) ]`
	`// aSub[1] = 1, aSub[2] = 3`
	`aSub := oGetVar:subscript`

TABLE I-7. Get Class Exported Instance Variables (Cont.)

Variable	Description
type	This variable returns the type of the get variable. These are the same types described in the ValType( ) module of this manual. You use the type variable as follows. `cSomeVar := oGetOBJ:type`
typeOut	Use the typeOut variable to determine if the most recent method attempted to move the cursor outside the get or if the get does not contain any editable positions. If the user can no longer move the cursor in a specific direction or if there aren't any editable positions, this variable returns true. You use the typeOut variable as follows. `lSomeVar := oGetOBJ:typeOut`

There are more types of exported methods provided with the Get class than other classes described so far. These different types of methods give the Get class more flexibility than the commands provided by strictly X-Base compatible commands. For example, the state change methods determine when and how a get object performs certain tasks. There are methods for displaying the object on screen, giving it input focus, and even undoing user input. The cursor movement methods allow the programmer to determine which keys are functional and what task they will perform. There are methods for skipping a single word or moving the beginning of the get object. You can use the different editing methods to determine how the user removes text from the get object. Finally, the text entry methods determine how the user adds text to the get object. Table I-8 contains a complete listing of all these methods and a description of how to use them.

TABLE I-8. Get Class Methods

Method	Description
State Change Methods	
assign( )	This method assigns the value in the editing buffer to the get object by evaluating the get code block. You may only use this method when the get object has the input focus.
colorDisp( )	Use this method to reassign the colors used by a get object, then redraw the screen. It is equivalent to setting the color using the colorSpec instance variable and issuing a display( ) method. This method is available in Clipper version 5.01 and above.
display( )	The display( ) method redraws the get object on screen. If the get object has the input focus, it places the cursor in the position indicated by the pos variable and uses the selected color. Otherwise, it redraws the get object using the unselected color.
killFocus( )	Use this method to remove the input focus from a get object. Once the input focus is removed, the get object redisplays itself and discards any internal state information.
reset( )	The reset( ) method resets a get object's internal state information. It also places the current value of the get variable into the editing buffer. Finally, it places the cursor in column one of the buffer. You may only use this method when the get object has the input focus.

TABLE I-8. Get Class Methods (Cont.)

Method	Description
setFocus( )	Use this method to give a get object the input focus. Once the get object receives the input focus, it creates and initializes the internal state information. This includes the exported instance variables: buffer, pos, decPos, and original. Finally, the get object displays the editing buffer in the selected color.
undo( )	This method copies the contents of the original instance variable to the editing buffer, returning the buffer to its unedited state. You may only use this method when the get object has the input focus.
updateBuffer( )	Use the updateBuffer( ) method to update the editing buffer with the current value of the get variable. This method automatically redisplays the get. You may only use this method when the get object has the input focus.

Cursor Movement Methods

Method	Description
end( )	This method moves the cursor to the rightmost column in the object and redraws the screen.
home( )	This method moves the cursor to the leftmost column in the object and redraws the screen.
left( )	This method moves the cursor one column left in the object. If the cursor is on the last column, the cursor position remains unchanged.
right( )	This method moves the cursor one column right in the object. If the cursor is on the last column, the cursor position remains unchanged.
toDecPos( )	Use this method to move the cursor to the first column position to the right of the decimal point. This method is valid only when editing numeric values.
wordLeft( )	This method moves the cursor one word left in the object. If the cursor is on the last editable column, the cursor position remains unchanged.
wordRight( )	This method moves the cursor one word right in the object. If the cursor is on the first column, the cursor position remains unchanged.

Editing Methods

Method	Description
backspace( )	The backspace( ) method moves the cursor one column to the left in the object. It removes the character to the left of the original cursor position. If the cursor is on the first column, the cursor position remains unchanged.
delLeft( )	Use this method to remove a character to the left of the cursor.
delRight( )	Use this method to remove a character to the right of the cursor.
delWordLeft( )	Use this method to remove a word to the left of the cursor.
delWordRight( )	Use this method to remove a word to the right of the cursor.

Text Entry Methods

Method	Description
insert (<cChar>)	The insert( ) method inserts cChar at the current cursor position in the object. It moves the contents of the buffer to the right of the cursor enough space to accommodate the entry. cChar may contain a single character or a string. Once the get object inserts the string, it moves the cursor to the first position to the right of the last insertion column.
overStrike (<cChar>)	The overStrike( ) method places cChar at the current cursor position in the object. It overwrites the contents of the buffer to the right of the cursor. cChar may contain a single character or a string. Once the get object overwrites the string, it moves the cursor to the first position to the right of the last overwritten column.

USING THE ERROR CLASS

The Error class is one of the most misunderstood and unused portions of Clipper. Yet, its effective use can reduce the number of undetermined errors that a user must face when using an application. In most cases the programmer does not need to rewrite the error system code or change the code block that determines how the error class functions. The most important thing that the programmer can do is interpret the error codes and exported instance variables correctly and provide procedures that help the user recover from the error. Common examples of how the programmer can achieve this include detecting and preventing file open and printer errors. For example, instead of allowing Clipper to display a cryptic error message when the printer is out of paper, the programmer could create a procedure that displays a message like "Check Printer Paper" and then retries the print routine. The following paragraphs describe how to detect errors and recover from them. They also provide a description of the exported instance variables provided by the error class.

The first step in helping the user overcome an error condition is error detection. One of the best ways of doing this is to place critical code sections within a Begin Sequence control structure. For example, in the following code sequence, the critical code section checks to see that two variables are of the same type before comparing them.

```
local nCount := 0
local cString := "Help Me"
local lEqual := .F.
do while .not. lEqual
   begin sequence
     if valtype(nCount) <> valtype(cString)
       break
     endif
     iif(nCount == cString, lEqual := .T., lEqual := .F.)
     ? nCount
     ? cString
   recover
     ? "Couldn't compare the two variables."
     nCount := cString
   end
enddo
? "The variables are now equal."
```

If the two variables don't compare, then the error recovery code after the Recover clause takes effect and makes them equal. The program can then proceed to print out the two strings and tell the user that they are equal.

Of course, this isn't necessarily the best way to do things. The programmer would need to include a great deal of error recovery code to trap errors using this technique. Fortunately, another method exists for trapping this error. By modifying the ERRORSYS.PRG to allow you to recover from the error, you can trap every occurrence of an error without adding much code to your programs. The following code shows a code fragment from the ERRORSYS.PRG included on your Clipper disk. The required code additions are highlighted.

NOTE
There is an error in some versions of ERRORSYS.PRG. The two defines, OUT and OUTNL resolve to the __OUTSTD( ) function. Remove the initial underscores from the OUTSTD( ) function to allow the program to execute properly.

You must use the /N command line switch when compiling
ERRORSYS.PRG. Otherwise, you will receive a runtime error stating
that there is a redefinition error in the program.

```
static func DefError(e)
local i
local cTryAgain := "Y"

    if ( e:genCode == EG_OPEN .and. NetErr() .and. e:canDefault )
        return (.f.)   /* ignore */
    end

    if (!Empty(e:operation) .and. e:operation == "==")
        OUTNL("Tried to compare two different types of variable.")
        accept "Try to fix error? " to cTryAgain
        if (cTryAgain == "Y" .or. cTryAgain == "y")
            e:args[1] := e:args[2]
        return (.f.)
        end
    end
```

As the code example shows, a programmer can intercept some of the messages contained in
exported instance variables and provide a custom error handler to recover from noncritical
errors. In this case, the error system handler displays a message that the user has tried to
compare two different types of variables. It then offers the user a chance to recover from the
mistake. If the user types Y and presses Enter, then the program makes the two offending
variables equal in type and returns .F. to the error handling code block. Using the program that
follows, the user would see the error message, recover from it, then see .F., the first variable,
and then the second variable. This error handler now provides a higher level of information to
the user about the exact nature of the problem. If the user simply presses Enter at the fix prompt,
the error handler displays the standard error message and exits to the DOS prompt.

```
local nCount := 0
local cString := "Help Me"
? nCount == cString
? nCount
? cString
```

Since the language developer had to create a handler that would work in all situations (generic)
and you have access to the code for your specific situation, you are in the position to enhance
the error handler provided as a default with the program. Table I-9 provides a listing and
description of the imported instance variables provided with Clipper. As shown in the previous
example, there are many ways in which to use these variables to create better error handling
routines for your programs.

TABLE I-9. Error Class Exported Instance Variables

Variable	Description
args	This variable contains a list of the arguments supplied to an operator or function when an argument error occurs. Monitoring this variable allows you to check the type and value of the parameters sent from one area to another area of your code. The args variable contains NIL for other types of errors.
canDefault	Use this variable to determine if the error can use the default error handler to recover. A return value of false means that it can't. The result is that the user will receive an error message and the program will end. By adding your own error handling routines, you can help the user recover from many errors. If the variable returns true, you can safely ignore the error because the default recovery routines will handle it. This variable never returns true if the canSubstitute variable is true.
canRetry	Use this variable to determine if the subsystem can retry the operation that failed. If the variable returns true, then the default error handler will allow the user to fix the problem and retry the operation. This variable never returns true if the canSubstitute variable is true.
canSubstitute	Monitor the canSubstitute variable to determine when the error handler can safely substitute a new value for a failed operation. This normally occurs when a function or operator receives invalid arguments. You must perform the substitution by returning a new result value from the code block invoked to handle the error. The canSubstitute variable is never true when the canDefault or canRetry variables are true.
cargo	This variable contains the value of any data type not used by the get system. You can use this variable to keep track of data that does not have a standard slot in the error object. For example, you could use it to store additional error information for a custom error handler to aid in recovery.
description	The description variable contains a string describing the failure condition. A zero length string indicates the system does not recognize the specific error that occurred. In most cases it is not safe to try to recover from unrecognized error conditions. If the genCode variable does not contain zero, a printable error description is always available.
filename	The filename variable contains the name of the file associated with the error condition. If this string is empty, then the error did not occur as the result of a particular file. Other conditions that output a null string include failure to provide a filename and loss of the filename by the subsystem.
genCode	Use the genCode variable to determine if the error is one of the generic errors described in ERROR.CH, or if it is subsystem specific. A subsystem specific error requires special handling. In most cases it results in a unrecoverable error unless your code contains special error handling code.
operation	This variable contains the name of the operation being performed when the error occurred. When the error occurs in an operator or function, the operation variable contains the name of the operator or function. If the error occurs due to an undefined variable or function, operator contains the name of the variable or function. In most cases you can use this variable to determine the exact nature of an error. If the operator variable is blank, the subsystem doesn't recognize the particular operation in effect during the error.

TABLE I-9. Error Class Exported Instance Variables (Cont.)

Variable	Description
osCode	Use this variable to determine if the error is operating system specific. If the variable contains a zero, then the error is Clipper specific. Otherwise, the error occurred as the result of a DOS operation. The osCode variable returns the same value as the DOSError( ) function.
subCode	The subCode variable contains the subsystem error number. If this variable contains a zero, then the subsystem does not recognize a specific error code.
subSystem	This variable contains the name of the subsystem experiencing the error. For Clipper specific errors, the subSystem variable returns BASE. Database specific errors return the name of the database driver.
tries	The tries variable contains the number of times that the retry operation has failed. If this number is zero, then the subsystem does not allow retries for this particular error.

Appendix J
EXERCISES

1. About This Book
   a. What benefits will the advanced programmer receive from using this book?
   b. What are the hardware requirements for using Clipper?
   c. What should you know about your machine and its environment before using this book?

2. Clipper Overview
   a. What does the -l command line option do?
   b. What does the -m command line option do?
   c. What happens if you use capital letters when specifying a command line option?
   d. How do you specify the files to link when using the plink86 linker?
   e. Why should you use the /e option when using the standard linker supplied with Microsoft languages.

3. Creating a Program Diagram
   a. What steps do you need to perform when designing a database structure?
   b. Do memo fields create any special problems when creating a database? If so, what problems?
   c. Why should you use indexes with databases?
   d. Why should you use a flow chart to design your program?
   e. Who ultimately pays the cost for lack of program design? What are the disadvantages to ignoring the program design phase?

4. Creating the Basic Program Structure
   a. How do you use the flow charts created during the design phase when you begin creating your application?
   b. What do you do after creating the program skeleton?
   c. How do you complete the program after you create the various procedures and user-designed functions.

5. Creating a Database Using the DBU Utility
   a. When do you use the /M command line option?
   b. How do you open a database using DBU?
   c. What type of help does the Help command provide? How does this assist you in using DBU?
   d. Why would you use the Zap command on the Utility menu?
   e. Which Set menu command allows you to link two databases together?

6. Creating an Index Using the Index Utility
   a. When do you use the Index utility in place of DBU?
   b. What command line parameter do you have to provide for the Index utility?
   c. How do you specify the index key when using the Index utility?

7. Creating Reports and Labels Using the RL Utility
    a. What is the difference between a report and a label file?
    b. How do you enter the heading for a report file?
    c. How do you enter the information for each line of a label form?
    d. When should you use a label form instead of a report form?

8. ACCEPT
    a. When should you use the Accept command instead of an At (@) Say/Get command?
    b. What function does the optional prompt clause perform?
    c. Where does Accept place the user response?

9. APPEND
    a. What function does the Append command perform?
    b. When would you use the Append Blank form of the command?
    c. What does the scope clause specify?
    d. How does the while clause differ from the for clause?

10. AT (@) BOX
    a. How do you specify a fill character for the area encircled by the box?
    b. Which coordinate does EXPN2 specify?
    c. How would you draw a straight line using this command?

11. AT (@) CLEAR TO (Blanking Display Sections)
    a. When would you use this command?
    b. Where does Clipper erase to if you don't specify a lower right corner coordinate?
    c. What is an advantage of using this command instead of the Clear Screen command?

12. AT (@) PROMPT (Menu Creation)
    a. What function does the message clause perform?
    b. Why should you use this command?
    c. How do you determine where Clipper places the prompt?

13. AT (@) SAY/GET (Positioning/Retrieving Text and Data)
    a. What is the difference between a picture template and a picture function?
    b. What function does the valid clause perform?
    c. How does the valid clause differ from the range clause?
    d. When should you use this command?
    e. Can you use the get clause separately from the say clause?

14. AT (@) TO DOUBLE (Line Drawing)
    a. What function does the double clause perform?
    b. Can you draw angular (versus horizontal or vertical) lines using this command? If so, how?
    c. How do you draw a box using this command?
    d. When should you use this command in place of the At (@) Box command?

15. AVERAGE
    a. What task does the Average command perform?
    b. How do you specify the range of numbers to average?
    c. How does the while clause limit the number of records averaged?

16. BEGIN SEQUENCE
    a. Why should you use the Begin Sequence command?
    b. When should you use this control structure?
    c. How does this control structure provide protection from runtime errors?

17. CALL
    a. What type of routines does the Call command execute?
    b. When should you use the Call command?

18. CANCEL/QUIT
    a. What sequence of events occurs when you use the Quit command?
    b. Why should you use the Quit command instead of the Return command?
    c. Can you use the Quit command anywhere other than the end of a program? Where?

19. CLEAR ALL
    a. What sequence of events occurs when you use the Clear All command?
    b. When is the Clear All command especially useful?

20. CLEAR GETS
    a. Why would you want to clear all pending gets?
    b. Can you clear gets before a read statement?

21. CLEAR MEMORY
    a. What function does this command perform?
    b. How does this command differ from the Release All command?
    c. Why should you use this command?
    d. What runtime errors could occur when you use this command?

22. CLEAR SCREEN
    a. Where does this command place the cursor?
    b. What function does this command perform?
    c. Why would you use this command?

23. CLEAR TYPEAHEAD
    a. What function does the typeahead buffer perform?
    b. How do you change the size of the typeahead buffer?
    c. When would you use this command?

24. CLOSE
    a. What sequence of events occurs when you use the Close command?
    b. What types of files does this command affect?
    c. Which file does the alternate clause close?
    d. What is the default condition for this command?

25. COMMIT
    a. What types of failure does this command guard against?
    b. When should you use this command?
    c. Are there any drawbacks to using this command? If so, what?

26. CONTINUE
    a. Which command do you use before issuing the Continue command?
    b. Does this command use any of the conditional statements specified with the previous command?
    c. Why should you use this command?

27. COPY FILE
    a. How can you use this command to improve database access speed?
    b. How does this command differ from the Copy To command?
    c. What types of files can you copy using this command?

28. COPY STRUCTURE
    a. What is a database header? What type of information does it contain?
    b. What function does the fields clause perform?
    c. How does this command differ from the Copy To command?
    d. When should you use this command?

29. COPY TO (Data/Structure)
    a. What is an SDF file format?
    b. How does an SDF file differ from a delimited file?
    c. What types of information does this command copy?

30. COUNT
    a. What function does this command perform?
    b. Where does Clipper place the output from this command?
    c. How can you use this command in an application?

31. CREATE, COPY STRUCTURE EXTENDED, CREATE FROM
    a. How does the Create command differ from the Create From command?
    b. What type of file does the Copy Structure Extended command create? What information does it place in the file?
    c. When should you use the Create From command instead of the Create command?

32. DECLARE, FIELD, LOCAL, MEMVAR, STATIC
    a. What is an array?
    b. How does an array differ from other data structures?
    c. When should you use an array?
    d. Can you create more than one array at a time using this command? If so, how?

33. DELETE
    a. What function does the Delete command perform?
    b. Does the Delete command actually remove records from the database?
    c. What is the default scope of the Delete command?

34. DIR
    a. What function does the path clause perform?
    b. How do you tell Clipper which files to display?
    c. How would you use this command in an application?

35. DISPLAY
    a. What function does the To File clause perform?
    b. What type of information does this command display?
    c. What function does the off clause perform?
    d. When would you use this command?

36. DO CASE
    a. How does the Do Case command differ from the If command? How is it the same?
    b. What function does the otherwise clause perform?
    c. Why should you use this command?

37. DO (Procedure)
    a. What function does this command perform?
    b. When should you use the with clause?
    c. Why should you use this command?
    d. How does this command aid in creating more readable code?

38. DO WHILE
    a. What function does this command perform?
    b. How does the loop clause alter the way this command works?
    c. When should you use the exit clause.

39. EJECT
    a. How does the Eject command affect the printer?
    b. When should you use this command?

40. ERASE/DELETE FILE
    a. What function does this command perform?
    b. What hazards does this command present?
    c. When is this command especially useful?

41. EXTERNAL
    a. What runtime error does this command fix?
    b. When is the command required? Optional?
    c. How does this command affect the linker?

42. FIND
    a. What are the advantages to using this command instead of the Seek command? Disadvantages?
    b. Do you need to use an index with this command? If not, why not?

43. FOR TO (Execute a Loop)
    a. How does this command differ from the Do While command?
    b. Can you exit this command before the counter reaches the count value? If so, how?
    c. What function does the step clause perform?
    d. When should you use this command in place of a Do While command?

44. FUNCTION
    a. What is a user-defined function?
    b. How does it differ from a procedure?
    c. When should you use a function instead of a procedure?
    d. Do you always need to provide a return value for a function? If so, why?

45. GO/GOTO
    a. What three ways can you use this command?
    b. When should you use this command?

46. IF, ELSEIF, ELSE, ENDIF
    a. What is the difference between the else and elseif clauses?
    b. What is a conditional statement?
    c. How does the If, Elseif, Else, Endif command affect program execution?

47. INDEX ON
    a. What function does an index serve?
    b. What types of information can you include in the key expression?
    c. When would you use this command?

48. INPUT
    a. How does the Input command differ from the At (@) Say/Get command?
    b. Why would you use this command instead of the At (@) Say/Get command?
    c. Are there any problems associated with using this command?
    d. What are the disadvantages of using this command?

49. JOIN WITH
    a. What function does the Join With command perform?
    b. Where does the Join With place the result of a join?
    c. Why would you use this command?

50. KEYBOARD
    a. How does the Keyboard command affect program execution?
    b. When would you use the Keyboard command?

51. LABEL FORM
    a. How does the Label Form command differ from the Report Form command?
    b. What function does the sample clause perform?
    c. How does the for clause affect Label Form output?
    d. What is the default scope for the Label Form command?

52. LIST
    a. What function does the off clause perform?
    b. What type of information does the List command display?
    c. What is the essential difference between the Display and the List commands?

53. LOCATE
    a. What is the advantage of using the Locate command in place of the Seek command? Disadvantage?
    b. How do you find the second occurrence of an expression when using the Locate command?
    c. When would you use this command in place of the Seek command?

54. MENU TO
    a. What command must you use before using the Menu To command?
    b. Where does Menu To place the user response?
    c. Besides pressing Enter after highlighting the correct menu choice, how can you select a menu item using the Menu To command?
    d. What is a light-bar menu?

55. NOTE (*/&&)
    a. Why is it important to place notes within your code?
    b. When would you use the && in place of the * command?

56. PACK
    a. What function does the Pack command perform?
    b. What steps must you perform before using the Pack command?
    c. Why must you use the Pack command with caution?

57. PARAMETERS
    a. What is the purpose of the Parameters command?
    b. Where do you use this command?
    c. What does Clipper do with variables created using the Parameters command when you exit the procedure?

58. PRINT STATEMENT (?/??)
    a. What function does the Print Statement command perform?
    b. When should you use the ?? Command in place of the ? Command?
    c. When should you use this command in place of a report form or At (@) Say/Get command?

59. PRIVATE
    a. What is a private variable?
    b. Can you declare a variable private after you declare it? Why or why not?
    c. Why should you use private variables?

60. PROCEDURE
    a. What is a procedure?
    b. How does using the Procedure command help create more readable programs?
    c. When should you use a procedure?
    d. How do you get out of a procedure?

61. PUBLIC
    a. What is a public variable?
    b. How does a public variable differ from a private variable?
    c. Does a public variable exist outside the procedure that created it?
    d. When should you use public variables?

62. READ
    a. What command does the Read command work with?
    b. What function does the Read command perform?
    c. What function does the save clause perform?

63. RECALL
    a. When should you use the Recall command?
    b. What is the default scope of the Recall command?
    c. What function does the Recall command perform?

64. REINDEX
    a. Does the Reindex command create index files? If not, what does it do?
    b. When should you use the Reindex command?

65. RELEASE
    a. What is the default scope of the Release command?
    b. Why should you use the Release command?
    c. How does the all like clause limit the number of variables released?

66. RENAME
    a. What function does the Rename command perform?
    b. When should you use this command?
    c. What potential problems could occur when using this command?

67. REPLACE
    a. How can this command help prevent database damage due to power failures and hardware related failures?
    b. What is the default scope of this command?
    c. What is the function of the alias clause?

68. REPORT FORM
    a. What is a report form?
    b. When should you use a report form?
    c. What is the function of the summary clause?
    d. What is the function of the heading clause?
    e. What is the function of the no eject clause?
    f. When should you use the plain clause?

69. RESTORE FROM
    a. What is a memory file?
    b. What does the additive clause do?
    c. When should you use the Restore From clause?
    d. How can you use the Restore From clause within an application?

70. RESTORE SCREEN
    a. How can you use the Restore Screen command within an application?
    b. What command must you use before using the Restore Screen command?
    c. What is the function of the from clause?

71. RETURN
    a. What is the function of the Return command?
    b. What does the expression clause contain?
    c. What sequence of events occurs when you use the Return command?

72. RUN/!
    a. What environment entry should you make using the DOS Set command before using this command?
    b. How do you return from a DOS shell to the current application?
    c. Are there any problems with using this command?

73. SAVE SCREEN
    a. What function does the Save Screen command perform?
    b. Does this command require you specify where to place the screen image? If so, why?
    c. When should you use this command?
    d. How will using this command enhance an application?

74. SAVE TO
    a. What function does the Save To command perform?
    b. What type of applications can you create using the Save To command?
    c. Where does Save To place the variables?

75. SEEK
    a. Why should you use the Seek command?
    b. How do you find the second occurrence of an expression found using the Seek command?
    c. Does the Seek command require any special database conditions? If so, what conditions?

76. SELECT
    a. What are the three ways you can select a database?
    b. When do you use the Select command?

77. SET COMMANDS
    a. What is the general purpose of the Set commands?
    b. What function does the Set Bell command perform?
    c. What does the unselected clause of the Set Color command do? When does this setting become apparent?
    d. What date formats does Clipper allow you to use?
    e. What function does the Set Escape command perform?
    f. What function does the Set Margin To command perform?

78. SKIP
    a. How does the Skip command affect a database?
    b. What is ths purpose of the EXPN clause?
    c. How do you use this command within a loop?

79. SORT
    a. What is the purpose of the /A clause? The /D clause? The /C clause?
    b. How does using the Sort command reduce database access time?
    c. When should you use this command?

80. STORE
    a. Why would you use the Store command instead of the At (@) Say/Get command?
    b. What are the advantages/disadvantages of using the Store command?

81. SUM
    a. What function does the Sum command perform?
    b. How can you use the for or while clauses to control how Sum creates a total?
    c. For what applications is the Sum command useful?

82. TEXT TO PRINT/FILE
    a. How can you use the Text To Print/File command within an application?
    b. How can this command assist you in error recovery?

83. TOTAL ON
    a. How does the Total On command differ from the Sum command?
    b. What function does the fields clause perform?
    c. When do you use this command within an application?

84. TYPE TO PRINT/FILE
    a. How does the Type To Print/File command differ from the Text To Print/File command?
    b. Where would you use this command within an application?
    c. How do you pause the text appearing on a display as the result of using this command?

85. UNLOCK
    a. When would you use the Unlock command?
    b. Are there any circumstances where this command could damage the database or associated index files?
    c. What types of database conditions does this command unlock?

86. UPDATE ON
    a. What is the purpose of the Update On command?
    b. What function does the random clause perform?
    c. How do you use this command within an application?
    d. Do you need to use an index with this command? If so, when?

87. USE
    a. What is the purpose of the exclusive clause?
    b. What is the purpose of the alias clause?
    c. When do you use this command?

88. WAIT
    a. Does this command supply a prompt when you don't supply one? If so, what prompt?
    b. How do you retrieve the key pressed by the user when using this command?
    c. Where would you use this command within an application?

89. ZAP
    a. What are the potential hazards of using this command?
    b. What combination of commands does this command replace?

90. ABS( ), EXP( ), LOG( ), MAX( ), MIN( ), MOD( ), SQRT( )
    a. What math function does the MAX( ) function perform?
    b. How can you use the MAX( ) and MIN( ) functions within an application?
    c. When should you use the ABS( ) function within an application?

91. ACHOICE( ), AADD( ), ACLONE( ), ACOPY( ), ADEL( ), ADIR( ), AEVAL( ),
    AFIELDS( ), AFILL( ), AINS( ), ARRAY( ), ASCAN( ), ASIZE( ), ASORT( ),
    DBSTRUCT( ), DIRECTORY( )
    a. How does the AChoice( ) function work differently than the Menu To command?
    b. What are the advantages/disadvantages of using the AChoice( ) function?
    c. What information does the ADir( ) function retrieve?
    d. What information does the AFields( ) function retrieve?
    e. How do you use the AScan( ) function within an application?
    f. When should you use the ASort( ) function within an application?

92. ALTD( )
    a. What object module must you include with your program files to use the ALTD( ) function?
    b. What is the purpose of the ALTD( ) function?
    c. How can you use the ALTD( ) function while debugging an application?

93. ASC( ), CHR( )
    a. How do the ASC( ) and CHR( ) functions differ?
    b. When should you use the ASC( ) function within an application?
    c. When should you use the CHR( ) function within an application?

94. AT( )
    a. How does the AT( ) function differ from the RAT( ) function?
    b. When should you use the AT( ) function within an application?

95. BIN2I( ), BIN2L( ), BIN2W( ), I2BIN( ), L2BIN( ), WORD( )
    a. How do you use these functions within an application?
    b. What type of files can you use these functions with?
    c. How does the Word( ) function differ from the BIN2I( ), BIN2L( ), BIN2W( ), I2BIN( ), and L2BIN( ) functions?

96. BOF( ), DBF( ), EOF( ), LASTREC( )/RECCOUNT( ), RECNO( ), RECSIZE( ), ALIAS( )
    a. What do these functions have in common?
    b. How can you use these functions within an application?

97. CDOW( ), CMONTH( ), CTOD( ), DATE( ), DAY( ), DOW( ), DTOC( ), DTOS( ), MONTH( ), SECONDS( ), TIME( ), YEAR( )
    a. Which of the above functions work specifically with date information? Time information?
    b. How can you use these functions within an application?
    c. Why should you use the DTOS( ) function instead of the DTOC( ) function within index key expressions?

98. COL( ), MAXCOL( ), MAXROW( ), ROW( ), PCOL( ), PROW( ), SETPRC( )
    a. Which of the above functions work specifically with printer output? Display output?
    b. How do you use these functions within an application?
    c. When should you use the SetPRC( ) function?

99. CURDIR( ), DISKSPACE( ), DOSERROR( ), ERRORLEVEL( ), FKLABEL( ), FKMAX( ), GETE( ), GETENV( ), OS( ), VERSION( )
    a. How do these functions help you recover from equipment failure and other error conditions?
    b. When do you use the ErrorLevel( ) function?
    c. How do you tell the DiskSpace( ) function which disk to look at?

100. DBEDIT( ), BROWSE( ), DBCREATE( ), DBEVAL( )
    a. How do you use the DBEdit( ) function within an application?
    b. Which parameters does DBEdit( ) require you supply?
    c. How can the addition of a user-defined function add to the functionality of the DBEdit( ) function?
    d. How do you create column headings within the edit area?

101. DBFILTER( )
    a. What task does the DBFilter( ) function perform?
    b. How can you use the DBFilter( ) function within an application?

102. DBRELATION( ), DBRSELECT( )
    a. How do the DBRelation( ) and DBRSelect( ) functions complement each other in the task they perform?
    b. How do you use the DBRelation( ) function within an application?
    c. What does DBRSelect( ) return if the relation number you supply doesn't exist?

103. DELETED( )
    a. When should you use the Deleted( ) function?
    b. What value does Deleted( ) return if Clipper marked the current record for deletion?
    c. How does this function improve user displays?

104. DESCEND( )
    a. What is the purpose of the Descend( ) function?
    b. Can you use the Descend( ) function within an index? If so, how?
    c. When should you use the Descend( ) function?

105. EMPTY( )
    a. How do you use the Empty( ) function within an application?
    b. Can you use the Empty( ) function to determine if a database contains any records? How?

106. FCLOSE( ), FCREATE( ), FERROR( ), FILE( ), FOPEN( ), FREAD( ), FREADSTR( ), FSEEK( ), FWRITE( )
    a. What types of files do these functions work on?
    b. How would you use these functions within an application?
    c. What is the purpose of the FError( ) function.
    d. What is a file handle.
    e. How do the FRead( ) and FReadstr( ) functions differ?

107. FCOUNT( ), FIELD( )/FIELDNAME( )
    a. How does the output of the FCount( ) function differ from the Field( )/FieldName( ) function.
    b. What is the purpose of the FCount( ) function?
    c. How do you use the Field/FieldName( ) function within an application?

108. FLOCK( ), RLOCK( )/LOCK( )
    a. Why does a networked application require locks?
    b. What file does Clipper supply with sample programs you can use to learn how to create a network program?
    c. What is the difference between a record and a file lock?
    d. Why can't you lock a database opened using the exclusive attribute.

109. FOUND( )
    a. When does Found( ) become true?
    b. How do you use Found( ) within an application?
    c. Do you need an index attached to the current database to get an accurate response from Found( )?

110. HARDCR( )
    a. What is the purpose of the HardCR( ) function?
    b. How do you use the HardCR( ) function within a program?
    c. Does the HardCR( ) function change the contents of the memo field?

111. HEADER( )
    a. What is a database header? What information does it contain?
    b. How can you use the Header( ) function within an application?

112. IF( )/IIF( ), EVAL( )
    a. When can you use the If( )/IIf( ) function in place of an If command?
    b. What is the advantage to using an If( )/IIf( ) function instead of an If command?
    c. What three parameters do you have to supply to the If( )/IIf( ) function?

113. INDEXEXT( ), INDEXKEY( ), INDEXORD( )
    a. What do these three functions have in common?
    b. When should you use the IndexKey( ) function within an application?
    c. Why is the IndexEXT( ) function important?

114. INKEY( ), LASTKEY( ), NEXTKEY( ), READKEY( ), SETKEY( )
    a. What value does the InKey( ) function return? LastKey( )? NextKey( )?
    b. What happens if you specify 0 as the time element for the InKey( ) function?
    c. When should you use these functions within an application?

115. INT( ), ROUND( )
    a. What is the difference between the INT( ) and Round( ) functions?
    b. When would you use the INT( ) function instead of the Round( ) function?
    c. How do you use the Round( ) function within an application?

116. ISALPHA( ), ISDIGIT( ), ISLOWER( ), ISUPPER( )
    a. What type of value do each of these functions return?
    b. When would you use the IsAlpha( ) function in an application?
    c. What is the purpose of the IsLower( ) function?

117. ISCOLOR( )/ISCOLOUR( ), SETCOLOR( )
    a. How can you use the IsColor( ) function to automatically compensate for differences in display adapters?
    b. What function does the SetColor( ) function perform?

118. ISPRINTER( )
    a. How does the IsPrinter( ) function help you determine the status of a printer connected to LPT1?
    b. When should you use IsPrinter( ) within an application?

119. LEFT( ), RIGHT( )
    a. How are the Right( ) and Left( ) functions alike? Different?
    b. When should you use these functions within an application?

120. LEN( )
    a. What value does the LEN( ) function return?
    b. How can you use this value within an application?

121. LOWER( ), PAD( ), QOUT( ), SPACE( ), STR( ), STRTRAN( ), STUFF( ), TRANSFORM( ), UPPER( ), VAL( )
    a. What do all these functions have in common?
    b. How do the Upper( ) and Lower( ) functions differ?
    c. When should you use the Transform( ) function?
    d. How are the STR( ) and VAL( ) functions the same? Different?

122. LTRIM( ), SUBSTR( ), TRIM( )/RTRIM( ), ALLTRIM( )
    a. What is the purpose of the LTrim( ) function.
    b. When would you use the Trim( )/RTrim( ) function within an application?
    c. Explain how the SubSTR( ) acts like a combination of the LTrim and Trim( )/RTrim( ) functions?
    d. How are these functions useful in creating indexes to the current database?

123. LUPDATE( )
    a. When would you use the LUpdate( ) function?
    b. What value does the LUpdate( ) function return?

124. MEMOEDIT( ), MEMOLINE( ), MEMOREAD( ), MEMOTRAN( ), MEMOWRIT( )
    a. How are the MemoEdit( ) and DBEdit( ) functions the same? Different?
    b. Why would you use the MemoLine( ) function in place of the MemoEdit( ) function?
    c. What is the purpose of the MemoRead( ) function?
    d. How does the addition of a user-defined function to a MemoEdit( ) function create a more flexible environment?

125. MEMORY( )
    a. How can the Memory( ) function prevent runtime errors?
    b. What value does the Memory( ) function return?
    c. When should you use this function within an application?

126. MLCOUNT( ), MLPOS( )
    a. What value does the MLCount( ) function return?
    b. How can you use the MLCount( ) function in conjunction with the MemoLine( ) function to create more pleasing displays?
    c. When should you use the MLPos( ) function?

127. NETERR( ), NETNAME( )
    a. What value does the NetName( ) function return if the current workstation is not connected to a network?
    b. When should you use the NetERR( ) function?
    c. How can you use the NetName( ) function within an application?

128. PCOUNT( )
    a. How can you use the PCount( ) function as part of a procedure to retrieve DOS command line parameters?
    b. What value does the PCount( ) function return?
    c. Does PCount( ) return the correct number of passed arguments if you do not provide enough parameter variables using the Parameters command?

129. PROCLINE( ), PROCNAME( )
    a. What value does the ProcLine( ) function return? ProcName( )?
    b. How can you use these two functions within an error handling routine? Help routine?

130. RAT( )
    a. What order does RAT( ) use to search a string?
    b. What value does RAT( ) return if the search value does not appear in the target string?
    c. How can you use RAT( ) within an application?

131. READEXIT( ), READINSERT( ), READVAR( )
    a. What values do these three functions return?
    b. When should you use the ReadExit( ) function within an application?
    c. How can you use the ReadVar( ) function as part of a help routine?

132. REPLICATE( )
    a. How does the Replicate( ) function act like the Space( ) function?
    b. How do the Replicate( ) and Space( ) functions differ?
    c. How do you use the Replicate( ) function to draw lines similar to those drawn by the @ To command?

133. RESTSCREEN( ), SAVESCREEN( ), SCROLL( )
    a. How do the RestScreen( ) and SaveScreen( ) functions work like the Restore Screen and Save Screen commands?
    b. In what way are the RestScreen( ) and SaveScreen( ) functions superior to the Restore Screen and Save Screen commands?
    c. What task does the Scroll( ) function perform?

134. SELECT( )
    a. How is the Select( ) function different than the Select command?
    b. What task does the Select( ) function perform?
    c. How would you use the Select( ) function within an application?

135. SETCANCEL( ), SET( )
    a. What is the cancel program control key?
    b. How does the SetCancel( ) function affect the cancel program control key?
    c. Why would you use this function in an application?

136. SOUNDEX( )
    a. How does this function make it easier to find information in the database?
    b. What are the disadvantages to using this function?

137. TONE( )
    a. What is one use for the Tone( ) function?
    b. How would you use this function in an application?

138. TYPE( ), VALTYPE( )
    a. What value does Type( ) return for a character variable? An array? A memo field?
    b. Why would you use this function within an application?

139. UPDATED( )
    a. When does Clipper update the value of Updated( )?
    b. What value does Updated return if Clipper detects a change in a get?
    c. Why would you use this function within an application?

140. USED( )
    a. What is a work area?
    b. What value does Used( ) return if the current work area does not contain a database?
    c. When would you use this function within an application?

141. BREAK
    a. What is a break point?
    b. How do you set a break point using Debug?
    c. What is the difference between a line and expression break point?
    d. Where does Clipper display the status of the break points?
    e. How do you remove a break point?

142. BREAK TOGGLE
    a. Why would you want to toggle a break point between on and off?
    b. What does Clipper do when it encounters a break point that you toggled off?

143. DISPLAY EXPRESSION, DISPLAY TRACE, DISPLAY STATUS, DISPLAY DATABASE
    a. What are the four displays provided by the Display Database command? What do these displays contain?
    b. What information does the Display Status screen provide?
    c. How can you use the Display Expression dialogue box during a debug session?
    d. What type of errors does the Display Trace screen help you find?

144. DOS SHELL
    a. What menu does the DOS Shell command appear on?
    b. How do you return to Debug after exiting a program using the DOS Shell command?
    c. What limits the tasks you can perform while in the DOS shell?

145. GO, GO (ANIMATION), GO (KEY)
    a. What are the basic differences between the three Go commands?
    b. When do you use these commands?

146. HELP
    a. What type of information does the Help menu provide?
    b. Can you access help from within another command?

147. QUIT
    a. What should you do when you use the Quit command and the cursor disappears?
    b. Does the Quit command automatically close your files?
    c. How can you use the Quit command to exit a problem area in your program?

148. SINGLE STEP
    a. What is the main purpose for the Single Step command?
    b. How do you use the Single Step command for debugging an application?
    c. Does Single Step execute non-command lines of code?

149. VARIABLE ASSIGN PRIVATE, VARIABLE VIEW PRIVATE
    a. How can you use the Variable Assign Private command during a debugging session?
    b. What does the Variable View Private screen show you?

150. VARIABLE ASSIGN PUBLIC, VARIABLE VIEW PUBLIC
    a. When should you use the Variable Assign Public command?
    b. How does the Variable View Public command help you find global errors in your program?

151. WATCH
    a. What is a watch point?
    b. Where does debug display the contents of the watch points?
    c. How do you add watch points during a debug session?
    d. What word does debug display for watch point variables that are not currently defined?

Index

!/RUN, 22, 190
#Command, 430, 473
#Define, 431, 476
#Error, 477
#IfDef, 432, 478
#IfNDef, 432, 478
#Include, 432, 478
#Translate, 430, 476
#UnDef, 432, 478
#XCommand, 473
#XTranslate, 476
$/Macro, 430
%/Modulus, 245
&&/*/NOTE, 151
&/Macro, 115, 213
=, 217
?/??/PRINT, 156, 340

AADD( ), 249
ABS( ), 245
ACCEPT, 35, 324
ACHOICE( ), 139, 249, 324
ACLONE( ), 249
ACOPY( ), 249
ADEL( ), 249
ADIR( ), 98, 249
AEVAL( ), 249
AFIELDS( ), 249
AFILL( ), 249
AINS( ), 249
ALIAS( ), 266
ALLTRIM( ), 344
ALTD( ), 256
APPEND, 21, 36
ARRAY( ), 249
ASC( ), 258
ASCAN( ), 249
ASIZE( ), 249
ASORT( ), 249
Assignment Operators, 217
AT, (@)
    BOX, 39, 203
    CLEAR TO, 41, 203

PROMPT, 43, 93, 148, 203
SAY/GET, 45, 134, 202, 241, 324, 369, 371
TO DOUBLE, 50, 203, 371
AT( ), 260
Automatic Program Compilation, 429
AVERAGE, 52

BEGIN SEQUENCE, 55
BIN2I( ), 262
BIN2L( ), 262
BIN2W( ), 262
BOF( ), 266
BREAK, 389
BREAK TOGGLE, 393
BROWSE( ), 282

CALL, 57
CANCEL/QUIT, 58
CDOW( ), 269
CHR( ), 258
CLEAR ALL, 60
CLEAR GETS, 47, 61
CLEAR MEMORY, 62
CLEAR SCREEN, 64
CLEAR TYPEAHEAD, 66
CLOSE, 68
CLS, 66
CMONTH( ), 269
Code blocks, 472, 479
COL( ), 272, 340
Color Selection, 202, 331
Command Line Parameters, 3, 5, 17, 27, 30
COMMIT, 70
Compiler Directives, 429
Compiler Error Messages, 435
Compiler preprocessor, 472
Compound Assignment Operators, 217
CONTINUE, 75, 310
COPY FILE, 77
COPY STRUCTURE, 79
COPY STRUCTURE EXTENDED, 88
COPY TO, 21, 81

COUNT, 85
CREATE, 88
Create
    Database File, 9, 19
    Database Utility (DBU) Program, 24
    Index File, 10, 19
    Index Program, 27
    Label File, 31
    Report File, 32
    Report and Label Utility (RL)
        Program, 30
CREATE FROM, 88
CTOD( ), 269
CURDIR( ), 277

Data Types, 384
Database Runtime Errors, 439
DATE( ), 269
Date Types, 203
DAY( ), 269
dBASE III Functions not Supported by
    Clipper, 434
DBCREATE( ), 282
DBEDIT( ), 70, 139, 282, 324
DBEVAL( ), 282
DBF( ), 266
DBFILTER( ), 288
DBRELATION( ), 290
DBRSELECT( ), 290
DBSTRUCT( ), 249, 283
DECLARE, 91
DELETE, 96, 167, 242
DELETE/ERASE FILE, 113
DELETED( ), 292
DESCEND( ), 293
DIR, 98
DIRECTORY( ), 249
DISKSPACE( ), 277
DISPLAY, 100, 143
DISPLAY DATABASE, 395
DISPLAY EXPRESSION, 395
DISPLAY STATUS, 395
DISPLAY TRACE, 395
DO CASE, 104
DO (Procedure), 107, 155
DO WHILE, 109, 121

DOS Extended Error Codes, 278, 299
DOS SHELL, 401
DOSERROR( ), 277, 361
DOW( ), 269
DTOC( ), 269
DTOS( ), 269

Edit Keys, 164, 250, 282, 323
EJECT, 112
ELSE, 104, 128
ELSEIF, 104, 128
EMPTY( ), 296
ENDIF, 104, 128
EOF( ), 266
ERASE/DELETE FILE, 113
Error Class, 496
Error Class Exported Instance Variables, 498
Error Messages, Compiler, 435
Error Messages, Linker, 438
Error Messages, Runtime, 439
ERRORLEVEL( ), 277
Escape Key Status, 204
EVAL( ), 316
EXP( ), 245
Expression Runtime Errors, 440
Extended DOS Error Codes, 278, 299
EXTERNAL, 115

FCLOSE( ), 298
FCOUNT( ), 305
FCREATE( ), 298
FERROR( ), 298
FIELD, 91, 124, 157, 162
FIELD( )/FIELDNAME( ), 305
Field Types, 8
FILE( ), 298
File Attributes, 251, 299, 301
File Pointer Direction Modifiers, 302
FIND, 117, 310
FKLABEL( ), 277
FKMAX( ), 277
FLOCK( ), 213, 307
Flow Chart, 11, 15
FOPEN( ), 298
FOR TO, 121
Format Types, 46

FOUND( ), 146, 310
FREAD( ), 298
FREADSTR( ), 298
FSEEK( ), 298
FUNCTION, 124
Function Key Status, 205, 278, 324
Function Symbols, 46
FWRITE( ), 298

Get Class, 490
Get Class Exported Instance Variables, 491
Get Class Methods, 494
GETE( ), 190, 277
GETENV( ), 190, 277
GO, 403
GO (ANIMATION), 403
GO (KEY), 403
GO/GOTO, 23, 124

HARDCR( ), 312
HEADER( ), 314
HELP, 406

I2BIN( ), 262
IF, 104, 128
IF( )/IIF( ), 316
INDEX ON, 131, 213
INDEXEXT( ), 320
INDEXKEY( ), 320
INDEXORD( ), 320
INKEY( ), 241, 323, 329
INPUT, 134, 324
INT( ), 326
ISALPHA( ), 329
ISCOLOR( )/ISCOLOUR( ), 331
ISDIGIT( ), 329
ISLOWER( ), 329
ISPRINTER( ), 333
ISUPPER( ), 329

JOIN WITH, 136
Justification of Text, 340

KEYBOARD, 139

L2BIN( ), 262
LABEL FORM, 141
LASTKEY( ), 323
LASTREC( )/RECCOUNT( ), 85, 266, 314
LEFT( ), 336
LEN( ), 338
Line Program, 428
Link, 5
Linker Error Messages, 438
LIST, 143
LOCAL, 91, 124, 157, 162, 188
LOCATE, 23, 146, 310
LOCK( )/RLOCK( ), 307
LOG( ), 245
LOWER( ), 340
LTRIM( ), 344
LUPDATE( ), 346

Macro, 115, 213, 430
Make Program, 429
Match patterns, 473
MAX( ), 245
MAXCOL( ), 272
MAXROW( ), 272
MEMOEDIT( ), 312, 324, 348
MEMOLINE( ), 348, 359
MEMOREAD( ), 348
MEMORY( ), 190, 355
MEMOTRAN( ), 348
MEMOWRIT( ), 348
MEMVAR, 91, 124, 157, 162
MENU TO, 93, 148, 206
MIN( ), 245
Miscellaneous Runtime Errors, 440
MLCOUNT( ), 359
MLPOS( ), 359
MOD( ), 245
MONTH( ), 269

NETERR( ), 361
NETNAME( ), 361
NEXTKEY( ), 323
NOTE (*/&&), 151

Object oriented programming, 472
Open File Attributes, 301
OS( ), 277

PACK, 22, 153, 242
PAD( ), 340
PARAMETERS, 92, 155
PCOL( ), 272, 340
PCOUNT( ), 362
Picture
    Function Symbols, 46
    Template Symbols, 46
PLink86, 4
Pre-Processor Directives, 429
PRINT STATEMENT (?/??), 156, 340
Printing a Program, 428
PRIVATE, 91, 157, 162, 194
PROCEDURE, 124, 159
PROCLINE( ), 364
PROCNAME( ), 364
Program Execution Error Messages, 439
PROW( ), 272, 340
PUBLIC, 92, 162

QOUT( ), 340
QUIT, 408

RAT( ), 366
READ, 47, 164, 324
READEXIT( ), 369
READINSERT( ), 369
READKEY( ), 323
READVAR( ), 369
RECALL, 167
RECCOUNT( )/LASTREC( ), 85, 266, 314
RECNO( ), 266
RECSIZE( ), 266, 314
REINDEX, 82, 169
RELEASE, 62, 172
RENAME, 174
REPLACE, 22, 70, 176
REPLICATE( ), 371
REPORT FORM, 141, 180
RESTORE FROM, 184
RESTORE SCREEN, 186
RESTSCREEN( ), 373

Result patterns, 475
RETURN, 124, 159, 188
RIGHT( ), 336
RLOCK( )/LOCK( ), 307
ROUND( ), 326
ROW( ), 272, 340
RTLink, 7
RTRIM( )/TRIM( ), 344
RUN/!, 22, 190
Runtime Error Messages, 439

Sample
    Database Structure, 9
    Index Structure, 10
SAVE SCREEN, 186, 193
SAVE TO, 184, 194
SAVESCREEN( ), 373
SCROLL( ), 373
SECONDS( ), 269
SEEK, 23, 117, 196, 310
SELECT, 198
SELECT( ), 376
SET Commands, 23, 64, 98, 100, 201, 229, 290, 307, 320, 378, 395
SET( ), 378
SETCANCEL( ), 378
SETCOLOR( ), 331
SETKEY( ), 323
SETPRC( ), 272
SINGLE STEP, 410
SKIP, 23, 196, 210
SORT, 82, 213
SOUNDEX( ), 381
SPACE( ), 340
SQRT( ), 245
STATIC, 91, 124, 157, 162
STORE, 217
STR( ), 340
STRTRAN( ), 340
STUFF( ), 340
SUBSTR( ), 344
SUM, 219

TBColumn Class, 488
TBColumn Class Exported Instance
    Variables, 489

TBrowse Class, 481
TBrowse Class Functions, 481
TBrowse Class Exported Instance
    Variables, 482
TBrowse Class Methods, 484
Template Symbols, 46
Terms and Definitions, 423
Text Justification, 340
TEXT TO PRINT/FILE, 223
Text Transformation, 341
TIME( ), 269
TONE( ), 383
TOTAL ON, 226
TRANSFORM( ), 340
TRIM( )/RTRIM( ), 344
TYPE TO PRINT/FILE, 229
TYPE( ), 384

Undefined Runtime Errors, 441
UNLOCK, 234
UPDATE ON, 236

UPDATED( ), 324, 386
UPPER( ), 340
USE, 239
USED( ), 388

VAL( ), 341
VALTYPE( ), 384
VARIABLE ASSIGN PRIVATE, 412
VARIABLE ASSIGN PUBLIC, 416
Variable Type Determination, 384
VARIABLE VIEW PRIVATE, 412
VARIABLE VIEW PUBLIC, 416
VERSION( ), 277

WAIT, 241, 324
WATCH, 419
WORD( ), 262

YEAR( ), 269

ZAP, 22, 242

New Popular Applications Series Titles

Learn CorelDRAW! in a Day
Ed Paulson

With this book as your guide, open the door to your own creativity by exploring the power and flexibility of this popular illustration software. Designed with the beginner in mind, you'll find all the information you need to get started with the CorelDRAW! program.

128 pgs. • 6 x 9
1-55622-206-8 • $12.95

Learn DOS in a Day
Russell A. Stultz

The "down and dirty" information users need to tame the most popular operating system around, this book gives users all they need to know to start using DOS on their computers. Designed with the beginner in mind, you'll find the most common commands explained and clarified with hands-on activities.

144 pgs. • 6 x 9
1-55622-203-3 • $12.95

Learn Microsoft Works in a Day
Source disk included.
Jerry Funk

Spring into action and open the door to the power and flexibility of this integrated software package. Designed to get the beginner up and running as soon as possible, this book provides all the information you'll need to get started on the word processor, spreadsheet, database and communications functions.

128 pgs. • 6 x 9
1-55622-205-X • $12.95

Learn Quattro Pro in a Day
Versions 2.0 and 3.0
Source disk included.
Russell A. Stultz

If spreadsheets have got you covered, this book will provide the light at the end of the tunnel. Designed to give beginners all the information they need to unlock the power and flexibility of Quattro Pro, this book will have you up and running in no time.

128 pgs. • 6 x 9
1-55622-216-5 • $12.95

Creating Newsletters With Ventura
Source disk included.
Maria Hoath

With this book as your guide, learn to manipulate the powerful features of this desktop publishing program to give all of your newsletters that professional look. This book provides you with a solid Ventura foundation while taking you step-by-step through the creation of an actual newsletter. Source disk with ready-made Ventura style sheets.

120 pgs. • 6 x 9
1-55622-199-1 • $12.95

Desktop Publishing With WordPerfect
Source disk included.
Maria Hoath

If you want to create commercial quality newsletters, bulletins, or books using WordPerfect, this book is for you. Learn how to use WordPerfect to create desktop publishing effects including the manipulation of text attributes, fonts, and style sheets.

120 pgs. • 6 x 9
1-55622-197-5 • $12.95

Learn Paradox in a Day
Source disk included.
Tim Colman

Designed to get new Paradox users up and running in less than a day, this book guides you through the basic operations, table creation, data entry, reporting, and more. Source disk with ready-to-use examples.

136 pgs. • 6 x 9
1-55622-210-6 • $12.95

Object-Oriented Programming Using Turbo C++
Source disk included.
Norman Smith

Unlock the mysteries of object-oriented programming with a book dedicated to the hottest new area of computer programming. Source disk containing ready-to-run "OOP" source code.

136 pgs. • 6 x 9
1-55622-204-1 • $14.95

New Illustrated Books from Wordware

Illustrated AutoCAD
RELEASE 11
Paul Schlieve
A complete revision of the classic *Illustrated AutoCAD*, this book brings the power and flexibility of Release 11 to the full range of drawing activities from lines to three-dimensional solids.
572 pgs. • 7 ½ x 9 ¼
1-55622-178-9 • $24.95

Illustrated PageMaker 4.0
William Harrell
From basic setup to the final printout, explore the expanded features of this powerful desktop publishing program with this book as your guide. Following the easy step-by-step instructions, novice and experienced users will be mastering the program and its new features in no time.
336 pgs. • 7 ½ x 9 ¼
1-55622-217-3 •$23.95

Illustrated MS-DOS 5.00
And All Previous MS/PC-DOS Versions
Russell A. Stultz
Get up to date with the latest version of the most popular operating system on the market. Hands-on examples and extensive illustrations give the advanced user insight to the new features and the novice a complete learning guide.
312 pgs. • 7 ½ x 9 ¼
1-55622-214-9 • $21.95

Illustrated Turbo Pascal 6.0
Paul Schlieve
This book will lead you through the expanded features of the latest version of Borland's Turbo Pascal. Work your way through the sample programs and hands-on examples to get up to speed on Turbo Vision and all the new features.
384 pgs. • 7 ½ x 9 ¼
1-55622-202-5 • $23.95

Illustrated Ventura 3.0
DOS/GEM EDITION
George Sheldon
This reference-tutorial introduces users to all the features of this best selling, desktop publishing software. This book has novice users up and running fast while providing the experienced user with direct access to the new, expanded features.
384 pgs. • 7 ½ x 9 ¼
1-55622-213-0 • $23.95

Illustrated Windows 3.0
Whitsitt & Bryan
With this indispensable reference/tutorial at your side, learn to work with several applications simultaneously using the Windows operating environment. Designed with both the novice and expert in mind, this book is a must for the serious Windows user.
380 pgs. • 7 ½ x 9 ¼
1-55622-211-4 • $23.95

New Advanced Computer

Understanding 3COM Networks
Bulette & Chacon
From networking concepts through management techniques, this book provides examples, comparisons, and insight to simplify the complexities of 3COM networks. Detailed information about physical topologies, workgroup components, hardware, installation planning, and more are included.
192 pgs. • 7 ½ x 9 ¼
1-55622-209-2 • $23.95

The Desktop Studio: Multimedia with the Amiga
David Johnson
This book provides an overall assessment of the Amiga computer including the different models and their capabilities, professional uses, an in-depth look at the graphic options, descriptions and explanations of hardware options, and helpful recommendations for the creation of professional studio graphics presentations.
256 pgs. • 7 ½ x 9 ¼
1-55622-215-7 • $21.95

Other Books from Wordware Publishing, Inc.

Business-Professional Books
Business Emotions
The Business Side of Writing
Confessions of a Banker
Hawks Do, Buzzards Don't
How to Win Pageants
Innovation, Inc.
Investor Beware
MegaTraits
Occupying the Summit
Steps to Strategic Management
To Be or Not to Be an S.O.B

Computer Aided Drafting
Illustrated AutoCAD (Release 10)
Illustrated AutoCAD (Release 11)
Illustrated AutoCAD for the Mac
Illustrated AutoLISP
Illustrated AutoSketch 1.04
Illustrated AutoSketch 2.0
Illustrated GenericCADD Level 3

Database Management
The DataFlex Developer's Handbook
Illustrated dBASE III Plus
Illustrated dBASE IV 1.1
Illustrated FoxPro
Illustrated FoxPro 2.0
Illustrated Paradox 3.0 Volume II (2nd Ed.)

Desktop Publishing
Achieving Graphic Impact with Ventura 2.0
Desktop Publisher's Dictionary
Illustrated PFS:First Publisher 2.0
Illustrated PFS:First Publisher 2.0 & 3.0
Illustrated PageMaker 3.0
Illustrated PageMaker 4.0
Illustrated Ready, Set, Go! 4.5 (Macintosh)
Illustrated Ventura 2.0
Illustrated Ventura 3.0 (Windows Ed.)
Illustrated Ventura 3.0 (DOS/GEM Ed.)
The Desktop Studio: Multimedia with the Amiga
Ventura Troubleshooting Guide

General and Advanced Topics
Illustrated DacEasy Accounting 4.1
Illustrated Harvard Graphics 2.3
Illustrated Novell NetWare 2.15 (2nd Ed.)
Illustrated Novell NetWare 3.1.1
Novell NetWare: Adv. Tech. and Applications
Understanding 3COM Networks

Integrated
Illustrated Enable/OA
Illustrated Framework III
Illustrated Microsoft Works 2.0
Illustrated Q & A 3.0 (2nd Ed.)

Programming Languages
Illustrated C Programming (ANSI) (2nd Ed.)
Illustrated Clipper 5.0 (2nd Ed.)
Illustrated QBasic for MS-DOS 5.00
The DataFlex Developer's Handbook
The FOCUS Developer's Handbook
Graphic Programming with Turbo Pascal
GUI Programming with C

Programming Languages (cont.)
Illustrated Turbo C++
Illustrated Turbo Debugger and Tools
Illustrated Turbo Pascal 5.5
Illustrated Turbo Pascal 6.0

Spreadsheet
Illustrated Lotus 1-2-3 2.01
Illustrated Lotus 1-2-3 Rel. 3.0
Illustrated Lotus 1-2-3 Rel. 2.2
Illustrated Microsoft Excel 2.10 (IBM)
Illustrated Microsoft Excel 1.5 (Macintosh)
Illustrated Quattro
Illustrated SuperCalc 5

Systems and Operating Guides
Illustrated Microsoft Windows 2.0
Illustrated Microsoft Windows 3.0
Illustrated MS/PC DOS 3.3
Illustrated MS/PC DOS 4.0 (6th Ed.)
Illustrated MS DOS 5.00
Illustrated UNIX System V

Word Processing
Illustrated DisplayWrite 4
Illustrated Microsoft Word 5.0 (PC)
Illustrated WordPerfect 1.0 (Macintosh)
Illustrated WordPerfect 5.0
Illustrated WordPerfect 5.1
Illustrated WordPerfect for Windows
Illustrated WordStar 6.0
Illustrated WordStar Professional (Rel. 5)
WordPerfect: Advanced Applications Handbook
WordPerfect Wizardry Adv. Tech. and Applications

Popular Applications Series
Cost Control Using Lotus 1-2-3
Creating Newsletters with Ventura
Desktop Publishing with WordPerfect
Learn CorelDRAW! in a Day
Learn DOS in a Day
Learn Lotus 1-2-3 in a Day
Learn Microsoft Works in a Day
Learn PAL in a Day
Learn Paradox in a Day
Learn PlanPerfect in a Day
Learn Quattro Pro in a Day
Learn WordPerfect in a Day
Mailing Lists using dBASE
Object-Oriented Programming using Turbo C++
Presentations with Harvard Graphics
WordPerfect Macros

Regional
Exploring the Alamo Legends
Forget the Alamo
The Great Texas Airship Mystery
100 Days in Texas: The Alamo Letters
Rainy Days in Texas Funbook
Texas Highway Humor
Texas Wit and Wisdom
That Cat Won't Flush
They Don't Have to Die
This Dog'll Hunt
Unsolved Texas Mysteries

Call Wordware Publishing, Inc. for names of the bookstores in your area
(214) 423-0090